Controversies
in Canadian Sociology

Controversies in Canadian Sociology

M. REZA NAKHAIE

UNIVERSITY OF WINDSOR

THOMSON

NELSON

Australia   Canada   Mexico   Singapore   Spain   United Kingdom   United States

THOMSON

NELSON

Controversies in Canadian Sociology

by M. Reza Nakhaie

Associate Vice President, Editorial Director:
Evelyn Veitch

Editor-in-Chief, Higher Education:
Anne Williams

Executive Editor:
Cara Yarzab

Director of Marketing:
Kelly Smyth

Developmental Editor:
Sandy Matos

Permissions Coordinator:
Sandra Mark

Senior Content Production Manager:
Natalia Denesiuk Harris

Production Service:
Graphic World Inc.

Copy Editor:
Graphic World Inc.

Proofreader:
Graphic World Inc.

Manufacturing Coordinator:
Loretta Lee

Design Director:
Ken Phipps

Interior Design:
Graphic World Inc.

Cover Design:
Jack Steiner

Cover Image:
Stephen Simpson/Stone/Getty Images

Compositor:
Graphic World Inc.

Printer:
Thomson/West

Library and Archives Canada Cataloguing in Publication

Nakhaie, Mahmoud Reza, 1952–
Controversies in Canadian sociology / M. Reza Nakhaie.

Includes bibliographical references.
ISBN-13: 978-0-17-610468-9
ISBN-10: 0-17-610468-2

1. Canada—Social conditions—Textbooks. 2. Sociology—Canada—Textbooks. I. Title

HM586.N35 2007   301.0971
C2006-903727-2

Contents

Unit Four
CRIME AND DEVIANCE

Unit Five
FAMILY

Unit Six
SOCIAL INEQUALITY

Preface

In teaching sociology for twenty years, I was always challenged on how to help students develop critical thinking skills and understand the relevance of sociology for their everyday life. This challenge was more pronounced when teaching introductory sociology students. How does one teach introductory sociology students both continuity and discontinuity of sociological explanations? How does one make students aware of the gatekeepers' agreement and disagreement about what sociology is and why it is important? Moreover, how does one walk the fine line of showing various controversies and at the same time maintaining that this discipline has something to offer in understanding our past, explaining our present, and predicting our future? In a nutshell, how does one keep them interested, engaged, and involved in sociology? Of course, there is no clear answer to any of these questions. In an attempt to introduce sociology to students, this book contains extensive introductions, original empirical evidence, newspaper clippings, and one set of authentic debates in order to challenge students to develop a critical imagination and allow them to expand on their previous and new knowledge.

Basically, this book explores theoretical, conceptual, and empirical contacts and debates on key sociological issues, with three main objectives. The first is to introduce key sociological concepts and theories through detailed introductions, examples, and evidence. The second objective is to introduce twelve sociological debates and controversies that are relevant to an understanding of these concepts, theories, and research in sociology so that undergraduate students can grasp how sociologists view the work of their colleagues. In this regard, each article presents an in-depth look at a specific sociological issue. The third objective is to teach critical thinking by studying sociologists as they debate each other. Each article is followed by a comment about or criticism of concepts, research, theories, or theorists discussed in the previous article. The debate format will encourage students to re-examine their preconceptions and submit their views to critical reasoning.

These twelve sociological debates are intended for students to have access to a clear and concise rebuttal of existing knowledge in order to assess various aspects of an issue, concept, or theory; to evaluate the arguments on their merits; and to choose on the basis of their own autonomous thought. Therefore, students will be exposed to a real sense of the excitement and heated debates regarding the fundamental issues, concepts, and theories

prevalent in sociology. Students will understand that issues and interpretations are not necessarily agreed upon in sociology but that some are questioned and critically reevaluated. Such understanding allows students to develop critical imagination, which is pertinent to sociological endeavour. Students will have the opportunity to access authentic and critical information and methods of weighing and considering various sociological issues and assumptions. The point–counterpoint method, as presented in this textbook, will help students acquire a realistic image of the processes of sociological understanding and develop autonomous, authentic critical knowledge.

However, the articles are written by scholars, for scholars, and their language, therefore, can be daunting for undergraduate students. With this in mind, the complex debates and concepts have been edited, while still keeping the integrity of the author's main message intact. Furthermore, at the beginning of each debate, a detailed general introduction is provided in order to facilitate students' understanding, clarifying the basic terms and concepts and making them relevant to the everyday lives of students. The result for the students is that they will master the vocabulary of the discipline, both through the introduction and their exposure to the debates. In addition, students are encouraged to build on and not just tear down the existing knowledge. Ultimately, they must decide for themselves whether any of the sociological arguments and research are valid and/or interesting. To do this students need to assess how criticism sheds light on the issues and how it helps in the process of developing and building new ideas. At the end of each point–counterpoint pair of articles, students are encouraged to contemplate each issue and its criticism and to ponder their own related questions. To foster the stance of criticism and build theories, students are afforded the opportunity to write a short essay on any aspects of the debate that can be salvaged after the critical commentary. This will enable them to rethink the major issues and controversies present in the debate. In the process, students can employ their sociological knowledge and evaluate these debates. They may also recognize that there are often more than two sides to any debate. Rather, such debates among sociologists are aimed at developing and improving the knowledge on various social issues. Finally, each debate includes a recent newspaper clipping and/or empirical evidence or other learning aids that will highlight the relevance of the readings to everyday life.

The selection of debates is guided by three criteria:

1. They are recent debates and commentaries—all are published after 1990.
2. They are challenging, yet not too complex for first-year students. Debates that were methodologically complex were excluded. The necessary but complex debates are edited so that they are comprehensible to undergraduate students.
3. The majority of the debates were written by Canadians and are about relevant Canadian issues.

ACKNOWLEDGMENTS

◆ ◆ ◆

In preparing this book, I was fortunate to benefit from the encouragement of Cara Yarzab, Executive Editor; Sandy Matos, Developmental Editor; Natalia Denesiuk Harris, Senior Content Production Manager; Anne Williams, Production Editor; and all from Thomson Nelson.

Maria Frances Cachon and Ayda Rezaian from the Department of Sociology, University of Windsor, were always ready to assist me in preparing this book. I thank them both. My colleagues at the University of Windsor, Drs. Booth and Zaidi, have given me valuable advice. Many thanks also to Shelly Ungar, University of Toronto; George Pollard, Carleton University; Patricia Kachuk, University of British Columbia; Ivan Emke, Memorial University; and Marilyn Belle-McQuillan, University of Western Ontario, who all reviewed the book during its development and provided seasoned advice. I am fortunate to have Vince Sacco and Larry Comeau as my buddies. Last but not least, my love and companion for twenty years, my *hamsar,* Abby, and the three best children anybody could have—Sheeva, Farrah, and Ali—were essential in giving me encouragement, sanity, and patience.

M.R.N., Windsor
August 2006

Introduction to Sociology

What is sociology? Why should I take this course? What is it good for? Some of you may have pondered questions such as these before. Basically, sociology will help you refine your thought processes in a critical, systematic, and orderly way. However, it is not about all aspects of your thoughts, but only those that focus on group-based relations. That is to say, sociologists are interested in studying individual characteristics within groups, institutions, and structures. When we say that we are interested in group-based relations, we mean that we like to study individuals in group settings. For example, we may want to know how university education shapes students' knowledge, values, beliefs, consciousness, and future access to scarce resources (e.g., income). In order to do this we study the impact of education on students. We can **observe** students in a class setting in order to see how they interact with each other and with the instructor. We may **experiment** on them in order to see if students taught, let us say, in a lecture hall, learn differently from those who are taught via new electronic technology (e.g., e-mail, online courses, etc.). We may **compare** different groups of students (e.g., males and females) in order to see if there are differences in their values as they move through the education system or at different times. Similarly, we may study students by following them through life in order to see where they end up in the socioeconomic **hierarchy** (i.e., by paying attention to their **history**).

Once we have learned more about student life we can use this information to **predict** future events and improve their life. For example, if we find out that students who go to university earn more income than those who go to college, we can predict that this difference will emerge again and again with different data and perhaps at different times and places. Therefore, we can recommend that students attend university rather than college as a means of upward mobility.

In all of these examples, we used scientific methods of observation, experimentation, comparison, and prediction, as used in the natural sciences but also included in the historical method, which applies more to human society. We used these methods in order to understand students' values and behaviours, which took place in group settings. We would then use our study to provide a tentative explanation of students' values, behaviours, and so on. Therefore, we may say that sociology is a science that intends to construct **theories** about social relationships. Sociology is a science similar to chemistry, biology, or other natural sciences, because it, too, aims at systematically constructing and validating tentative explanations (i.e., theories) about the real world. But we should also recall that human subjects are not like inanimate objects in the natural sciences. Humans have feelings, emotions, and values that may guide their understandings. In fact, as your sociological knowledge grows you will be exposed to other sociological theories (e.g., feminism) that challenge our notion of sociology and that present science, itself, as a social construction (e.g., postmodernism). Despite different theories and empirical findings, as sociologists we aim to further improve our understanding of the social world by accumulating knowledge and evaluating our theories.

What is theory? Theory involves summarizing, connecting, condensing, and organizing ideas or a great deal of information about the social world. Theories are logical and consistent statements. They guide our research and are themselves modified as well. That is, theories are consistent with known facts and thus are testable in the real world. They are also general statements that apply to a large group of people but may exclude some people. For example, when we say that male students are more likely to be violent than female students, we do not mean that every male student is violent and every female student is nonviolent. We are merely pointing to the violent tendency, probability, and likelihood of male and female students.

There are four broad sociological theories that dominate our discipline.

- **Functionalists** are interested in explaining a particular social institution by its function and how it helps meet the needs of the system and/or helps the survival of larger society. Therefore, functionalists are interested in identifying the basic functions of any institution or social system and then explaining how it is held together. As an example, in his book *Suicide* (1951 [1938]), Émile Durkheim (1858–1917), one of the principal founders of sociology, theorized that suicide varies with the degree of integration of individuals in society. Those who are married or have many friends are less likely to commit suicide than their counterparts. Therefore, marriage and having friends is functional to individual survival. In other words, functionalists tend to view human society as an organism that has many parts and each part performs a function that meets society's needs and helps its survival. Accordingly, even crime is functional because it helps produce jobs for locksmiths, police officers, lawyers, judges, and many government officials. Similarly, a function of education is to help students learn the necessary skills for the employment market, and so on.

- **Conflict theorists** derive their views from Karl Marx (1818–1883), who stated that the history of all previous societies is a history of class struggles. This means that in any class-based society there are people and groups who are unequal in wealth, power, and resources. Those who have more tend to dominate those who have less, and the latter struggle to minimize or eliminate such domination. Marxist theorists tend to focus more on the economic structure of society than on other aspects because for them, those who control the economic process tend to control other aspects of society. It is not that the economic structure operates independent of politics or ideology. Rather, economic interests, politics, and ideology are often interrelated. Marxists point to the strong relationship between large businesses and government policies, which tend to favour business interests. They note how the prevalent views on private property, the judicial system, and religion tend to promote and protect the interests of the capitalist class in modern societies. For example, Marx used the example of religion and suggested that "religion is the opium of the masses" because it tends to make people accept their lower position in the system of inequality as "god's will," in exchange for the hope of finding a better place after life. It is not that people live in an illusion. Rather, their minds are subject to contradictory types of awareness that may confuse and fragment their judgment about the nature of the world they inhabit. In other words, the dominant groups are able to control the production of ideas and therefore subject the masses to such cultural and ideological production.
- **Symbolic interactionists** pay attention to **microstructures**, individuals, and agencies. Functionalists and Marxists tend to emphasize the importance of macrostructures. Symbolic interactionists are interested in finding out how face-to-face interaction between individuals helps explain human behaviour and produce shared meaning and stable social systems. George Herbert Mead (1863–1931) argued in *Mind, Self and Society* (1962 [1934]) that society emerges from the ability of individuals to refer to themselves as objects and to act accordingly. This is

possible because individuals use symbols (language and signs) in order to identify and distinguish themselves. They use words such as "I" and "me." However, individuals are able to use these self-referent terms because some element of community is embedded in these terms. "I the woman," "I the barber," "I the student," and so on, all have social characters. Therefore, individuals refer to themselves and interact in the society because they use self-referent terms and terms that have some communal status. From this, we can conclude that self is always symbolically connected to others in the society. Moreover, symbols constrain individuals' behaviour. Women, barbers, and students all think and behave according to social values, norms, and constraints associated with these terms. As an example, Sherif (1936, 1937) experimented in an autokinetic situation (the apparent movement of a point of light in a light-proof room lacking visible anchorages). He had a group of people sit in a dark room and observe a stationary pinpoint of light that was placed in front of them. Participants, not knowing that the light was stationary, stated that the light was moving in an erratic and random manner. Next, Sherif suggested to them that the light was moving in a horizontal manner and asked them to inform him about the extent of the movement. Subjects modified their understanding and stated that indeed the light was moving back and forth. Finally, after soliciting their views on the length of such movement, Sherif asked them to discuss the length of light with each other. Subsequently, those who had stated that the light was moving a large distance reduced their original estimate, and those who stated that the light was moving a short distance increased their original estimate. The conclusion drawn from this is that Sherif's symbolic assertion that the light moved, and moved in a horizontal manner and distance, was a coercive symbolic construction of individuals' perception. It also meant that individuals construct a disposition to act in specific situations and that the definition of the situation is learned, based on our symbolic experiences. In addition, the mind is a social process arising out of social interactions and changes according to future interactions.

- **Feminists** are mainly interested in evaluating and explaining why women have less power and resources than men, and how to challenge and transform such imbalance. Feminist theory is wide-ranging but basically it refers to a body of knowledge that aims to offer critical explanations of women's subordination and to undermine and expose it. In sum, feminists tend to explain male domination (i.e., patriarchy) by examining the structures of society, power relationships, and conventions. The unit on gender relations provides a detailed discussion of feminist theories. Here, a discussion of Nancy Chodorow's (1978) book, *Reproduction of Mothering,* gives us an example of how feminists explain female subordination. Chodorow is concerned with the social construction of the gender-based psyche, how women become mothers and men become fathers. She states that the organization of family life and childcare helps produce men and women who have different "rational capacities." In such an environment, girls experience a lesser sense of separateness from their mother than do boys. Despite turning to their father in order to develop a sense of separateness, girls never complete their separation from their mother. In fact, girls develop gender identity through identification with their mother. Consequently, as adults, women find themselves most comfortable in intimate relationships and seek to reproduce with a man in order to replicate the same triangular emotional configuration, by having a baby, that they experienced in childhood. Following a line of argument similar to Freud's, Chodorow states that boys undergo a process of sexuality development (see the unit on socialization) and repress their need for a love relationship. Therefore, for Chodorow, masculine personality comes as a denial of intimate companionship and connections, or a denial of femininity. Boys' painful separation from their mother through repression of Oedipal sexuality is also what pushes males to seek domination when in a relationship. In fact, Chodorow argues that intimacy with a woman evokes fear in men because it (unconsciously) symbolizes their early repression. In other words, boys' hostility toward their mother is entangled with the acquisition of masculinity, which is then generalized toward all women.

Recall that theories are developed about social relationships. Social relations are binding relationships that connect individuals to groups or society, such as friendship, family, motherhood, university culture, criminal culture, community, and so on. In *The Rules of Sociological Method,* Durkheim referred to such social relationships as "**social facts.**" Social facts have distinctive characteristics, are external to individuals, endure over time, and have coercive power over individuals, independent of individual will. For example, individuals are born into an ongoing society that already has a definite organization and structure and that conditions their personality and exercises constraints upon individuals. In another example, when you enter university you are exposed to a culture that is external to you and constrains your behaviour: you must respect the class environment, you must not cheat, you may identify with your university, and so on. Similarly, individuals become father, mother, student, friend, employee, among other roles, all of which are subject to external social constraints that are identified with these roles. For example, fathers and mothers provide and rear children, and friends do not betray each other. Finally, sociologists study these social facts the same way that natural scientists study an object. Therefore, sociologists are concerned with the study of these large-scale structures, shared moral beliefs, institutionalized laws—and their impact on individuals. We treat social facts as "things," such as atoms or organisms, and study them.

By now you may have realized that being a sociologist requires having what C. Wright Mills (1959) called a **sociological imagination.** Such an imagination allows for creative thinking that enables an individual's awareness in relationship to the wider society. It helps us to comprehend the links between our immediate personal social setting and a more remote impersonal social world. A key element of this imagination is to view one's society as an outsider. Anthony Giddens (1987: 13–22) decomposes the sociological imagination into a threefold exercise of sensitivity: historical, anthropological, and critical. As you sit in class in your comfortable clothing, enjoying your laptop, audio, and PowerPoint presentations and feeling free to challenge your instructor or those outside the university, you may ask yourself whether such comfort and freedom would be possible without the industrial revolution of the latter part of the 18th century, primarily in England, and the political revolution, primarily in France. These "two great revolutions" brought the world into your home via radio, TV, Internet, and satellites, and gave you the democratic citizenship rights within a nation state and globally. They enabled the Chinese to watch *I Love Lucy* or *American Idol* in Beijing, and Americans to consume Chinese-made products in the United States. They enabled a Canadian Aboriginal woman to take her government to the International Court and win her Aboriginal title right. These are changes that can be attributed to the last 200 to 300 years. We can go even further and understand that without the Muslims providing the Greeks and Europeans with the number zero, we may have not developed the binary code so important in computer technology. There are many other examples that illustrate how our present comfort and knowledge is the result of our past. However, suffice it to say here that our knowledge of past history is an important type of sensitivity necessary for understanding our present world.

The second type of sociological imagination refers to anthropological sensitivity. This requires us to break away from the notion that our way of life, and particularly the Western way of life, is superior to other life forms and cultures, or that all societies must undergo a similar process of evolution as that of the Western world. This tendency is referred to as ethnocentrism or Eurocentrism and should be challenged through our anthropological imagination. A cursory knowledge of different cultures and societies will inform us that many such cultures existed long before ours and had far fewer social problems (e.g., crime and violence) than ours. They seem to have developed institutions that were necessary and sufficient for peaceful coexistence. The tendency to use Western culture to judge others is rooted in the history of colonization and capitalist expansions aiming to exploit cheap labour and raw materials of other societies and to make them a consumer heaven for capitalist commodities. In order to colonize and exploit, Western capitalist powers viewed First Nations Aboriginals and Africans as godless savages who needed to be brought to the civilized world. For example, in Canada, such ideas justified forcing the First Nations people onto reserves and their children into white Christian schools away from their parents. Similar justifications were used for enslavement of Africans and other groups. Anthropological imagination allows us to comprehend and appreciate the diversity of human life. Such an appreciation also helps us to understand ourselves— the human race—better.

Finally, by combining historical and anthropological imagination we will arrive at critical imagination, allowing us to break away from thinking only in terms of the society we are part of here and now. This enables us to see alternative societies, futures, and forms of development. It also helps us critique existing societies. You will note that such critique is based on analysis and evidence. A discussion of types of sensitivity helps us understand that, despite the fact that we use the methods of the natural sciences, our discipline is different from theirs. Human beings and human societies are not like inanimate objects, which are similar in kind and governed by some natural laws. Human society is diverse and its history shows alternative paths.

A BRIEF DISCUSSION OF STATISTICS
◆ ◆ ◆

Sociologists interested in quantitative research often use concepts such as dependent and independent variables. A variable is simply the observable equivalent of a concept and is formed by a range of different observable values. For example, sex has two categories: males and females. Income is measured in dollars. Political party affiliation consists of Liberal, Conservative, Bloc Quebecois, New Democratic Party, and others. A variable that can be changed by another variable is called a dependent variable. A variable that causes change in another variable is called an independent variable. Thus, for example, we can say income causes well-being. In this case income is the independent variable and well-being is the dependent variable. If our causal statement is correct, then a change in income should produce a change in well-being.

Sociologists also use various statistical techniques in order to summarize their research and discuss their findings. These techniques are highly specialized and require some knowledge of mathematics and statistics. The brief below will help students understand information and tables provided in most sociological research. Sociologists often summarize information by showing the **frequency** distribution of their findings. For example, if there are 20 male subjects and 30 female subjects, then we can say that 40% of subjects are males (= 20 * 100 / 20 + 30) and 60% are females (= 30 * 100 / 20 + 30).

Sometimes, sociologists summarize information by showing the **mean** or average. Mean is a common measure of central tendency and applies to variables that are ranked and the distance between the categories is equal. These variables may or may not have a true or absolute zero point. If such variables do not have a true zero point, they are called **interval** variables (e.g., IQ, Fahrenheit). On the other hand, if they do have a true zero point, they are called **ratio** level variables (e.g., income in dollars, Kelvin scale). For example, $10 is half as much as $20 and a quarter of $40. In order to calculate the mean, we simply add the frequencies and divide it by the number of categories in the data. For example, if one person has $20, another $50, and yet another $140, then their mean would be $70 (= 20 + 50 + 140 / 3).

Other times, sociologists are interested in knowing how dispersed individuals' or groups' scores are from their mean. Here they may be interested in **variance** on **standard deviation.** Variance is simply a measure of the differences between the individuals' score and their mean:

the higher the variance, the more the dispersion of individuals from their mean. The square root of variance is called **standard deviation.** The reason for this has to do with the calculation of variance, which is based on the sum of squared deviations across cases and then divided by the number of cases.

Sociologists sometimes analyze two or more variables at the same time. For example, they may wish to know how many males versus females have a university education and how many have a college education. This is done through **bivariate** analysis: examining the relationship between two variables. Other times, sociologists would like to know the effect of one variable or phenomenon on another when

---

"What can I do with a BA in sociology?" As a strong liberal arts major, sociology provides several answers to this important question:

A BA in sociology is excellent preparation for future graduate work in sociology in order to become a professor, researcher, or applied sociologist.

The undergraduate degree provides a strong liberal arts preparation for entry-level positions throughout the business, social service, and government worlds. Employers look for people with the skills that an undergraduate education in sociology provides.

Since its subject matter is intrinsically fascinating, sociology offers valuable preparation for careers in journalism, politics, public relations, business, or public administration—fields that involve investigative skills and working with diverse groups.

Many students choose sociology because they see it as a broad liberal arts base for professions such as law, education, medicine, social work, and counseling. Sociology provides a rich foundation of knowledge that directly pertains to each of these fields.

"What can I do with an MA or PhD degree in sociology?" With advanced degrees comes the likelihood that a job will have the title sociologist, but many opportunities exist—the diversity of sociological careers ranges much further than what you might find under "S" in the Sunday newspaper employment ads. Many jobs outside of academia do not necessarily carry the specific title of sociologist:

Sociologists become high school teachers or faculty in colleges and universities, advising students, conducting research, and publishing their work. Over 3000 colleges (in the United States) offer sociology courses.

Sociologists enter the corporate, non-profit, and government worlds as directors of research, policy analysts, consultants, human resource managers, and program managers.

Practicing sociologists with advanced degrees may be called research analysts, survey researchers, gerontologists, statisticians, urban planners, community developers, criminologists, or demographers.

Some MA and PhD sociologists obtain specialized training to become counsellors, therapists, or program directors in social service agencies.

Today, sociologists embark upon literally hundreds of career paths. Although teaching and conducting research remains the dominant activity among the thousands of professional sociologists today, other forms of employment are growing both in number and significance. In some sectors, sociologists work closely with economists, political scientists, anthropologists, psychologists, social workers, and others, reflecting a growing appreciation of sociology's contributions to interdisciplinary analysis and action.

Source: American Sociological Association
(URL: http://www.asanet.org/page.ww?section=Careers+and+Jobs&name=Sociology%3A+A+World+of+Opportunities). For more information see http://www.sociologyinourtimes3e.nelson.com/degrees.html.

they take into account the importance of other variables or phenomena. That is, they would like to know the net effect of a variable, holding the effect(s) of other variable(s) constant. This is done through **multivariate** analysis. In this book you will encounter two multivariate statistical techniques: **ordinary regression** and **logistic regression**.

Ordinary (least square) regression technique relies on an interval or ratio type of dependent variable. Regression statistics give researchers a summary coefficient that can be easily interpreted as one unit change in the dependent variable being accompanied with one unit change in the independent variable. For example, if income, the independent variable, was to change from $100 to $200, and number of health problems, the dependent variable, was to change by 1 unit (from 0 to 1), then, when income changes from $200 to $300, health problems will change by 1 unit (from 2 to 3). Similarly, if income were to change from $500 to $600, health problems would change by 1 unit (from 5 to 6). Ordinary regression is called least square regression because of its property, which is that the sum of the squared deviation from the regression line is a minimum. Regression technique also provides a measure of variation, which is called R-squared or explained variance. It amounts to the percentage of change in the dependent variable, which is accounted by the independent variables in the regression model.

There is little difference between bivariate and multivariate regression analyses, except that in the **multivariate** models, one unit change in independent variable produces one unit change in dependent variable, holding the effects of other variables constant. This simply means that multivariate models produce a net effect of each independent variable on the dependent variable, taking into account the effects of other independent variables.

Logistic regression coefficients are similar to ordinary regression, with two basic differences. First, the dependent variable is dichotomous (e.g., vote or not vote, good or bad, high or low, Protestant or Catholic, etc.). Second, when interpreting the logistic regression coefficients, instead of saying one unit change in independent variable produces a unit change in dependent variable, one says that the odds of, for example, voting (dependent variable), is so many times higher or lower for males compared to females (independent variable). Logistic regression calculates estimates (B coefficients) that point to the log odds on voting (dependent variable) for those in a category of independent variable compared to anther category in the independent variable called the reference. Since the log odds have little intuitive meaning, researchers often use the exponential of a coefficient. The exponential of a coefficient is the factor by which the unlogged odds on the dependent variable are multiplied for one unit of change in the predictor variable (e.g., gender). If the exponential value is more than 1, then the relevant category in the independent variable has a higher effect on the dependent variable than the reference category. In contrast, if the exponential is less than 1, then the relevant category has a lower effect on the dependent variable than the reference category.

Unit One

CULTURE
Introduction: Canadian–American Cultural Similarities and Differences

♦ ♦ ♦

In everyday life, you might notice that some people do not follow society's norms, or that their values and norms are different from yours. For example, some may think that eating frog legs is a sign of high culture, whereas others view it with disdain. In some societies premarital sex is acceptable and is a test of love and compatibility, whereas in other societies the same behaviour is viewed as promiscuity and even prostitution. What these examples suggest is that people adhere to different cultural values, beliefs, and norms. In this sense, **culture** refers to a set of values, norms, mores, laws, and so on that prevails in a given society. **Values** are abstract principles, which in and of themselves are neither true nor false. They are cultural conceptions about desirable goals that result in judgment of actions. Therefore, being good has meaning only in relation to being bad, and such meaning differs by place, time, and context. For example, during **slavery,** slaves were subject to the will of the master. They were sold and bought without having any rights. At that time, slavery was acceptable, at least among the slave owners. In modern times, we look at slavery with disdain and refer to it as our dark past.

Once values become institutionalized they are referred to as **norms.** Institutionalization of norms means that they are supported by an organized system of social relationships. Norms are rules and expectations about what we should or should not do. To be quiet during a lecture in class is a norm. Norms are not necessarily stable. They change over time. For example, before the

1960s it was the norm not to have premarital sex. Now the norm has changed. The new norm is that if you have premarital sex, you should have safe sex. **Mores** are a much stronger set of norms. They must be followed because they are essential for the survival of the society. For example, eating pork is forbidden by Jews and Muslims. Once norms become formally legislated, they become **laws.** For example, today there are laws against slavery, incest, and genocide. Therefore, generally, all laws are based on norms, and all norms are based on values. However, not all values are norms, and not all norms are laws.

Culture is more than values, norms, and laws. It includes both material and nonmaterial aspects of a society. For example, houses differ from one society to another. Some houses are made of wood, and others are made of bricks. Some societies have TVs, cars, and computers, and others do not. It is important to remember that all shared products of a society are part of that society's culture.

Culture is one of the most important elements of human society, distinguishing us from animals. It allows individuals to pass their values, norms, laws, discoveries, and products from one generation to another and across societies. Animals act instinctively and start anew in each generation. Humans, in contrast, produce culture (material and nonmaterial) and pass it to the next generation. In turn, culture produces people and their future generations. Imagine trying to learn how to hunt, to build a house or car, or to go to the moon.

If we were to rely on each generation starting from scratch, none of these things would have been possible. Accumulation of culture across generations resulted in our unprecedented success when compared to other species.

The implication of our discussion on culture is that we should be critical of assertions that humans are aggressive or acquisitive by "nature." Or that we have an instinct for survival, or sex, or food gathering. In fact, some individuals are aggressive and acquisitive whereas others are less so or not at all. Some people commit suicide, others remain celibate for life, and yet others go on hunger strikes. If these attributes were "natural," we should not be able to find variations in these attributes by people and culture. However, it is also a mistake to consider nature and culture (nurture) as unrelated. Nature and nurture complement each other. Nature provides us with the raw materials that can be shaped by culture.

The aforementioned discussion also points to the diversity of human culture. This diversity cannot be understood if we look at others just through our own way of life—**ethnocentrism.** We also need to adopt an outsider's point of view—**cultural relativism.** That is, we need to recognize that other cultures cannot be judged by our own cultural standards. We may not like that the Japanese criticize us for abandoning our elderly by leaving them apart from the family in old-age homes. But we criticize the traditional Inuit culture that left the aged to die in the snow. We may be quick to view our religion as the one true faith and others as full of superstitions. These examples suggest that it is often hard to view one's own culture objectively. One of the reasons for ethnocentrism or a sense of cultural superiority is that it tends to develop social cohesion, faith, and confidence in one's culture.

What are some of the common values Canadians share? How are these values different across regions and between the French and others? Table 1.1 provides a snapshot of Canadian values and attitudes in 2000. Canadians seem to favour a traditional type of family (83.3%) and view people as responsible for their position in society (71.9%). They also agree that the gap between rich and poor needs to be reduced (81.2%). Canadians tend to be tolerant of other ways of life (73.4%) and sympathetic toward feminism (68.1%). Nevertheless, they do not view a need for more immigrants (14.1%) or that minorities should have special rights (18.1%). However, Canadians differ on these issues by region and ethnicity. Support for the traditional family is higher among people in Eastern regions; English Quebeckers are more likely to believe that individuals should be responsible for their position in society; tolerance of other ways of life is higher in the Eastern regions; sympathy toward feminism is higher among French Quebeckers, and so on.

However, people often develop a better understanding of their own culture and society by comparing themselves to others. Canadians, for example, have a tendency to compare themselves to Americans. Canadians view themselves as polite, shy, and timid, and Americans as nationalistic, loud, and disrespectful. In recent times, however, there are signs that Canadians are as nationalistic and loud as their neighbour to the South. For example, in a beer commercial aired in the spring of 2000:

> "The Rant," a spot for Molson Canadian, featured a young man known only as "Joe," who stands on stage before a screen which flashes Canadian images while he outlines what makes Canada unique. Joe begins his rant shyly, hesitantly, but slowly gains confidence, building to an heroic crescendo and climaxing with the tag line, "My name is Joe, and I am Canadian!". . . Within days of its release, "The Rant" was being discussed in media across the country (and beyond), parodied on the radio, and repeated live to cheering crowds at hockey games (Wright et al., 2002).

This is not the only example of Canadianism. Other examples include T-shirts stating that "Canada kicks ass" or "Canadian girls kick ass." The popular rock song "American Woman," by the Guess Who, is arguably an anti-American song written by Canadian musicians. Although these examples suggest that Canadians are becoming more similar to their American neighbour in being loud and nationalistic, it is not clear from these examples if this similarity has been there in the past or is even present now. To know this we need comparative sociological studies.

Seymour Martin Lipset, one of the eminent American sociologists, has been involved for decades in comparing Canada and the United States. He has argued that Canada and the United States differ from each other on the basis of a five-value system that he called the American Creed: **liberty, egalitarianism, individualism, populism,** and **laissez faire.** Lipset has argued that the root of these differences is in the American Revolution, which produced enduring cultural differences between the two countries. The Canadians,

Table 1.1   Values and Attitudes of Canadians by Regions, 2000 (Percentage Agree or Strongly Agree)

				Quebec Population			
Inequality Issues	*East* %	*Ontario* %	*West* %	*French* %	*English* %	*Other* %	*Total* %
More needs to be done to reduce the rich and poor gaps	80.9	87.1	92.7	83.6	83.7	71.8	81.2
Unions need to have more power	14.8	20.1	16.5	9.2	12.4	7.8	13.2
Business needs to have more power	42.8	18.2	44.1	26.7	14.1	18.6	25.3
People who don't get ahead should blame themselves not the system	71.4	69.3	73.7	72.5	77.7	71.4	71.9
Gender Issues							
Society would be better off if more women stayed home with their children	44.4	43.6	52.6	46.4	45.3	47.9	46.8
I favour political parties having equal number of male and female candidates	44.8	32.4	27.7	56.6	54.1	43.8	40.3
I am sympathetic towards feminism	67.8	65.1	61.3	76.6	72.7	50.7	68.1
The best way to protect women's interests is to have more women in Parliament.	55.4	48.3	46.6	61.9	64.7	25.1	52.8
Ethno-Racial Issues							
Minority groups need special rights	17.6	15.7	13.2	24.1	38.9	12.5	18.1
We have gone too far for pushing for equal rights in this country	42.7	37.6	46.9	37.6	19.4	14.3	40.4
Canada should admit more immigrants	13.5	15.1	14.8	10.9	23.8	34.9	14.1
Immigrants make an important contribution to this country	77.1	89.3	85.8	71.6	91.2	99.1	72.1
I favour political parties to have more members of racial minorities as candidates	50.1	44.4	37.1	50.1	55.5	80.1	47.3
We should be more tolerant of people who choose to live according to their own standards	81.7	72.8	67.6	75.3	78.4	66.6	73.4
Canadian unity is weakened by those of different ethnic and culture sticking to their old ways	41.1	36.6	42.2	41.4	26.5	0	39.5
We have gone too far in pushing bilingualism in Canada	55.5	58.8	68.1	23.7	25.8	25.1	50.5
Religion							
Religion is important in my life	84.6	75.6	72.4	65.4	71.3	76.6	72.8
The Bible is the actual world of God and is to be taken literally word for word	31.1	21.2	22.4	18.4	20.6	28.6	22.2
Crime							
I favour death penalty for persons convicted of murder	40.2	44.2	51.6	44.1	39.1	28.6	45.2

Continued

Table 1.1 Values and Attitudes of Canadians by Regions, 2000 (Percentage Agree or Strongly Agree) *Continued*

Family	East %	Ontario %	West %	Quebec Population French %	Quebec Population English %	Other %	Total %
It is important to promote traditional family values	91.9	83.2	81.5	81.2	80.5	81.3	83.3
Only people who are legally married should have children	35.3	30.6	39.1	9.6	35.1	50.1	28.1
Gays and Lesbians should be allowed to get married	51.7	53.4	51.7	58.7	56.7	37.8	54.2

Note: Quebec population is divided by language spoken at home.

Source: Elections Canada, National Election Study, 2000.

exemplified by the United Empire Loyalists, left the United States as an opposition to the American Revolution and in support of the Empire (Britain). Thus, Canada was born out of counter-revolution whereas the United States was born of revolution. In a series of articles and a book, Grabb, Curtis, and colleagues have argued that Lipset is wrong in that there is little U.S./Canada difference in these core values. Michael Carroll takes up this debate and argues that this debate is irresolvable because each side has come to the table adhering to unacknowledged ideology in terms of which is the best type of democracy: Canadian or American. Lipset (1963, 1965, 1986, 1990, 2001) believes that the American democracy is best, and Grabb and his colleagues argue that Canadians and Americans are similar because they share a British culture. Curtis and Grabb respond that Carroll misunderstood their arguments.

As you read the debate on the following pages, ponder these questions:

1. What are the key elements of being Canadian, and how are these, if any, distinguishable from American culture?
2. What are key differences between Canada and the United States? How did these differences emerge?
3. What is the "best" sort of democracy? How does one come to an understanding of the "best" democracy?
4. Should one nation invade another in order to establish her visions of democracy upon the other?
5. Are there Canadian attributes that are not identified in the debate? What are they?
6. Which groups in Canada are more likely to agree or disagree with the Canadian attributes identified in questions 1 and 5?
7. Why do you think Canadians differ in their views on gender, inequality, religion, and so on?

Who Owns Democracy? Explaining the Long-Running Debate over Canadian/American Value Differences

Michael P. Carroll

University of Western Ontario

◆ ◆ ◆

For more than forty years, in a steady stream of articles and books, Seymour Martin Lipset (1963a: 248–73; 1963c; 1965; 1986; 1990a; 1990b; 2001) has argued that the American Revolution produced enduring cultural differences between Canada and the United States. In the first instance, he argues, this was because the United Empire Loyalists, who left the new Republic to settle in Upper Canada, had explicitly rejected the values of the American Revolution whereas the Americans left behind were more likely to be committed to those values. In his own words (Lipset 1996b, 23),

> [T]wo nations came out of the American Revolution: Canada the country of the counterrevolution, and the United States the country of the revolution. The northern nation is much more statist, Tory (noblesse oblige), communitarian, elitist, group oriented, and deferential. The southern is much more individualistic, antistatist, antielitiest, supportive of laissez-faire, and less obedient.

For Lipset, these initial cultural differences were subsequently reinforced by other institutional patterns (most notably, by different religious traditions).

Lipset's work has generated a continuing series of articles by Edward Grabb, James Curtis and a variety of co-investigators (hereafter: Grabb et al.) whose consistent message is that Lipset's core argument is wrong (Baer, Grabb and Johnston 1990; Curtis, Grabb and Baer 1992; Baer, Grabb and Johnston 1993; Grabb, Baer and Curtis 1999; Grabb, Curtis and Baer 2000; Grabb, Curtis and Baer 2001; Grabb and Curtis 2004). Lipset himself (2001, 97) has called attention to the fact that his critics are for the most part English-Canadian academics. What makes the English-Canadian background of Lipset's critics worth noting is that their critique of Lipset is not what someone familiar with Canadian popular culture might expect.

Thus, it has been common since the 1960s for many English-Canadian nationalists to emphasize the ways in which Canada is different from the U.S. Lipset (1965) himself took note of this process by pointing out that English-Canadian nationalists were attempting to depict Canada as a more humane and democratic society as compared to the U.S. Although today there is no shortage of commentators writing on the "Americanization" of Canadian culture (a position, note, which itself presupposes that Canada and the U.S. were once relatively distinct cultures), there are still a great many Canadians who continue to emphasize the cultural differences between the two countries. . . .

Basically, Grabb et al. have advanced two claims. First, they argue that if we pay attention to ordinary people rather than elites, then there is much historical evidence suggesting that local English-speaking populations in the U.S. and Canada around the time of the Revolution shared more or less the same cultural values. In particular, they argue that the United Empire Loyalists were little different (in terms of cultural values) from the Americans who stayed behind. Second, Grabb et al. argue that survey data collected in recent years fail to support the con-

From Michael P. Carroll, "Who Owns Democracy? Explaining the long-running debates over Canadian/American value differences," *Canadian Review of Sociology and Anthropology*, Vol. 42 No. 3, August 2005, pp. 267–282. Reprinted with permission of the Canadian Sociology and Anthropology Association.

tention that there are significant differences between Canadians (outside Quebec) and Americans on attitudinal and behavioural measures relevant to the Lipset thesis.

But perhaps the most curious feature of this long-running debate is precisely that it has been so long-running. Even writing more than a decade ago, Baer, Grabb and Johnston (1990) could call the debate over the Lipset thesis "one of the most well-known and longstanding arguments in comparative social analysis." This is all the more true today. What no one has yet asked is why this debate is still on-going after more than four decades.

The participants themselves would likely give a two-part answer. First, I suspect that they would argue—as in fact both sides have argued over the years—that studying Canada and the U.S. in comparative perspective is the best way to gain insight into each society individually. . . . Second, I also imagine that both sides would explain the longevity of this debate by invoking modernist conventions suggesting that the pursuit of empirical truth is what social science is all about. In other words, I suspect they would argue that even in this postmodern age there is some value in using data to decide if the Lipset thesis is right or wrong.

What I want to do in this article is suggest that answers of this sort do not fully explain the durability of this on-going debate and that in fact the debate has been sustained mainly by unacknowledged ideological claims implicit in the arguments being advanced by each side. As a first step in demonstrating all this, it will be useful to imagine the ways in which the debate between Lipset and his critics might have proceeded differently if the stated concerns of the participants had truly been the concerns fueling the debate.

COMPARING NATIONAL CULTURES
◆ ◆ ◆

Suppose, for example, that the concerns were indeed with assessing whether or not there were important cultural differences between Canada and the United States, how might we proceed? Lipset has undertaken to focus on the five political values that constitute his American Creed: liberty, egalitarianism, individualism, populism, and laissez-faire. Grabb et al. have increasingly come to focus on a list of four political values: liberty, legal equality, pluralism (tolerance of diversity) and popular sovereignty. Although there are differences between the two lists, even when the same word (like "liberty") is being used, what they have in common is that both lists restrict our attention to a relatively small number of political values. But why such a narrow range? Furthermore, why the exclusive focus on political values?

The fact that Lipset peppers his work with terms like "the American Creed," "national identity," "American character," "national character," etc. easily creates the impression that the values he is discussing are somehow "central" in American culture. Grabb et al. create the same impression for the values on their list. Not only do they also use terms like "national character" . . . , but in fact say quite explicitly that the four values they identify are "core principles [that] were crucial to the social-structural and cultural development of Canada and the United States" (Grabb and Curtis 2004, 57). The fact is, however, that neither Lipset nor Grabb et al. have ever established the centrality of the particular values they discuss to either Canadian or American culture, or presented any evidence establishing that the values on which they focus are more central than other values in the culture (Canadian or American) being studied. . . .

Lipset might presumably justify his focus by suggesting (1) that the five values constituting his American Creed were central to the rhetoric of the American Revolution and (2) that his original goal was not really to assess Canadian/America cultural difference generally but rather to assess the continuing influence of the American Revolution on American culture. Fair enough, but if in fact the concern driving the debate were indeed to establish the continuing effects (or, in the case of Grabb/Curtis, the non-effects) of the American Revolution, then it is still the case that the debate might have proceeded quite differently. This can be demonstrated by considering a body of literature, very visible among American historians but generally ignored both by Lipset and by Grabb et al., that is directly relevant to the matter of the Revolution's continuing cultural impact.

REVOLUTIONARY RELIGION
◆ ◆ ◆

Lipset has always argued that the cultural values which came into force as a result of the Revolution were subsequently reinforced by the particular Protestant sects that have predominated in the U.S. (Lipset 1986, 124–128; Lipset 1990a, 74–89) For some time now, however, a number of historians (Mathews, 1969; Hatch, 1989; Schneider, 1991) have advanced a much stronger argument: the success of the Revolution created a cultural climate in the U.S. in which people were encouraged to make the values associated with the Revolution central to their religious experience. Nathan O. Hatch's (1989) version of this argument has been particularly influential (on

Hatch's influence, see Albanese 2002, 13–14). Hatch's argument, in a nutshell, is that the tremendous success of the Revolution (1) eroded traditional authority, (2) empowered ordinary people to think for themselves independently of established authority and (3) generated a passion for equality. Carried into the religious realm, mainly by the Methodists and Baptists, Hatch argues, this led people (1) to reject the traditional view that the clergy were a special class set apart from other believers, (2) to take their "deepest emotional impulses" at face value and (3) to believe that they could create a quite different and much better world in which to live. Concretely, this means that Methodists and Baptists were more likely than, say Presbyterians, Congregationalists and others, to grant local congregations a great deal of autonomy and to not make formal education a requirement for the ministry. The great success of the Methodists and Baptists in the aftermath of the Revolution, in other words, which was always at the expense of other Protestant groups (Finke and Stark, 1992), derived from the fact that the Methodists and Baptists embodied the values associated with the American Revolution in a way that these other groups did not.

So, what happens if we do what neither Lipset nor Grabb et al. have done and bring the Hatch thesis, that is, the contention that populist and anti-elitist impulses of the Revolution (hereafter: the Revolutionary Ethos) were incorporated into evangelical Christianity, to bear on the issue of the Revolution's continuing effect on American culture? It seems to me that doing this leads to a fairly straightforward prediction: *we are most likely to find a lingering commitment to the Revolutionary Ethos in those U.S. contexts where the influence of evangelical Christianity has been greatest*—and this in turn brings us to an interesting feature of the work by Grabb et al.

ON IGNORING THE CASES
THAT ARE MOST RELEVANT

◆ ◆ ◆

Lipset's (1963a, 1965) early work suggested that Americans were more likely to participate in voluntary associations on account of the individualism and distrust of the state that were among the legacies of the Revolution. . . . The Hatch thesis leads us to expect that religious contexts are precisely where we are most likely to find a lingering commitment to the Revolutionary Ethos and so to the notion that people should shape their society through voluntary associations. . . . In fact, as

Curtis, Grabb, and Baer's (1992) own data demonstrate, when religious organizations and associations are included, America does surpass Canada and thirteen other Western nations with regard to participation rates in voluntary associations—which is, just to repeat, what the Lipset/Hatch thesis leads us to expect. Curtis, Grabb and Baer (1992), however, then go on to exclude religious organizations from their analysis. Doing this, they find . . . that U.S. participation rates are not especially high, and so conclude that their data falsify the Lipset thesis. In the end, in other words, they challenge Lipset's contention that the Revolution has had a continuing cultural impact but only by excluding the cases, religious organizations, which the Hatch thesis suggests are most relevant to that contention. Still, a far more serious example of "ignoring the evidence that is most relevant" is to be found in Grabb et al.'s treatment of the U.S. South.

THE SOUTH AND THE REVOLUTION

◆ ◆ ◆

In the popular imagination the South is likely most of all associated with slavery and American Civil War. Then too there is no denying that in the post-Civil War period, the South was routinely characterized by patterns of political organization that disenfranchised black (and a large number of white) voters and concentrated power in the hands of a relatively small number of white males. Given these associations and patterns, it may at first be difficult to associate the South with the Revolution's emphasis on equality and liberty. Yet the fact is that the South and Southern leaders played a crucial part in securing the success of the Revolution and the Revolutionary Ethos. It is something of a cliché in American history texts, for example, to say that the Revolution started in the North but ended in the South. Partly, this means that as the British increasingly turned their attention to what they regarded as easier targets in the Carolinas and Georgia, many of the crucial battles in the last few years of the Revolution were fought in the South. But it also means that the South—Virginia in particular—supplied some of the most recognizable leaders of the Revolution, including George Washington, Thomas Jefferson, Francis Lightfoot Lee, and Patrick Henry.

Furthermore, as much as it may seem odd to modern audiences, the Southern commitment to the Revolution generally and to the rhetoric of "equality" in particular, was not at all incompatible with slavery. Indeed, in the late eighteenth century, Southern slaveholders were among those Americans *most* likely to express a commitment to equality. . . . This alone might lead to the prediction that if the Revolution shaped American culture, then any lingering remnants of that "shaping" should be more evident in the U.S. South than in the U.S. West.

Still, the strongest grounds for expecting that the Revolution's cultural effects might be especially apparent in the U.S. South derives from the Hatch thesis given that the forms of evangelical Christianity that embraced and perpetuated the Revolutionary Ethos have always been predominant in the South in a way that has never been true of the rest of English-speaking North America. The historical data presented by Finke and Stark (1992, 282–288), for example, make it clear that by 1850 Methodists and Baptists outnumbered all other religious groups (combined) in almost all areas of the South and that this sort of Methodist/Baptist predominance was not characteristic of other areas in the U.S. . . .

All in all then, if the Revolutionary Ethos was incorporated into evangelical Christianity (which is the Hatch thesis), then we should be most likely to encounter the continuing effects of this Revolutionary heritage in the one area, the South, where the sort of evangelical Christianity that emerged in the wake of the Revolution has been "in place" the longest—and in fact we do.

THE PERSISTENCE OF THE REVOLUTIONARY ETHOS IN THE SOUTH

◆ ◆ ◆

Lipset has made clear (Lipset 1996a, 275–280) that by "individualism" he means that type of individualism that leads people to maintain the civil order through voluntary associations and self-made decisions rather than by relying on the state and hierarchical authority. In fact, this emphasis on the right of individuals to decide for themselves how to engage and shape the civil order, and a corresponding disdain for rules imposed top down by the state, seems to be the common thread that underlies at least four of the five elements in his American Creed (namely, individualism, liberty, populism, and laissez-faire). These four elements, in other words, might profitably be collapsed into a single cultural category called "laissez-faire individualism." Using Hatch's formulation, laissez-faire individualism is thus the value that derives from the Revolutionary belief that ordinary citizens can and should shape both their own destiny and the nature of the community in which they live without need of guidance by elites.

All this is relevant to the matter of the South because studies of (white male) Southern culture routinely mention that precisely this sort of individualism, tightly linked as it is to notions of community and civic responsibility, has been a continuing theme in that culture. . . .

The South, in other words, can plausibly be regarded as providing strong evidence in support of the contention that the Revolution and the Revolutionary Ethos has had (does have) a continuing effect on American culture. And yet, neither side in the debate over the Lipset thesis has really ever taken the work by Hatch (and others) on the links between the Revolutionary Ethos and evangelical Christianity to heart, and examined what we know about southern culture in light of this thesis. Lipset himself, for example though sensitive to the matter of regional culture in Canada (evidenced in his discussions of Quebec) has generally ignored regional culture within in the U.S. Grabb et al., by contrast, *have* taken the South into account but in an odd way.

EXPLAINING (AWAY) THE SOUTH

◆ ◆ ◆

Baer, Grabb and Johnston (1993) used survey data from a multi-nation "Class structure and Class consciousness" study to argue that there are in fact three distinct regional subcultures in North America: (1) Quebec, (2) the U.S. South, and (3) the U.S. outside the South combined with Canada outside Quebec. Their evidence for singling out the South as a distinct regional subculture consists mainly in demonstrating that Southerners are less committed to gender equality in the workplace and more committed to family discipline. Although the authors cite this as evidence that Lipset is wrong (since there seems to be little difference between Americans outside the South and Canadians outside Quebec), the fact is that these gender/family measures bear only a tenuous relationship to the strong emphasis on local autonomy, anti-elitism, laissez-faire individualism, etc. that (if Lipset and Hatch are correct) is the main cultural heritage of the Revolution.

In their most recent work, Grabb and Curtis (2004) continue the sort of analysis used earlier in Baer, Grabb and Johnston (1993), i.e., they show that if you exclude Quebec and the American South, then English Canadians and Americans outside the South appear similar on a variety of attitudinal and behavioural measures. I must add that in doing so they quite inadvertently call attention to data that can be read as supporting the Lipset/Hatch thesis. For example, a central part of Lipset's original argument was that the disdain for hierarchical authority that flowed from the American Creed produced higher rates of crime in the U.S. Given this, the Hatch thesis, suggesting as it does that the Revolutionary Ethos is most entrenched in the U.S. South, would lead us to expect that crime rates should be especially high in the U.S. South. And indeed, as Grabb and Curtis (p. 160) themselves point out, this is true. . . .

[T]he main point to be kept in mind here is this: the one paragraph just mentioned notwithstanding, both sides in the debate over the Lipset thesis—despite any number of passing references to religion in America—have for decades now ignored the clear implications of a very visible body of scholarly literature on American religion (the Hatch thesis) that leads easily to predictions which are directly relevant to the matter of the Revolution's continuing cultural impact. A parsimonious way to explain this is on the hypothesis that the goal has never really been, for either Grabb et al. or Lipset, to assess the lingering cultural effects of the Revolution, just as it has never been to assess whether Canadian culture and American culture differ in important ways. So then: what *has* driven the debate?

LIPSET ON "THE BEST SORT OF DEMOCRACY"

◆ ◆ ◆

As most readers will know, Lipset's work on Canadian/ American value differences is one thread in a larger body of work concerned with "democracy"—and a second thread in this same body of work is concerned with the "social prerequisites" of democracy. In regard to this second issue, Lipset (1963b) early on argued that stable and continuing democratic traditions were fostered most of all by economic development (which muted discontent in the lower classes); by Protestantism; by legislatures based on geographical (rather than proportional) representation; and by two-party (rather than multi-party) systems. Thirty years later, in his presidential address to the American Sociological Association, Lipset (1994) was still making this same argument using the same list of characteristics.

Reviewing the various attempts to assess the empirical adequacy of Lipset's argument on democracy is beyond the scope of this article and indeed not relevant to my concern, which is simply to determine how Lipset's theory functions ideologically. Clearly, it functions to legitimate the ideological claim that English-speaking democracies

(which are associated with high levels of economic development, Protestantism, two party systems, geographic representation, etc.) represent the form of democracy that is to be preferred over other forms of democracy (assuming that stability and continuity are desired).

If we now fold Lipset's work on the social prerequisites of democracy into his work on political values, then the full ideological message legitimized by Lipset's theoretical work would seem to consist of three elements: democracy is good, the democracy found in English-speaking countries is best, and American democracy is the best of the best. This last statement (that American democracy is the best of the best) flows easily from Lipset's analysis given that the United States not only has all the structural prerequisites for a stable and continuing democracy but also the additional advantage of a democracy reinforced by the cultural heritage of a Revolution that did not occur in England, Canada, or Australia.

As an aside, I might note that Lipset himself does little to hide the way in which his vision of American democracy has shaped his view of the "best" sort of democracy. Thus, for example, in his 1993 Presidential Address to the American Sociological Association, he (1994, 2) says:

> In discussing democracy, I want to clarify my biases and assumptions at the outset. I agree with the basic concerns of the founding fathers of the United States—that government, a powerful state, is to be feared (or suspected, to use the lawyer's term), and that it is necessary to find means to control governments though checks and balances.

Given that he so clearly bases his view of the ideal democracy on the American experience, it hardly seems surprising that he finds the American experience to be ideal.

ON THE OTHER HAND . . .

◆ ◆ ◆

But if the ideological claim implicit in Lipset's analysis seems clear, what is the ideological claim implicit in the work of Grabb et al.? Initially, I suspect, it was simply a rejection of the final element in Lipset's claim (that American democracy is the best of the best). Over time, however, the ideological underpinnings of the Grabb et al. argument have become more positive. The shift seems to have come with Baer, Grabb and Johnston (1993), who argued, remember, that on a number of attitudinal measures, having mainly to do with family and gender issues, there is little difference between Canadians living outside Quebec and Americans living outside the South. At the time, these findings were presented simply as falsifying the Lipset thesis. In their recent book, however, Grabb and Curtis (2004) provide a theoretical rationale for the three region model that contains a more precise ideological claim.

Grabb and Curtis develop what they call "a deep structures" approach, the main thrust of which is that "the English regions of North America, particularly the sub-societies that now form English Canada and the northern United States, were imbued historically with a similar set of core values, or deep-structural principles, that are traceable to their common origins as colonies of Britain" (p. 248). These core values, they argue, originated in England during the Middle Ages and include things like equality under the law; an independent judiciary; secret ballots; free elections; the right to choose from among different political parties; an emphasis on political checks and balances; and more generally, a love of personal freedom and liberty. It is their contention—and here they draw heavily on the writings of Winston Churchill, Montesquieu, Alexis de Tocqueville, and Ralf Dahrendorf—that these cultural deep structures have made the democratic traditions of the English-speaking world distinctive.

Unfortunately, just what "deep structures" are (to the extent that the term is not synonymous with "tradition") is unclear. Grabb and Curtis tell us, for example, that the term has been used both in linguistics and anthropology—and here they cite the work of Noam Chomsky and Claude Lévi-Strauss, respectively. Unfortunately, in both Chomsky's work on language and Lévi-Strauss's work on myth, "deep structures" refers to innate qualities of the human mind, which is clearly not what Grabb and Curtis intend. . . .

Still, my main concern here is not really with the empirical adequacy of the Grabb/Curtis theory but rather—as in the case of Lipset's theory—with the ideological claim that the Grabb/Curtis "deep structures" theory legitimizes. And here again, the ideological claim being made seems clear: taken at face value, Grabb and Curtis's deep structures argument suggests that what best promotes democracy is the collective weight of a centuries-old cultural tradition that developed originally in England and that was exported off-island through colonization. Like Lipset, in other words, their argument suggests that the sort of democratic systems found in England and former English colonies are best; unlike Lipset, their theory does not single out American democracy as being the best of the best.

Grabb and Curtis, I believe, are a might (sic) less obvious than Lipset in making clear the value judgments that shape their analysis, but those judgments (which in this case involve a high valuation of things English, and in particular a high valuation of English political traditions), I suggest, can be detected in a number of the remarks they make. These would include, just to take two examples, their characterization (p. 31) of Winston Churchill as "arguably the most important historical figure of the twentieth century" (I suspect that a great many people in the Republic of Ireland, not to mention the former Soviet Union, China, India, and Africa would disagree) and the fact that they cite approvingly the claim, made both by Ralf Dahrendorf and Jeane Kirkpatrick, that "democracy . . . was really a form of social and political organization peculiar to the Anglo-Saxon world" (p. 47).

SUMMARY AND CONCLUSION
◆ ◆ ◆

One goal of this article has been to demonstrate that if the stated concerns of the participants in the debate over the Lipset thesis—namely, that they were concerned with assessing cultural differences between Canada and the U.S. or with assessing the continuing cultural impact of the American Revolution—then the debate could easily have branched off into any number of directions not taken. Along the way, I have suggested that evidence from the U.S. South provides strong support for the view that the Revolution *has* had a continuing cultural impact.

But the more important goal has been to suggest that the Lipset/Grabb et al. debate has been fueled mainly by unacknowledged and competing ideological claims about "the best sort of democracy." Recognizing this, I now want to suggest, allows us to understand some otherwise puzzling features of the debate. First, it helps us to understand why the debate has lasted so long. As Steven Seidman (1994) has proposed, one reason why so many disputes in social science go on endlessly, no matter how much evidence is gathered, is precisely because the clashing interpretations involved derive ultimately from incompatible ideological claims. Second, this formulation also helps us understand why both sides in the debate have focused on a relatively narrow range of cultural variables: since the concern is with "who owns democracy" it make little sense for the participants to concern themselves with cultural values, no matter how central to the culture being studied, that do not connote "democracy" to intended readers. Finally, it helps to explain why both sides have ignored the Hatch thesis and explained away the South.

Thus, for example, under the argument offered here Lipset is predisposed to ignore the evidence from the South because his ideological goal is to establish the superiority of the form of democratic government in place at the national level in the U.S.; calling attention to the survival of the Revolutionary Ethos in one sub-region of the U.S. would not aid that goal. The fact that the sub-region in question (the South) rose in rebellion against the national government that Lipset identifies as the "best" form of democracy only makes it that much easier to ignore the South.

Grabb et al. have also been predisposed to ignore the Hatch thesis, and so the South, but for different reasons. First, as a purely practical matter, splitting the South off from the rest of the U.S., allows them to say that there is no difference between English Canadians and Americans outside the South on a variety of attitudinal measures—something they can (and do) then bring forward as evidence that both falsifies the Lipset thesis and supports their claim that English Canadians and Americans are culturally similar as a result of a common English heritage. More importantly, however, the South's association with slavery, segregation, Jim Crow, etc. is inconsistent with the "gradual but inexorable unfolding of the four core principles that are part of our great English heritage" vision that pervades their work. Given this, the South must be explained away—which, as I have suggested, is what they do. Calling attention to the Hatch thesis, and so to evidence that the Revolutionary Ethos is alive and well in the South as a result of evangelical Christianity, would only make that harder to do.

There is obviously nothing novel in the general contention that sociological theorizing can be influenced by ideology. Quite the contrary, it is a contention central to a long tradition in the sociology of knowledge, and—if anything—gained renewed currency with the rise of postmodernism and feminist theory in the 1980s and 1990s. Moreover, it is a contention that has increasingly come to be applied to sociological theorizing of times past (see Connell, 1997; Pederson, 2001; Wallerstein, 2004). . . . Nevertheless, while the idea of a possible link between ideology and theorizing might seem entirely unproblematic in the abstract, or in the case of theorizing in times past, I suggest that a lingering commitment to positivist ideals in mainstream sociology often prevents us from seeing ideological influence in sociological arguments close at hand. Here again, of course, the general point is not original.

Some time ago Judith Stacy and Barrie Thorne (1985) argued that mainstream sociology's commitment to positivism made sociology more resistant to the influence of feminist theory than was the case for other disciplines—like anthropology, literary studies and history—less committed to positivism. More specifically, they suggested (p. 309) that mainstream sociology's commitment to positivism made it less open to the feminist contention that political and social circumstances can shape the ways in which knowledge is created and received. The fact that the Lipset/Grabb et al. debate has lasted for decades without being problematized, i.e., without anyone raising the possibility that more is going on here than the simple pursuit of empirical truth, is for me evidence that Stacy and Thorne's judgment still has some merit.

Rejoinder to "Who Owns Democracy?"

James Curtis
University of Waterloo

Edward Grabb
University of Western Ontario

◆ ◆ ◆

CONCERNING THE ARGUMENT THAT WE BELIEVE THE ENGLISH-SPEAKING NATIONS ARE "BEST"

◆ ◆ ◆

. . . It is suggested in the commentary (279) that we believe "the sort of democratic systems found in England and former English colonies are best." However, it is evident from our work that this is not our view. In *Regions Apart* (Grabb and Curtis, 2005: 51), for example, we explicitly reject any claims of English "superiority." We do conclude, like many scholars, that English-speaking societies are *different* from others in certain respects. The list of researchers who draw this same conclusion is long, and includes Montesquieu, Tocqueville, Bryce, Weber, Hartz, Dahrendorf, Goldstone, Hopcroft, and numerous others (see Grabb and Curtis, 2005: 46–53).

The substance of our research provides the clearest evidence of what democratic nations we think are "best." Our published work reflects the belief that the best societies are those that are more socially inclusive, have more civic participation, are more apt to promote equality of both opportunity and condition, are relatively free of violent and other crimes, and have better health and life expectancy profiles (e.g., Curtis, Grabb and Guppy, 2004 [and earlier editions]; Tepperman and Curtis, 2004). Even if confined to the small number of our studies that are mentioned in the commentary, we demonstrate that several *non-English* nations, including European social democra-

cies (e.g., Sweden and Holland), generally surpass English-speaking societies on such criteria (e.g., Curtis, Grabb and Baer, 1992; Curtis, Baer and Grabb, 2001). In *Regions Apart,* we show that the one clearly *non-English* region, Quebec, ranks highest on most of these indicators of the best society. In short, neither our international studies nor our four regions analyses support the conclusion that we portray the English-speaking societies as the best.

Studying the English-speaking countries is one part of our broader cross-national research, and stems from: 1) the fact that Canada is included among them; 2) the wish to comprehend Canadian social structures and culture; and 3) the belief that Canada, like any society, is best understood if studied comparatively. Hence, notwithstanding suggestions in the commentary (269), our continuing research comparing Canada and the U.S. (and many other nations) is not driven by "a long-running debate" with Professor Lipset over "incompatible ideological claims." Instead, our work is motivated by the desire to understand relationships among nations over the longer term. Clearly, the only way to map and account for the trajectory of these relationships is by studying them comparatively over time, and not doing so would mean that any important changes would go undetected. Such studies go back at least to Montesquieu and Tocqueville, and comprise a large and diverse contemporary literature. Included here are the more than 700 books, articles and other sources we cite in *Regions Apart,* written by authors with a variety of perspectives. Undoubtedly researchers will

From James Curtis and Edward Grabb, "Rejoinder to 'Who Owns Democracy?'" *Canadian Review of Sociology and Anthropology,* Vol. 42, No. 4, 2005, pp. 467–478. Reprinted with permission of the Canadian Sociology and Anthropology Association.

continue this work well into the future, given the abiding interest in comparing patterns of change across nations.

CONCERNING OUR CANADA-U.S. COMPARISONS OF CONTEMPORARY SOCIAL STRUCTURE

◆ ◆ ◆

In the commentary, it is stated (269) that we "fail to . . . [show] significant differences between Canadians (outside Quebec) and Americans, on attitudinal and behavioural measures relevant to the Lipset thesis." Actually, along with similarities, our research results show some marked Canada-U.S. differences, and numerous smaller but significant differences, many of which are the reverse of Professor Lipset's predictions. For example, in chapters 7–11 of *Regions Apart* alone, we compare contemporary Canada and the U.S. on approximately 90 separate dependent measures, and report significant differences in fully *two thirds* of these comparisons. Some of the largest differences are that Americans are "more religious than Canadians according to virtually all measures," are "more conservative on . . . family values and sexuality," and "experience much higher homicide rates" (Grabb and Curtis, 2005: 242–43). Among many other differences detailed in *Regions Apart*, we find that, compared with Americans, Canadians are more likely to: vote, support interracial marriage, accept ethnic and religious minorities and various "outgroups" as neighbours, favour increased immigration, promote personal responsibility and unselfishness in children, engage in political protest and civil dissent, distrust their politicians and government agencies, be optimistic about change, find cheating on their taxes acceptable, favour gay rights, support women's rights, experience lower economic inequality and higher state spending, be victims of non-violent crimes (e.g., auto theft and burglary), and so on. . . .

While describing many Canada-U.S. differences, we show as well that these differences often are more thoroughly understood when the countries are divided internally, i.e., when Quebec, English Canada, the U.S. North, and the U.S. South are compared. We find that the

> four regions are, indeed, often distinctive, and on a diverse set of issues. . . . Although there are some clear exceptions, the four sub-societies frequently array themselves in a consistent pattern or order . . . in which Quebec occupies one end of the continuum . . . , the American South stands at the other end, and the other two regions fall relatively close to one another and between the two extremes. . . .

Also, in *Regions Apart* (e.g., Chap. 12) we stress the central finding that Canada-U.S. comparisons show no simple, stable trend of either sameness or difference. Our long-term analyses reveal a pattern that varies considerably over time, with regular *"periods of both convergence and divergence"* and "alternating phases of greater or lesser distinctiveness" (Grabb and Curtis, 2005: 271, 272, original emphasis). All of the above, as well as the book's title, make it evident that we report and discuss many significant Canada-U.S. differences. . . .

CONCERNING THE HISTORICAL CANADA-U.S. COMPARISONS

◆ ◆ ◆

It is suggested in the commentary (268–69) that we see no real Canada-U.S. differences historically. In fact, we show clear differences involving both the elites and the general populations, especially (but not only) due to internal divisions involving the South and Quebec. We do find that English-speaking Canadians and U.S. *northerners* were much alike in various ways and shared many similarities historically, certainly more than Professor Lipset's research indicates. However, this is not surprising to those who know the literature. Indeed, we would have to ignore almost all the pertinent historical research to conclude otherwise. Professor Lipset's assumption of substantial historical differences, which seems to be accepted in Professor Carroll's commentary, is decidedly the minority view.

Consider just a few examples of the majority view. First, there is Tocqueville, who observed both nations firsthand during the 1830s. This was a *half-century after* the Revolution, the event that Professor Lipset says made the two peoples forever different. Tocqueville, however, concluded that Americans, especially in the North, were still "identical" to English Canadians (see Grabb and Curtis, 2005: 45). Bryce, another first-hand observer and the leading historian to study the two countries in the 19th century, wrote in 1889 (*100 years after* the Revolution) that when comparing English Canadians and Americans, "it need hardly be said that there is little difference between the populations" (see Grabb and Curtis, 2005: 267). Finally, S.D. Clark, whom Professor Lipset (1990: l0) calls "the foremost Canadian analyst of North American values and institutions," concluded that the two *populations*, in contrast to the *elites*, were highly similar. Professor Clark found "it was only a small minority of the [Canadian] population, individuals or groups identified with the vested interests of empire or, later, nation, who had any real desire to remain politically separate from their American neighbours. . . . Had the [Canadian] people at the time had their way, in 1760, and again in 1775, 1812 and 1838, and possibly even in 1860, the society growing up on the northern half of the Continent [Canada] would have joined forces politically with the society growing out of the Atlantic seaboard [the U.S.]" (Clark, 1968: 223).

CONCERNING THE INTERNATIONAL STUDIES OF VOLUNTARY ASSOCIATION ACTIVITY

◆ ◆ ◆

It is stated in the commentary (271–72) that we omit "the cases that are most relevant," i.e., religious organizations, in our voluntary association research. Because Americans have higher numbers of religious association memberships than Canadians, such a procedure could "minimize Canadian/American differences" in association involvement (276), thereby making Canadians look as good as the "best," i.e., the U.S. (277). In fact, however, this is not the procedure we follow.

First, it is asserted in the commentary (271) that Curtis's (1971) study of associations in Canada and five other nations "did not include religious organizations." But, as shown on page 874 of that paper, responses about religious organizations were included in all analyses (1971: 874 ff.). It is then stated (272) that "Curtis, Grabb and Baer (1992) . . . exclude religious organizations from their analysis." Actually, the 1992 study does include religious organizations; this study compared Canada, the U.S., and 13 other nations, using three dependent measures: all memberships (religious organizations included), memberships with unions excluded (but religious organizations included), and memberships with unions and religious organizations both excluded (1992: 142–48). Rather than ignoring religious organizations, we used these measures throughout the analysis to highlight the central role of religion in the association involvements of some nations, including the U.S.

For virtually all our voluntary association studies, analyses using religious associations are always included, as are *additional* analyses showing the effects for religious and union memberships (see also Grabb and Curtis. 2005: Chap. 11). For several decades, researchers have followed this procedure (i.e., doing analyses with religious and union organizations both in and out of the membership counts) because of concerns that these two types of membership, unlike others, may not be fully voluntary (see, e.g., Smith, 1975: 249–50). Reviewers of our research, including assessors of the three articles in the *American*

Sociological Review, have consistently expected this procedure to be followed. The commentary does not acknowledge this convention in the literature, although we repeatedly mention it in our publications. It is notable that we follow the convention of conducting analyses that distinguish unions as well (a point not discussed in the commentary), even though Canada is regularly higher in terms of union memberships than the U.S. . . .

CONCERNING HATCH'S THESIS AND RELIGION IN CANADA AND THE U.S.

◆ ◆ ◆

In the commentary (271–76), it is remarked that we mention but do not feature Hatch's (1989) "Revolutionary Ethos" thesis, which links presumed changes in American values (for example, the erosion of traditional authority, the growth of independent thought, the desire for equality) to the rise of Protestant sects, especially evangelical Baptists and Methodists. The suggestion is that our not discussing Hatch's argument in detail reflects an ideological bias on our part.

In fact, we subscribe to Hatch's thesis, as far as it goes. Indeed, like him (and others), we find that many American Protestant groups had a strong sense of their rights to religious freedom, personal independence, local autonomy from elites, and so on. (Grabb and Curtis, 2005: 68–73). However, we also go beyond the Hatch analysis, which focusses only on the U.S., to show similar beliefs were also evident among *Canadian* Protestants (Grabb and Curtis, 2005: 78–83, 95–96). Indeed, along with several other researchers, we report that, until *the middle decades of the 1800s,* English-Canadian religious adherents were like Americans in that most belonged to a range of Baptist, Methodist, and other Protestant faiths (Grabb and Curtis, 2005: 95–97, 111–16, 128). Such findings have led historians to conclude that Protestant "evangelicalism . . . [was] . . . in the nineteenth century . . . the dominant religion in both the United States and English Canada" (Rawlyk and Noll, 1994: 1819; also Clark, 1959: 421–24; Noll, 1992: 265–76; Adamson, 1994; Deming and Hamilton, 1994). . . .

CONCERNING THE U.S. SOUTH AND SLAVERY

◆ ◆ ◆

In the commentary (272–74), the Hatch thesis is extended. The inference is drawn that, if the Revolutionary Ethos was especially strong among evangelical Baptists and

Methodists, then the South was in effect even more Revolutionary than the North, since these religions were more prevalent in the South (Finke and Stark, 1992: 282–88). The suggestion in the commentary is that we have overlooked this possibility. In fact, we do discuss the religious distinctiveness of the South compared with the North, but, for reasons outlined below, we conclude that a different inference is more compelling.

We, too, report the relatively higher levels of evangelical Protestantism in the South (e.g., Grabb and Curtis, 2005: 110, 141), and discuss the South's distinctiveness regarding ideas that Hatch subsumes under the Revolutionary Ethos. These include anti-elitism and the desire for local autonomy, plus related beliefs in "states' rights," "intense localism," and "local communalism" (Grabb and Curtis, 2005: 69, 109, 124, 176; Shain, 1994: 37–38, 55; Reed, 1982: 170–72; 1991: 231–32). However, we find that the research on this question shows such differences were not sufficient by themselves to make Southerners more Revolutionary. Previous studies also do not support the interpretation that the existence of a larger proportion of evangelical Protestants in the South than in the North was the crucial variable distinguishing these regions historically, or the main reason why the South today is still distinct, both from the rest of the U.S. and from North America generally. We suggest that such an interpretation does not account for the elephant in the room, i.e., the social and economic organization of slavery and its consequences for the fundamental rights of Blacks over the past 300 years. While Blacks have endured ill treatment throughout North America, these injustices have unquestionably been more prevalent and deep-seated in the South. Recall, for example, that Southern Blacks were still being lynched in the second half of the 20th century (Dray, 2003), and that Black-White intermarriages were generally *illegal* in the South until at least the 1950s (Romano, 2003: 3, 58–59). We cite recent studies showing that Southerners still oppose Black-White unions more than other interracial marriages (e.g., White-Asian) (see Grabb and Curtis, 2005: 208). All of this indicates to us that Southern Blacks have experienced unique inequities that go beyond other prejudices, and that are traceable, not to religious composition differences, but to the legacy of slavery.

In the commentary (272), the role of slavery is minimized, based on the argument that "the Southern commitment to . . . the rhetoric of 'equality' . . . was not at all incompatible with slavery." Unfortunately, however, compatibility in some Southerners' minds does not alter the structural realities of extreme racial inequality in the South. Hence, many scholars—Alexis de Tocqueville, Nathan Hatch, Edgar T. Thompson, John Shelton Reed, etc.—emphasize these realities and, like us, conclude that slavery *did* make the South distinctive, and in ways that *were* incompatible with equality and other Revolutionary principles (e.g., Grabb and Curtis, 2005: 105–06).

Professor Reed's work is significant here. On the historical role of religion in the South, he says, as we do, that evangelical Protestantism was "not translated directly into Revolutionary sentiment." There is no *necessary* connection between evangelical Protestantism and values like equality, as shown in Professor Reed's research on the Southern Baptist Convention. This "thousand-pound gorilla of Southern religious life," which has long dominated religion in that region, broke with its northern Baptist counterpart in 1845, and did so precisely because the Southern Baptists supported slavery (Reed and Reed, 1996: 237).

Then there is Professor Hatch, whose thesis is the basis for the commentary's extrapolation about the South. He also agrees with us about slavery and its disjuncture from Revolutionary values. Writing with Mark Noll and George Marsden (1983: 56–57, 97–100), Professor Hatch discusses the gross "hypocrisy" of arguing that slavery could somehow be compatible with Revolutionary ideals like equality, and cites Southerners and others who decried this same hypocrisy.

We also note instances where Americans, including Baptists and Methodists, deemed slavery an inversion or "perversion" of both Revolutionary and Christian principles (Grabb and Curtis, 2005: 106–08). One especially blunt example of this Southern inversion involves Alexander Stephens, the Confederate Vice-President. In 1861, Stephens explicitly rejected the founding principle in the Declaration of Independence that "all men are created equal": "Our new government is founded on exactly the opposite idea. Its cornerstone rests upon the great truth that the negro is not equal to the white man" (McPherson, 1998: 18). Ultimately, slavery's blatant negation of Revolutionary tenets helped precipitate "the second American Revolution," the Civil War (McPherson, 1991). . . .

CONCLUSION

◆ ◆ ◆

We would conclude by simply reiterating our appreciation for being given the chance to clarify these issues that were raised by Professor Carroll's commentary.

Despite American Culture Creep, Canadian Values Remain

Alan Kellogg

As we get closer to our neighbours to the south, so grows in intensity the illumination of the things that separate us.

For decades, those of us who call ourselves Canadian nationalists have long maintained that true political independence is all but impossible without a strong measure of economic sovereignty. When ultimate decisions on jobs, research and development, investment, etc., are made by absentee owners, human nature, patriotism and head office logic are likely to rule more often than not, even if we call the latest edition of foreign control "globalization."

It's not a matter of being anti-American or assigning evil motives to corporate greed-hounds from afar, because the model also works internally, as almost any former local employee of Edmonton Telephones or AGT will tell you now that the shots are called in Burnaby. It only makes sense that geography and power go hand in hand. They didn't call it "political economy" for nothing when I was in university.

Although some of us still wring sweaty hands over the latest Texas purchase of another Calgary oilpatch firm, the imminent passing of Molson to the Coors organization or the increasing dominance of Wal-Mart in our retail sector, Canadians have generally greeted the acceleration of foreign economic control with a collective yawn. Times are pretty good for many in this country, and not surprisingly, the importance of where the cheques are finally cut is lost on us, as long as they keep coming. We shop where we want to, watch and listen to our favourites. It's not so much unpatriotic, it's real life. Freedom.

At the same time, the potency of U.S. culture, in spite of our many advances over the years at home, has never seemed stronger. We love the American Story in almost all its forms, and like much of the world (but also more than most) demonstrate our affection where it really counts, with our TV remotes, tourism dollars and conversations.

Given this and dozens of other indicators, you wonder if we've finally sold out completely, happily. Travelling outside the country, we're often mistaken for Americans, which we find mildly irritating. But you take their point.

Still, a funny thing is happening that can't be easily dismissed. As we get closer to our neighbours, so grows in intensity the illumination of the things that separate us. Forget about the politicians and the media. It lives in the hearts and minds of the people, the real, unfiltered thing. We see the world in our own way, for better or worse, and it hasn't gone unnoticed.

Seven days ago, in a performance far better than his shaky tete-a-tete with George W. Bush, Paul Martin appeared on CNN's fourth-place Sunday pundit show hosted by the resolutely uncontentious slo-pitcher Wolf Blitzer. The PM was in the midst of discussing our current difficulties as a family matter when Blitzer hauled up a recent poll. When it came to "values," 80 percent of Canadians found us on a separate page than our neighbours, while 50 percent of Americans responded in kind. Sputtering ensued.

Surveys of this dicey ilk might well be taken with a grain of salt, but three events this past week hinted at potentially important differences between the two countries on fundamental conceptions of justice, equality and democracy. None of these things have been resolved here, and the outcome remains unclear in each case. But the very fact that they have moved to the front burner of public discourse—with many of our politicians ducking for cover—is something in itself.

In a nation where cautious incrementalism underpins our history, it's a bit odd that Canada would find itself having to decide on same-sex marriage, potentially putting us in a very tiny kaffeeklatsch with Belgium and the Netherlands.

The recent narrow decision by New Zealand's parliament to sanction civil unions would seem much more our style. But Thursday's Supreme Court ruling—so clear on three of four points—has forced the federal government to ante up definitive legislation very quickly.

A victory will be neither assured, bloodless nor forgotten when the next election is called. At the moment, a slim majority of Canadians seems to support same-sex marriage, but many of them voted for the Bloc Quebecois and NDP, a fact well-known by the Liberal braintrust.

On the surface, the case for Jeremy Hinzman, the U.S. army deserter whose political asylum hearings wrapped up Wednesday, doesn't seem promising, a fact all but admitted by his own lawyer. There is no precedent in Canada to allow refuge for enlistees of foreign armed forces.

Continued

But there are other ways to enter the country than political asylum, as thousands of Vietnam War resisters, now solid citizens with Canadian children and grandchildren, can testify. As the war drags on, Hinzman will be (in fact, already has been) joined by others who have experienced a change of heart, particularly from the ranks of the National Guard, who never bargained for an interminable assignment in a murky undertaking.

Another Texas president, Lyndon Johnson, once cursed and slapped Lester Pearson up against a kitchen wall for criticizing the Vietnam War and accepting draft dodgers and deserters. A call will have to be made.

Friday, the B.C. Citizens' Assembly on Electoral Reform—a historic, randomly selected body with teeth—officially tabled its recommendations for proportional representation, to be voted on in May. Its final selection for change, the single transferable vote system—a halfway PR measure—is fraught with marketing problems and difficult to explain in a sound bite. That said, its genesis is unassailable, standing in marked contrast to the money politics of the day.

Equality for gay and lesbian Canadians, safe haven for war resisters, fundamental electoral reform via people's tribunals—none of these potential initiatives are particularly revolutionary or unique. But the fact that we're talking seriously about them opens a portal to the national soul.

We may not be masters of our own house in many ways, but we are still capable of showing spine, a dogged independent streak, when it counts. Tolerance, fairness, justice count.

Source: Alan Kellogg, "Despite American culture creep, Canadian values remain," *Edmonton Journal*, Dec. 12, 2004, p. A2. Material reprinted with the express permission of CANWEST NEWS SERVICE, a CanWest Partnership.

Unit Two

SOCIALIZATION
Introduction: Socialization and Dominant Ideology in Education

◆ ◆ ◆

How do helpless babies survive and grow to become full participatory members of society? Can children develop cognitive, emotional, and behavioural attributes without help from family, peers, schools, and media? The answer is no. Children learn a language, develop identity and survival skills, manage everyday life, communicate with others, play roles according to social expectations, adjust to changing situations, and develop selfhood. The process of learning these attributes and becoming a participant in society is called **socialization.** It includes the acquisition of values, norms, motives, and knowledge in informal (e.g., family and peers) and formal (e.g., schools and universities) settings.

There are many explanations of the socialization process. Ivan Pavlov's (1849–1936) experiment suggests that we learn in relation to certain stimuli. He noticed that dogs salivate at the sight of meat. Subsequently, he experimented by ringing a bell every time he gave meat to a dog for a period of time. Then Pavlov rang the bell without providing meat to the dog. He noticed that the dog salivated when the bell rang. Do humans similarly learn based on stimuli? Do you automatically look at your car's speedometer or push the brake when you see a police car? Do you feel hungry at about 12 noon? If the answer to these questions is yes, then perhaps your responses may be due to the fact that you have been conditioned in relation to a stimulus (i.e., police, time).

Sigmund Freud (1856–1939) argued that biology plays an important part in human development. How-

ever, humans do not act instinctually. They respond to basic drives, such as love and survival. He identified three elements of human personality: **Id, Ego,** and **Super-Ego.** According to Freud, all humans are born with certain innate drives that seek pleasure. These drives could include eating, touching, or other diffused sexual or physical pleasures. He called the innate drives that seek pleasure the "Id." Infants also develop strategies of satisfying Id's desires. For example, infants may learn that by crying they will get attention or food. Freud called the sum total of all strategies that seek to please Id as the "Ego." However, children also develop beliefs that inhibit Id's desire. Such beliefs are part of what Freud called the "Super-Ego." An example, which is perhaps fitting of Freud's concern with sex, is that you are walking down the street and see a very beautiful or good-looking member of the opposite (or the same) sex. What goes through your mind? Freud would say that perhaps your Id may want to have sex with that individual. Your Ego will find a strategy of meeting Id's desire by, for example, "wining and dining" that person. However, your Super-Ego may jump in and encourage you to take a cold shower. You may notice that, according to Freud, Super-Ego is important for socialization, without which human civilization would not have been possible. In this example, the Super-Ego inhibits all kinds of harmful strategies that the Ego may imagine in order to satisfy Id's desires.

How does Super-Ego come about? According to Freud (1964), all children pass through three sexual stages. This simply means that as children grow, different types of physical activities give them pleasure. Thus, at the *oral* stage, the act of sucking; at the *anal* stage, the act of excreting; and at the *phallic* stage, the act of playing with their genitals is pleasurable to children. Freud was most interested in the third (phallic) stage. During this stage, the male child, who tends to view his mother as his "love object," notices that he has a competitor—his father. However, the child also notices that this competitor is very powerful and more than twice his size. According to Freud, this observation allows the child, consciously or subconsciously, to think that his father will retaliate against him by preventing Id's pleasure. Since the child is at the phallic stage, he conceives this retaliation as being directed at the source of his pleasure, his genitals, with the possibility of castration. The child, fearful of castration, therefore abandons his desire for his mother as his love object and replaces it with a desire for another female as his mate. This transformation, in Freud's opinion, formed the development of the prohibition of incest, which in turn lifted human beings out of biological relations into social relations.

Jean Piaget (1896–1980) was also interested in knowing how humans learn to think and understand the social world (see Delaney, 2005: 219). Piaget argued that children pass through four stages of development:

1. Sensorimotor stage occurs up to the age of two. At this stage our senses play important roles in experimenting about the world. We learn through seeing, hearing, touching, and feeling the important objects and individuals in our life.

2. Preoperational stage (around two to six years of age) is when children start to have a more stable conception of the world. However, children at this stage do not know the reason why things happen. They have a perception or an "understanding" of this because they see and interact with their parents or someone else who meets their needs every day, repetitively. At this stage, children are extremely egocentric, because they can only look at the world from their own point of view. They have not learned to play various social roles yet.

3. Concrete operational stage occurs around the age of seven. At this stage, children are able to look at the world from a concrete, but not abstract, position. For instance, they may understand death by experiencing the loss of a pet, without having an understanding of death or life, in general. That is to say, children do not have a philosophy of death

and dying. Nevertheless, they are able to do some simple operations and to understand concepts such as weight, numbers, and so on.

4. Formal operational stage starts about the age of twelve. This is a stage of formal and abstract thought. Adolescents are able to understand and develop theories and explanations and are able to form their own opinions.

Piaget argued that, generally, all children go through this process of social and cognitive development. However, the developmental process varies from culture to culture.

Development of a sociological explanation of socialization is heavily indebted to the work of George Herbert Mead. Other scholars had emphasized biological instincts, economic interests, and survival instincts, among others, for human development. Mead, in *Mind, Self and Society* (1962), instead emphasized the symbolic nature of the human world. According to Mead, symbols (e.g., language, signs) allow us to have a conception of ourselves and of others, and of life and death. Such abstract concepts enable us to reflect on ourselves, to communicate and be communicated to, and to judge and be judged. For example, in the case of Hamlet, who ponders "to be or not to be," he is attempting to play the dual role of executioner and victim, or the murderer and murdered. In order to answer this question, Hamlet must have a symbolic conception of himself and of death and dying. He must be aware of his place in the world and be able to judge himself in order to decide whether or not to execute himself (see Ritzer, 1996).

However, at birth, individuals do not have a self-concept. They do not even have a conception of a lack of self-concept. As they acquire symbols (e.g., language and signs), they develop self-referent concepts such as "**I**" and "**me.**" These concepts not only enable individuals to distinguish themselves from others but also allow them to bond to a community. "I" is the unpredictable and creative aspects of the self. It is a key source of novelty and self-actualization. "I" enables individuals to project themselves into the future. "Me" is organized around the attitudes of others. It is the social self and is consciously responsible. In order for individuals to develop a self-identity that allows them to be connected to society, individuals pass through three stages.

1. **Preparatory** stage: This is the stage of imitation. Children mimic the behaviour of their **significant others** (e.g., mother). By copying adults children

become prepared to take adult roles. For example, a 2- or 3-year-old child may want to get the attention of her mother by calling out, "Mom." The mother, working on the computer, responds "Wait a minute, I am working on my thesis." Several minutes later, the mother calls up to the child, "Jill, come, supper is ready." The child, playing a game on her toy computer, responds "Wait a few minutes, I am working on my thesis." Similarly, a child may pretend to read the newspaper as she sees her mother or father reading the paper.

2. **Play** stage: In this stage, children learn to take roles and learn others' points of view. Children develop self-awareness by taking the social roles of a mother, a father, a storekeeper, among other roles. They may play with a truck or doll and act as a truck driver or a mother, and so on.

3. **Game** stage: In this stage children learn to take general and multiple roles. Thus, in playing baseball, for example, they learn to be a pitcher by relating to the runner at first and the batter who stands before them, but they also relate to the catcher, the infielder, the outfielder, and the fans. Children learn to symbolically relate themselves to the **generalized others** and to place themselves in their community.

Therefore, according to Mead, it is false to argue that either society or individuals have primacy over the other. Rather, individuals emerge out of a society that exists prior to them, but the very existence of society presupposes self-conscious individuals. In Mead's opinion, individuals and society are welded together as parts of a common process.

In his study, "On Becoming a Marijuana User," Howard Becker (1953) highlighted the importance of the learning process. Becker suggests that there is nothing intrinsically pleasurable about using this drug. In other words, becoming "high" is not just due to smoking marijuana. Those who start using marijuana must learn the relevant techniques, interpretive framework, and the rationale of becoming a smoker. They must learn to interpret their feelings and sensations created by the drug. Becker interviewed 50 marijuana smokers and found that most beginners thought that the effects were frightening and unpleasant. They were calmed down by experienced users who told them that such effects were normal. The experienced users stated to the new user: "The same thing happened to me," or that "You'll get to like that after a while." In other words, a favourable definition of the experi-

ence by others introduced a feeling of enjoyment into the act of smoking marijuana.

The same is true for acquiring a taste for eating oysters, frog legs, sushi, or drinking vodka—smokers will learn to interpret feelings of dizziness, thirst, scalp tingles, and misjudgment of time as being "high" and will attribute pleasure to these feelings. You may have heard a drug user or an alcohol drinker brag that, "I was so high that I did not know where I was for a long time," or "I was so drunk that I lost my jacket and was bruised all over." These experiences are not necessarily pleasurable. However, drug users and alcohol drinkers learn to interpret them positively. These examples do not mean that drugs or alcohol do not have any effect on the human body; rather, the examples suggest that we learn to interpret the effect positively or negatively through our social relationships.

You may have noticed that socialization is a life-long process, and that in the process of being socialized a child encounters many agents of socialization (family, peer groups, schools, mass media—see Table 2.2 for minutes of TV viewing by age and gender). Each of these agents plays an important role in shaping one's personality. The debate in this section pays attention to the role of education in shaping students' attitudes and ideas.

Students seek higher education primarily to improve skills, get a degree and a job, and, consequently, to improve their standard of living. But does education have other functions? Does it help us to question inequities? Or alternatively, does education ensure that we support the existing system, which may be unjust? If education has any effect on our attitudes, does the effect vary by different disciplines? Are some disciplines more critical of social injustices than others? These questions have been the subject of much debate. Baer and Lambert re-evaluate previous research by Guimond et al. and suggest that higher education does not have the liberalizing effect that is hypothesized. Baer and Lambert study the extent to which higher education is related to support for profit motive, big business, compliant labour unions, and maintenance of the military. Ideas such as these are often referred to as the "dominant ideology," because they tend to be supportive of the interests of upper (dominant) social classes. Baer and Lambert's study shows that higher educated individuals tend to support the dominant ideology more than the less educated. However, there is no evidence of such effect for social sciences, arts, and natural sciences. The only support for the higher educated being more supportive of the dominant ideology is for those with business and professional degrees. Baer and Lambert conclude that social science does not produce students with a more critical view of the society. Guimond and Palmer respond that international and national studies, as well as those provided by Baer and Lambert, are consistent with their own conclusion, and therefore Baer and Lambert's conclusions are misleading. In fact, Guimond and Palmer argue that Baer and Lambert's study indicates that within social sciences there is resistance to change in the direction of dominant ideology. Moreover, Guimond and Palmer maintain that the findings on business and professional degree students' support for the dominant ideology are consistent with their views.

TABLE TALK

Table 2.1 shows percentages of different Canadian households that used the Internet between 1999 and 2003. First, it shows that a majority of households are now connected to the World Wide Web and use it. Substantial change took place between 1999 and 2000, where the percentages of households using the Internet rose from 28.7% to 40.1%. The table also shows that the elderly (65 years of age and older) are least likely to use the Internet. Why do you think that the elderly are least likely to use the Internet?

Table 2.2 shows the amount of time Canadians spend viewing TV. It shows that, on average, Canadians spend more than two hours per day watching TV.

Table 2.1   Household Internet Use by Household Type

	1999 %	2000 %	2001 %	2002 %	2003 %
All households	28.7	40.1	48.7	51.4	54.5
Age of head of household	28.7	40.1	48.7	51.4	54.5
Under age 35	32.8	46.8	56.8	56.2	60.8
Age 35 to 54	38.0	52.2	60.6	64.3	68.2
Age 55 to 64	24.6	35.3	44.6	48.9	52.4
Age 65 and over	8.2	12.2	17.3	19.9	22.7

Source: Statistics Canada: CANSIM, Tables: 358-0003, 358-0004, 358-0005, and 358-0017.

Table 2.2   Television Viewing per Day by Sex (Minutes)

Age group	Females	Males
15 to 17	127.7	141.0
18 to 19	101.6	108.9
20 to 24	99.1	122.6
25 to 29	97.2	127.0
30 to 34	92.9	110.5
35 to 39	96.1	115.0
40 to 44	88.3	121.1
45 to 49	99.2	139.3
50 to 54	118.7	149.1
55 to 59	123.6	158.3
60 to 64	158.3	170.6
65 to 69	169.3	230.3
70 to 74	206.4	223.6
75 to 79	221.6	236.8
80+	206.6	260.4
Total	124.2	145.5

Source: Statistics Canada, General Social Survey, 1998.

However, this varies by age and gender. Young males and particularly those over 60 years of age watch more TV than females and middle-aged groups. Note that it does not show the amount of TV viewing for those under 15 years of age. Younger age groups, particularly those under six years of age, watch more TV than any other age groups. In fact, TV is called the "electronic baby sitter" mainly for this young age group. What do you think the implications of watching more TV are for socialization of younger age groups?

MORE QUESTIONS

1. What drew you to study sociology? Are your reasons aligned with the liberal social sciences and humanities argument discussed by Guimond and Palmer?
2. Do you think that your friends in sciences and engineering are less liberal or radical than those in social sciences? Why?

3. Do you think that there is a dominant ideology in Canada? If yes, what are its various aspects?

4. What are the functions of education? Explain how each function works.

5. After reading the debate, which side of the argument seems to be more accurate? Why?

6. Do you think that business and corporation's involvements in universities have a negative effect on academic freedom and/or scientific knowledge? Why?

Socialization into Dominant vs. Counter Ideology among University-Educated Canadians

Douglas E. Baer
University of Western Ontario

Ronald D. Lambert
University of Waterloo

✦ ✦ ✦

The institution of education serves a host of social functions, some of them mutually reinforcing, but many of them contradictory. At one and the same time, schools are expected to provide job training and meet the needs of the economy, inspire critical and inquiring minds, transmit moral sensibilities, produce a law-abiding and patriotic citizenry, rectify inequalities in society, provide custodial services, and so on. Given the educational system's remarkable diversity in curricula, mandate, personnel and students, it would appear to be a challenge to uncover any generalized effects on people's beliefs about society . . . . Our interest in this study is to explore the boundaries between the general ideological effects of higher education and the potential differentiation in people's beliefs produced by their academic fields of study.

. . . A number of investigators have reported that exposure to higher levels of education is associated with greater support for the status quo (Bowles and Gintis, 1976). Alternatively, education has been seen as a source of liberalism and enlightenment (Lipset, 1971; Ladd and Lipset, 1975). This apparent contradiction can be resolved if we suppose that the first relationship pertains to socio-economic beliefs and the second to social and religious beliefs. This resolution has its origins in the idea that liberalism/conservatism or left/right really comprises two dimensions (socio-economic and social/religious), and that education affects them in opposite ways. . . .

Whether higher education has a conservatizing or liberalizing effect, Guimond, Palmer and Begin (1989) have shown, depends on the disciplines in which individuals major. At the one extreme, these investigators found that university students in business and the professions were more likely to subscribe to dominant ideology and the status quo which it defends than other students; at the other extreme, students whose training was in the social sciences tended to reject dominant ideology. In their cross-sectional Quebec City study, they found that social science university students were more supportive of the concept of 'socialists' and less supportive of the concepts of 'conservatives' and the 'military' than students in comparison groups composed of a sample drawn from two selected Quebec City high schools and two area CEGEPs. A similar pattern was observed when social science university students, especially those at the second year level, were compared with students in science and business administration. In sum, the findings support the claim that higher education produces greater attachment to dominant

From Douglas E. Baer and Ronald D. Lambert, "Socialization into dominant vs. counter ideology among university-educated Canadians," *Canadian Review of Sociology and Anthropology*, Vol. 27, No. 4, 1990, pp. 487–504. Reprinted with permission of the Canadian Sociology and Anthropology Association.

ideology within some faculties, but cultivates counter ideology in other faculties (Guimond et al., 1989: 207).

Moreover, the radical effects are seen as neither transient nor temporary. 'As social science students enter a job after graduation, even a high status job in the academic world,' Guimond and his colleagues argue, 'they do not appear to leave their liberal beliefs behind' (1989: 207). . . .

DOMINANT VS. COUNTER IDEOLOGY

◆ ◆ ◆

In what sense is dominant ideology 'dominant'? One criterion holds that ideology is dominant insofar as it is promulgated by the most powerful groups in society, whose position it legitimizes for them, if not for others (Abercrombie et al., 1980). A second criterion for dominance is to be found in majority public opinion (Marchak, 1988: 14–15). Sometimes what is dominant satisfies both standards (cf. Mann, 1970). We hold that the beliefs examined in this paper are dominant in the first sense, and sometimes dominant in the second sense. Thus, support for the profit motive, the continuing dominance of big business in the Canadian economy, compliant labour unions, and maintenance of the military were clearly status quo positions in 1983, the year in which the survey data we employ were collected. Conversely, rejection of these propositions indicates, at the least, qualified support for dominant ideology and, at the most, support for some version of counter ideology. These content domains closely parallel the areas of investigation (unions, the military, socialists, conservatives) which were the subject of the Quebec City study. . . .

PREDICTIONS

◆ ◆ ◆

The purpose of the present study is to test the claim that support for dominant ideology depends on respondents' area of study at the post-secondary level. Guimond et al. (1989: 207) favour a strong version of the hypothesis which predicts socialization into dominant ideology among business and professional graduates and socialization into counter ideology among social science graduates. In addition, they anticipate that the differences among students 'are likely to persist in their later life' (Guimond et al., 1989: 207). A weak version of the hypothesis predicts a dominant ideology or conservative effect among respondents whose post-secondary education was in business or the professions, but no effect or a

reduced effect among respondents who were educated in the social sciences.

It was necessary to control for a number of antecedent variables, such as sex, age, parental education, and region. These controls were warranted because there are theoretical and empirical grounds to believe that they are associated with our independent variables and the kinds of dependent variables used here. We also controlled for respondents' occupation and income because these variables refer to important processes intervening between the termination of (most) respondents' formal education and the interviews for the study from which our data were derived. They represent alternative sources of ideological beliefs and therefore need to be taken into account in assessing education's independent effects, as well as the persistence of these effects.

Data Source and Procedures

The data analysed in this paper were taken from the Canadian Class Structure and Class Consciousness (CCSCC) study, conducted in 1983 by John Myles of the Department of Sociology and Anthropology at Carleton University. The original data were sampled from three sub-populations: 1) individuals in the workforce (part time or full time); 2) housewives; and 3) unemployed individuals. Of the 2,577 people who were interviewed, 1,785 were in the workforce sub-sample on which our analyses are based. The sample we employ is nationally representative of workforce participants from the 'non-institutionalized, non-adult population (ages 15–65) of Canada's ten provinces' (I.C.P.S.R, 1986: xi) at the time of the survey. The CCSCC study is, to our knowledge, the only national survey which collected information on the relevant dependent variables and which also asked university-educated respondents the following question: 'What was your major subject or field of study?'

The CCSCC study included a number of measures which tap the same domain of dominant ideology as the dependent variables employed in the Quebec City study. Paralleling the latter's measure of attitudes toward the military, respondents were asked whether 'the government should be spending a great deal more on the military, somewhat more on the military, the present amount, somewhat less, or a great deal less.' A series of items dealt with the importance of the profit motive ('it is possible for a modern society to run effectively without the profit motive'), whether corporations have 'too much power,' whether corporations 'benefit owners at the expense of workers and consumers,' and whether the government should spend more money or less money on social services such as health and education. Finally, attitudes toward labour unions were measured with three items that asked whether hiring 'scabs' should be prohibited, whether workers are justified in physically preventing strikebreakers from entering the workplace, and the importance of strikers winning their demands before returning to work. . . .

Results

Tables I and II report the results of multiple regression analyses in which the various dependent measures were regressed, before and after statistical controls, on the six dummy variables representing exposure to different types of university education. Table I deals with the disciplines of respondents who have had some exposure to post-secondary education, while Table II categorizes only respondents who have obtained at least a bachelors degree. The 'reference' category consists of individuals who have not attended university (in the case of Table I) or individuals

who have either not attended or have not graduated (in the case of Table II). The differences between these two tables help us to address the question of whether the effects are simple educational effects or credential effects (Collins, 1979). The coefficients presented in the tables refer to differences between the means for university-educated individuals with a given type of disciplinary education (social science, science, business, etc.) and the non-university-educated population. The column headed 'All' presents the results of a separate analysis in which all university-educated individuals (or, in the case of Table II, all graduates) are pooled together and coded '1' and compared with all others who are coded '0.' In these tables, negative coefficients indicate a conservative effect or an effect in the direction of dominant ideology for university as a whole, relative to the reference category. Positive coefficients indicate an effect in the direction of counter ideology or 'radicalism.'

Table I   Relationship between Some University Education and Political Attitudes, without and with Statistical Controls

Variables (N =)	Social Science (69)	Business (44)	Profess. (54)	Arts (61)	Science (35)	Other (146)	All
Corporate Power & Profits							
1. Corporations	−.090	−.694**	−.527***	+.088	+.001	−.068	−.170***
benefit owners	−.025	−.419***	−.272*	−.007	+.064	−.032	−.100*
2. Profit motive	−.291*	−.376*	−.366**	−.018	−.216	−.121	−.202***
is unnecessary	−.160	−.272	−.141	−.027	−.131	−.072	−.129*
3. Big corporations	−.131	−.599***	−.369**	+.005	−.306**	−.089	−.193***
have too much power	−.030	−.445**	−.205	+.002	−.283	−.075	−.147**
Social Services							
4. Support social	+.084	−.400**	−.466***	+.022	−.055	−.108	−.130*
service expenditures	+.140	−.298*	−.332*	+.032	−.043	−.090	−.099
Unions							
5. Prohibit	−.072	−.509***	−.473***	+.056	−.075	−.202*	−.200**
hiring scabs	−.065	−.543*	−.303	+.076	−.081	−.155	−.171
6. Workers can	−.222	−.387*	−.184	−.120	−.145	−.197*	−.203***
prevent scabs	−.152	−.272	−.095	−.037	−.179	−.138	−.150*
7. Achieve strike	+.016	+.116	−.159	+.144	−.024	+.153	+.024
objectives	+.018	+.124	−.087	+.101	−.063	+.035	+.033
Military							
8. Favour military	−.016	−.086	+.074	−.124	+.252	−.094	−.032
spending	−.140	−.110	−.086	−.127	+.125	−.207	−.100

Note: Values are unstandardized regression coefficients; first rows are from analyses without statistical controls and second rows are from analyses with controls. Controls are for sex, age, parental education, region, occupation and income. See text for measurement of variables. Significance levels: *p < .05; **p < .01; ***p < .001.

Table II Relationship between Possession of University Degree and Political Attitudes, without and with Statistical Controls

Variables (N =)	Social Science (51)	Business (29)	Profess. (45)	Arts (44)	Science (29)	Other (83)	All
Corporate Power & Profits							
1. Corporations	−.084	−.660**	−.609**	+.190	−.066	−.107	−.189**
benefit owners	−.011	−.347*	−.299*	+.090	+.014	−.026	−.088
2. Profit motive	−.144	−.364	−.406**	−.017	−.260	−.134	−.197**
is unnecessary	+.011	−.197	−.130	−.018	−.159	−.059	−.094
3. Big corporations	−.218	−.731**	−.457**	+.044	−.487**	−.178	−.284***
have too much power	−.132	−.553**	−.283**	+.047	−.455"	−.139	−.223***
Social Services							
4. Support social	+.084	−.643**	−.508**	+.023	−.106	−.109	−.171**
service expenditures	+.143	−.492**	−.379"	+.030	−.067	−.070	−.124
Unions							
5. Prohibit	−.045	−.680***	−.541***	+.256	−.111	+.086	−.161*
hiring scabs	−.143	−.713*	−.288	+.356	−.081	+.064	−.069
6. Workers can	−.161	−.421*	−.178	−.048	−.142	−.107	−.155*
prevent scabs	−.068	−.293**	−.059	+.059	−.141	−.014	−.080
7. Achieve strike	+.067	+.051	−.169	+.111	+.020	−.009	+.007
objectives	+.060	+.065	−.087	+.047	−.003	+.006	+.020
Military							
8. Favour military	−.074	−.383	+.136	−.154	+.107	−.178	−.097
spending	−.143	−.430	−.062	−.172	−.009	−.297*	−.178*

Note: Values are unstandardized regression coefficients; first rows are from analyses without statistical controls and second rows are from analyses with controls. Controls are for sex, age, parental education, region, occupation and income. See text for measurement of variables. Significance levels: $*p < .05$; $**p < .01$; $***p < .001$.

TESTING FOR OVERALL EFFECTS

♦ ♦ ♦

Previous research led us to expect that the net effect of higher education without regard to discipline would be in the direction of dominant ideology (Curtis and Lambert, 1976; Baer and Lambert, 1982). The 'All' columns of Tables I and II provide continuity between the original studies that prompted the Guimond et al. (1989) paper and the present analyses. In Table I, there were significant higher-order effects in the direction of dominant ideology for the three corporate items, the social service item, and the item permitting strikers to prevent the hiring of replacement workers. All statements, except the one about strikers achieving their objectives before returning to work, yielded negative

signs. The 'All' column in Table II produced generally consistent but less significant results. . . .

TESTING FOR DISCIPLINE EFFECTS

♦ ♦ ♦

We are mainly concerned with testing the working hypothesis that higher education 'radicalizes' social science students and indoctrinates business and professional students into dominant ideology. The findings in the first three columns of Tables I and II bear on this hypothesis. On the evidence, it is clearly wanting. In Table I, the only positive coefficients for social science graduates appear for social service expenditures and the importance of strikers achieving their objectives. In neither case were the coefficients for these items statistically significant. The coefficients for business and professional graduates were generally negative and in the direction of dominant ideology, as expected. The results in Table II are similar.

It is noteworthy that there is little difference in support for dominant ideology between respondents who have studied the social sciences and those who have studied arts subject. Neither is there much to choose between the social sciences and the sciences. Given the peculiar properties of the social sciences that are said to engender 'radicalism,' the failure of the expected *pattern* of differences among disciplinary areas to emerge must also be regarded as damaging to the strong version of the hypothesis.

TESTING FOR FRENCH-ENGLISH DIFFERENCES

● ● ●

There is reason to believe that the kinds of relationships discussed here might vary between English Canada and Quebec. Certainly the social sciences have played a role in Quebec that has been unmatched in the rest of Canada. The social sciences in Quebec contributed to the articulation of Québécois nationalism throughout the 1960s and 1970s, with profound consequences in terms of people's orientations toward social movements, labour unions, and the legitimacy of capitalism and the Canadian and Quebec states (but see Laurin-Frenette, 1989). . . .

Table III [not shown here] shows that the tendency for business and professionally educated individuals to endorse corporate power might not be quite as strong in Quebec, at least for business graduates. And, while there is a greater tendency for Québécois arts and social science graduates than non-university educated individuals to believe that corporations are too powerful (the coefficients are + .270 and + .281), there is no such effect in English Canada. This single interaction suggests that any 'liberalizing' effect of social science education, if it exists, is confined to Quebec. The column labeled 'All' in Table III indicates the net effect of university education across all disciplines. Overall, university education in English Canada is associated with a higher level of disagreement with the statement that 'corporations have too much power,' while in French Canada it is associated with a higher level of agreement. . . . Our ability to make claims regarding French-English differences is limited by the relatively small numbers of French Canadian university graduates in our sample. While we cannot discount the possibility that there is a more 'liberalizing' effect of social sciences education in Quebec, the data we employ do not support a strong version of this hypothesis, since the effects are certainly not very strong. . . .

Discussion and Conclusions

At the heart of the analysis reported here is Guimond et al.'s (1989) hypothesis that post-secondary programs of study produce different ideological effects, and the specific prediction that studying social sciences 'radicalizes' students. It is true that respondents who had studied business and the professions were more likely to express dominant ideological beliefs than those who had studied the social sciences. At the same time, though, social science-educated respondents were somewhat more conservative than arts graduates; and they did not differ appreciably from those who had studied science. The most important comparison is between social science graduates and their reference category, people who had not obtained a bachelor's degree. This comparison demonstrates quite convincingly that social science graduates have not been 'radicalized.' How then shall we explain the differences between the present findings and those reported by Guimond et al. (1989)?

First, we differ from these authors in their depiction of the social sciences in Canada. In part, this has to do with their use of the 'radical' label. Education in the social sciences can, of course, be properly described as 'radical' if it 'gets to the root of things.' Surely, any academic discipline makes at least the pretense of fostering this perspective, even if it is not labelled as radical. 'Getting to the root of things' is a matter of perspective, the kinds of questions that are asked, and how one sets about answering these questions. 'Radical,' in this sense, implies nothing about whether the analyst is disaffected or alienated from the object of analysis. The enthusiasm of social science students, understandably excited by their 'discovery' of society and flexing their newly acquired verbal skills, is occasionally mistaken by their elders for radicalism in the more conventional sense of the word, which equates it with a militant opposition to the status quo. In our view, there is little evidence that Canadian social scientists—students or faculty—are radical in this second sense of the word.

To support their case about radicalism in the social sciences, Guimond et al. offer anecdotal evidence for the 'real' nature of higher education. '[T]heories to the effect that education generates support for the dominant ideology,' for example, 'do not predict that the capitalist school system would produce sociologists, often claiming Marxist allegiance, who have somehow escaped the ideological indoctrination of the school system' (Guimond et al., 1989: 207). We recognize these occurrences as 'exceptions' to the kinds of trends envisaged by the dominant ideology thesis (cf. Miliband, 1973: 230). A few harmless pockets of 'radicalism' may, if not rooted in a larger set of social institutions providing for the implementation of a 'radical' political agenda, deflect any criticism that the educational system is closed to contrary ideas. Indeed, a number of writers have argued that academe is part of a process whereby left radicalism has been domesticated (cf. Jacoby, 1987; Piccone, 1989; Berman, 1989; Etzkowitz, 1988). Closer to home, it has been argued that English Canadian academics, compared to those in Quebec, the United States and Britain, have been singularly disengaged from public policy debate (Brym and Myles, 1989). However, in the absence of more direct evidence on how many Canadian social scientists apply one or other of the conventional radical labels to themselves, we suggest that the findings presented here offer little support for Guimond et al.'s depiction of social science graduates or, by inference, their instructors. Indeed, on the evidence, one might be tempted to conclude that social scientists, including more than sociologists, have little discernible impact on their students' opinions.

Although Guimond et al. believe that the social sciences generate 'radicalism,' it is also instructive that they seem to have only sociology in mind. All of their examples of social science radicalism make reference to sociology and sociologists. We wonder if this is because it would be more difficult to sustain the argument in the case of other disciplines that fall within the social science camp, namely economics, geography, political science, anthropology, demography, social psychology, and so on.

Second, the samples used in the two studies differed in a number of significant respects. In contrast to the nationally representative sample which we used, Guimond et al. (1989) based their observations on a highly selective sample of students from Quebec City. They justify their sample on the grounds that 'none of the institutions selected either has any reputation for being radically different from other schools in terms of its ideology, or is especially small, or has a student population drawn from a particularly privileged or deprived background' (Guimond et al., 1989: 200). Although the high school students are probably residents of the Quebec City area, the Laval University students are more likely to come from across the province and beyond, thus leaving open the question of whether the differences between the high school students and the university students will generalize beyond the specific Quebec City comparison which was undertaken.

The studies differed also in how the education variable was sampled. Respondents' highest level of education in the Quebec City study was partial completion of the second year of university. This makes it impossible to address the question of how much of the education effect is attributable to education as such, as opposed to credentialization (Baer and Lambert, 1982: 177, 189). 'Idealization' in the early years of higher education may well be replaced with a degree of 'realism' as students approach graduation and the necessity of finding employment. . . . On the other hand, if area-specific socialization occurs throughout students' undergraduate years, as Guimond et al.'s hypothesis and results seem to suggest, we should expect the ideological differences between business and the professions, on the one hand, and the social sciences, on the other, to increase among those who graduated in these areas. Our analyses provide no support for this inference.

Third, in our analysis, the reference category of people who did not attend post-secondary schools provided an invaluable benchmark for deciding what 'meaning' we should assign to the scores of respondents who were educated in the different disciplines. Without this benchmark, we might overinterpret the lower mean scores obtained by social science graduates compared with business and professional graduates. When we compare social science graduates with people who did not attend university, we can see that there is no basis for labelling the beliefs of social science people as 'radical.' If we are to say anything about their beliefs, they are marginally more conservative than the population at large, and they are somewhat less so than business and professional graduates. The Quebec City study failed to provide the necessary comparison points for imputing radicalism to social science students.

Our analyses could be subject to the criticism that respondents' orientations reflect the effects of at least three kinds of experiences: factors prior to post-secondary education, which shape beliefs and attitudes and which may select respondents into post-secondary education and into different academic programs; factors associated with higher education itself, the specific focus of the radicalism hypothesis; and factors in the job setting which intervene between completion of higher education and the interviews from which the data are taken. The first and third sets of variables represent potential threats to our test of the Guimond et al. hypothesis. If Guimond and his colleagues were correct in their ideological characterization of academic disciplines, it is reasonable to expect that students who select the social sciences are more liberal, leftist, or 'radical' than students who opt into business and professional programs.

We might note in passing that Guimond et al. make no such claim; instead, they find few significant differences between high school students enrolled in 'work-entry' programs as opposed to those in more general programs where post-secondary education might be expected (1989: 204), and few differences among high school students indicating a preference for 'science,' 'administration' or 'social science' (1989: 205, Figures 1–3). Still, given the limitations of the high school sample in the Quebec City study, we might leave open the question of whether students who opt for social sciences are more leftist or 'radical' to begin with. If this is the case, though, we should expect to observe ideological orientations which exhibit not only the effects of socialization from the putatively 'radical' social sciences but also the effects of prior beliefs (pre-selection). We need not worry about distinguishing between these independent effects, however, because our analysis suggests that there is no evidence that social science graduates are more radical than anybody else. For experiences that intervene between graduation and the interviews, we have attempted to control for some of the more salient factors that may affect ideology. These included parental education, as a proxy for the social standing of respondents' families of origin; income, occupation and region, to capture some of the material basis for ideology; as well as gender and age, which are important dimensions within which people's experiences in society are organized and which undoubtedly contribute to ideology.

In our view, the present exercise has not been without merit. We could say the same about Guimond et al.'s hunch that there might be an interaction between higher education and academic discipline, although we think that they have overstated their case. While there is no evidence to support their conclusion of social science 'radicalism,' it appears that socialization into dominant ideology is more successful in some disciplines than in others (cf. Abercrombie et al., 1980). The fact that dominant ideology is transmitted most effectively in business programs is consistent with our view of the content of dominant ideology and the hypothesis that socialization into such beliefs is a byproduct of higher education.

The Politics of Canadian Social Scientists: A Comment on Baer and Lambert

Serge Guimond
Royal Military College of Canada

Douglas L. Palmer
Royal Military College of Canada

◆ ◆ ◆

Baer and Lambert (hereafter referred to as B & L) were able to show, using a national sample, that two fields of study were more effective than others in disseminating dominant beliefs in Canada. They found that 'respondents who had studied business and the professions were more likely to express dominant ideological beliefs than those who had studied the social sciences' (p. 498). These findings have a number of important theoretical implications that unfortunately are not considered by B & L. Instead, their objectives appear to be to downplay any possible counter effects of studying the social sciences. In that process, they make several claims about our 1989 paper in *The Canadian Review of Sociology and Anthropology* (CRSA) (Guimond, Palmer and Bégin, 1989, hereafter GPB) and about their own results that are far from justified. Indeed, B & L cite the GPB study several times but fail to mention two other relevant papers that we have published during the same period (see Guimond, Bégin and Palmer, 1989; Guimond and Palmer, 1990). This enables them to present a somewhat distorted view of our work and to put forward criticisms that are simply not valid. After noting the limitations of their arguments, we will present an alternative interpretation of their results that is more consistent with existing evidence.

PROVING THE NULL HYPOTHESIS

◆ ◆ ◆

Baer and Lambert (1990: 501) assert that we 'overstated' our case in our 1989 paper because we interpreted our results as evidence that university-level education in the social sciences has a liberalizing effect on intergroup attitudes. They state that their comparisons between social science graduates and people without a degree 'demonstrate quite convincingly that social science graduates have not been "radicalized"' (p. 499). There are some serious problems with this presentation of the facts.

The first and most basic problem is that such a conclusion is based entirely on null finding. Within the social sciences, B & L find no differences, no effects of education whatsoever. . . . Thus, if their study failed to provide evidence of liberalization of attitudes within the social sciences, *it failed as well to show that social science graduates become more conservative or more likely to support dominant ideology.* . . . As we all know (or should know), the failure to find a difference does not prove that there is no difference. In the words of Mitchell and Jolley (1992): *"the failure to find a treatment effect does not mean the treatment has no effect.* If you had looked more carefully, you might have observed an

From Serge Guimond and Douglas L. Palmer, "The politics of Canadian social scientists: A comment on Baer and Lambert," *Canadian Review of Sociology and Anthropology*, Vol. 31, No. 2, May 1994, pp. 184–195. Reprinted with permission of the Canadian Sociology and Anthropology Association.

effect" (p. 175; emphasis in original). Thus, on this ground alone, the conclusion reached by B & L that 'social science graduates have not been radicalized' is misleading.

. . . In our CRSA paper, we reported the results obtained with dependent measures consisting of evaluations of group labels (e.g., 'the military,' 'unions,' 'socialists') on a scale running from 'very unfavourable' to 'very favourable.' While the measures used by B & L have some similarities, they are far from identical. For example, their measure of attitudes towards the military asked whether the respondent felt that military spending was too high or too low, probably tapping attitudes towards government spending, deficits, and taxation levels as well as (if not rather than) attitudes towards the military as a group. Thus, if there are differences in results, it is quite possible that they are due to differences in the dependent measures used in the two studies. . . .

However, the strongest effect reported by GPB (1989) concerned attitudes towards 'socialists.' Education had a positive effect on ratings for this group among social science students and a negative effect among commerce and science students. . . . What do B & L find here? This is a crucial question and the answer is difficult to find because B & L (1990) have no measures that tap attitudes towards 'socialists'. . . .

B & L do offer several alternative explanations for the difference in results. Unfortunately, none of these explanations are consistent with existing national and international evidence.

DIFFERENT DEPICTIONS OF THE SOCIAL SCIENCES IN CANADA

◆ ◆ ◆

. . . B & L (1990: 499) believe that 'there is little evidence that Canadian social scientists—students or faculty—are radical(s)' while GPB (1989) apparently believe that there is. Two points to note here. First, GPB (1989) were concerned with liberalism, not radicalism as B & L assume, and second, though it might be true that there is little evidence of radicalism among social scientists in Canada, this is not the case with respect to liberalism. . . .

. . . Astin (1986) reports the results of an American study among 'some 200,000 students and a national sample of more than 300 postsecondary institutions of all types' (p. 3). One of the findings is that 'Majoring in the social sciences was associated with greater-than-average increases in liberalism and majoring in either engineering,

mathematics, or physical sciences was associated with less-than-average increases' (p. 38). Similarly, in *The power of protest,* Astin (1975) notes that 'both faculty and students who lead, participate in, or otherwise support protests show a number of traits in common: they are likely to be Jewish or to have no religious preference, to be left or liberal in their politics, and to be from the humanities or the social sciences' (p. 63). Note here the mention of humanities.

GPB (1989) have chosen to study the social sciences because research suggests that it is the most liberal field of study. But, people in arts or humanities are also typically found to be fairly liberal. We confirmed this in a study of English Canadian university students from various regions (Guimond, 1990). Thus, when B & L (1990: 494) find 'that there is little difference in support for dominant ideology between respondents who have studied the social sciences and those who have studied arts subject [sic],' this is not surprising nor necessarily 'damaging' to the hypothesis of fields-specific effects as B & L appear to believe. Rather, such a finding is consistent with past research (see Altemeyer, 1988; Astin, 1975; Feldman and Newcomb, 1969; Ladd and Lipset, 1975). . . .

B & L (1990: 500) also criticize our use of sociology as an example and 'wonder if this is because it would be more difficult to sustain the argument in the case of other disciplines that fall within the social science camp, namely economics. . . .' Again, a more extensive consultation of research in the area suggests that while the social sciences as a group are more liberal, there are indeed differences within that group. In their study of 60,000 faculty in American colleges and universities, Ladd and Lipset (1975) found that economists tend to be the least liberal and sociologists the most liberal within the social science group. Thus, when focusing on liberalism and perhaps even more so on radicalism, sociology may provide the clearest examples (see also Lipset and Ladd, 1974). . . .

FIELDS OF STUDY AND THE INTERPRETATION OF SOCIAL INEQUALITY

◆ ◆ ◆

. . . [B]aer and Lambert (1982: 174) have pointed out that the essential meaning of the concept of dominant ideology has to do with the interpretation of social inequality. 'What is important about dominant ideology,' they write 'is its capacity to explain, justify and even in some cases, to see justice itself in social inequality. It does this, for example, by ascribing to personal character (motivation, hard work), rather than to systemic or institutional factors, the ultimate responsibility for worldly success or failure.'

On the basis of a factor analysis, Guimond, Bégin and Palmer (1989) have constructed two scales to measure this important dimension of dominant ideology: a four-item scale measuring an individualistic explanation which ascribes inequality to personal character and a five-item scale measuring a structural explanation. They find that in contrast to studies in science or commerce, 'an education in social science, regardless of one's employment prospects or social class background, is associated with a decreasing tendency to attribute poverty to personal failure' (Guimond, Bégin and Palmer, 1989: 137) which is exactly the opposite of what the dominant ideology thesis predicts (see Baer and Lambert, 1982; Bowles and Gintis, 1976). Moreover, the results indicate, in *Quebec and in Ontario,* an increasing tendency to ascribe inequality to systemic or institutional factors among social science students but not among commerce or engineering students (see Guimond, Bégin and Palmer, 1989; Guimond and Palmer, 1990). . . .

DIFFERENCE IN SAMPLES
◆ ◆ ◆

A second explanation proposed by B & L concerns the different samples used in the two studies. They used a nationally representative sample while ours was a 'highly selective sample of students from Québec City' (B & L, 1990: 500). Their main argument here is that the high school students in our sample probably come from the Quebec city area but not the university students. This leaves 'open the question of whether the differences between the high school students and the university students will generalize beyond the specific Quebec city comparison which was undertaken' (B & L, 1990: 500). . . . [E]ven if our results could possibly be valid within the Quebec context, B & L would argue that they certainly do not apply to English Canada where social scientists are known for their lack of political involvement. On these points, we invite B & L to consult the two publications referenced above (i.e., Guimond, Bégin and Palmer, 1989; Guimond and Palmer, 1990). They will find that the study carried out in Ontario (Guimond and Palmer, 1990) did not use high school students but only first-year and upper-year university students. The results revealed effects similar to those obtained with the Quebec sample (see Guimond, Bégin and Palmer, 1989), which sug-

gests that the findings reported by GPB (1989) were *not* due to the alleged difference between high school students and university students and further that they *could* apply equally well to English Canada as to Quebec (see also Guimond, 1990; 1992a).

DIFFERENCE IN COMPARISON GROUPS
◆ ◆ ◆

The third and final explanation offered by B & L concerns differences in comparison groups or reference categories used in the two studies. They have an 'invaluable benchmark' for interpreting scores of respondents in various fields of study: 'the reference category of people who did not attend post-secondary schools' (1990: 500). In contrast, they note that 'the Quebec city study failed to provide the necessary comparison points for imputing radicalism to social science students' (B & L, 1990: 500). B & L seem to have misread the purpose of our research which is not to impute radicalism to social science students. Two issues appear to be confused here. One could ask what is the percentage of a particular population that can be classified as, say, 'radicals.' To answer such a question, a representative sample of the population in question is vital. But one could also ask: what are the causes of 'radicalism'? How can we explain the fact that some people become 'radicals' while others become 'conservatives'? The latter are the issues with which we are concerned and to answer such questions, there is no absolute need for a nationally representative sample. There is a need for a theory, an hypothesis, and a sufficient number of appropriate cases to permit an empirical test of that hypothesis. GPB's (1989) Quebec study was designed in that context and consequently, it had little or nothing to say about the former issue. Rather, the aim was to examine whether education in a given field of study had ideological effects that differed from education in another field. . . .

ALTERNATIVE INTERPRETATION OF BAER AND LAMBERT'S RESULTS
◆ ◆ ◆

. . . In no way did B & L report evidence that contradicted what was found in the Quebec study. To the contrary, B & L observed that there were some overall effects of education but that these effects could be attributed mainly to the role of two fields of study which they called business and the professions. . . .

If, as B & L maintain, the social sciences have no lib-eralizing or radicalizing effect, why do individuals with such an education appear to remain attitudinally iden-tical to other members of society who lack the privileges and vested interest in the status quo that accompanies the obtaining of academic credentials and the ensuing occupational status? Are there not important implica-tions if a group of individuals, possessing greater social power because of educational and occupational status, share the same attitudes towards society as those who are disadvantaged?

In that context, and in the context of existing evi-dence concerning the greater liberalism of the social sci-ences in English Canada, in Quebec, and elsewhere, an alternative interpretation of B & L's results is that the null effect obtained in that field may reflect a *resistance to change in the direction of dominant ideology*. Such an interpretation is consistent with Feldman and Newcomb's (1969) theoretical analysis of the impact of higher educa-tion. . . . [F]eldman and Newcomb (1969: 55) note that the attitude may have a firmer basis in the student's con-sciousness or that it may have become more strongly related to other attitudes and beliefs. When this occurs, they suggest that the process of attitude maintenance really reflects what they call *reinforcement* of an attitude.

Evidence for the existence of such a process among Ontario social science students was found recently (see Guimond, 1992b; Guimond and Palmer 1993). This lon-gitudinal study essentially confirms earlier cross-sectional results (see also Guimond, 1992a). At the beginning of their academic program, social science students were found to be very similar to commerce students in terms of their socio-political views. Two and a half years later, these *same* anglophone students differed significantly in their attitudes towards socialists, capitalists and immi-grants, as well as in their mode of explaining social inequality. In each case, a more liberal response was given by social science students compared to business students. This evidence, which is clearly at variance with a self-selection explanation, implies that each field of study has different ideological effects. Yet, if one looks at the changes occurring within each field, one finds relatively few significant changes among social science students. . . .

CONCLUSION
◆ ◆ ◆

We arrive then at a very different conclusion. B & L claim to have shown that there is no radicalization process within the social sciences. We have presented arguments to suggest that such a claim is methodologically incorrect, theoretically questionable and inconsistent with a body of research evidence. We have argued that their study may indicate to the contrary, that there is, within the social sci-ences, a resistance to change in the direction of dominant ideology. B & L *may* claim that there is no radicalization process within the social sciences but they have not shown that. Neither have they shown that social science students and graduates are more conservative than others. They found that there is no difference between social science graduates and people without a degree, which is an ambiguous result that can mean many different things.

Apart from this, our comments should not detract from the fact that their study is an important contribu-tion. One of their key findings (B & L, 1990: 501) that 'socialization into dominant ideology is more successful in some disciplines than others,' obtained with a nationally representative sample, clearly suggests that discipline-specific effects of higher education have some generality beyond Quebec city and, as such, that research taking into account such effects may greatly enhance our under-standing of some critical aspects of Canadian social and political life.

The Ruling Class and the Ruling Ideas. How the Hegelian Conception of the Domination of the Spirits in History Arose

Karl Marx and Frederick Engels

The ideas of the ruling class are in every epoch the ruling idea: i.e., the class which is the ruling *material* force of society is at the same time its ruling *intellectual* force. The class which has the means of material production at its disposal, consequently also controls the means of mental production, so that the ideas of those who lack the means of mental production are on the whole subject to it. The ruling ideas are nothing more than the ideal expression of the dominant material relations, the dominant material relations grasped as ideas; hence of the relations which make the one class the ruling one, therefore, the ideas of its dominance. The individuals composing the ruling class possess among other things consciousness, and therefore think. Insofar, therefore, as they rule as a class and determine the extent and compass of an historical epoch, it is self-evident that they do this in its whole range, hence among other things rule also as thinkers, as producers of ideas, and regulate the production and distribution of the ideas of their age: thus their ideas are the ruling ideas of the epoch. For instance, in an age and in a country where royal power, aristocracy and bourgeoisie are contending for domination and where, therefore, domination is shared, the doctrine of the separation of powers proves to be the dominant idea and is expressed as an "eternal law."

The division of labour, which we already saw above (pp. [15–18]) as one of the chief forces of history up till now, manifests itself also in the ruling class as the division of mental and [31] material labour, so that inside this class one part appears as the thinkers of the class (its active, conceptive ideologists, who make the formation of the illusions of the class about itself their chief source of livelihood), while the others' attitude to these ideas and illusions is more passive and receptive, because they are in reality the active member of this class and have less time to make up illusions and ideas about themselves. Within this class this cleavage can even develop into a certain opposition and hostility between the two parts, but whenever a practical collision occurs in which the class itself is endangered they automatically vanish, in which case there also vanishes the appearance of the ruling ideas being not the ideas of the ruling class and having a power distinct from the power of this class. The existence of revolutionary ideas in a particular period presupposes the existence of revolutionary class; about the premises of the latter sufficient has already been said above (pp. [18–19, 22–23]).

Source: Karl Marx and Frederick Engels, "The ruling class and the ruling ideas. How the Hegelian conception of the domination of the spirits in history arose," *The German Ideology*, pp. 67–68. Progress Publishers (Moscow, Russia), 1976.

Universities and Ideology: Political Correctness May Be Rampant in the U.S., but in Canada, There Are Other Pressures on Academic Freedoms; [Final Edition]

Mark Abley, The Gazette

"The universities have been destroyed by ideology."

—Harold Bloom

It's a striking notion. In the United States, where Harold Bloom is a well-known literary critic, it may even have a grain of truth. But here in Canada, Bloom's glum emphasis on political correctness and postmodern trendiness hardly seems to fit what professors themselves are feeling.

Universities are in a tricky position right now. The expectations on them are enormous: to educate an ever-growing percentage of young and not-so-young adults; to be a wellspring of scientific innovation and economic renewal; and, increasingly, to meet the demands of business as well as government. The oldest expectation of them all—to nurture top-flight scholarship, free from society's daily concerns—can seem virtually archaic.

The kind of radicalism endemic in North American universities during the late '60s and early '70s—the days when strikes and demonstrations would routinely shut a campus down—are long past.

Many of today's students are preoccupied by the need to find a good job at the end of their long and expensive formal education. And excesses of political correctness (banishing the word "history" as sexist, for example, as happened at a college in northern England) seem largely remote from the four universities in Montreal.

"The whole debate about political correctness never became a burning issue in Quebec," says Yves Gingras, a professor at the Université du Quebec á Montreal who specializes in the sociology of science. "The intensity of the argument was mostly an American phenomenon, with English Canada somewhere in between."

"Political correctness can be an occasional pain in the ass," Decarie admits. "If I say 'Indian,' someone in my class might tell me to say 'First Nations.' It's a bit annoying.

"But look, in some cases it's good. In my own department, it's made us more conscious of women and minorities than we were. You can't use history as an opportunity to boost the morale of anybody; what you have to show, as accurately as possible, is what happened. So, in my history of recreation and leisure course, I show how women were systematically kept out of organized sports because organized sports were meant to foster leadership, and leadership was defined as male."

"There are fashions in ideas, just as there are fashions in clothes," says McGill's principal, Bernard Shapiro. "The challenge for a university is always to make sure it sits at a slight angle to society, so that the current fashion is not the only one young people are exposed to.

"In the McCarthy era in the U.S., staying at a slight angle to society became somewhat more problematic. But I haven't seen anything even remotely like that in my time here." Shapiro took over the reins at McGill in 1994, the year after the Lief affair.

"It's difficult to move against the current fashion," Shapiro admits. "If you are opposed to Women's Studies as an idea, this is difficult at the moment. Now there are good reasons for not having it and there are wonderful reasons for having it. If you're opposed to it, some people may suspect you of being in league with the devil.

"But even so, you would not be frozen out. I don't get the sense that political correctness is overwhelming this or any other debate."

Shapiro's confidence is not shared by Bloom, the American literary critic, who has sneeringly deplored the arrival in the academy of "professors of hip-hop . . . ideologues of gender and of various sexual persuasions . . . multiculturalists unlimited." From Bloom's standpoint, the study of literature and the other humanities has fallen into a warring disarray in which ideology matters more than pure scholarship.

Certainly the humanities are no hotbed of intellectual conservatism (which is, of course, an ideology in its own right). Today's campus activists are as likely to emerge from departments of cultural studies as from more traditional disciplines such as economics or political science. But the postmodernist tendencies that Bloom so deplores have grown in strength at the exact moment when many universities are confronting a much greater force: the corporate agenda.

This may not be wholly accidental, suggests Anthony Pare, who is chairman of the Department of Educational Studies in McGill's Faculty of Education: "A lot of post-

Continued

modern theory is a playfulness, a resistance to hard fact. It dwells in uncertainty and it resists truth as being something provable in the world.

"That may form part of an ideology of resistance to the kind of pragmatism that is so evident in corporate culture. More and more, universities are being asked to produce people who will fit into the economy in particular places. And there is a real danger of the humanities and social sciences being frozen out—wilting on the vine."

Even in Harold Bloom's field of literary studies, business has shown a keen if indirect influence. The Parisian dominance of literary theory through the '70s and '80s has been supplanted, to some degree, by an American-led movement called "New Historicism." It's not a right-wing movement. But still, when the New Historicists look at texts from the past, the terms they prefer to use are ones like "exchange," "circulation," "negotiation" and "commerce."

In other words, the metaphors of the marketplace have even filtered into Shakespeare studies.

Nowhere, perhaps, are the changes more dramatic than in McGill's Faculty of Management, which boasts an academic staff of over 60. Back in the late 1950s, the university merely had a "School of Commerce" that fell under the Faculty of Arts and Science. In those days, literature was compulsory for an aspiring businessman.

Today, by contrast, the management faculty offers up-to-the-minute courses like "Asia/Pacific Management," "Technological Entrepreneurship" and "Applied Time Series Analysis for Managerial Forecasting."

"There's been an enormous growth in Commerce at Concordia, too," Graeme Decarie points out. "And to a very wide extent at universities, it has meant a kind of sellout to the corporate world."

"I don't think there's anything wrong in teaching commerce; we should be of service to the corporate world. But our job should also be to criticize what's going on in our field. We should be independent enough of business to also be critical of it. And that's what I don't see."

"It's a very sad scene," adds Howard Ripstein, a retired professor of accounting at Concordia. "The students are so narrow. Universities are supposed to be places for free thinking, but as far as I can see, all they do now is train people for jobs."

Universities have turned to businesses partly out of sheer need. Between 1993 and 1998, federal and provincial governments cut their spending on higher education by a staggering total of $800 million.

"The governments," says Shapiro, "all Canadian governments, have found it impossible to support both the access agenda and the quality agenda. They don't have the money.

"So if you want to support the quality agenda, you'd better be out there finding the other sources of money that make that possible." . . .

Universities across Canada faced a financial crunch in the '90s, but in most provinces the purse strings have begun to loosen. In Quebec, where the provincial government has chosen to keep tuition fees low, universities remain in poor financial shape. The six campuses of the Université du Quebec are running a deficit of greater than $70 million; in the case of the Abitibi-Temiscamingue campus, the deficit is over 34 percent of operating budget.

What Canadian universities do not enjoy is the luxury of relying on their own endowments. Last year, the endowment funds at all Canadian universities added up to about $5.4 billion. Yale University alone had twice that amount, Harvard four times as much.

When new funding arrives from governments, it often comes with conditions attached. "Targeted funding," as it's called, allows governments to direct money to specific areas (mostly science and technology) while ignoring subjects that are supposedly less productive (such as the humanities). Pare, of McGill's education faculty, fears that targeted funding may lead to "the university becoming the servant of the state in producing the workers that the state wants."

"But targeting is not the same as cutting," notes Gingras, the UQAM professor. "Governments have a logical right to target their funds. They just shouldn't do it in a way that takes money away from other areas, or is directed at only short-term results."

Ontario universities, notably Waterloo and Guelph, have led the movement to forge links with private businesses. It's a movement that can have unwieldy results, as when the University of New Brunswick announced the creation of something called the "NSERC-SSHRC-N.B. Power-Xerox chair in management of human resources, technology, learning and work in a digital economy."

The influx of business money has very little to do with altruism. Allan Taylor, then chairman of the Royal Bank of Canada, let the cat out of the bag in the early '90s when he urged corporations to "get directly involved with funding for universities, but also with a direct involvement in setting courses, setting the curricula, so that they will get the kind of student they want."

Through the '80s and early '90s, Pare observes, many companies cut their staff development programs in the rush to appear lean and mean. The leaders of those companies are often the same people who have been urging universities to offer training that neatly fit the demands of business.

On March 13, the Canadian Association of University Teachers released an open letter to Jean Chretien signed by more than 1,400 scientists. They told the prime minister, "We are deeply concerned about the growing commercialization of university research." If university research is tied closer to corporate demands, they warned, "scientists would be perceived as beholden to special interests."

Universities don't always accept money proffered by the corporate world. Shapiro recalls one case in which a company (he discreetly avoids naming it) wanted to co-operate with McGill researchers. But the company expected to keep the research private for a significant time, thereby preventing the academics from publishing the fruits of their work. McGill said no.

Other universities might have made a different choice. Some have already done so in the U.S. Earlier this year, "The Kept University," a cover story in The Atlantic Monthly, gave numerous examples of deals between big companies and major universities that appear to overstep the traditional concept of academic freedom.

In 1996, for instance, a Brown University scientist named David Kern was serving as a paid consultant to Microfibres, a Rhode Island company that makes nylon flock. He found evidence of a serious lung disease among the company's employees. Microfibres tried to persuade him to keep silent—and Brown University too asked him not to publish his findings.

He went ahead anyway. The Centres for Disease Control recognized the new disease ("flock worker's lung"), but Kern's job was eliminated.

"When I look at our society," Pare says, "I see us flying ahead in technology and science. Where we seem to be lagging behind is in understanding the ethical implications— the human implications—of some of these things.

"If you ask me what universities should be producing, it would not be better technocrats. It would be better thinkers."

Source: Mark Abley, "Universities and Ideology: Political correctness may be rampant in the U.S., but in Canada, there are other pressures on academic freedoms," *The Gazette*, Montreal, June 23, 2000, p. B1. Reprinted with permission of *The Gazette*.

Unit Three

GENDER RELATIONS
Introduction: Feminist Theory and Gender Relations

◆◆◆

We often refer to "sex" as biological, and "gender" as cultural. Sex refers to the differences in human anatomy, such as penis and vagina. Gender refers to social differences between men and women, such as masculinity and femininity. However, this distinction is not cast in stone. For example, Hird (2000) argued that both sex and gender are social constructions, not just gender. By focusing on **intersexuality** and **transsexuality,** she identified varieties of sexes (e.g., XXY, XXXY, XXXXY, XXYY, XXXYY). In fact, all fetuses spend their first six weeks as an XX (female) in the amniotic fluid, until the release of testosterone for most XY (male) fetuses. She also points out that, historically, physicians and surgeons have at times decided whether or not one is to be a male by looking at penile growth at an early age. Physicians reasoned that if there was little or no penile growth then the male sex should be replaced by female genitals. That is, physicians determined the male sex by size of the penis rather than by chromosomes or the ability to produce sperm. In this regard, an infant with an XY chromosome is "constructed" as male, both in terms of the body and how "he" should be raised.

When we look at the well-known example of a male infant (John) who was surgically constructed as female (Joan), we notice how she at first liked dolls and female toys (i.e., she became feminine). However, she later asked doctors to reconstruct a penis for her, and then "she" married a woman and they adopted three children. Now he identifies himself as male. Hird pointed out that there has been an increase in the number of

intersexual individuals, which points to the variability of sexual identification beyond the male/female binaries. The increase of intersexuals and transsexuals also raises the question of whether one can experience the world authentically as female or male. This problem thus challenges feminist and male movements. Hird also asked that, if sex itself is a construction, then on whose behalf do feminists or male movement groups speak? That is to say, is male or female identity sexed or gendered? Hird argued that this example suggests that we cannot use "nature" to define the constitution of sex or how individuals know their gender. As Mead said long ago, self cannot exist without society. Hird similarly argued that sex itself is a construction.

Almost all societies are stratified along sex or gender lines. Even though there have been some changes in recent times, there is a general tendency for females to be viewed as sentimental, emotional, and subjective, whereas males are viewed as independent, logical, and objective. If a male is weak, he is called a sissy, and if a girl is tough, she is called tom boy. Males tend to become physicians, engineers, and firefighters, and females tend to become nurses, secretaries, and kindergarten teachers. Moreover, females earn less than males. For every dollar that males earn, females earn about seventy cents (see Table 3.1). Why are there such differences in perceptions, attitudes, behaviours, and outcomes? There are various explanations for these differences.

Some provide a biological explanation. For example, Doreen Kimura (2002) argued that men and women display different cognitive and behavioural patterns because of differences in hormonal influences on brain development. Others question this argument by showing that the so-called association between hormonal level and behaviour is not universal and varies by culture.

Another explanation searches for the sources of gender inequality in early human history. For example, Marvin Harris (1977) argued that gender inequality and the tendency for males to be aggressive and females passive can be traced to early societies where males were the principle combatants. He argues that early combats were dangerous and that many men did not want to fight despite the fact that the existence of the whole community could depend on it. In order to motivate and psychologically prepare males' involvement in warfare, a system of reward was developed where victorious warriors were awarded wives and concubines. In fact, military alliance in some societies were solidified by exchanging women. These practices, Harris argues, may have been the source of male aggression and dominating characteristics.

Others suggest that women's involvement in childbearing and childrearing resulted in a sexual division of labour in the early history of humanity. Accordingly, bearing and rearing children prevented women's geographical mobility. Instead, they developed domestic skills. Men, not being limited to their immediate domestic environment, became hunters, were involved in warfare and religion, and controlled cultural ideas. These differences and outcomes became the sources of male privileges compared to females.

The difference in types of socialization of boys and girls is another source of gender differentiation (Figure 3.1). Socialization of boys and girls in the family differ by giving them either a boy's name or a girl's name, blue or pink clothing, different curfew times, among other things, which help shape different types of gender identities. Similarly, boys and girls may rely on the same-sex parent as a role model. Since traditionally fathers tend to have more authority at home than mothers, boys and girls might develop different authority personalities. As well, the types of games boys and girls play differ. Boys tend to be involved in games with larger numbers of individuals, which fosters competitiveness and aggressiveness. Females tend to play in small groups, which allows development of emotional attachment to playmates. Other agents of socialization also play important roles in shaping differential gender identities. School officials may direct boys and girls toward different subject matters based on sex. Lan-

guage, religion, and media also may help shape their perception of authority along gender lines. For example, in everyday language we may tend to refer to human beings as "mankind."

Another explanation for these differences focuses on social structure. Friedrich Engels, Karl Marx's close friend and collaborator, argued that the development of private property in agricultural society was an important

Figure 3.1

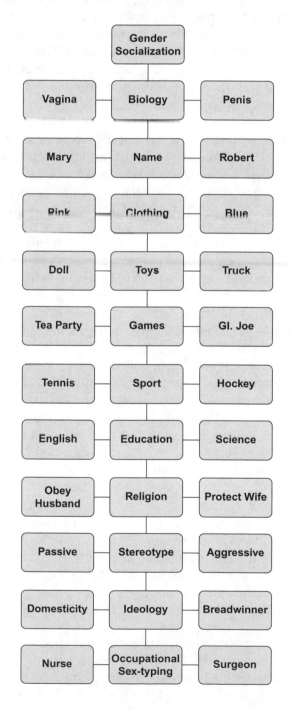

source of gender inequality (see Unit 5 on Family). In modern days, Marxists argue that society tends to value commodities produced for exchange and undervalue commodities produced for use at home. For example, people in the capitalist system tend not to consider household labour (such as childbearing, cooking, cleaning, etc.) as real work and do not pay women for this work. Because men generally work outside the house and produce **exchange value,** and women generally work inside the house and their work has only **use value,** the work of women is undervalued. Consequently, despite the fact that the work women do is essential for perpetuation of capitalist society (e.g., producing and socializing future labourers and ensuring that existing labourers are properly rested and taken care of, thus ready for another day of work), women's work has lower status, and women get paid less.

Similarly, Marxists argue that capitalists use women's labour as a **"reserve army of labour."** Women are called into the labour force when they are needed and sent back to the home when there are extra workers. According to this argument, the cultural value that "a woman's place is in the home" helps the capitalist system because it gives just cause to send women home when they are no longer needed in the labour force. Therefore, the capitalist system tends to consider women's work as secondary and dependent on men. This differential treatment places men in the position of power and allows them access to more resources. A Marxist's solution, short of a revolution for communism, is for women to enter the labour force and take control of property and resources, not against men, but with men.

Marxists have historically tended to subsume women's **oppression** as another aspect of class **exploitation** and **domination.** Therefore, women's work in the house is seen as necessary for capitalist production and reproduction. Feminists have long been dissatisfied with the Marxist explanation of women's oppression that tends to subsume women's liberation under the working-class struggle for socialism. They argue that men and women have different positions in society that are crucially significant in explaining women's oppression as long as sex structure remains significant in the society. Therefore, feminists insist that they should produce a theory about women's lives that is directly relevant to challenging the oppression of women and improving women's position in society.

There are many variants of feminist theory. Liberal feminists challenge the boundaries of gender differences. Their main solution is for women to educate themselves as well as joining the labour force, which would allow women to acquire status and position independent of their husbands' or partners'. Marxist feminists relate women's oppression to that of capitalism, as discussed above. Radical feminists focus on the biological source of women's oppression and the use of violence by men to control women. For these feminists the most important social division is not based on class, as Marxists would suggest; but rather, the main division is based on sex where men strive for power over women. This form of domination is called **patriarchy:** a social system characterized by male domination over females. Socialist feminists agree with Marxists on the importance of class relations for understanding women's oppression but focus on the interconnection between sex oppression and class oppression. For them, *both* patriarchal and capitalist oppression needs to be eradicated. There are other schools of feminism as well (e.g., poststructuralists, psychoanalysts, cultural, and antiracist feminists). In general, all feminists agree that gender inequality is a pervasive feature of most (if not all) societies and that gender inequality requires a distinct theoretical framework because women's oppression is distinct from other forms of oppression.

The debate that follows is one among feminists themselves. The key issue is whether there is such a thing as feminist theory and if so, is it a sociological theory? Janet Saltzman Chafetz answers this question by defining four key concepts: social sciences, theory, methodology, and feminism. She views science as an attempt to provide an explanation for the how and why of human behaviours, whereas much of feminist theory (particularly those related to **standpoint** and **postmodern** theories) is oriented toward questioning an empirically rooted sociology. This empirical aspect of science, she argues, is fundamental to the discipline of sociology where it is believed that the empirical world exists and is knowable. The empirical aspect is also related to the development of **theory**(ies) in sociology, where we develop abstract explanations of empirically testable social phenomena. She argues that feminism is a theory but not necessarily a sociological one. Sociological theories are directed at explaining aspects of a knowable world and are evaluated in substantial part by how well the theory accords with what we find empirically. Feminist theory is a more philosophically oriented discussion of the nature of social life and the nature of a good or just society. Feminist theory, for example, is concerned with the issue of gender inequality, which is evaluated negatively and needs to be eliminated. She further argues that feminist theorists need to improve their empirical support for their theories. Alexis Walker's comments are generally in agreement with Chafetz's. However, Walker argues that feminism is more diverse than what is suggested by Chafetz, and that similar methods of studying human behaviour may result in different answers because of the different questions that can be asked from the subjects.

TABLE TALK

◆ ◆ ◆

Figure 3.1 shows schematically how various social relations ensure different types of personality development for males and females. Do you think that these social relations are still powerful in socialization of masculinity and femininity? In which area are they more or less powerful?

Table 3.1 shows the average earnings of men and women who worked full time and for the full year. It shows that, on average, working women earn about 70 percent of what working men earn. As well, there are some signs that the gender wage gap has slightly increased during the last ten years. Why do you think women earn less than men?

QUESTIONS

◆ ◆ ◆

1. In your mind, what is the best explanation of gender differentiation? Why?
2. In your mind, what is the best explanation of gender inequality? Why?

Table 3.1   Average Earnings by Gender 1995–2004, Constant $2004

| Year | Full-Time, Full-Year Workers | | |
	Women	Men	Ratio W/M
1995	35,500	49,100	72.4
1996	34,900	48,300	72.3
1997	34,600	50,700	68.3
1998	37,100	51,700	71.9
1999	35,700	52,200	68.4
2000	36,900	52,200	70.6
2001	37,200	53,300	69.9
2002	37,500	53,400	70.2
2003	37,300	53,200	70.2
2004	38,400	54,900	69.9

Source: Statistics Canada, CANSIM, 202-0102.

3. What are your views on the various schools of feminism? Explain your views on those that you agree with and also those that you disagree with.
4. Do you think that sex is biological or a social construction?
5. What is your opinion about predetermined roles that are based on sex? Does it vary by culture?
6. Are men and women fundamentally different from each other? Why?
7. To what extent do you think men's and women's career choices are based on gender socialization and gender stereotypes?
8. What roles do empirical investigation play for scientific theories?

Bridging Feminist Theory and Research Methodology

Janet Saltzman Chafetz
University of Houston

◆ ◆ ◆

On and off over the past 25 years I have pondered the question of whether it makes any sense to talk about feminist theory—and relatedly, although mostly outside of my area of expertise, feminist methodology—in sociology (and by extension the social and behavioral sciences). Any answer to such a question requires one to first define four basic terms, each of which currently has multiple and contested meanings. Of course, I will present what these terms mean to me, recognizing that many of you may not share these definitions. The terms are social/behavioral sciences (specifically as it pertains to my discipline, sociology), theory, methodology, and feminist. . . .

DEFINITIONS
◆ ◆ ◆

I begin my discussion by defining what the four terms mean to me, but first I have an admission to make: I am quite old-fashioned in my approach to what it is that we are and should be doing in the social sciences. The goal of the social and behavioral sciences is to develop explanations (theories)—that is, attempts to answer questions of why and how—of empirically documentable phenomena concerning human behavior and the structures and processes they create in the present and have created in other times and places. I distinguish doing sociology/social science from other related but, nonetheless, inherently philosophical issues of epistemology and ontology. Much of what is currently presented as feminist theory in my discipline is, in fact, largely epistemology (e.g., much of standpoint theory), and much of the

postmodernist literature—feminist and otherwise—is substantially oriented to debunking a scientific ontology and epistemology. An empirically rooted sociology of knowledge/sociology of science leads me to assume a limited version of standpoint theory, which I will discuss a bit further later. However, I think that if one basically dismisses the possibility that the social sciences can ever know a reality out there with a level of certainty greater than just anyone's knowledge, then one should cease to identify with a discipline that is conventionally defined as a social/behavioral *science* by most of its practitioners, financial supporters, and the general public. No matter how broad they may be, disciplines have boundaries that define the nature—although not necessarily all of the content—of their endeavors, and work outside that boundary is work of a fundamentally different discipline (e.g., philosophy rather than sociology). No discipline's boundaries are so permeable that anything, no matter how idiosyncratic, done by its officially credentialed members automatically falls within that discipline or the very term discipline becomes irrelevant. I might add that interdisciplinary work is important precisely because it melds two or more distinctive ways of understanding the world to enhance general understanding of something.

One of the two components that makes social sciences in some sense sciences and distinguishes them especially from philosophy is an emphasis on the use of systematic approaches to learning about the empirical world, what I take to be the meaning of methodology in our disciplines. Although it is certainly appropriate to talk about methodologies of theory development (indeed about methodologies of doing any type of intellectual work), the social and behavioral sciences conventionally use the word to refer to the means by which we access the empirical world while simply and necessarily assuming that such a world indeed exists and is potentially knowable with at least a substantial degree of validity and reliability. Methodologies include approaches to issues of research design and techniques of data collection and analysis. Sociology, indeed all of the social and behavioral sciences, enjoy large kit bags of methodological tools, each more appropriate for some purposes and less so for others.

The other component that makes a social science a science is the development of at least relatively abstract explanations of empirically testable and documentable phenomena (i.e., theory). Among theorists in sociology it is routine to distinguish between sociological and social theory. The former is directed at explaining aspects of the empirically knowable world and should be evaluated, in substantial part, according to how well it accords with what we find empirically. Social theories, on the other hand, are more philosophically oriented discussions of the nature of social life and the nature of the good or just society. They are not designed explicitly to be tested against data (i.e., to be empirically falsifiable). I have come to define my own work theorizing systems of inequality between men and women as gender theory to stress that it is sociological rather than social theory. Social theory pertaining to gender may properly be called feminist theory—assuming that it is feminist in content.

This brings me to the fourth term, *feminist*. Given the substantial disagreements among those who during the past 35 years have called themselves feminist and in the absence of any definition agreed on by the majority to those who self-label as feminist, we need a definition that avoids privileging any one minority view of the term's meaning. We need, in other words, a minimalist definition that would encompass virtually all uses among the self-identified. The word is a sociopolitical or ideological label that minimally includes four tenets:

1. Whatever else it may also be, gender is a system of inequality between males and females as sex categories by which things feminine are socially and culturally devalued and men enjoy greater access to scarce and valued social resources.
2. Gender inequality is produced socioculturally and is not immutable.
3. Gender inequality is evaluated negatively as unjust, unfair, etc.
4. Therefore, feminists should strive to eliminate gender inequality.

Note that even with this minimalist definition there is plenty left to debate concerning the causes of gender inequality (often termed patriarchy), how best to change the system, and even the meaning/components of the very term *gender inequality*. I think, however, that virtually all who self-label as feminist would accept these four elements as a fundamental part of what they include in the term even if few would want to stop here.

Given these four definitions, it should come as no surprise that I think that sociological/social scientific theory should be testable (i.e., potentially falsifiable) and that, therefore, careful attention should be paid to employing or developing research methodologies that represent, as closely as possible, adequate tests of theory(ies). When more than one theoretical explanation for a given phenomenon has been proposed, the research process should focus on directly comparing the theories to generate hypotheses that predict different outcomes and testing these. For instance, several theoretical explanations have been offered to explain the well-documented finding, repeated over time among different subpopulations and in other nations, that among dual-earner couples women continue to perform a far greater proportion of domestic and childrearing work than their husbands. These theories include: (a) a power inequality approach that centers around discrepancies in men's and women's earnings; (b) a *doing gender* approach derived from symbolic interaction theory that claims that men and women perform gender-traditional, domestic tasks to reaffirm their gender identities; (c) a theory of least-interest approach that assumes that females are socialized to care more than men about such things as clean and neat homes; and (d) a normative argument that others expect women, but not men, to be responsible for domestic work and therefore blame them when it is done inadequately. It is likely that several of these so-called competing theories are simultaneously partially useful rather than one being right and the others wrong. At any rate, theory development, which I consider the ultimate goal of social sciences, should be a major result of successive empirical tests and theoretical refinements based on new data. In recent years in my discipline, network exchange and expectations states theories are models of this kind of interaction between theory development, empirical testing, and theory refinement. However, in most instances sociologists are more inclined to apply one or more theoretical approaches, often ex post facto, to explain their findings than to test theory from the outset of a research project—a habit that may or may not be as applicable to the other disciplines represented here today.

In sociology, too much effort is expended on developing theory that is never adequately tested—and in many instances is not even apparently testable—and in conducting research the design of which precludes it from serving as an adequate test of any theory, especially sampling on the dependent variable (e.g., in-depth analyses of one category of people—such as poor, unmarried mothers; Hispanic, domestic workers; or equally sharing married couples—in the absence of any kind of others to whom to make comparisons). Another way of saying this is that researchers tend too often to make short shrift of the research design phase by failing to consider the basic nature of the conclusions they will be able to legitimately draw given their sample composition and the nature of the data collected. Convenient samples are grabbed and people are interviewed and/or observed without much thought about the logic of research vis-à-vis explanation.

An example of this problem can be seen by looking at the copious literature within the hot topic among gender sociologists today: the intersection of race, class, and gender. Edited books abound and a new section of the American Sociological Association has been organized under this rubric. I grabbed three of the more popular anthologies off my shelf: Anderson and Hill Collins (1995), Rothenberg (1998), and Rosenblum and Travis (2003). All have titles or subtitles that include the words *race, class,* and *gender.* A quick list of some of the chapter titles from their tables of contents include: "Asian-American Panethnicity"; "Who Is Black?"; "Our Classroom Barrios"; "The Social Construction of Gender"; "Deconstructing the Underclass"; "Masculinities and Athletic Careers"; "Are You Middle Class?"; and "Rap, Race and Politics." Very few chapters in any of these books analyze more than two—and many only one—of the three dimensions, and none looks simultaneously at the full range of variation on the three dimensions of gender, race, and class and their interactions. This kind of one-or two-at-a-time descriptive work logically precludes the very possibility of understanding how these three statuses simultaneously affect people, which is supposedly the goal of the enterprise; research design fails to flow from theoretical concern. What, for instance, can we conclude about poor, Mexican American women in the absence of comparable data on middle-class, Mexican American women; poor, Mexican American men; and poor women of other ethnic/racial backgrounds? The answer is nothing. Too often we end up with piles of incommensurable descriptive works that cumulate to nothing generalizable. Please note that I am not arguing that any one form of theory—as long as it is potentially falsifiable with data—or any particular research methodologies are better or best regardless of the uses to which they are put.

FEMINISM, GENDER, AND THEORY
◆ ◆ ◆

I turn now to examine more closely the relationship between feminism, gender, and theory. The popular resurgence of feminist activism beginning in the late 1960s quickly affected the often very few female professionals in the various social and behavioral sciences. During the 1970s, we simultaneously undertook to accomplish two very different activities: (a) to demonstrate the inadequacies and downright errors created in our disciplines because of the fact that knowledge creation had long been almost entirely a monopoly of one social type, White males, and (b) to create new knowledge about gender (often specifically only women) and about the role gender plays in social, political, economic, and cultural institutions; in interpersonal interactions; and in intrapsychic phenomena.

Although critiques of existing theory and knowledge traditions constitute a starting point for efforts to correct problems and produce improved understandings, they do not constitute theory per se. There is no question in my mind that a discipline dominated overwhelmingly by people of one social type (e.g., White males) will have collective blinders that, because of various processes and professional pressures, are likely to blind the few members of other social types in the profession as well. Such blinders will focus attention on some issues (e.g., paid labor-force work) and ignore others (e.g., unpaid household labor) and on some processes (e.g., the rationalization of social institutions) but not others (e.g., the emotional content of virtually all human interactions). Practitioners will likely assume that their own type constitutes the norm against which the attributes, skills, values, and behaviors of others are measured and usually found wanting. In other words, in the social and behavioral sciences, scholar homogeneity produces highly biased, poor quality, or at best woefully inadequate knowledge. There is fairly widespread agreement about this assumption in my discipline, the explanation of which can be found in a theoretical and empirical tradition that dates back to the founders of our discipline and demonstrates that people—which presumably includes scholars—perceive the social world substantially as a function of their social location(s) in that world. As long as it was overwhelmingly White males who developed the sociology of knowledge, variation in social location was defined only in terms of social class. Now we include, along with social class, gender, race/ethnicity, and often sexual preference in our understanding of what constitutes the crucial dimensions of one's social location. It is important to note, however, that the link between location and perception is provided by experience; people who occupy different locations tend to have different experiences that tend to result in different perceptions. To ignore this understanding is to reify the statuses that constitute social location.

To the extent that standpoint theory asserts that our life experiences, as rooted in our social locations, color scholars' substantive interests, the questions they raise, their interpretations of data, and their overall view of social life, I agree with it. However, one must be careful in what else one assumes here. Standpoint theorists sometimes assume that the perspective of less powerful (more oppressed) actors—women, the poor, racial/ethnic minorities—are more accurate than, not just different from, that of members of a social majority group (e.g., Farganis, 1986; Harding, 1986; Mies, 1983). There is neither logic nor data to support such an assumption; all views must be accepted as equally partial. They also often reify broad categories of highly heterogeneous human beings such that we end up reading about masculinist and even White heterosexual masculinist thinking, which logically presupposes that men and women have fundamentally different thought processes, not just average differences in what they think about, rooted in average differences in their experiences (e.g., Hill Collins, 1986; Smith, 1990). To say that a given way of thinking (e.g., deductive theorizing) was developed by men at a time when virtually all theorizing was done only by men does not logically result in the assertion that, therefore, deductive thinking is a masculine cognitive style and by implication, if not explicit statement, that feminine and/or feminist thinking must be otherwise. There is no systematic evidence to support such essentialist thinking and no way of making the case short of positing significant innate sex differences in fundamental cognitive processes, which is a position most sociologists today, including most feminist ones, would reject. A further problem for standpoint theory flows from a failure to analytically separate women's perspective(s) from a feminist one. Dorothy Smith (1990), the most prominent proponent of standpoint theory in sociology, wrote as if a women's perspective (a gender term) will automatically lead a scholar to appreciate her sex's oppression (a feminist understanding). As women, we have substantially different experiences, yet Smith seemed to assume that female scholars, but not male ones, will have experienced and been significantly affected by childrearing and housework and therefore reach similar feminist insights. This is an empirical, not theoretical, issue and probably varies substantially among academic women and academic men as well as between them.

The point in this discussion of standpoint theory is that although our social locations undoubtedly do affect what we think about, (a) they do so by affecting our experiences, and these are substantially variable within each gender, and (b) there is no evidence that they affect how we think—except essentialist stereotypes, which are largely unsupported by any systematic evidence (Epstein, 1988). As feminists, we often will be motivated to study gender and to include issues of gender in whatever else we study. We will be inclined, for instance, to perceive that family, along with religion, the economy, polity, and other institutions, are deeply gendered sites in which the reproduction of inequality between women and men occurs. To understand and to explain how gender reproduction occurs, we have revised and extended all sorts of theoretical perspectives created initially by men (e.g., Marxist, Freudian, symbolic interactionist, and ethnomethodological in my discipline) as well as fashioned new ones, often syntheses that also incorporate male-created theories. Why are such masculinist theories not deemed inappropriate as bases for feminist theoretical efforts by those who espouse fundamental differences in the cognitive processing of men and women?

To the extent that our theories represent attempts to explain empirically observable phenomena, they constitute gender theory, and such theory could as well be developed by nonfeminists if they were somehow motivated to do so. As a feminist, I personally have sought to understand how systems of gender stratification arise, reproduce themselves, and change (Chafetz, 1984, 1990; Collins, Chafetz, Blumberg, Coltrane, & Turner, 1993) and why feminist social movements arise and grow only in specific times and places (Chafetz & Dworkin, 1986) because I believe that such understanding will provide better ideas about how more effectively to create social change that enhances gender equity. However, my theoretical efforts were explicitly and closely tied to an accumulated empirical record, primarily in sociology and anthropology but in history as well, and were presented in a form that encourages their systematic testing (and therefore potential falsification). Moreover, when I theorized gender system change, I examined why and how such systems sometimes change to exacerbate inequality whereas at other times change to reduce it (Chafetz, 1990), despite my feminist commitment to the latter. Another way of saying this is that my feminism is neither true nor false nor even subject to such an assessment; my gender theory is subject to the issue of how well it can stand up to empirical test.

I do not think that I am merely splitting hairs when I distinguish gender from feminist theory to argue that the former is social scientific and the latter substantially to entirely philosophical. Much self-styled feminist theory in sociology is in fact a mishmash composed of both types (along with critiques of "malestream" sociology), often doing each less well than they could. As feminists—that is, people espousing a sociopolitical ideology—our chief concern should be focused on how to change systems of gender inequality. Recently (Chafetz, 1999), however, I demonstrated that little of the theory produced by feminist sociologists even makes the attempt to systematically explain change processes or, for that matter, how feminist consciousness comes to arise in given times and places but not others. The little theory that makes such an attempt is plagued by problems, especially the problem of presupposing an undefined, mystical agency and a developed feminist consciousness and agenda that themselves must be explained. In an effort to be optimistic about the possibility of change toward a more equitable system, a requirement of any movement ideology on behalf of a subordinate category of people, much feminist sociological theory resorts to deus ex machina devices: unsupported and often unrecognized assumptions and circular logic. By temporarily bracketing one's feminist (ideological) commitments one can more readily perceive the logical skeleton of theory and the extent of empirical support, possibly resulting in questions—even tentative answers—that may be less than completely politically correct. But I believe that I am a better feminist to the extent that I am a better gender theorist because I can thereby potentially provide a more realistic understanding of the gender system and the means by which it is most, as well as least, amenable to change. I do not think that activist strategies that lack such underpinnings are likely to work; I do not think that collective ignorance enhances our ability to create a better world.

FEMINIST METHODOLOGY

◆ ◆ ◆

Although there is such a thing as feminist theory—even if I do not think of it as social scientific—I find the very idea of feminist methodology in the social and behavioral sciences fundamentally untenable. I defined social scientific methodology in terms of logics of empirical examination and a tool kit of techniques, which are both used to access the empirical world as relevantly and accurately as possible. The research design and tools of data collection and analysis one selects ought to be chosen on the basis that they are the most appropriate to answering a given re-

search question (ideally rooted in one or more theories). In fact, at least in my discipline, researchers too often specialize in a specific methodology (e.g., quantitative or qualitative) and employ it regardless of the research question, which may, in fact, be developed or altered along the way to fit the method.

In an excellent exposition and critique, Sprague and Zimmermann (1993) argued that self-styled feminist methodology arises from a critique of positivism and focuses on four dichotomies: object/subject, rational/emotional, abstract/concrete, and quantitative/qualitative (p. 261). The second half of each pair—subject, emotional, concrete, qualitative—together are said to constitute a feminist methodology. It treats the objects of research as subjects, presumably to be empowered rather than dominated by the researcher. This raises the following issue: What if the subjects' definition of empowerment is antithetical to that of the feminist researcher? Because women's subjectivity constitutes the main focus of feminist research, intuition and emotion, as accessed via in-depth qualitative techniques, are to replace rational, quantitative methodologies, which are described as masculine. The goal of feminist research is rich description of the concrete experiences of women's everyday life rather than abstract theorizing. However, as I argued elsewhere (Chafetz, 1997), it is difficult to see how this kind of research strategy can lead to any theoretical understanding of gender, indeed, any explicit and direct means of conceptualizing the macro-level of gender inequality (patriarchy) that all feminists at least implicitly assume. Social scientific (including gender) theory is inherently abstract and focused on creating generalizations that are stochastic in nature. They do not pretend to describe all the rich contextual details of the unique case, which is precisely the focus taken by self-styled feminist methodology (Sprague & Kobrynowicz, 1999). This approach to methodology also raises very real questions about how to deal with subjects whose subjectivity is nonfeminist and especially antifeminist. Does the researcher have the right, not to mention the duty, to attempt to convert subjects? Is not this exactly antithetical to respecting subjects and empowering rather than dominating them? Speaking for myself, I see no obligation to attempt to empower right-to-life adherents, although I may wish to understand their motives and perceptions of the world, and I would find it unethical to attempt, as a researcher, to convert them. Moreover, feminist methodology, as defined above, substantially narrows the range of appropriate research questions to those concerning women's subjective understanding of their everyday experiences which, as far as I can see, is only one issue among a whole host of gender issues we ought to be (and in fact are) examining. . . .

Ironically, the attributes of so-called feminist methodology match very well with the stereotypes of women and men that antifeminists have espoused for at least 150 years. You know—men are more rational and objective than women, women are overly emotional and focused on the mundane, math is a guy thing, etc. For reasons that are not altogether clear to me, self-styled feminist methodologists have rejected techniques developed and employed by some men as masculinist while proclaiming that other techniques, especially qualitative data gathering ones, also developed and employed by some men, are appropriately feminist using an essentialist logic—really stereotypes—to get there. To reiterate, virtually the entire tool kit of research strategies and techniques was originally developed by men because few social/behavioral scientists were women until pretty recently. We ought to be exploiting the full array of these tools to the utmost to conduct the highest quality research on gender. The master's tools can indeed dismantle the master's house if that is what the tool wielder intends to do. The truth is that we collectively are using the full array of research tools despite those who appear to think they are speaking for all sociologists/social scientists with a feminist commitment.

CONCEPTUAL IMPEDIMENTS TO LINKING THEORY TO RESEARCH

◆ ◆ ◆

A major problem often standing in the way of carefully linking feminist/gender theory on one hand and research on the other is ideologically laden, inadequately and vaguely defined basic theoretical concepts. I will focus on three: patriarchy, oppression, and agency.

Depending on the writer, patriarchy may refer to an ideology—secular and/or religious—to one or more properties of family, economy, or polity, or most often to some combination thereof. To the extent that the definition of patriarchy subsumes more than one of these—as is typical—it is truth asserting, that is, an empirical hypothesis about relationships between various phenomena is smuggled into the definition and therefore assumed to be true. One does not usually research relationships between phenomena if one assumes their isomorphism by definition. For instance, the issue of precisely how gender inequality in the economy (or polity or hegemonic ideology) gets translated into gender inequality within the

family, and vice versa, may be overlooked or given short shrift to the extent that high levels of all of these are assumed to be part of the same basic phenomenon, patriarchy. The term patriarchy is often reified by the use of an active verb, as in "Patriarchy creates, causes, requires, encourages, etc." The result is meaningless verbiage masquerading as an explanation. Finally, one virtually never hears patriarchy used as a variable, as in "The contemporary United States is less patriarchal than Saudi Arabia." Extensive empirical evidence demonstrates that the level of gender inequality (which, after all, is fundamentally what the term *patriarchy* means) varies over time and space; it is not just the same old, same old in different guises as implied when patriarchy is implicitly, if not explicitly, treated as a constant.

The term *oppression* is bandied about so frequently today that it has become virtually synonymous with disadvantaged. To be at the lower end of any system of inequality is to be oppressed, unlike its dictionary meaning of "to keep down by cruel or unjust use of power," which is a far more severe notion of disadvantaged position. Unlike patriarchy, oppression is never defined. But like patriarchy, oppression is never used as a variable. Surely, American women were more oppressed 150 years ago when they lacked the vote, were legally excluded from various occupations and educational opportunities, lost their children on divorce, and did not even control their own money or income if married than they are today.

The term *agency* is likewise never defined but commonly, carelessly, and, in fact, mystically used (see Chafetz, 1999, for a more extensive discussion of this term). In an effort to avoid displaying women merely as passive victims of oppressive patriarchy, many feminist scholars use the term agency as a way of noting the myriad ways women have resisted and worked to create freer social spaces for themselves. It is mystical in the sense that it appears to assume the existence of an uncaused and unexplained attribute of individuals that, however, has considerable power to cause or influence individuals' behaviors. However, feminists cannot logically argue that women are both oppressed and experience more than trivial amounts of agency. To make sense of the term, and in the absence of other social scientific definitions of which I am aware, I offer the following one: "The extent to which one enjoys the opportunity to make choices among alternatives that are perceived as variably rewarding choices that do not incur heavy social penalties." To choose between your life and relinquishing your purse to a mugger is not a meaningful exercise in agency, and where women are truly oppressed, that is likely the type of choice they will *enjoy*. When a given choice is associated with a steep penalty, especially relative to socially accepted or expected ones, very few are likely to make it and it becomes trivial for social analysis. The level of agency, conceptualized as I have above, is a variable that will be highly related to position within a stratified system but also to the type of system itself. Surely an impoverished African American woman living in Texas today enjoys somewhat more agency than her equally poor grandmother did under Jim Crow, not to mention her slave ancestors.

Without clearly and unambiguously defined concepts that include the logic of variability, there is no way to directly link research to theory testing and potential falsification and no way of knowing how to go about developing adequate research methodologies to test theory. In practical terms, the persistent use of ideologically laden but imprecise terminology impedes the development of understanding in a variety of different ways, muddying rather than clarifying the way we theorize and conduct research.

CONCLUDING THOUGHTS

◆ ◆ ◆

People committed to a sociopolitical ideology have different skills they can offer to a social movement designed to bring about social change. It is my conviction that fem-inist social and behavioral scientists can maximize their movement contributions by doing excellent social science on gender issues; that is their unique contribution. I have offered my view of what that entails, namely, the development of gender theory including well-defined and empirically relevant concepts and the use of the most appropriate methodologies available to answer the specific questions raised by such theories. Our feminist commitments should rightfully provide the energy and insights that lead us to new questions, new sources of data, and new interpretations and explanations of the empirical world, but there is no one way to do theory or research that is feminist. There are no ways of thinking that are inherently masculine, feminine, or feminist. Most of us get furious when we hear stereotypes about women's rational deficit and emotional surfeit, yet many of us have bought into the idea that as feminist social scientists we ought to privilege the intuitive and emotional and devalue the rational and quantitative and concentrate on rich description and eschew abstract, deductive theorizing. We have to reject such essentialist nonsense in our disciplines and get on with doing the best social and behavioral science we can. A social movement cannot prosper in the long run on the basis of ignorance or self-delusion. It is best served when its most highly trained and educated adherents concentrate on developing the most empirically well-supported theories we are capable of producing, regardless of the techniques we use to get there.

Methods, Theory, and the Practice of Feminist Research: A Response to Janet Chafetz

Alexis J. Walker
Oregon State University

◆ ◆ ◆

There is nothing so practical as a good theory.

—Kurt Lewin

Janet Chafetz dismisses Audre Lorde's dictum that you cannot dismantle the master's house using the master's tools. Instead, she argues compellingly that feminists draw from the same tool kit from which all social scientists draw and not from feminist theory and feminist methodology. It is perhaps an indication of how far we have come that four feminists, Janet and the three discussants (Allen, Baber, and me), disagree with each other on the extent to which this is true. Thirty-five years ago, feminist theorists and researchers focused on family might have gathered in one room excited to find others who saw the world in the same way. It is no longer, however, we (i.e., the unitary feminist voice) and them (i.e., hostile and uninformed others; Rapping, 1994). With maturity, our own and feminist family studies, we have developed a variety of theories and practices and simultaneously created healthy disagreements among us. Diversity among social scientists, even feminist social scientists, is inevitable. It is a mistake to assume that feminists share homogenized theoretical perspectives and commitments to specific methodologies. Furthermore, although some might describe standpoint theory as a feminist theory, many nonfeminists recognize the importance of social position in influencing what we see (Denzin & Lincoln, 2000; Furstenberg, 1999). And, as do other social scientists, feminists change over time in adherence to particular theoretical perspectives or methodological approaches (e.g.,

Thompson & Walker, 1995). Nevertheless, I agree with Janet's minimalist definition of feminism: (a) gender is a system of inequality, (b) gender is a social construction, (c) inequality is unjust, and (d) feminists work to eliminate gender inequality.

Janet points to the mismatch between the feminist goal of understanding the interaction of race, class, and gender and feminist theoretical and empirical work that falls far short of this goal. Although I agree that we have yet to theorize or study this intersection adequately, I am perhaps somewhat more forgiving of my feminist sisters and brothers—and of myself as well—than is Janet. The goal of understanding intersectionality is difficult in the extreme, and the master's tools, in this case the theories and methodologies at hand, for the most part, are inadequate to this task. The rich description emerging from these admittedly inadequate approaches, however, might be the building blocks from which an advanced, integrated theory will eventually be constructed. What better way to develop theory than to move back and forth from ideas to data and from data to ideas? Surely rich description, from multiple perspectives, will enable us to produce a full understanding of social life in all its complexity.

Although Janet dismisses within-group studies, I stand with feminist scholars who argue that recognizing and documenting diversity within groups is essential to building this understanding (e.g., Bowles and Klein, 1983; Rutenberg, 1983). Janet states that the perspective of the less powerful is not more accurate but just different from that of members of a social majority group (Chafetz, 2004 [this issue]). Although I agree that all knowledge is partial, I also agree with the many feminist and minority social scientists (e.g., Du Bois, 1983; Stanley and Wise, 1983; Westkott, 1979) who contend that life on the margins requires that we see things from our own view as well as the view of those to whom we are held accountable. Doing so is essential for survival (e.g., Tedlock, 2000). As scientists, therefore, we need to attend to the perspectives of both the more and the less powerful.

Janet takes particular issue with feminist standpoint perspectives. In my view, one of the primary advantages feminists bring to the scientific enterprise is a willingness to acknowledge—perhaps an insistence on acknowledging—our perspectives and biases. Such acknowledgement is often missing from the nonfeminist social science literature. The attempt to understand intersectionality is, in fact, an effort to see things from the worldview of others and not simply from our own unique standpoints. Compared with theory developed by so-called objective observers, acknowledging our own perspectives and asking how the world looks to others eventually will lead to rich theory closely linked to social life.

To make her point, Janet highlights a small group of feminists who focus primarily on epistemology. The majority of feminist researchers are, like Janet, however, practicing their feminism using theories and methods developed and employed by nonfeminist social scientists. I do not agree that all or even most feminist researchers uniformly aim to produce "rich description" (Chafetz, 2004, p. 972); although, as I noted earlier, such description has both empirical and theoretical value. Too often, regardless of theoretical orientation, researchers conduct survey research without a foundation of rich description. In this instance, limited knowledge of the subject matter leads to narrow, superficial, or even inaccurate measurement. Such an approach to science cannot advance our understanding (Walker, 2000). Nor do I agree that feminist researchers focus narrowly on "women's subjective understanding" (Chafetz, 2004, p. 972). The feminist research I read is theoretically explicit and is related to the "accumulated empirical record" (p. 970). Surely, research that fails to meet these standards is not scientific; it is neither replicable nor would it stand up to peer review.

Janet states unequivocally that there can be no such thing as a feminist methodology. On a purely definitional level, I agree. And yet, as Kurt Lewin noted so long ago, method is driven by theory. Scientists' ways of studying the world emerge from their ideas about the world. Although Janet argues that one's standpoint affects what we think about but not how we think, I am skeptical of this view because the two cannot be unrelated. Whereas synapse firing is the same in all people, surely the thoughts we have and how we put them together are influenced by what we think. Such differences in thinking make it possible for feminists to employ theories such as Marxism and symbolic interactionism, tools also employed by nonfeminists, with different research questions, different procedures, and different conclusions.

Consider an example: Two researchers, a structural functionalist and a feminist social constructionist, design and carry out separate observational studies of adults (women and men) at an amusement park accompanied by children in strollers. Because structural functionalism, the framework implicit in most studies of families, is focused on families as unities, the structural functionalist would observe the building of family solidarity during this family outing. Front-stage behavior would be seen as evidence of family interaction in the privacy of the home, not as an opportunity for social display. Women unaccompanied by men, presumably mothers with their children, would be problematic to the extent that opportunities for family interaction were missed. Of greater significance, many such families, along with few heterosexual couples with children, could signal social decline. These women might not have husbands and their children would not then have coresidential fathers. Opportunities for children, especially boys, to observe a male role model would be missed.

Feminist social constructionists would observe family outings as opportunities to "do gender" (e.g., West and Zimmerman, 1987). They would see family interaction as evidence of the stratification of family-life experience by age and especially by gender. Whereas a structural functionalist would describe parents caring for their children, a feminist would see mothers and fathers and would observe differential involvement by gender, especially in White families, both in terms of tasks and in terms of time. The researcher would highlight how often men push strollers, for example, whereas women feed and diaper toddlers and comfort crying children, thus drawing attention to the family labor invisible to a structural functionalist. Men who carry children might be seen as exhibiting on-stage behavior in response to the current cultural demand for fathers to be involved.

This admittedly simplistic, superficial scenario lacks nuance but serves a pedagogical purpose. Two researchers use the same method but ask different questions, observe different phenomena, and analyze data differently. Inevitably, they reach different conclusions. Strictly speaking, the method is the same but, because theory shapes method, the two approaches cannot be described as identical.

Janet laments the reliance of some feminists on what she describes as vaguely defined theoretical concepts of patriarchy, oppression, and agency (Chafetz, 2004). Reliance on poorly defined constructs is not solely the province of feminists. Social scientists generally are too quick to adopt such constructs—a current favorite, social capital, is an example—as shorthand for an entire complex of structures and processes that can be measured, at best, only approximately. Feminists do not have the market cornered on terms used "commonly," "carelessly," and even "mystically." Think of how the social capital perspective privileges those of us who are White, well educated, middle class or upper middle class, and who live in so-called good neighborhoods, not to mention those who are heterosexual and married and whose friends share these same characteristics. By implication, if poor, minority, and espe-

cially poor minority families were just more like us, their children in particular and society in general would be so much better off. All social scientists should pay more attention to precision in theory and in measurement.

Although my response highlights points of contention, on broader and overarching issues Janet and I agree. I share her goal of developing explanations of human behavior and the social world through systematic approaches, a goal we no doubt have in common with most feminist social scientists. Furthermore, I agree that feminists should use every methodological tool available, assuming its appropriateness to the research question, from in-depth interviews to demography to pursue our understanding of gender. Doing so is essential not just to advance the goals of feminism but also to advance the goals of social science.

Is Gender a Question of Socialization or Surgery?

Pamela Walker, Toronto Star

Vested Interests: Cross-Dressing as Cultural Anxiety

by Marjorie Garber

What is gender? While recent writing on gender has explored how certain behaviors and attributes have come to be understood as masculine and feminine, they have usually done so within a framework that retains the binary opposition of male/female.

In Vested Interests, Marjorie Garber, a professor of English at Harvard University, argues that transvestism forces us to move beyond such binary thinking. Garber asserts that the cross-dresser is not a third sex, an androgyne or a figure struggling to become fully male or female. Rather, the transvestite "puts into question identities previously conceived as stable, unchangeable, grounded and 'known'."

Garber argues that becoming male or female is a complicated social process and never complete. One of the ways gender is interpreted and communicated is through clothing; men and women learn how to dress appropriately.

Garber notes that John Malloy's dress-for-success books, intended as guides to professional dress codes for the upwardly mobile business person, are highly valued by cross-dressers. A woman wishing to dress like a man often ends up looking like a young boy, but Malloy's book can help achieve an authoritatively masculine look.

Many would argue that while clothes can easily be assumed, the body does not lie. But if the body itself is the true ground of gender identity, what of the transsexual? Garber points out that "to make a man" has a very different meaning than "making a woman." Likewise, becoming a woman is usually seen as a passive process of biological maturation while becoming a man involves hard work, overcoming obstacles and perhaps some male-bonding.

Not surprisingly, it is far easier to obtain male to female transsexual surgery than female to male. Garber argues that "in sex reassignment surgery there remains an implicit privileging of the phallus, in a sense a 'real one' can't be made, but only born." But if one argues that an individual's congenital sex is the true sex, does that mean anatomy is destiny? Or does it mean, Garber asks, that gender is a question of life-long socialization not surgery. But if that is the case, why is surgical construction any more artificial than social construction?

Having raised these questions, Garber demonstrates their importance by showing how often they arise in our culture. She draws material from Shakespearean drama and Hollywood films, Liberace and Elvis, Madonna and Flip Wilson, autobiographies and medical literature on transsexuals. Some of her material is overtly concerned with cross-dressing, like the film *Some Like It Hot*. She also interprets cross-dressing where it is less obvious, as in the work of Josephine Baker and Elvis Presley.

Although Garber addresses current questions in psychoanalytic and literary theory, she does not write in the dense and jargon-laden language fashionable among many academics. Certainly the reader already familiar with her material, be it Shakespeare or Elvis, will appreciate her argument more fully. But this is a readable, provocative book. Readers may find themselves pausing the next time they are guided to a washroom based on the presumption that the clothing on the small signs actually represents their "real" gender.

Pamela Walker is Professor of History at Carleton University, Ottawa.

Source: Pamela J. Walker, "Is gender a question of socialization or surgery?" *Toronto Star*, March 7, 1992, p. J17. Reprinted with permission of the author.

Unit Four

CRIME AND DEVIANCE
Introduction: Deviance, Crime, and Racial Profiling

◆◆◆

What is deviant behaviour? Why do people commit crime? These questions have challenged social scientists and lawmakers for centuries. If we were to examine different places and different times in human history, we would notice substantial diversity in what is considered as deviance or crime. Generally, we look at deviance as a departure from the social norms. Since norms differ by time and place, not all behaviours known as deviant in Canada are considered as such in other countries or in other times. Moreover, conceptualization of an act as deviant changes to the same extent as the act is perceived as harmful and actually is harmful. For example, there is little disagreement that murder is deviant or a crime. But there is much disagreement on whether prostitution is a criminal act. Similarly, there is substantially less agreement on whether extramarital sex or adhering to new fashion is deviant. It is often the case that people who are powerful and who control main institutions of the society play a key role in defining what is or isn't deviant or a crime.

There are several explanations as to why some people are deviant or commit crime. Deviant behaviour can be the result of labelling of individuals (Becker, 1963). It may be that certain actions if ignored will not be repeated. But if people bring attention to those acts by labelling the individual as deviant or a criminal, the person may internalize the label and commit more crimes. For example, if a boy is involved in an altercation in the school yard, the principal may call him in and ask him to stop "bullying" the other students. He is suspended from school for the day. Once at home, the parents remind their son that "bullying" is not tolerated. They may punish him further. The next day at school, the boy's peers may call him a "bully" and exclude him from their social circle. Consequently, it is possible that the child will internalize the bullying self-concept and further repeat such actions. In this example, the first act, or **primary deviance,** resulted in a response to the others and consequently produced more unacceptable actions, or **secondary deviance.** In fact, this child could grow up to become a violent criminal. In other words, negative labelling could substantially change a person's self-concept and identity.

Deviants and criminals are also involved in an active definition of their deeds. Sykes and Matza (1957) theorized that the deviant individual often qualifies the normative imperatives in such a way that violations become acceptable. Such justification and rationalization of deviant behaviour is referred to as **techniques of neutralization.** In this process the offender "denies responsibility" and attributes the act to forces outside individual control (e.g., "I stole the money because I was hungry"). Similarly, the offender "denies the victim" by neutralizing the moral indignation of self and others (e.g., "I kicked my wife because she was abusing me"). Other obvious types of neutralization include "the condemnation of condemner" (e.g., "the judge was racist"); "appeal to higher loyalties" (e.g., "suicide bombing was in response to subjugation of our people"); and "blaming the victim." For example, Scully and Marolla's (1985) study of convicted rapists' vocabulary of motives showed that these rapists often undergo a process of justification by blaming the victim. Women are seen as seductresses or as "not nice girls," since "nice girls do not get raped."

Another way of looking at crime is to view the extent to which social forces control one's behaviour. Before discussing **control theories,** we will discuss Emile Durkheim's explanation of suicide and evaluate the importance of social integration for deviant acts. Durkheim, in *Suicide* (1951), noted that individuals are not satisfied by their lot in modern society as shown by an increase in the suicide rate. He defined suicide as "every case of death resulting directly or indirectly from a positive or negative act performed by the victim himself." To shoot oneself is a positive act that entails some expenditure of energy. Going on a hunger strike is a negative act that entails a conscious refusal to take action necessary for survival. Shooting oneself with a gun is a direct act, and refusing to leave a burning house is an indirect act.

Durkheim noticed that suicide is higher among Protestants than Catholics; older than younger; single, divorced, and separated than married people; and higher among men than women. As an example, Durkheim argued that suicide is higher among Protestants than Catholics because Catholics are more integrated to the church than are Protestants. A similar argument applies to groups that have lower suicide rates. Women, married people, and younger people are more integrated into the society than are their counterparts. Therefore, the reason for higher suicide rates among certain groups of people has to do with their lower degree of integration in and involvement with the society and its social organizations.

Durkheim distinguished four types of suicide:

1. **Anomic** suicide entails a breakdown in social regulations that control and influence individuals. Under these circumstances individuals are left to themselves to manage their own life. Such a state of affairs is called **anomie** or conditions of relative **normlessness** in society or part of it. Anomie is not a state of mind but is a property of the social structure. It characterizes a condition in which an individual's desires are no longer regulated by common norms, and individuals are left without moral guidance in pursuit of their goal. This type of suicide tends to increase during drastic economic depression or social disorders (e.g., the 1929 Depression).

2. **Egotistic** suicide varies in inverse ratio to the degree of integration of the individual to the social groups or society. Here, individuals feel little connection to the larger society and are not affected by social constraints against self-destructive behaviour. This may include suicide by an individual without friends and family and who is perhaps living in an isolated environment.

3. **Altruistic** suicide, opposite to egotistic suicide, is mostly characteristic of traditional societies. In this case, in contrast to egotistic suicide, individuals are substantially integrated into society and its social organizations. One kills oneself because one is obliged to do so. Kamikaze and "suicide bombers" commit suicide for the larger good of society. This type of suicide rests upon a strong collective conscience.

4. **Fatalistic** suicide occurs when individuals feel powerless to regulate their own life. For example, a prisoner may see suicide as a "way out."

You may have noticed that Durkheim was interested in finding out how social control influences individuals' self-destructive behaviour. Merton (1964) extended Durkheim's argument on normlessness and argued that deviance and crime are due to lack of correspondence between societal goals and the means of achieving such goals. For example, becoming economically successful is a societal goal in Western societies. Means of achieving such success include acquiring higher education, hard work, and business investment. Most people are **conformists.** They use accepted means to achieve their goals. But if opportunities are not available, individuals may choose alternative routes for success. Individuals may innovate by cheating in school, robbing a store or a bank, or committing business fraud. Merton calls these individuals **innovationists.** Others are called **retreatists** because they tend to retreat from social goals and use drugs. Finally, some individuals may **rebel** against both the means and goals and join a revolution.

Generally, **control theories** explain criminal behaviour in terms of a weak internal control mechanism developed in early childhood, in combination with weak or absent social rules. Social control can be external or internal. **External control** or social bonds (Hirschi, 1969) includes attachment to significant others (peers or parents), commitment or investment in conventional society (such as education), involvement in conventional behaviours (such as participation in recreational activities), and belief in society's values (respect for law and authorities).

Internal control refers to early parental childrearing and school practices that can help inhibit a child's undesirable immediate act and ensure internalization of values and lessons that prevent future deviance (Gottfredson and Hirschi, 1990). According to Gottfredson and Hirschi, parents need to monitor a child's behaviour, recognize deviant behaviour, and punish it. Similarly, children need to learn to delay gratification, be sensitive to the desires of others, become more independent, be more willing to accept restraints in their activities, and be less likely to use force or violence to attain their goals. If children do these things properly, they internalize self-control so that when given the opportunity they will resist deviant and criminal behaviours.

What role does power play in explaining crime? Is there a tendency to define some activity and individuals as more criminal than others, depending on who is in the position of power and authority? **Conflict theory** reminds us that we tend to see crime as **street crime** while ignoring much of **corporate crime,** which may be significantly more harmful. A business that pollutes the environment can slowly kill large numbers of people by decreasing peoples' longevity and life expectancy. Similarly, capitalists owning the means of production tend to exploit those who have nothing to sell in the market but their labour power. If they could, capitalists would pay lower wages in general, and to women and visible minorities in particular. The workers have no choice but to work for whatever is the "going rate" in the market. Therefore, capitalists tend to get relatively rich whereas workers remain poor. Capitalists can take advantages of all social amenities. Workers, in contrast, tend to live in an unhealthy environment and thus are prone to all kinds of illnesses. Therefore, the misery of workers and the prosperity of capitalists tend to be intertwined. But these differences are legitimated and accepted. There is no law on overexploitation and far less in controlling the expanding appetite of the business class to take advantage of the property-less multitude. The point is that capitalist society tends to define certain acts as acceptable and others as criminal and thus punishable. A corporation that evades taxes, pollutes the environment, and exploits workers is not seen as criminal. In contrast, marijuana or drug users (street crime) who primarily harm themselves are criminalized. We tend to have more severe punishments for the latter (i.e., street crime) than the former (i.e., corporate or white-collar crime).

Similarly, the definition of crime and criminals affects the identification of who is categorized as deviant or criminal. For example, there may be a perception that the poor, unemployed, and some visible minorities are more criminal than the rich, working population and whites, respectively. . . . If such a perception is prevalent, particularly among police officers and criminal justice officials, then areas where minorities and the poor are concentrated would be targeted for crime control. Consequently, police officers may find a higher number of criminals in these areas, not so much because minorities and the poor are more deviant or criminal, but because police officers have failed to look for such individuals in the middle- or upper-class neighbourhoods or among the working and white population.

This discussion brings us to the debate in this section. **Racial profiling** is based on the tendency to define certain groups as criminal and then to target them for crime control. Such behaviours tend to target some groups and ignore others. Therefore, the question is raised: "Do certain police forces in Canada engage in racial profiling?" You can judge for yourself by reading the debate that follows this section, the summary of which is presented below (also see the box insert).

In October 2002 the *Toronto Star* published a series of articles and showed that based on data from the Toronto Police Service, the Toronto police had engaged in racial profiling. Toronto police strongly rejected this assertion. Subsequently, Edward Harvey, a professor at the University of Toronto, "cleaned" the same data and focused on individuals who were charged only once. He re-evaluated the racial profiling hypothesis and concluded that the data did not provide support for the allegation by the *Toronto Star*.

Wortley and Tanner provide national and international evidence that the black population has been subjected to racial profiling far more than any other ethnoracial group. Moreover, they argue that Harvey's exercise in "data cleaning" is questionable because it tends to reduce the chance of discovering racial profiling. For example, they argue that by focusing on single events, Harvey made sure that incidences of racial profiling were minimized. Accordingly, Harvey's procedure eliminated all offenders who were charged with a crime on more than one occasion during the six-year study period. However, by doing so, he eliminated the very population that experienced the greatest degree of police discrimination. In other words, Wortley and Tanner argue, if racial profiling exists—and black people do come under greater police surveillance than whites—one would expect that black people would have a much higher probability of being arrested on multiple occasions. Harvey's elimination of multiple cases, therefore, diminished the actual rate of racial profiling. Nevertheless, Wortley and Tanner used data provided by Harvey and showed that even with such data, blacks have been subject to far more racial profiling than whites.

Does this discussion suggest that we should limit police's choice in use of needed information for crime control? Gabor argues that by the very fact that the crime rate is unevenly distributed in the population, police should use the information related to this differential for budget allocation, community relations, and crime control. He suggests that the problem with Wortley and Tanner's definition of racial profiling is that it does not distinguish between "law enforcement practices that are based on pure bigotry and those that may be entirely reasonable as a result of systematic analyses of crime patterns, intelligence work, information obtained from the community."

TABLE TALK
◆ ◆ ◆

Table 4.1 shows distribution of crime rate by types of crimes. **Crime rate** is calculated by multiplying the number of crimes by 100,000 and then dividing the result by the total population. Overall, the crime rate in Canada has somewhat increased during the last four years. However, property and violent crimes have, in

Table 4.1   Crime Rate per 100,000 Population by Type of Offence

	2000	2001	2002	2003	2004
All incidents	8,432.6	8,453.7	8,504.0	8,904.9	8,834.9
Criminal Code offences (excluding traffic offences)	7,666.5	7,655.4	7,705.6	8,146.4	8,050.6
Crimes of violence	984.4	983.8	968.8	965.5	916.1
Homicide	1.8	1.8	1.9	1.7	2
Attempted murder	2.5	2.3	2.2	2.2	2.2
Assaults (level 1 to 3)	761.6	763.9	75.3	747.9	731.8
Sexual assault	78.2	77.5	78.1	74.3	73.7
Other sexual offences	10.2	8.7	8.8	8.1	8.2
Robbery	88.1	88.0	85.0	89.8	86
Other crimes of violence	42.1	41.7	41.6	41.4	42.3
Property crimes	4,080.9	4,003.5	3,973.2	4,122.6	3,990.9
Breaking and entering	955.9	900.9	878.4	899.9	859.9
Motor vehicle theft	522.4	543.5	516.1	550.2	530.7
Theft over $5,000	69.6	67.2	63.2	61.3	54.1
Theft $5,000 and under	2,160.5	2,126.3	2,127.1	2,212.9	2,131.3
Possession of stolen goods	93.0	86.9	95.8	104.7	110.8
Fraud	279.6	278.8	292.7	293.5	303.9
Other Criminal Code offences	2,601.2	2,668.1	2,763.6	3,058.3	3,113.6
Criminal Code offences (traffic offences)	366.4	387.6	374.8	369.9	372.1
Impaired driving	258.2	266.7	255.1	245.2	247.2
Other traffic offences	108.2	120.9	119.6	124.7	124.9
Federal statutes	399.8	410.7	423.6	388.7	412.3
Drugs	287.0	288.2	295.7	274.1	304.1
Other federal statutes	112.7	122.5	127.9	114.5	108.2

Source: Statistics Canada, CANSIM, table: 252-0013.

fact, decreased. Also note that despite the media's glorification, homicide and attempted murder constitute a fraction of the total crime rate. Why do you think the media glorifies crime?

OTHER QUESTIONS

1. In your view, does Durkheim's explanation of suicide make sense? Do you find any problem with his explanation?
2. Among the various theories of deviance and crime, which one(s) makes sense to you? Why?

3. More broadly, why do people commit crime?
4. Explain the role of culture in explaining people's attitude toward terrorism.
5. What are the various implications of racial profiling for a just society?
6. Do you think that racial minorities are subject to racial profiling? Why or why not?
7. Do you think police officers and security forces should be involved in racial profiling? Why or why not?
8. Do you think that Muslims have been subjected to racial profiling since 9/11? Do you think it is appropriate for police to target Muslims?

Data, Denials, and Confusion:
The Racial Profiling Debate in Toronto

Scot Wortley
Centre of Criminology, University of Toronto

Julian Tanner
Department of Sociology, University of Toronto

◆ ◆ ◆

RESEARCH ON RACIAL PROFILING
◆ ◆ ◆

. . . In his report, Professor Harvey claims to provide evidence that systematic racial profiling does not exist in the Toronto area (Harvey 2003: 39). In fact, Harvey does not actually examine racial-profiling data at all. Indeed, his entire report is based on an examination of the Toronto police *arrest* data set (CIPS). It is our contention that such arrest data are only produced *after racial profiling has already taken place*. In the criminological literature, racial profiling is said to exist when the members of certain racial or ethnic groups become subject to greater levels of criminal justice surveillance than others. Racial profiling, therefore, is typically defined as a racial disparity in police stop and search practices, racial differences in customs searches at airports and border-crossings, increased police patrols in racial minority neighbourhoods and undercover activities, or sting operations that selectively target particular ethnic groups (see Weitzer and Tuch, 2002; Meehan and Ponder, 2002; Engels et al. 2002; Harris 1999). Racial profiling, therefore, is associated with racial bias in police investigation—not racial bias in arrest decisions or racial bias in police treatment after arrest. This is not to say that arrest statistics do not *reflect* profiling. For example, the over-representation of blacks in Toronto arrest statistics could mean that blacks are, indeed, subject to greater police surveillance. However, it could also mean that blacks are simply more involved in certain criminal activities. Thus, the racial-profiling hypothesis cannot truly be proven or rejected unless we first examine information on police surveillance activities. Harvey, unfortunately, makes no attempt to look at such data.

Do black people come under greater criminal justice surveillance than people from other racial backgrounds? Are black people more likely to be stopped, questioned, and searched by the police? Police data from both England (Bunyan 1999) and the United States (see Engel et al. 2002; Harris 1997) suggest that they are. . . . Police statistics from 1997–1998 reveal that black people were stopped and searched at a rate of 142 per 1,000, compared to 45 per 1,000 for Asians and 19 per 1,000 for whites. Overall, the English data suggest that blacks are approximately eight times more likely to be stopped and searched by the police than whites (Bunyan 1999; Brown 1997).

Unfortunately, unlike England and the United States, the police in Canada are not required to record the race of the people they stop and/or search. Thus, official police statistics cannot be used to investigate the presence or absence of racial profiling in this country. However, a number of field studies have uncovered evidence that racial profiling may exist. For example, James (1998) conducted intensive interviews with over 50 black youth from southern Ontario. Many of these youths reported that

From Scot Wortley and Julian Tanner, "Data, denials, and confusion: The Racial Profiling Debate in Toronto," *Canadian Journal of Criminology and Criminal Justice,* 2003, 45(3), pp. 367–389. Reprinted by permission of Canadian Criminal Justice Association.

being stopped by the police was a common occurrence for them. James concludes that the adversarial nature of these police stops contributes strongly to black youths' hostility towards the police. Neugebauer's (2000) interviews with 63 black and white teenagers from Toronto produced very similar results. Although the author found that teenagers from all racial backgrounds often complain about being hassled by the police, both white and black youth agreed that black males are much more likely to be stopped, questioned, and searched by the police than youths from other racial backgrounds.

Although these ethnographic studies provide great detail about police encounters and document the "lived experiences" of black youth, they are based on rather small, non-random samples. They thus risk being dismissed as anecdotal and not truly representative of police behaviour. However, similar evidence of racial profiling has been recently uncovered by two surveys that utilized much larger, random samples. To begin with, a 1994 survey of over 1,200 Toronto residents found that black people are much more likely to report involuntary police contact than either whites or Asians. For example, almost half (44%) of black male respondents reported that they had been stopped and questioned by the police at least once in the past two years, and one third (30%) reported that they had been stopped on two or more occasions. By contrast, only 12% of white males and 7% of Asian males reported multiple police stops. Multivariate analyses reveal that these racial differences in police contact cannot be explained by racial differences in social class, education, or other demographic variables (see Wortley forthcoming; see also Commission on Systemic Racism, 1995). In fact, two factors that seem to protect white males from police contact—age and social class—do not protect blacks. In general, whites with high incomes and education are much less likely to be stopped by the police than whites who score low on social class measures. By contrast, blacks with high incomes and education are actually more likely to be stopped than lower-class blacks. Black professionals, in fact, often attribute the attention they receive from the police to their relative affluence. As one black respondent stated, "If you are black and you drive something good, the police will pull you over and ask about drugs" (Wortley forthcoming).

A recent survey of approximately 3,400 Toronto high school students (Tanner and Wortley 2002; Wortley and Tanner 2002) provides further evidence of racial profiling. Over 50% of the black students in the study reported that they had been stopped and questioned by the police on two or more occasions in the previous two years, compared to only 23% of whites, 11% of Asians, and 8% of South Asians. Similarly, over 40% of black students claimed that they had been physically searched by the police in the previous two years, compared to only 17% of their white and 11% of their Asian counterparts. However, the data also revealed that students who engage in various forms of crime and deviance are much more likely to receive police attention than students who do not break the law. For example, 81% of the drug dealers in this sample (defined as those who sold drugs on 10 or more occasions in the previous year) reported that they had been searched by the police, compared to only 16% of those students who did not sell drugs. . . .

While our data revealed that white students have much higher rates of both alcohol consumption and illicit drug use, black students did report higher rates of both minor property crime and violence. Furthermore, both black and white students reported higher rates of participation in public leisure activities than students from all other racial backgrounds. These racial differences, however, do not come close to explaining why black youth are much more vulnerable to police contact. In fact, after statistically controlling for criminal activity, drug use, gang membership, and leisure activities, the relationship between race and police stops actually got stronger. Why? Multivariate analysis revealed that racial differences in police stop and search practices were actually greatest among students with low levels of criminal behaviour. For example, 34% of the black students who had not engaged in any type of criminal activity still reported that they had been stopped by the police on two or more occasions in the previous two years, compared to only 4% of white students in the same behavioural category. Similarly, 23% of black students with no deviant behaviour reported that they had been searched by the police, compared to only 5% of whites who reported no deviance. . . .

These findings strongly suggest that racial profiling does, in fact, exist in Toronto. Our research further suggests that, due to racial profiling, black people are much more likely to be caught when they break the law than white people who engage in similar forms of criminal activity. For example, 65% of the black drug dealers in our high school study reported that they had been arrested at some time in their lives, compared to only 35% of the white drug dealers (Worley and Tanner 2002). This finding is completely *consistent* with the fact, reported by the *Star*, that blacks are highly over-represented in drug-related arrests (Rankin et al. 2002a). It must be stressed that Harvey totally ignored these stop-and-search findings when writing his report—despite the fact that these studies were extensively covered by the *Toronto Star* as part of their investigative series on race and crime. . . . The fact that Professor Harvey totally ignored previous Canadian, American, and British research on racial profiling is very difficult to explain. How could he come to a "no profiling" conclusion, without examining all of the empirical evidence? At best, this situation *might* be viewed as unprofessional and reflecting a general ignorance of the academic literature on racial profiling. At worst, it might represent a deliberate attempt to mislead the public about the true nature of the racial-profiling debate. . . .

HARVEY'S "CLEANING" OF THE TORONTO ARREST DATA

◆ ◆ ◆

. . . To begin with, Harvey complains that "as a database, CIPS was designed as an administrative tool to assist TPS officers in the conduct of their duties. It is not and was never intended to be a research database" (Harvey 2003: 10). Harvey seems to be implying that this arrest data should never have been examined by the *Star* and that any conclusions drawn from such data are questionable. We believe that this statement is completely incorrect. Indeed, any cursory glance at the published literature in the social sciences—including history, political science, sociology, and criminology—would reveal that a great deal of research examines administrative or archival data that was not originally intended for research purposes. For example, many important court-processing studies—including research that examines racial and gender bias in bail decisions and sentencing—effectively use court records that were not originally designed for empirical analysis (see reviews in Bowling and Phillips 2002; Kellough and Wortley 2002; Cole 1999; Williams 1999; Roberts and Dobb 1997; Mann 1993; Hood 1992). As long as arrest data are adequately described and subjected to appropriate analysis, there is absolutely no intrinsic problem with using them for research purposes.

Harvey goes on to state that it "should be noted that CIPS is only a sample (and not a scientifically designed sample) of the millions of contacts with the public the TPS had over the 1996–2002 time-frame" (Harvey 2003: 10). This is another misleading statement. In fact, the CIPS data set is not supposed to be a sample at all. It is a data set that was designed to represent the *total population* of criminal charges (and certain traffic charges) that were laid by the Toronto police during the study period. It was never intended to represent *all* police contacts with the public—which would include everything from arrests to traffic stops to citizen requests for service to informal

interaction at community events. Furthermore, the *Star* *never* described CIPS as anything but a source of data on police arrests. Unfortunately, Harvey's suggestion that CIPS is based on an "unscientific" sample may unjustifiably convince some members of the public that the *Star*'s analysis does not warrant serious consideration.

After questioning whether the data should be used for research at all, Harvey states that he will, nonetheless, attempt to replicate the *Star*'s analysis. He begins by outlining the various "data cleaning" procedures he utilized to prepare the data for analysis (see Harvey 2003: 10–13). Firstly, Harvey eliminated all cases with missing information. This is a perfectly acceptable social science practice. However, in our opinion, Harvey then engages in some very questionable "data cleaning" procedures. For example, he eliminates all "multiple offenders" from the CIPS data. This strategy eliminates over half the completed cases from the offender data set (reducing it from 418,148 completed cases to 204,373). Harvey's only justification for dropping 213,775 "multiple offenders" from his analysis is that their inclusion "has the potential of skewing the data and biasing analytical outcomes" (Harvey 2003: 11). Although we do not understand this reasoning (advanced statistical analyses could easily control for multiple offenders), we do agree that excluding these offenders from the analysis could have a major impact on the results. Specifically, it could greatly reduce the size of the racial disparities that emerge in the subsequent analysis.

Harvey first eliminates all offenders who were charged with a crime on more than one occasion during the six-year study period. In other words, if a person was charged with one crime in 1996 and another crime in 2002—s/he was automatically eliminated from the analysis (Harvey 2003: 11–13). However, if racial profiling exists—and black people do come under greater police surveillance than whites—we would expect that black people would have a much higher probability of being arrested on multiple occasions. Furthermore, by focusing exclusively on those who had been charged with a "single count" of a criminal offence, it appears that Harvey also eliminated those offenders who were charged with more than one crime during a specific arrest incident (Harvey 2003: 12). For example, if an offender was charged with both assault and drug possession at the time of their arrest, they were apparently left out of Harvey's investigation. Interestingly, previous research suggests that black people are much more likely to be charged with multiple crimes than whites—a phenomena referred to as over-charging (Commission on Systemic Racism 1995;

Kellough and Wortley 2002). In sum, we feel that by eliminating multiple offenders, Professor Harvey likely excluded from his analysis the very population that experienced the greatest degree of police discrimination and thus reduced the extent of the racial disparities in his findings. If racial profiling exists, blacks should be greatly over-represented among multiple offenders.

While the *Star* focused on racial differences in arrest statistics at the aggregate level, Harvey decided to focus on racial differences at the division level. His only rationalization for this decision is that there are "extensive sociodemographic differences among the various TPS divisions" (Harvey 2003: 13). We can see no reason for not looking at the data at the divisional level. In fact, it might produce some interesting comparisons. However, we totally disagree with Harvey's decision to focus only on those divisions that have a black population of greater than 6% (see Harvey 2003: 20). Harvey justifies this decision by stating that the exclusion of divisions with less than 6% black population "is based on concerns about the validity of statistical analysis based on such small proportions" (Harvey 2003: 20). Importantly, we could not locate a single statistics manual or academic publication that would support this position—and Harvey does not provide a single reference to justify his argument. Furthermore, we must remember that the CIPS data set is not a random sample—it represents the total population of arrests made by the police from 1996 to 2002. It is, therefore, not subject to the normal statistical concerns related to probability theory. Secondly, Harvey's decision suffers from a basic methodological problem known as the *ecological fallacy*. He seems to assume that all offenders are arrested for crimes and charged with traffic offences in the very same areas that they live in. There is absolutely no evidence to support such a claim. Indeed, research suggests that people often travel outside of their neighbourhoods to engage in certain types of criminal behaviour—including prostitution and drug use (see Wortley, Fischer, and Webster 2002). In addition, it is logical to assume that many traffic charges are administered to citizens while they are travelling in their automobiles, some distance away from their home residences. Finally, Harvey's exclusion of those police divisions with less than 6% black population totally ignores previous research which supports the "out-of-place" hypothesis—the idea that minorities are actually treated more harshly by the police when they live in or venture into predominantly white neighbourhoods (see Meehan and Ponder 2002). In other words, Harvey's elimination of police divisions with small black populations—and his refusal to discuss the data at the aggregate level—may further reduce the size of the racial disparities revealed in his analysis. Nonetheless, despite Harvey's extremely questionable "data cleaning" procedures, we ultimately feel that his results remain quite consistent with the *Star*'s conclusion that racial profiling exists.

INTERPRETING ARREST STATISTICS
◆ ◆ ◆

The original *Star* analysis focused on racial differences with respect to four different types of offence: simple drug possession, cocaine possession, out-of-sight traffic offences, and violence (see Rankin et al., 2002a, 2002b, 2002c, 2002d). The over-representation of minorities in drug arrests has long been linked—both theoretically and empirically—to the racial-profiling debate (see Mauer 1999; Harris 1997 1999; Tonry 1995). Out-of-sight traffic offences (including driving without a licence, driving with a suspended licence, and driving without proper insurance) have also been linked to racial profiling. After all, such behaviours can only be discovered *after* the police have stopped and questioned a driver. Thus, racial differences in out-of-sight charges may reflect racial differences in police stop-and-search activities. This is particularly true when the police have not charged the driver with a moving violation like speeding or running a red light (violations that would justify the initial traffic stop). Although the *Star* articles also discuss black over-representation in violent crimes, Harvey decides not to focus on such arrests because they include too many multiple offenders (see Harvey 2003: 17). However, Harvey does include both prostitution and impaired driving in his independent analysis—two offences that were not discussed by the *Star*. Harvey provides no justification for including these two new offences.

Harvey's findings suggest that while blacks are over-represented in charges for simple drug possession, cocaine possession, and out-of-sight traffic offences, whites are over-represented in charges for both prostitution and impaired driving (Harvey 2003: 39). Harvey seems to suggest that white over-representation in certain crime categories constitutes proof that racial profiling does not exist. We disagree totally with this assessment. First of all, the fact that Harvey only focuses on police divisions with a greater than 6% black population completely distorts his analysis. Fortunately, Harvey actually does provide complete arrest data for all divisions—and a summary table for the entire city—in Appendix B of his report. This allows us to scrutinize his findings more closely.

Tables 1 through 3 present arrest statistics from the City of Toronto. These data were drawn directly from Appendix B of Harvey's report. In order to illustrate the extent of racial over-representation, we calculated a ratio statistic by dividing the percentage of blacks and whites in the various charge categories by their percentage in the total population. Table 1 provides the arrest figures for 42 Division—one of the divisions Harvey focuses on because it has a relatively large black population. Consistent with Harvey's conclusions, the statistics from this division reveal that blacks are indeed over-represented in drug possession and out-of-sight traffic offences, while whites are over-represented in both prostitution and impaired-driving charges. However, what Harvey fails to discuss in his report is the fact that the level of black over-representation in drug and out-of-sight traffic offences is much greater than the level of white over-representation for either prostitution or impaired driving. For example, our calculations reveal that blacks are almost 4 times over-represented in out-of-sight driving offences, 3.8 times over-represented in cocaine possession, and 2.1 times over-represented in simple drug possession. By contrast, whites are only 1.5 times over-represented in prostitution offences

and 1.4 times over-represented in impaired driving charges. It is, therefore, difficult to understand how Harvey could imply that these figures cancel each other out and prove that racial profiling does not exist.

The situation gets more problematic when we examine those divisions that Harvey deliberately dropped from his analysis. Table 2, for example, presents data from 52 Division—an area of the city with a relatively small black population. In our opinion, this is a very important division to include in the analysis because it incorporates much of the downtown core. It is the heart of Toronto's business, shopping, and entertainment district. Thus, while only 4% of the permanent residents of this area are black, it is logical to assume that many more blacks regularly travel to this area of the city to work, shop, and seek entertainment (including sports events, nightclubs, restaurants, and the theatre). Interestingly, data from this division indicate that blacks are over-represented in all five offence categories—including prostitution and impaired driving. This finding totally contradicts Harvey's conclusions. Furthermore, the ratios suggest that blacks are even more over-represented in police divisions with low black populations than in divisions in which they make up a larger

Table 1: Selected Arrest Statistics for 42 Division, by Race of Offenders

Categories	% Black Offenders	% Blacks in Population	Ratio of Black Offenders/Black Population	% White Offenders	% Whites in Population	Ratio Offenders Population
Out-of-Sight Traffic Charges	42.9	10.9	3.936	36.1	39.8	0.907
Drug Possession	23.3	10.9	2.138	50.6	39.8	1.271
Cocaine Possession	41.0	10.9	3.761	48.7	39.8	1.224
Prostitution	6.7	10.9	0.615	60.4	39.8	1.518
Impaired Driving	10.2	10.9	0.936	54.3	39.8	1.364

Table 2: Selected Arrest Statistics for 52 Division, by Race of Offenders

Categories	% Black Offenders	% Blacks in Population	Ratio of Black Offenders/Black Population	% White Offenders	% Whites in Population	Ratio Offenders Population
Out-of-Sight Traffic Charges	29.7	4.2	7.071	50.77	69.4	0.731
Drug Possession	15.8	4.2	3.762	73.4	69.4	1.058
Cocaine Possession	17.0	4.2	4.048	73.0	69.4	1.052
Prostitution	12.2	4.2	2.905	66.9	69.4	0.964
Impaired Driving	5.9	4.2	1.405	74.8	69.4	1.078

Table 3:   Selected Arrest Statistics for All Police Divisions, by Race of Offenders

Categories	% Black Offenders	% Blacks in Population	Ratio of Black Offenders/Black Population	% White Offenders	% Whites in Population	Ratio Offenders Population
Out-of-Sight Traffic Charges	34.3	8.1	4.235	51.8	62.7	0.826
Drug Possession	24.3	8.1	3.000	63.3	62.7	1.010
Cocaine Possession	29.3	8.1	3.654	61.2	62.7	0.976
Prostitution	11.9	8.1	1.496	68.1	62.7	1.086
Impaired Driving	7.0	8.1	0.864	73.6	62.7	1.174

proportion of the total population. For example, while blacks are approximately four times over-represented in out-of-sight traffic offences for 42 Division (Table 1), they are more than seven times over-represented in this offence category for 52 Division (Table 2). This finding is consistent with the idea that blacks are treated more harshly by the police when they venture into predominantly white areas.

Table 3 presents arrest data for Toronto at the aggregate level. It includes statistics for all police divisions. These data clearly indicate that Harvey's final conclusions are both misleading and inaccurate. First of all, contrary to Harvey's statements, blacks are actually over-represented with respect to prostitution charges. Importantly, blacks are more over-represented (1.5 times) in this offence category than whites (1.1 times). Additional analysis reveals that impaired driving is, in fact, the only offence category in which blacks are under-represented and whites over-represented. However, it must be stressed again that the degree of black over-representation in drug and out-of-sight offences is much greater than the degree of white over-representation in impaired driving charges. Indeed, blacks are 4.2 times over-represented in out-of-sight traffic offences, 3.7 times over-represented in cocaine charges, and 3.0 times over-represented with respect to simple drug possession. By contrast, whites are only slightly over-represented (1.2 times) in impaired driving arrests.

Clearly these findings do not in any way disprove the existence of racial profiling. Indeed, researchers have long argued that black over-representation in both drug offences and out-of-sight traffic violations is completely consistent with the racial-profiling hypothesis. Experts maintain, for example, that drug offences are often discovered by the police when they engage in racially biased stop-and-search tactics. This argument is supported by survey research that consistently reveals that although blacks are over-represented in drug arrests, whites actually have higher rates of illegal drug use (see Tonry 1995; Mauer 1999). By contrast, neither prostitution nor impaired driving arrests have been theoretically linked to racial profiling. For example, prostitution arrests are often made during sting operations in which prostitutes or their clients must approach and communicate their intentions to undercover police officers (see Wortley et al. 2002). In other words, prostitution is rarely uncovered by police stop-and-search practices. Similarly, impaired driving charges often result from RIDE programs in which all drivers—regardless of their race—are stopped and questioned. This is not to say that Harvey's findings actually prove that racial profiling exists. We feel that more data—including official police statistics on stop-and-search practices—are needed before such a conclusion can be reached. However, we do feel that Harvey's findings are completely consistent with the idea that racial profiling may be a problem in the Toronto area. Harvey's manipulation and interpretation of the CIPS data only serves to mask this reality and deflect charges of racial bias.

POLICE TREATMENT AFTER ARREST

◆ ◆ ◆

The *Toronto Star* also used the CIPS data set to examine the treatment of offenders by the police after they had been charged with a crime. The *Star* found that for simple drug possession (over 10,000 cases), blacks were less likely to be released at the scene (61.8%) than their white counterparts (76.5%). Of those taken to the station for processing, blacks (15.5%) were held for a bail hearing at twice the rate of whites (7.7%). The *Star* maintains that if the drug in question was cocaine (over 2,000 cases), the police treatment of blacks became even harsher. For example, only 41.5% of blacks charged with cocaine possession were released at the scene, compared to 63% of whites charged with the same offence. Similarly, over 40% of blacks charged with one count of cocaine possession were held for a bail hearing, compared to only 20% of their white counterparts. The *Star* maintains that these racial differences in police treatment persist after statistically controlling for other relevant factors—including the offender's criminal history, age, employment status, immigration status, and whether or not the suspect had a permanent home address (Rankin et al, 2002a).

In his report, Harvey argues that the *Star's* analysis is not transparent and that his re-analysis of the CIPS data reveals no evidence of racial bias in police treatment. It is interesting to note that in his 156-page report (including appendices) Harvey devotes only a half page to this important issue. In fact, we feel that Harvey's re-analysis of the *Star's* treatment data is so poorly done and incomplete that we have reproduced the entire section of the report below. Harvey writes,

> In its reporting on possession of cocaine, the *Toronto Star* states, "If the drug was cocaine, the treatment was tougher: 63 percent of Whites were released at the scene but only 41.5% of Blacks." Using the cleaned-up CIPS database, I re-analysed the numbers controlling for a number of factors available in the CIPS database. These factors are: CIPS, MANIX, BAIL, PROBATION, PREVIOUS CONVICTION, TAP PAROLE, WARRANT. The purpose of these controls was to come up with a population of Blacks and a population of Whites who were "clean" with respect to police records and the criminal justice system. Put in plain language, I wanted to ensure I was comparing "apples" with "apples." This analysis revealed no difference in the "release-at-scene" (Form 9) rates for Blacks and Whites. The rate for Blacks was 74.0% and the rate for Whites was 74.3%. (Harvey 2003: 36–37)

That is all that Harvey has to say about the matter. In our opinion, this is a totally misleading attempt to discredit the *Star's* analysis. First of all, by stating that he has controlled for "a number of factors available in the CIPS database," Harvey suggests that he has actually conducted a multivariate analysis. However, he does not directly discuss the multivariate procedures that he has employed, nor does he present his results in tabular form. Harvey goes on to identify the names of the variables that he has apparently taken into statistical account. However, he does not provide any definitions for these variables—a tactic that can only serve to confuse the reader. Finally, Harvey suggests that he has eliminated all offenders with any kind of criminal history from his analysis. It is among this group that he apparently finds no evidence of racial bias in the release decision. However, Harvey does not exactly define what he means by offenders who are "clean" with respect to police records and the criminal justice system. Has he only eliminated those offenders with previous criminal convictions—or has he eliminated all offenders with a previous record of arrest or other form of contact with the justice system? It is unclear. Importantly, Harvey does not disclose how many of the original 2,000-plus cocaine offenders remain after he has eliminated those with a criminal history. What is his final sample? We suspect that his selective "cleaning" procedures may have greatly reduced the total number of offenders in his analysis and consequently rendered his findings meaningless. Finally, we find it particularly disturbing that Harvey blasts the *Star* for lack of transparency, then produces his own analysis which is equally—if not more—vague and difficult to follow.

It is also very difficult to understand why Harvey did not provide a complete replication of the *Star's* original analysis. As you recall, the *Star* actually conducted four different statistical analyses on this issue: (1) an analysis of the release decision for all those charged with drug possession; (2) an analysis of the release decision for all those charged with cocaine possession; (3) an analysis of the bail decision for all those charged with drug possession; and (4) an analysis of the bail decision for all those charged with cocaine possession. Harvey, however, only "replicates" one of these four analyses—the release decision for cocaine offenders. Why did Harvey not examine the release decision for all offenders charged with a single count of drug possession? Why did Harvey not examine the bail decision for those charged with drug possession or the bail decision for those charged with cocaine possession? Is it possible that—even using his questionable statistical techniques—these analyses still produced evidence of racial bias? Is it possible that, in his report, Harvey only discussed the release decision for those charged with cocaine possession because it was the only analysis that produced a "no racism" result? Whatever the reason, we feel that it is blatantly misleading for Harvey to suggest that he has replicated the *Star's* analysis and found no evidence of racial bias.

DISCUSSION

◆ ◆ ◆

As our above review suggests, Harvey's re-analysis of the CIPS database is plagued with both methodological issues and problems of interpretation. Unfortunately, critics of Harvey's report have not yet had a full opportunity to discuss these issues in the public arena. They were supposed to be given that opportunity at a special meeting of Toronto's Police Services Board on 28 April 2003—more than two months after Harvey originally presented his findings. However, a coalition of minority organizations actually walked out of this meeting after learning that the Board would only give them five minutes to respond to Harvey's report and his conclusion that the police do not engage in racial profiling . . . Harvey and his colleagues, incidentally, were given over two hours to present their results to the very same Police Services Board. . . .

In the meantime, social science in general—and the discipline of criminology in particular—has taken a beating over its part in the racial-profiling debate. Most damaging are accusations that social scientists can be hired to provide support for any side of an argument. This sentiment was perhaps best expressed by Councillor Gloria Luby—the vice-chair of the Toronto Police Services Board. In response to the *Star's* analysis, Luby claimed that statistics can be used to prove anything. . . . We obviously disagree with this argument. However, we strongly believe that, under ideal circumstances, statistical analyses of sensitive issues (like racial profiling) should be subject to intensive review by academic experts before the figures are released to the public. This is why academic journals usually adopt a strict peer review process that ensures the basic integrity of published research. Clearly, such a system of quality control has not been applied to media discussions of racial profiling.

Almost as damaging to the reputation of criminology are accusations that research can actually cause social problems. Chief Fantino expressed this opinion when he was initially asked to comment on the *Star's* investigation: "It seems that . . . no matter what honest efforts people make, there are always those who are intent on causing trouble. Obviously this (story) is going to do exactly that" (quoted in "Racism" 2002: A14). Consistent with this view, Fantino recently dismissed community attempts to further discuss the racial-profiling issue as "mischief-making" (Lakey and Duncanson 2003: A20). Councillor Luby expanded on this theme when she stated that "we've been getting along quite well. Police discrimination has not been an issue. So why should it suddenly become one? Because the *Star* did this research?" (quoted in "Analysis" 2002: A9). The argument seems to be that studies that document racism within the justice system do more harm than good. That public discussion of evidence of racism creates distrust, damages relationships with specific minority communities, and lowers morale among criminal justice personnel ("Racism" 2002: A14). We could not disagree more. Good, objective social research does not create social problems—it merely documents them. Research has not caused the apparent problems that exist between certain racial minority groups and the police. It has only documented a situation that already exists. The discomfort of having to talk about racism—and deal with it in the policy arena—should not be used as an excuse to prevent further research in this area.

In conclusion, it is clear that the controversy over the issue of racial profiling is far from over. It is also clear that the criminological community must take a much more active role in this debate. We must provide more detailed commentary on the research than has already been conducted—and demand that research funds be set aside to conduct more thorough investigations of this phenomenon. Most importantly, we must vigorously defend our right to examine sensitive topics and conduct research that may not coincide with the interests of major players within the criminal justice system.

Inflammatory Rhetoric on Racial Profiling Can Undermine Police Services[1]

Thomas Gabor

Department of Criminology, University of Ottawa

◆ ◆ ◆

. . . I share with many commentators the concern about "racial profiling"; however, this mutual concern has little meaning when the term has such varied connotations. My preference is for a more narrow usage, as broader definitions include law enforcement practices that, arguably, are legitimate. Therefore, "racial profiling," as defined here, is a form of racial bias whereby citizens are stopped, questioned, searched, or even arrested on the basis of their minority status per se, rather than due to a demonstrated, elevated risk of lawbreaking.

Several rigorous studies undertaken in the United States provide evidence of such "racial profiling." For example, John Lamberth of Temple University (cited in Harris 1999) sent out teams of observers to the New Jersey Turnpike and, based on observations of over 42,000 vehicles, found that black and white drivers violated traffic laws at virtually identical rates. However, police records indicated that 35% of those stopped and 73% of those stopped and arrested were black, while only 13.5% of the cars on the road had a black driver or passenger. Lamberth concluded that "it would appear that the race of the occupants and/or drivers of the cars is a decisive factor [in the number of stops of blacks] or a factor with great explanatory power" (Harris 1999: 198).

Lamberth's study illustrates what I consider to be the two main elements of "racial profiling": (1) members of a visible minority group have a significantly elevated likelihood of being subject to some form of police action, and (2) the more aggressive targeting of that group is due to the group's visible minority status, rather than to behavioural differences that might warrant a higher level of police scrutiny.

Alan Gold, one of Canada's most prominent barristers, adopts a precise definition and one that is consistent with the above: "racial profiling is thus profiling (i.e., identification of target criminals) based upon one characteristic: race. It is an attempt to identify previously undetected criminals based upon the single factor of race" (2003: 394).

According to the above definitions, "racial profiling" is a consistent tendency on the part of members of a police service to target a group in the absence of credible evidence that might warrant such targeting. Unfortunately, definitions of this phenomenon are often so broad that they include reasonable and legitimate police practices.

It is worth contrasting the definition provided by Scot Wortley and Julian Tanner with those advanced above. They write,

> In the criminological literature, racial profiling is said to exist when the members of certain racial or ethnic groups become subject to greater levels of criminal justice surveillance than others. Racial profiling, therefore, is typically defined as a racial disparity in police stop and search practices, racial differences in customs searches at airports and border crossings, increased police patrols in racial minority neighbourhoods and undercover activities, or sting operations that selectively target particular ethnic groups. (2003: 369).

From Thomas Gabor (2004), "Inflammatory Rhetoric on Racial Profiling Can Undermine Police Services," *Canadian Journal of Criminology and Criminal Justice,* 46 (4), pp. 457–466. Reprinted by permission of Canadian Criminal Justice Association.
[1]The author would like to thank colleagues Julian Roberts and Ronald Melchers for their valuable comments.

While Wortley and Tanner are careful to attribute this definition to the criminological literature, they appear to adopt it at various points in their discussion.

My concern is that this definition fails to distinguish between law enforcement practices that are based on pure bigotry and those that may be entirely reasonable as a result of systematic analyses of crime patterns, intelligence work, and information obtained from the community. It is legitimate for a police service to deploy additional personnel in neighbourhoods experiencing high levels of illegal activity, regardless of whether or not the residents tend to be members of visible minority groups. In fact, members of besieged minority communities, including Toronto neighbourhoods beset by gang warfare, have been known to demand more rather than less attention from their local police service.

The definition provided by Wortley and Tanner (2003) fails to address the motives underlying a higher police presence in some minority neighbourhoods. As Gold (2003) indicates, the term "racial profiling" suggests that race plays a critical role in the disproportionate emphasis on a minority group in a particular context. Wortley and Tanner's definition appears to include any police operation aimed at a criminal network of minority persons or conducted in a minority neighbourhood. Their definition of "racial profiling" includes increased police activity in a minority community even where segments of that community seek additional protection or where crime patterns indicate the need for a greater police presence.

CRIME IS UNEVENLY DISTRIBUTED IN MOST JURISDICTIONS

◆ ◆ ◆

The uneven deployment of police resources in an area is justified by the fact that crime is rarely, if ever, evenly distributed in a city. The concentration of crime in certain zones has been demonstrated in geographic studies conducted as long ago as the 1800s, as well as in studies of crime "hot spots" and of repeat victims of crime.

In 1862, for example, Henry Mayhew and his associates charted crime in London, England, and identified persisting criminal areas, popularly known as "rookeries" (Mayhew 1968). Since then, numerous studies have shown that crime tends to be concentrated in certain neighbourhoods within a city (Brantingham and Brantingham 1981).

The evidence indicates that high-crime neighbourhoods are often poor and contain a more transient population (Sacco and Kennedy 2002: 55). Particularly striking is the finding that, in contrast to pockets with high crime,

many sites within a city are relatively crime-free. In Montreal, André Normandeau (1987) found that most subway stations had low rates of crime and that a small number of stations accounted for most of the crime within the subway system. H. A. Bullock (1955), documenting urban homicide in Houston, TX, found that many homicides occurred along the same four streets.

The most influential recent study concerning the concentration of crime is that conducted by Sherman and his collaborators in Minneapolis, MN (Sherman, Gartin, and Buerger 1987). Monitoring 323,979 calls for police assistance over a one-year period, they found that three percent of the locations (addresses or intersections) in the city accounted for half of all calls. Their study underscored the need to identify crime "hot spots" within a city as a focal point for preventive efforts.

In the same vein, recent studies of victimization have revealed that a relatively small number of repeat victims account for a disproportionate number of victimizations. Lifetime victimization data drawn from Canada's General Social Survey indicate that 13% of the close to 26,000 respondents experienced over half of all victimizations (Gabor and Mata 2004). An Australian study found that, in the Beenleigh section of Brisbane, one percent of the addresses experienced 32% of the breakins during an 18-month period (Guidi, Townsley, and Homel 1997). Such findings have paved the way for prevention efforts that have focused on the most vulnerable people and locations—a potentially empowering approach from the perspective of repeat victims (Pease and Laycock 1999).

THE POLICE DILEMMA AND NEWER RESPONSES TO CRIME

◆ ◆ ◆

In a highly diverse metropolis such as Toronto, repeat victims and "hot spots" are often found in impoverished neighbourhoods that may house a high proportion of visible minorities. Police services may find themselves in a no-win situation in these circumstances. If they fail to respond to the concerns of residents in these areas, they may be accused of insensitivity toward the relevant minority group. If they take aggressive measures, however, they may face accusations of profiling and of overpolicing minority neighbourhoods.

Studies over the last 30 years have shown the limits of unfocused preventive patrol (Kelling 1974). New models of policing emphasize the analysis of crime patterns, rather than a reliance on hunches, to identify problematic spots and situations (Goldstein 1979). The emphasis today is on a pro-active approach in which officers attempt to deal with the flashpoints in a community before they erupt, rather than merely reacting once offences have occurred. Furthermore, newer models of policing, such as community policing, emphasize a more decentralized approach in which front line officers are given greater latitude in tackling problems and conflicts in the community (Trojanowicz and Bucqueroux 1990).

THE PERILS OF BASELESS ACCUSATIONS

◆ ◆ ◆

Caution ought to be exercised in making the type of serious allegations levelled against the Toronto Police Service. Headlines such as "Police target black drivers" (Rankin, Quinn, Shephard, Simmie, and Duncanson 2002) appearing in the *Toronto Star* and statements to the effect that the police were engaging in the "practice of stopping people for little reason other than their skin colour" (Rankin et al. 2002) can obviously inflame conflicts in the community and discredit the police and justice system. Such allegations must be carefully documented. . . . In addition, the term "racial profiling" must be defined precisely. If such profiling comes to mean anything other than a documented, systemic racial bias, the cost will be high in terms of the effectiveness of the police department concerned. Such departments will be reluctant to use analytical tools, such as geographic mapping, to identify areas in need of more attention if this elicits adverse media publicity. . . .

One example of misuse of the term "racial profiling" is found in Wortley and Tanner (2003: 371). They cite their own study of high school students as providing evidence of this phenomenon. In their survey, a higher percentage of black than white, Asian, or South Asian students indicated that they had been stopped and questioned by the police more than once over the previous two years. However, Wortley and Tanner also acknowledge "that students who engage in various forms of crime and deviance are much more likely to receive police attention than students who do not break the law" (2003: 372). Wortley and Tanner's survey also revealed that students spending more of their leisure time in public spaces are more likely to be stopped by the police than those spending their time in private spaces or in the company of their parents. The authors then concede that their data do not allow them to determine whether the greater police

attention received by black students is due to their skin colour or whether it is due to higher levels of criminality and their greater use of public spaces. In fact, black students reported more violence and minor property crime (Wortley and Tanner 2003: 372). Why, then, use the pejorative term "racial profiling" when the police may simply be doing their job? . . .

ALLEGATIONS OF RACIAL PROFILING OUGHT TO BE SUPPORTED BY CONCLUSIVE EVIDENCE OF SYSTEMIC RACIAL BIAS

◆ ◆ ◆

The concept of "racial profiling" is a complex one, which, if it is to be relevant to policy, must mean more than allegations of bias by individuals against some members of a police service. It must mean that an ethnic or racial group is being targeted, predominantly or exclusively, because of race, rather than because of a disproportionate involvement in some form of lawbreaking. Given the serious repercussions of such allegations in terms of ethnic conflict and police operations, there ought to be a strong onus on those claiming that the police are engaging in "racial profiling."

Ethnic or racial "profiling" must be documented empirically, rather than through anecdotes. The evidence must show that a disproportionate emphasis on minorities or minority communities, in a particular context, is unwarranted; that is, that it is not supported by the official crime or survey data available. Also, such evidence should include recruitment data, training materials, interviews with police personnel, internal documents, and other organizational sources.

For their part, police services might be advised to commission independent studies on a regular basis to ensure that crime prevention activities focusing on a particular group or neighbourhood are justified by solid evidence of disproportionate involvement in certain crimes, rather than based on stereotypes held about that group. External studies are useful not only because they are at arm's length but because they may rely on alternative data sources. Studies that rely exclusively on police data to show that minorities are over-represented in certain crimes are vulnerable to the criticism that these data reflect biased practices in the first place. Periodic external studies can increase the transparency, effectiveness, and efficiency of police operations, as well as avert accusations and instances of racial bias.

Vietnamese Welcome 'Racial Profiling' Decision; Court Stayed Charges in Grow-op Case OPP Search Breached Charter, Judge Said [ONT Edition]

Stan Josey

Toronto's Vietnamese community welcomes a Superior Court decision that found police had used "racial profiling" to find a marijuana grow operation run by a Vietnamese Canadian.

"For some time our entire community has been under the microscope when it comes to illegal marijuana grow operations," said Kim Trinh, program co-coordinator with the Vietnamese Association of Toronto.

She was reacting to a decision by Justice Emile Kruzick last month to stay charges against a man of Vietnamese background who was arrested on Feb. 26, 2003, after police found 596 marijuana plants in his Orangeville-area home.

The judge ruled that the method an OPP officer used to target Van Trong Nguyen was a violation of an individual's right to safety and security under the Charter of Rights and Freedoms.

In this case, the officer had searched land registry records in the area to find people of Vietnamese descent because some people from that ethnic community had been charged in past investigations of illegal grow operations.

Kruzick concluded that Nguyen's house had been targeted for investigation because of "a stereotypical assumption that because some grow operations have been run by East Asians, that anyone purchasing a new home who is Vietnamese must be conducting a grow operation."

Trinh said this decision should be a wake-up call for police who may target one particular ethnic community for particular types of criminal activity.

"We know for a fact that there are lots of people from other ethnic and Canadian communities involved in the same illegal activities," she said. "But whenever it is someone from our community it seems to be bigger news."

She said there are about 50,000 people of Vietnamese descent in the GTA and 67,000 in Ontario.

"Most of them are hard-working people in all of the professions and careers that are available," she said. "But it is true that a few people trying to make a new life in Canada make the wrong choice to try and quick-start their life in Canada with an illegal marijuana operation."

Trinh said the sad thing is that it is usually the grower, the lowest person in the drug production network, who is charged while the "big bosses"—not usually of Vietnamese descent—get away.

"We have been pushing the courts to give stiffer sentences for this offence as a further deterrent to people getting into it," Nguyen said.

She said her organization, which mainly assists with the resettlement of new Canadians of Vietnamese origin, has applied for a provincial grant to mount an extensive public and community education program on the dangers of marijuana grow operations.

OPP Supt. Bill Craig said they are reviewing transcripts of the judge's ruling before deciding if further action should be taken or an appeal pursued.

Craig said the OPP takes a "zero tolerance" approach to racism and racial profiling during investigations.

"This is not standard operating procedure, but I would like to have all the information to see what led the officer to do that in the first place," Craig said.

He said a breach of operating procedures could subject an officer to disciplinary measures.

"We would have to look at all of the factors involved before deciding what action to take," he said.

Source: Stan Josey, "Vietnamese welcome 'racial profiling' decision," *Toronto Star*, Feb. 9, 2006, p. B05. Reprinted with permission—Torstar Syndication Services.

Unit Five

FAMILY
Introduction: Family and Responsible Fathering

◆ ◆ ◆

Historically, the human family has undergone substantial transformation. Friedrich Engels, in his book *The Origin of the Family, Private Property and the State* (1970 [1884]), relied on historical and anthropological writings, particularly that of Louis Henry Morgan, and argued that methods of producing the necessities of life were important in the emergence and formation of the family institution. Accordingly, in the lowest stage of human development, people were mainly tree dwellers, living in forests, relying on fruits, nuts and roots for food, and slowly developing speech. Later on, they relied on fish for food; used fire; invented tools such as bows, arrows and canoes; smelted iron ore; domesticated animals; cultivated plants; made pottery; and kept records through development of the alphabet. These experiences and changes enabled people to become independent of a particular locality, construct houses, settle in villages, produce a large surplus of goods, and so on.

In the early stages of humanity, parents, children, brothers and sisters, and male and female cousins were all potential husbands and wives for one another. This type of partnership is based on **endogamous marriage.** That is, people married within their own blood clan or group. Later on, according to Morgan, parents, children, and brothers and sisters were all excluded from sexual intercourse. That is, partnership slowly became exogamous, or marriage was outside one's blood clan. Engels took Morgan's evidence, conjectures, and arguments and extended his own argument on the role and status of women in such a communal society. Engels argued

that, in communal societies, women had high status and were held in respect. This meant that women from one tribe had the right and power to decide who would be their husband in another tribe.

Engels also said that with domestication of animals, women slowly lost their power. At first, all domesticated animals belonged to the community as a whole. As sexual division of labour developed, men became responsible for obtaining food and producing tools. Private property in the form of herds and tools slowly emerged, with men coming to own the tools they made, rather than the tools belonging to the community as a whole. Because of the social custom prevalent at the time, men were able to take those instruments wherever they went. Still, children remained with the wife's clan. This meant that children were unable to inherit herds and instruments of production from their fathers.

Again, according to the rules of clan **exogamy** (marriage outside one's clan) and **matrilineal** descent (where descent is traced through mother), the herds and other goods were given to the men's clan brothers and sisters and their children. Therefore, the men's own biological children were disinherited, since their mothers belonged to a different clan. As wealth increased, and also men's control of such wealth, men decided to change the traditional order of inheritance. The mother-right, or matrilineal descent, was slowly brought to an end and was replaced with **patrilineal** descent (where descent is traced through the father) and father-right. Men's children now belonged to their own clan and were able to inherit wealth from their father. Similarly, development of **monogamy** (one man and one woman as partner), in contrast to **polygamy** (having more than one partner), was the result of men wanting to establish undisputed paternity, which was necessary if fathers were to give property to their natural heirs.

For Engels, therefore, the monogamous family as an institution came about as a consequence of the victory of private property over communal property. According to Engels, the family institution emerged so that individuals, particularly those with property, could pass their wealth to their legitimate heirs (see Zeitlin, 2001:181–93). This short historical evolution of family in Engels' view meant that the institution of family is not natural but is socially constructed. The main purposes of the institution of family has been to reproduce itself across generations through childbearing and childrearing, to regulate sexual intercourse, and to ensure economic cooperation through division of labour.

In modern societies **nuclear families** have replaced **extended families,** which were prevalent in hunting and gathering and agricultural societies. Nuclear families are independent institutions established through marriage and include parents and children. Extended families, on the other hand, include several families, such as parents, children, their spouses, and their children, all living in the same residence (see Tables 5.1 and 5.2 for types of family and the recent historical trend in Canada). In almost all families the division of labour has developed along sex lines. Men worked outside the house and were the breadwinners, whereas women worked at home, rearing children and doing domestic labour. However, in recent times, the majority of married women are also involved in paid work outside the home, resulting in them doing a **double day of work,** or **"second shift."**

The reasons for the increase in female participation in the labour force vary. These include the women's liberation movement, decreases in real wages where one wage-earner cannot meet the family's needs (see Table 5.3), increases in availability of "female types" of work, and changes in people's expectations. Despite their increasing participation in paid work, women still do the majority of the housework (see Table 5.4). In other words, as women have entered the labour force, their proportional share of housework has not declined and that of their partner has not increased. There are several reasons for women doing most of the housework and childcare.

- There is an understanding that housework is undesirable, and powerful persons (i.e., men) give it to the less powerful persons (i.e., women) to do.

- According to the "New Home Economic" theory (Becker, 1976), the operation of the house is based on free choice. In this model, household units seek to maximize the aggregate utility of the partner's labour power in both the home and the market by deciding what is to be produced at home as against what is produced in the market and by whom. Since women earn less in the market than men, then households can maximize utility by adopting a gendered division of labour, where women do most of the housework and husbands are more involved in paid work.

- Housework performance distribution can also be a negotiated process and is based on availability of time. If husbands have less time for housework because of their involvement in paid work, wives may do more housework due to their lower involvement in paid work.

- Housework contribution may be due to one's ideological orientation. The key argument here is that the principle of sexual equality or men's and women's gender attitudes, beliefs or ideas, are instrumental in the division of housework. For example, men who believe in gender equity do more housework, and women having similar views do less housework.

- Researchers have also suggested that "doing gender" in itself is important for distribution of housework. Accordingly, the intimate marital relationship is viewed as a setting for enactment of displays about one's identity as a woman or a man. Daily interaction between partners in the house about what the role of men and women should be infuses gender into the relationship and symbolically enacts gender relations. Women and men carry the traditional symbolic meaning of what is a good wife and a good husband in accordance with the ideology of domesticity for wives and breadwinner for husbands. Thus, women suppress their resentment for doing housework and conceptualize it as labour of love in order to maintain harmony in the family. On the other hand, men view housework as inconsistent with and threatening to their "manly" identity, which is historically constructed around their role as provider for the family.

Various studies in Canada and other countries have provided evidence for all of these explanations. Nevertheless, after accounting for these explanations, gender is still the best predictor of housework, with women doing about 60 percent and men about 40 percent of all housework (for Canada, see Nakhaie, 1995, 2002; McQuillan and Belle, 1999; McFarlane et al., 2000).

Spousal abuse and violence is another type of social problem experienced in modern families. Dobash et al. (1992) reviewed the evidence from the courts, the police, women shelters, divorce records, hospital records, and victimization and self-report surveys, and concluded that there is clear sexual **asymmetry** in conjugal violence. Males are significantly more likely to engage in violent activity in conjugal relationships than females. Women are about three or four times more likely to be killed by their husbands than are men by their wives (see Table 5.5). This evidence tends to support the feminist argument that males use violence to establish their patriarchal power within the family. Other research, however, relying primarily on self-report surveys, has pointed to sexual **symmetry** in conjugal violence. About 12 percent of men and women have stated in social surveys that they have been subject to some form of violent abuse from their spouse (see Straus et al., 1990).

The latter evidence moves away from a single-cause explanation and searches for the root of conjugal violence in such factors as education, income, occupation, employment status, class culture, age, alcohol use, and so on. For example, Nakhaie (1998) showed that conjugal violence is age-graded. It is asymmetrical among young couples and more symmetrical among older ones. In the early years of marriage, males are more capable of inflicting violence on their younger and physically weaker partners than females are on their older and stronger partners. In later years, however, males' physical strength deteriorates faster than their partners', both because of the differences in their age at marriage and the lower life expectancy for males compared to females. This deterioration results in a husband's lower capability of violence against his wife, a greater need for care, and a higher degree of physical and mental impairment. It is therefore important to understand that there are many reasons for conjugal violence, and its dynamics are not clear.

It is evident that family relations are not constant. It changes as one goes through the life cycle. For example, marital satisfaction not only depends on the relationship between partners but also on their participation in the labour force and types of occupation, and whether they have children and the children's age. Lupri and Frideres (1981) showed that marital satisfaction steadily declines while children are growing up and then returns to a high level after all children have left home. Lupri and Frideres showed that, on average:
- Husbands are less satisfied with their marriages than are wives.

- Wife's employment status has an important positive effect on both the wives' and husbands' marital satisfaction. The positive effect, however, is higher for husbands than wives.
- The presence of teenagers in the home has a more pronounced negative effect on wives' marital satisfaction than it does on husbands'.
- The higher the occupational status of the husband, the higher the marital satisfaction of the wife. In fact, men with higher occupations tend to be less happy with their marriage than men with lower paid and status occupations.

Finally, there has been an increase in the rate of divorce (see Table 5.2). Evidence also shows that about two-thirds of divorces are likely to take place in the first 10 years of marriage. There are several reasons for divorce and its increasing rate, including childlessness, religiosity, ethnic and educational differences among partners, sexual incompatibility, and breakdown of traditions due to urbanization. Other explanations include the difference between the perception of love and reality of marriage, increasing uncertainty in sex roles, lower stigma about divorce, higher economic independence of women, development of the women's liberation movement, and the substitution of family functions by other institutions, such as education, recreation, and economic production.

One consequence of divorce is an increase in women's poverty. In an important study of economic consequences of divorce, Lenore Weitzman's (1985) research in the U.S. showed that women's standard of living after divorce declined by 73 percent and men's increased by 42 percent following divorce. She attributed these radically diverse consequences of divorce to a court system that rarely awards wives alimony, the increasing household costs for wives after divorce because they often assume the responsibility of the children, and husbands' ability to take advantage of a high salary resulting from years of career enhancement while wives had the primary responsibility of the household. That is to say, marriage is a liability for a wife's career, whereas it is an advantage to her husband's. Weitzman's research has subsequently been criticized because the differences in standards of living after divorce has been shown to be substantially lower than the evidence in her study (i.e., men's income increased only by 10 percent and women's income decreased by 27 percent [Peterson, 1996]). Nevertheless, women and children experience substantial economic hardship after divorce.

This brings us to the debate articles on the importance of responsible fathering. Doherty, Kouneski, and Erickson reviewed the literature on responsible fathering and suggested many pathways that can help the quality of father-child relationships. These pathways are developed through a conceptual model. Generally, responsible fathering depends on:

- Contextual factors such as experience of unemployment and inequality, level of social support, and cultural expectations rooted in race and ethnicity.
- Coparental relationships such as the extent of support and cooperation by mothers and custodial arrangements.
- Father's role identification, commitment, and past relationship with his own father.
- Mother's attitude toward father.
- Child's attitude toward father, as well as his/her behavioural difficulties and temperament.

Walker and McGraw question the basic assumption of responsible fathering, which is that children *need* involved fathers throughout their childhood and adolescence. They argue that there is no empirical support that the needs of children should be provided by a parent of a certain gender. Moreover, they argue that there is a lack of empirical support to show that biology predisposes fathers to be responsible and involved.

TABLE TALK

◆ ◆ ◆

Table 5.1 shows the distribution of Canadian families. It shows that the traditional type of family (married couples with or without children) accounts for about 70 percent of all families, followed by single-parent and common-law families. Why are most lone-parent families headed by female parents?

Table 5.2 shows the Canadian family types during the last four decades. It points to an increasing percentage of divorced individuals, particularly after 1961. Why has divorce increased in Canada?

Table 5.3 shows the average family income in constant 2004 dollars. It reveals a declining family income from 1990 to 1994. Among all families, lone-parent families, particularly if female-headed, have the lowest income, followed by elderly families. These families often live with an income that is below the poverty line. Why do lone-parent families have a lower income than other types of families?

Table 5.1 Canadian Family Structure

	Number	%	%	Avg. Number of Children
All Families	8,371,020		100	1.1
Without children at home	3,059,225	36.5		
With children at home	5,311,795	63.5		
Families of Married Couples	5,901,430		70.4	1.1
Without children at home	2,431,720	29.0		
With children at home	3,469,700	41.4		
Families of Common-Law Couples	1,158,410		13.8	0.8
Without children at home	627,505	7.5		
With children at home	530,900	6.3		
Lone-Parent Families	1,311,190		15.6	
Male parent	245,825	2.9		1.4
Female parent	1,065,365	12.7		1.5

Source: Statistics Canada, Census of Population, 2001.

Table 5.2 Social Family Types

	Single	Married	Widowed	Divorced
1951	28.92%	64.16%	6.59%	0.33%
1961	26.49%	66.61%	6.46%	0.44%
1971	28.25%	64.38%	6.22%	1.15%
1981	27.70%	63.35%	6.14%	2.65%
1991	26.41%	63.16%	6.22%	4.21%

Source: Statistics Canada, Catalogue No. 93-310.

Table 5.4 shows attitudes of Canadians for mate selection. It reveals that, on average, commonality of values and ideas is the most important aspect of finding a desirable spouse. Similar political views, ethnic background, class background, religion, and attitudes toward work and leisure are viewed as the most important for choosing a spouse. However, there are some differences by age and gender. For example, on average,

Table 5.3   Average Total Income by Economic Family Types

	1990	1991	1992	1993	1994
			Constant $ 2004		
Economic families, two people or more	67,900	66,000	65,600	64,500	65,200
Elderly families	51,300	50,200	48,500	49,200	48,900
Non-elderly families	70,700	68,800	68,600	67,200	68,100
Married couples only	66,000	65,200	67,400	65,400	63,500
Two-parent families with children	75,700	73,800	74,100	72,400	73,700
Married couples with other relatives	96,100	91,000	90,300	90,600	91,600
Lone-parent families	31,300	30,200	31,400	29,700	30,600
Male lone-parent families	47,200	47,600	48,800	42,100	42,300
Female lone-parent families	28,600	27,800	29,100	27,800	28,800
All other non-elderly families	56,100	54,300	48,800	52,500	53,000

Source: Statistics Canada, CANSIM, table 202-0403 and Catalogue No. 75-202-XIE.

Table 5.4   Attitudes Towards Mate Selection

If someone is choosing a spouse it is important that both people share:	Years of Age					
	Between 18 and 30			Over 30		
	Male	Female	Total	Male	Female	Total
Similar attitudes towards family and children	1.54	1.36	1.44	1.41	1.33	1.36
Similar moral values	1.62	1.42	1.51	1.49	1.39	1.43
Similar sense of humour	2.00	1.92	1.96	1.93	1.82	1.87
Similar attitudes towards work and leisure	2.04	1.89	1.96	1.83	1.79	1.81
Similar religion	2.88	2.64	2.74	2.67	2.40	2.51
Similar educational background	2.83	2.73	2.78	2.55	2.45	2.49
Similar political views	2.88	2.84	2.86	2.93	2.74	2.82
Similar class, that is, economic background or income	3.00	2.89	2.94	2.72	2.64	2.67
Similar ethnic background	3.12	3.04	3.08	2.89	2.79	2.83

1 = very important 4 = not important

Source: The CRIC-Globe and Mail Survey on "The New Canada" (2003).

these values and attitudes tend to be more important for the young (30 and under years of age) and for females than for the older cohort (over 30 years of age) and males. Females also scored higher on the importance of other values and attitudes than males did.

Table 5.5 shows the distribution of time-use in Canada in minutes per day. It reveals that women do most of the housework, and men are mostly involved in paid work. Women spend most of their time socializing and personal care, and men spend time watch-

Table 5.5   Time-Use among Married and Cohabiters by Gender

	Females	Females	Males	Males
Child care	50.4		26.3	
Housekeeping	73.3		22.9	
Cooking	76.6		27.8	
Meal preparation	67		74	
Shopping	54.3		41.7	
House maintenance	6.1		21.1	
Other domestic activities	26.8		32.5	
Total		354.5		246.3
Paid work activities	165.5		261.8	
Other paid activity	1.7		3.2	
Travel to work	73.2		84.7	
Total		240.4		349.7
Watching TV	111.1		143.1	
Other leisure activities	87		97.6	
Other leisure	3.9		5.1	
Movie/sport	8.4		9.4	
Restaurant	14.3		16.2	
Socialization	93.8		76.2	
Other personal	77.6		71.3	
Total		396.1		418.9
Education	8.8		5.7	
Civic volunteering	24.5		25.6	
Total		33.3		31.3
Other activities	415.7		393.8	
Total		415.7		393.8
Total minutes per day	1440	1440	1440	1440

Source: Statistics Canada: General Social Survey, 1998.

ing TV and doing other leisure activities. Why do men not do more housework?

Table 5.6 shows pattern and trends in victimization. Women are about three times more likely to be killed by their spouse than are men. Males are more subject to elderly victimization than are women. Sexual and physical assaults of children and youth are often done by nonfamily members, though family members are also responsible. Why are children assaulted by their family members?

QUESTIONS

◆ ◆ ◆

1. What does Engels see as the cause for the fall of mother-right and the institution of monogamy?
2. Is the family in crisis? Why?
3. In your mind, how should the family be defined?
4. Assume that you are involved in a cohabitation or marital relationship. What do you think are the most important factors for the persistence and stability of your relationship?
5. Do you think that motherhood is devalued in society? Why?
6. Can a woman be successful by taking the lion's share of domestic work and doing paid work? Why?
7. Will an egalitarian family resolve the conflict between the world of work and the private world?
8. Do children need their biological fathers or mothers for their well-being and development?
9. What are some of the main functions of fathers for children's well-being and development?
10. What does responsible fathering mean to you?
11. Same-sex marriage is another contemporary and contentious issue in Canada. What types of people or groups tend to oppose this change in Canadian families and why? What are your views on same-sex marriage?

Table 5.6   Trends in Victimization Rate by Population Groups

Year	Rate in 1,000,000 Homicide Victimization by Spouse		Rate in 100,000 Elderly Violent Victimization		Rate in 100,000 Children and Youth Victimization			
					Sexual Assault by:		Physical Assault by:	
	Male	Female	Female	Male	Family	Nonfamily	Family	Nonfamily
1988	3.1	10.4	114	157	57	117	112	389
1999	3.8	10.6	130	171	55	116	113	382
2000	2	6.3	139	189	60	124	123	423
2001	2.1	8.2	131	187	62	122	121	412
2002	1.9	7.9	127	183	68	126	130	407
2003	1.7	7.5	114	180	65	118	119	388

Source: Statistics Canada, Centre for Justice Statistics, Family Violence in Canada: A Statistical Profile, 2005. Catalogue No. 85-224-XIE, Tables 3.2, 5.5 and 6.5.

Responsible Fathering: An Overview and Conceptual Framework

William J. Doherty
University of Minnesota

Edward F. Kouneski
University of Minnesota

Martha F. Erickson
University of Minnesota

◆ ◆ ◆

. . . The recent upsurge of interest in fathering has generated concern among supporters of women's and mothers' rights that the emphasis on the important role of fathers in families may feed longstanding biases against female-headed single-parent families, that services for fathers might be increased at the expense of services for single mothers, and that the profatherhood discourse might be used by the fathers' rights groups who are challenging custody, child support, and visitation arrangements after divorce. On the other hand, feminist psychologists have recently argued for more emphasis on fathering and have suggested that involved, nurturing fathers will benefit women as well as children (Phares, 1996; Silverstein, 1996). Only an ecologically sensitive approach to parenting, which views the welfare of fathers, mothers, and children as intertwined and interdependent, can avoid a zero-sum approach to parenting in which fathers' gains become mothers' losses. . . .

This post-1970s interest in fathering has been fueled by the reappraisal of family roles for women and by unprecedented demographic changes in the American family. . . . With more than half of mothers in the work force, with new marriages breaking up at a rate of 50%, and with nearly one third of births to single women, the landscape of fathering has been altered substantially. . . .

Sociological and historical work on fathering makes it clear that fathering (at least beyond insemination) is fundamentally a social construction. Each generation molds its cultural ideal of fathers according to its own time and conditions, and each deals with the inevitable gap between what LaRossa (1988) terms the "culture" of fatherhood and the "conduct" of fathers in families. Sociological and historical analyses also make it clear that fathering cannot be defined in isolation from mothering, mothers' expectations, and social expectations about childrearing in the society, and that these social expectations have been fairly fluid in the United States in the twentieth century. LaRossa (1997) has demonstrated how the culture of fatherhood and the conduct of fathers change from decade to decade as social and political conditions change.

In addition to this historical and social constructivist perspective, fathering also lends itself to a systemic framework, which views fathering not primarily as a characteristic or behavioral set of individual men or even as a dyadic characteristic of a father-child relationship, but as a multilateral process involving fathers, mothers, children, extended family, and the broader community and its cultures and institutions. Fathering is

From William J. Doherty, Edward F. Kouneski, and Martha F. Erickson, "Responsible fathering: an overview and conceptual framework," *Journal of Marriage and Family* 60 (May 1998), pp. 277–292. Copyright © 1998 by the National Council on Family Relations, 3989 Central Ave. NE, Ste 550, Minneapolis, MN 55421.

a product of the meanings, beliefs, motivations, attitudes, and behaviors of all these stakeholders in the lives of children. . . .

RESPONSIBLE FATHERING

◆ ◆ ◆

The use of the term "responsible fathering" . . . reflects a recent shift by academics and professionals away from value-free language and toward a more explicit value-advocacy approach. "Responsible" suggests an "ought," a set of desired norms for evaluating fathers' behavior. The term also conveys a moral meaning (right and wrong) because it suggests that some fathering could be judged "irresponsible. . . ."

The term "responsible fathering," as we use it, applies to fathers across all social classes and racial groups, not narrowly to men in lower social classes or minority groups. . . . James Levine and Edward Pitt (1995) have made an important start in their delineation of responsible fathering. They write:

A man who behaves responsibly towards his child does the following:

- He waits to make a baby until he is prepared emotionally and financially to support his child.
- He establishes his legal paternity if and when he does make a baby.
- He actively shares with the child's mother in the continuing emotional and physical care of their child, from pregnancy onwards.
- He shares with the child's mother in the continuing financial support of their child, from pregnancy onwards (pp. 5–6). . . .

Research on Responsible Fathering

The major areas of research on responsible fathering reflect the domains outlined by Levine and Pitt (1995), with the addition of attention to whether the father resides with the child. These domains can be categorized as (a) establishing legal paternity, (b) nonresidential fathers' presence versus absence, (c) nonresidential fathers' economic support for their children, and (d) residential fathers' level of involvement with their children. . . . The review of literature . . . will be organized by the four research traditions delineated above. In order to delimit the review, we focus on heterosexual, biological fathers and not gay fathers, stepfathers, adoptive fathers, or father surrogates—groups deserving considerably more research and programmatic attention.

Fathers and Legal Paternity   Declaring legal paternity is the sine qua non of responsible fathering. With legal paternity comes a variety of economic, social, and psychological benefits to the child and some degree of protection of the father's rights. Tangible benefits for the child include health care if the father is employed, social security, mandated child support, and armed forces benefits if the father is in the military. They also include the intangible benefit of knowing one's biological heritage and having a clearer sense of social identity (Wattenberg, 1993).

Unfortunately, only about one third of non-marital births in the U.S. are followed by paternity adjudication (Adams, Landsbergen, & Hecht, 1994). There is limited research on the reasons, but they appear to involve lack of information about the benefits of legal paternity, the dynamics of the couple relationship, opposition from mothers, cultural issues, social policy barriers, and low priority actions on the part of social institutions. . . .

Father Presence versus Absence   After the declaration of paternity, the bedrock of fathering is presence in the child's life. The two major structural threats to fathers' presence are nonmarital childbearing and divorce. In 1993, 6.3 million children (9% of all children) were living with a single parent who had never married, up from 243,000 in 1960 (.4% of all children). In terms of percentages of all births, nonmarital births have risen from 4% of births in 1940 to 31% in 1993; the biggest increases occurred in the 1970s and 1980s. . . .

In nearly all cases, children born outside of marriage reside with their mothers. If fathers do not live with the mother and child, their presence in the child's life is frequently marginal and, even when active for a while, tends to be fragile over time. . . . Lerman (1993), using data from a nationally representative group of over 600 unwed fathers, found that about three fourths of young fathers who did not reside with their children at birth never lived in the same household with them. About 50% of these fathers visited their child once a week, but about 20% never visited or visited once a year. The pattern over time was toward less contact as the children got older. . . .

Overall, there appears to be a strong negative effect of nonmarital fathering on the father-child bond. Furstenberg and Harris (1993), reporting on their 20-year follow-up of new unmarried African American parents in Baltimore (a group who were generally representative of African American unmarried parents nationally), found that only 13% of the young adults reported a strong bond with their biological father if he had not lived with them. The figure was 50% for fathers who lived with the child. . . .

. . . Research has documented a declining presence of noncustodial fathers over the years after a divorce. One national study of school-aged children found that 2 years after a divorce about half had not seen their father for a year. . . . A more recent study, using 1990 data from the Survey of Income and Program Participation, reported that about one third of divorced fathers did not spend time with their children in the previous year. . . . In general, although father involvement after divorce seems to be increasing and some fathers are quite involved with their children after a divorce, the predominant pattern among noncustodial fathers is one of gradual withdrawal from their children's lives. . . .

Much of the research on father's involvement with their children after divorce has focused on children's well-being. Although some studies have found that higher levels of father involvement were associated with greater psychological adjustment among children, other studies, especially those with nationally representative samples, have failed to support that conclusion (Furstenberg et al., 1987; Hetherington et al., 1982; Guidubaldi et al., 1986; Kalter et al., 1989). A number of scholars who reported no effects for father involvement suggested that, although contact with both parents is desirable in principle, the benefits of father involvement for the child may be neutralized when there is significant conflict between parents. That is, when there is a good deal of interparental conflict, higher contact with the father might create additional strains on the child, strains that offset the advantages of seeing the father more frequently. . . .

Fathers' Payments of Child Support   . . . The term "deadbeat dad" was coined to communicate moral indignation at the number of fathers who do not contribute to their children's economic well-being after a divorce. The research data are clear and consistent on the subject. According to a report on child support by the U.S. Bureau of the Census (1995), only 48% of the mothers who are awarded child support by the courts receive the full amount due. The remainder are divided more or less equally between those who receive partial payment and those who received nothing. Furthermore, other research has found that the amounts awarded and paid are not adequate to support a child, given mothers' often low incomes, even if the full amounts are forthcoming (Rettig et al., 1991).

. . . The most recent U.S. report (1995) . . . showed that noncustodial mothers, like noncustodial fathers, do not pay all the child support that is owed. Custodial fathers receive about 53% of the child support owed, and custodial mothers receive about 68%. Slightly more than

half of the noncustodial fathers (52%) and less than half of the noncustodial mothers (43%) pay all of what they owe. Mothers' nonpayment cannot be dismissed as stemming from their incomes being lower than the incomes of fathers because child support awards by the court are calibrated partly according to income.

These findings of nonsupport by noncustodial mothers suggest that there is something in the structure of nonresidential parenting, rather than in the culture of fatherhood, that is the principal inhibitor of economic support for children outside of marriage. Structural aspects of nonresidential parenting that may inhibit economic support might include having to send funds to an ex-spouse or to an ex-partner, having to provide economic support in the absence of day-to-day contact with one's children, and having no influence over how child support funds are spent. . . .

Residential Father Involvement with Children   . . . [I]t is clear that the quality of fathers' interactions with their children is tied to the father's success, real or perceived, as a breadwinner (McLoyd, 1989).

It appears that feeling like a failure in the breadwinning role is associated with demoralization for fathers, which causes their relationships with their children to deteriorate (McLoyd, 1990; Taylor et al., 1988). This phenomenon has particular relevance for African American fathers and other fathers of color, "who often face serious barriers to success in the provider role, with deleterious consequences for the ability to father. . . . At a conceptual level, this connection between fathering and breadwinning demonstrates the importance of taking an ecological approach to fathering (Allen and Connor, 1997). . . .

Overall, Pleck (1997) concludes that, in keeping with the shift toward a cultural ideal of the highly involved, coequal parent, there is evidence of the increasing engagement, accessibility, and responsibility of fathers in the lives of their children over the past 20 years. However, there remains a large gap between fathers' levels of involvement and mothers' levels. . . . Fathers tend to be more involved with their sons than their daughters, particularly with older children. Fathers are less involved with older children than younger children, although the decline of fathers' involvement as children get older is proportionately less than the decline in mothers' involvement. Fathers with larger numbers of children are more involved, although the research in this area is somewhat mixed. Fathers are more involved with firstborn than later-born children and with infants born prematurely and who have difficult temperaments; these trends are true for mothers as well. . . .

INFLUENCES ON FATHERING: A CONCEPTUAL MODEL

◆ ◆ ◆

. . . Based on the research literature, prior theoretical work on fathering, and the systemic ecological orientation described earlier, we present a conceptual model of influences on responsible fathering. (See Figure 1.) Unlike prior work, the model is intended to include fathering inside or outside marriage and regardless of coresidence with the child. The focus is on the factors that help create and maintain a father-child bond. The model attempts to transcend the dyadic focus of much traditional child development theory by emphasizing first the child-father-mother triad and then larger systems' influences.

The model highlights individual factors of the father, mother, and child; mother-father relationship factors; and larger contextual factors in the environment. Within each of these domains, the model outlines a number of specific factors that can be supported by the research literature. The center of the model is the interacting unit of child, father, and mother, each formulating meanings and enacting behaviors that influence the others. The three are embedded in a broader social context that affects them as individuals and affects the quality of their relationships. . . .

. . . The research reviewed for this article supports the notion that father-child relations are more strongly influenced than mother-child relations by three of the dimensions of the model: the coparental relationship, factors in the other parent, and larger contextual factors.

Coparental Relationship

A number of studies have shown that the quality of father-child relations both inside and outside marriage is more highly correlated with the quality of the coparental relationship than is true for the mother-child relationship (Belsky and Volling, 1987; Cox et al., 1989; Feldman et al., 1983; Levy-Shiff and Israelashvili, 1988). Fathers appear to withdraw from their child when they are not getting along with the mother, whereas mothers do not show a similar level of withdrawal. . . .

One reason that fathering is particularly sensitive to the marital or coparental relationship is that standards and expectations for fathering appear to be more variable than those for mothering. There is more negotiation in families over what fathers will do than over what mothers will do and hence more dependence among fathers on the quality and outcome of those negotiations. . . . [F]or most American heterosexual fathers, the family environment most supportive of fathering is a caring, committed, and

Figure 1   Influences on Responsible Fathering: A Conceptual Model

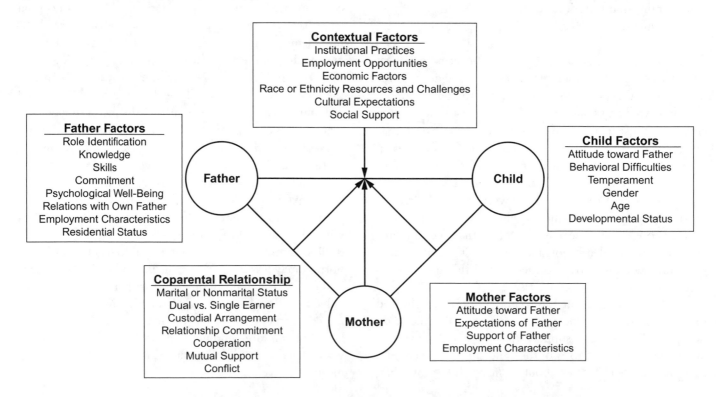

collaborative marriage. This kind of marriage means that the father lives with his children and has a good partnership with their mother. These are the two principal intrafamilial determinants of responsible fathering. . . .

We conclude that, in practice, the kind of mother-father relationship most conducive to responsible fathering in contemporary U.S. society is a caring, committed, collaborative marriage. Outside of this arrangement, substantial barriers stand in the way of active, involved fathering. . . .

Mother Factors

. . . [T]here is also evidence that, even within satisfactory marital relationships, a father's involvement with his children, especially young children, is often contingent on the mother's attitudes toward, expectations of, and support for the fathers, as well as the extent of her involvement in the labor force. . . . Indeed, studies have shown that many mothers, both inside and outside marriage, are ambivalent about the fathers' active involvement with their children (Baruch and Barnett, 1986; Cowan and Cowan, 1987). Given the powerful cultural forces that expect absorption by women in their mothering role, it is not surprising that active paternal involvement would threaten some women's identity and sense of control over this central domain of their lives. The evolution of a social consensus on responsible fathering, therefore, will necessarily involve a consensus that responsible mothering means supporting the father-child bond.

Contextual Factors

Lack of income and poor occupational opportunities appear to have a particularly negative effect on fathering . . . [F]athering is especially sensitive to changes in economic forces in the work force and marketplace and to shifts in public policy. It also suggests that fathering suffers disproportionately from negative social forces, such as racism, that inhibit opportunities in the environment. . . .

Our conceptual model also depicts the positive contribution of ethnic and cultural factors to fathering. One aspect of responsible fathering, that of economic support, is nearly universally expected of fathers by their cultures. . . . Allen and Connor (1997) have examined how role flexibility and concern for children in the African American community create opportunities for men to become involved in surrogate father relationships with children who lack day-to-day contact with their biological fathers. . . .

The final contextual factor in the model is social support, which McLoyd (1990) documented as a crucial factor in diminishing the negative effects of poverty on parenting behavior. . . . Pleck (1997) reviewed the limited research on extra-familial social support for fathering and found the studies skimpy and inconsistent, except for the pattern that highly involved fathers tend to encounter negative attitudes from acquaintances, relatives, and fellow workers. . . .

Child Factors

Individual child factors are included in the model for completeness, but the child factors studied in the research literature do not appear to be as important as the other dimensions in influencing fathering. Fathers do appear to find it easier to be more involved with their sons, especially older sons, presumably because they identify with them and are more comfortable communicating with them (Marsiglio, 1991). Most of the other child factors, such as age, appear to influence mothers as much as fathers, although Larson (1993) and Larson and Richards (1994) have documented how fathers withdraw more from parent-adolescent conflict than mothers do. . . .

Father Factors

Fathers' role identification, skills, and commitment are important influences on fathering (Baruch and Barnett, 1986; Ihinger Tallman et al., 1995; Pleck, 1997). These three appear to fluctuate from low to high levels along with a number of interpersonal and contextual factors, such as the mother's expectations and the father's residential status with his children. . . .

The variability of the individual father factors suggests two important implications of our conceptual model: that the positive support from mothers and the larger context can move men in the direction of more responsible parenting even in the face of modest personal investment, and that strong father commitment, knowledge, and skills are likely to be necessary to overcome negative maternal, coparental, and contextual influences. . . .

As for the father's experience in his own family of origin, some research suggests that the father's relationship with his own father may be a factor—either through identifying with his father or compensating for his father's lapses—in contributing to his own role identification, sense of commitment, and self-efficacy. . . .

The final father factors, psychological well-being and employment characteristics, have been studied extensively. Research examining psychological adjustment and parenting quality consistently shows a positive relationship between fathers' (and mothers') psychological well-being and their parenting attitudes and skills (Cox et al.,

1989; Levy-Shiff and Israelashvili, 1988; Pleck, 1997). The research on job loss and economic distress generally has examined declines in psychological well-being as mediating factors leading to poorer fathering. . . .

CONCLUSION

. . . The main premise [of this article], supported by a variety of studies, is that fathering is uniquely sensitive to contextual influences, both interpersonal and environmental. Fathering is a multilateral relationship, in addition to a one-to-one relationship. A range of influences—including mothers' expectations and behaviors, the quality of the co-parental relationship, economic factors, institutional practices, and employment opportunities—all have potentially powerful effects on fathering. These contextual factors shape the major domains of responsible fathering discussed here: acknowledgment of paternity, willingness to be present and provide economic support, and level of involvement with one's children. When these influences are not supportive of the father-child bond, a man may need a high level identification with the father role, strong commitment, and good parenting skills to remain a responsible father to his children, especially if he does not live with them. . . .

Who Is Responsible for Responsible Fathering?

Alexis J. Walker
Oregon State University

Lori A. McGraw
Oregon State University

◆ ◆ ◆

WHAT DO CHILDREN NEED?
◆ ◆ ◆

. . . A key, explicit assumption of the authors [Doherty, Kouneski and Erickson, 1998] is "that children *need* [italics added] and deserve active involved fathers throughout their childhood and adolescence" (p. 279). Although there might be an ideological basis for this assumption it lacks empirical support. Members of the scientific community may agree on what children need—broadly defined—for biological, physical, emotional, psychological, and social well-being. There is not agreement, however, that these needs must be met by a parent of a certain gender. In their study of children from single-parent households, Downey, Ainsworth-Darnell, and Dufur (1998) asked: "Do women and men play unique roles in shaping children's well-being?" (p. 878). They concluded that "the challenge for family researchers is to distinguish between familial characteristics that are necessarily important for creating positive family environments for children and those, such as sex of parent, that are not" (p. 892). We have no objection to children having actively involved fathers, but research has demonstrated that children's needs can be met within the full range of fathers' involvement, from no involvement to fathers raising children on their own (Acock and Demo, 1994; Risman, 1987).

Which Fathers Matter?

Doherty et al. focused on heterosexual, biological fathers "to delimit the review" (p. 279). Except for marital status, nothing in the authors' conceptual model accounts for their emphasis on biological fathers. Furthermore, there is no empirical evidence that biology predisposes fathers to be responsible and involved (Cooksey and Fondell, 1996). The authors deliberately excluded adoptive, gay, step, fictive kin, and other father surrogates, many of whom are involved, responsible fathers. They suggested that nonbiological and gay fathers deserve empirical and programmatic focus, but they saw such focus as beyond the scope of their paper. Given the authors' concerns about children's needs and the variety of ways through which men function as fathers in contemporary society . . . , we are at a loss to understand their decision. Because there are involved and engaged fathers who are meeting their children's needs in all of the excluded groups, a contextual model of responsible fathers would and should include them.

Mothers' "Gatekeeping," Fathers' Resistance

Doherty et al. exaggerated the problematic behavior of mothers and minimized the role fathers play in their own involvement with their children. . . .

Gatekeeping by mothers is an idea that has emerged to explain the relatively low levels of involvement of fathers with their children. It has been conceptualized in a variety of ways, most recently as a mother's cognitive schema that includes (a) high standards for housework and child care and enjoying control over family work; (b) an identity that is dependent on others' views of how well-groomed one's children are and how clean one's

From Alexis J. Walker and Lori A. McGraw, "Who is responsible for responsible fathering?" *Journal of Marriage and Family*, 62 (2000), pp. 563–569.

home is; and (c) a conventional attitude that women enjoy housework and find it easier to do housework and child care than men do (Allen and Hawkins, 1999). Note that interaction with children, other than through housework or child care, was neither part of this conceptualization nor measured as an outcome of gatekeeping. Allen and Hawkins did not include in gatekeeping the idea that fathers may play a direct or indirect role in setting standards for housework and childcare or in influencing the division of labor in other ways. . . .

In contrast to the idea that mothers keep fathers from their children, evidence suggests that women generally value and actively promote relationships between children and fathers. . . .

To emphasize women who are ambivalent about or act as gatekeepers of fathers' involvement does a disservice to mothers. We do not deny that some mothers make it difficult for fathers to connect with their children, but any instance of gatekeeping must be viewed in the larger context of mothers' facilitation and of men's authority in families. This empirical question has yet to be addressed: To what extent are mothers able to limit coresidential fathers' involvement when fathers have a strong interest in building connections with their children?

Fathers and Financial Support

Doherty et al.'s model and discussion of responsible fathering minimized children's dependence on fathers' financial resources. There is ample and compelling empirical support that the most important activity fathers can do for their children's well-being is to support them financially. . . . Regardless of family structure, fathers who provide economic resources improve their children's developmental outcomes (Acock and Demo, 1994). In our society, men have greater access to resources than women do and men are defined, in part, through their ability to be good providers (Bernard, 1981). Doherty et al. pay insufficient attention to this aspect of father involvement.

We intend neither to reduce men to their ability to provide money, nor to minimize the role mothers increasingly play in generating income for family members. Instead, we take issue with Doherty et al.'s decision to ignore the social context in which men's participation as fathers is grounded. . . .

That the social context creates differing financial imperatives and opportunities for women and men also makes it problematic to compare nonresidential mothers to nonresidential fathers. Doherty et al. minimized problems with noncustodial fathers' financial support by comparing it to that of noncustodial mothers. The causes and

consequences of noncustodial motherhood are not the same as those for noncustodial fatherhood. . . . At a minimum, being a noncustodial mother is far more nonnormative than being a noncustodial father. Furthermore, the reasons for noncustodial mothers' noncompliance with child support have yet to be determined. One cannot conclude, as Doherty et al. did, that "there is something in the structure of nonresidential parenting, rather, than in the culture of fatherhood, that is the principal inhibitor of economic support for children outside of marriage" (p. 282).

The authors attributed fathers' noncompliance, in part, to mothers' role in "misusing the funds and . . . withholding the children from the father" (Doherty et al., p. 282). What fathers describe as misusing funds, mothers describe as meeting children's needs. What fathers see as withholding children from them, mothers see as a strategy to gain fathers' compliance with child support orders. Stephens (1996) reported county data from Texas in which 14,000 complaints were registered for noncompliance compared with 700 complaints regarding visitation. Most noncustodial fathers were satisfied with the frequency and duration of their visits with children, and fathers' complaints were unrelated to compliance. Again, Arendell's (1992, 1995) research is relevant here. Some noncustodial fathers view child support payments as a loss of control over their income rather than as a way to enhance and support their children. This is lamentable because the problems caused by noncompliance are significant, particularly given the effect of such support on children's well-being.

Marriage and Father Involvement

The authors identified marriage as the best context for involved fathers. To support their position, they noted the problems fathers have interacting with and relating to their children, highlighting these problems for never-married and divorced fathers and minimizing the same problems for married fathers. For example, they cited research by Zill, Morrison, and Coiro (1993) showing that 65% of children aged 18 to 22 whose parents divorced reported poor relationships with their fathers. This same study found that nearly 1 in 3 (29%) children in the same age group with *married* parents also reported poor relationships with their fathers. Although the proportion is higher for divorced fathers, the proportion in stable families is alarmingly high. In contrast, mothers' relationships with their children, both inside and outside of marriage, are generally positive. . . .

Doherty et al. also overstated the role of marriage in father involvement in other ways. For example, they exaggerated fathers' involvement when wives are employed. They reported that fathers with employed wives perform a greater proportion of parenting activities than do fathers with nonemployed wives. They did not explain that the proportion is greater primarily because employed wives do less than nonemployed wives. They stated that "fathers are a significant source of primary care when mothers work" (p. 284). Careful attention to this literature demonstrates that fathers serve as primary care providers in response to their wives' paid work schedules (e.g., Brayfield, 1995; Presser, 1988). Care-giving fathers of younger children typically work for pay during daytime hours, and their wives typically work for pay during evening and nighttime hours. Most of the time during which fathers are responsible for young children is when their children are asleep. In contrast, fathers provide day-time, after-school care for older children who have less demanding needs for care.

By not attending to the context in which fathers are fully responsible for their children, Doherty and his colleagues risk exaggerating fathers' involvement, as well as fathers' interest in being involved. We agree that fathers are capable of caring involvement with their children. It is not necessary to exaggerate what fathers do to support this view. That some serve as primary child care givers provides hope that fathers indeed may be more involved in the future.

Doherty and his colleagues argued that "a caring, committed, collaborative marriage" (p. 290) fosters responsible fatherhood. Unstated is the fact that husbands' behavior is a major contributor to this type of marriage (e.g., Gottman, 1998). Husbands who are responsive to and appreciative of their wives and who facilitate their wives' sense of partnership and equality have better quality marriages (Hochschild, 1989; Schwartz, 1994; Thompson, 1991). Coltrane (1989) found that fathers who participate in child care from infancy also have more egalitarian partnerships with their wives. The connection between a collaborative marriage and an involved father may reflect something other than marital quality. The type of man who helps to develop a cooperative marriage may be the type of man who will be an involved father.

Collaborative marriages are not inevitable. Furthermore, prescribing marriage as a solution to the lack of father involvement is not without risk. Marriages characterized by conflict have a negative influence on children (e.g., Buehler et al., 1998; Gottman, 1998). An emphasis on marriage or other aspects of family structure absent of consideration of family process is misguided. . . . Indeed, Demo (1992) concluded that family structure has far less influence on child outcomes than is assumed. Data on fathering demonstrate that marriage is neither a sufficient nor a necessary context for responsible fathering. In considering her findings and those of others, King concluded that relationship quality, an important precursor to marital stability, is not changed easily by intervention or by social policy. . . .

Father Involvement

The literature in family science has attended increasingly to fathers, highlighting their importance to their children, and arguing that their contributions have been minimized. Although the authors reviewed a chapter by Pleck (1997) concluding that heterosexual, married, biological fathers are significantly more involved now than they were 20 years ago, empirical evidence suggests otherwise. In 1988, Ralph LaRossa highlighted the disjunction between the culture and the conduct of fatherhood. All evidence suggests that this disjunction continues to exist. Doherty et al. stated their intention to avoid between-gender comparisons but pointed out that fathers' involvement remains well below that of mothers. Our point is that fathers' involvement is well below that of the cultural standard for fathers.

Studies using nationally representative data sets show little change in residential and nonresidential father involvement over time, and no influence or weak influence on child outcomes when fathers are involved (e.g., Cooksey and Fondell, 1996; Harris, et al., 1998; Stephen, 1996). For example, despite public and scholarly discourse to the contrary, except during the 1990–1991 economic recession, there was virtually no change from the mid-1960s to 1993 in the proportion of preschoolers cared for by fathers when mothers are employed (Casper and O'Connell, 1998). King's (1994) research is illustrative of the literature on the involvement of nonresidential fathers. Using the National Longitudinal Survey of Youth, she reported "that there is only limited evidence to support the hypothesis that 'non-resident father involvement has positive benefits for children'" (p. 970). Other researchers (Mott et al., 1997) have found no significant long-term effects of father absence on children's behavior (see also Argys et al., 1998).

One consistent and key predictor of father involvement is education. . . . Highly educated men appear to have adopted a cultural standard for fathers that is at odds with fatherhood as practiced by the vast majority of men, most of whom have far less education. Given that education is so important in predicting fathers' involvement, policies and programs should stress greater access to and support for education for all men so as to encourage responsible fatherhood.

Fatherhood, Motherhood, and Social Location

Doherty and his colleagues suggested that, in comparison with mothers, fathers suffer disproportionately from negative social forces, such as racism, that inhibit them from being involved with their children. Fathers of color do suffer from racism, but so do mothers and children (e.g., Hill Collins, 1992). Oppression based on social location is a system of interacting influences: racism, classism, sexism, heterosexism, and ageism. Some individuals are affected by more of these influences than are others.

Additionally, fathers have greater access to economic resources than mothers do, and this fact shapes both fathering and mothering (Gerson, 1993; LaRossa, 1988). There are fewer deterrents to fathers' than to mothers' participation in paid labor, a highly valued activity, and fathers have greater discretion than mothers to participate in child care, a less valued activity. Fathers lose status when they participate in labor defined as "women's work" (Gerson, 1993; Hochschild, 1989). Thus, not all fathers choose to be involved. For fathers to become more responsible for child care and more involved with their children would require a restructuring of paid and unpaid work. This restructuring would necessitate fathers giving up paternal privilege (Goode, 1982).

Who Is Responsible for Responsible Fathers?

We do not agree that Doherty et al.'s model is a contextual, social constructionist one. Any such model would attend to a number of features absent from their analysis. We note, for example, their failure to attend to a key feature of the needs of children: that they are socially constructed. Children's "needs" have evolved over time to shape and control the behaviors of mothers as much as they have been about promoting children's development (Ambert, 1994; Ehrenreich and English, 1978; Gerson, 1985). Fatherhood, motherhood, and childhood are *all* social constructions. A fully contextual model cannot ignore this key fact, nor the patriarchal context in which this social construction occurs.

Another context the authors ignored is the gendered nature of mothering and fathering in the United States. Their model disproportionately placed responsibility for fathers' involvement with their children on women. Instead of identifying things mothers can do to "move men in the direction of more responsible fathering" (p. 288)—activities destined to be described as nagging—we ask what responsibility *men* have for being responsible fathers?

We share the authors' inclusive and flexible definition of who can nurture, discipline, and provide for children. In an ideal world, parenting—the activities of nurturing, disciplining, and providing for children—would be work taken up by women *and* by men according to their individual proclivities and within a climate of economic justice and an ethic of care at all levels of society (Okin, 1989). We do not live in such a society, however. In our society, women and men do not have access to the same level of economic resources, nor are they held equally accountable for the undervalued activity of caring for dependent people. Any definition of responsible fathering must reflect the real world, even if it aims for a better world in the future.

Does Father Figure? Do Children Really Need Their Fathers? New Studies Suggest They Do—Children Reared in Families with Fathers Are More Intellectually and Socially Capable

The Vancouver Sun

An old family friend leans over her pasta at the local nouvelle grill, smiles and tells you her sister-in-law has just had a baby via the stud services of an obliging man.

Everyone, she reports, is happy with the arrangement: the mother, because she wanted a baby but didn't want a husband; the father, because he can go back to his happy-go-lucky life in another city; even the grandparents, because now they have—to their surprise and delight—a granddaughter to dote on.

Your friend pauses, as if she had just sailed into a sudden qualm: "That's okay, right? I mean, the baby's a girl, so it's not like she really needs a father . . . is it?"

You've probably had or heard some version of this conversation. Certainly, unless you've been living underground, you've gotten the message through the media that for late 20th century style families, dads have become an optional attachment.

Not only have fathers become "unnecessary," but it has become politically incorrect to suggest otherwise. (Remember the abuse rained on former U.S. vice-president Dan Quayle when he impugned the single-motherhood of TV character Murphy Brown?)

We live in a climate where even to hint that kids might be better off with two parents is to insult all the single mothers struggling to raise children on their own. And they are many: A recent study by the Annie E. Casey Foundation showed that 24 percent of children in the U.S. lived in homes without fathers last year.

They are living this way because more mothers are having children without marrying, and more fathers are leaving their families or not making themselves part of the family in the first place.

But the question remains: Do children really need fathers? Is there any hard, scientific evidence that dads contribute anything to the healthful and happy development of their children that a mother cannot give them?

Actually, there is.

Fathers have a positive effect on their children in several ways. By nurturing, questioning, listening, sympa-thizing, stimulating and challenging them, they give their children intellectual and emotional food and drink.

Children reared with fathers will grow up to be more intellectually competent, socially capable and emotionally mature than children who are not, says Emory University psychologist John Snarey.

In *How Fathers Care for the Next Generation* . . . Snarey reports on his study of 176 grown-up children (25 years old and older) to determine whether their fathers' participation in raising them would predict their "educational and occupational success" in later life.

What he found may seem counterintuitive.

The daughters who were most successful as adults were those whose fathers had encouraged and supported them in athletic and competitive endeavors. The most successful sons were those whose fathers pushed them academically and intellectually.

And both had received high levels of social and emotional support from their fathers throughout their childhood and adolescence.

So the most successful daughters were those whose fathers played catch with them or taught them how to drive a basketball up to the net.

Such daughters, Snarey says, are "able to be persons in their own right, that is, to be autonomous, to be an individual. When a girl can go to the backboard in basketball against her father, she can also stand up against some other guy in the boardroom. There's a certain kind of ego-strength or gutsiness that comes out of that."

And the most successful sons were those whose fathers encouraged them to hit the books and to think about and question things.

"It's not that fathers shouldn't teach their sons how to pitch," Snarey says. "But if you really want to make a difference in your son's life, in addition sit down with the sports page with him."

And, he says, the best father is the one who listens, the one who asks "How did you feel when you lost that game?" and lets his son or daughter talk it through.

But what about children who don't have fathers, who live apart from their fathers through divorce or, because they were born to mothers unwed, never had fathers to begin with?

What are the prospects for those children?

Continued

Not good, says David Blankenhorn, author of *Fatherless America: Confronting Our Most Urgent Social Problem*.

Blankenhorn, the founder and president of the Institute for American Values, a nonpartisan group that focuses on family issues, has amassed evidence to show that boys and girls growing up in homes without fathers are disadvantaged.

Besides being—more often than not—poor, they "are far more likely than other children to be expelled or suspended from school, to display emotional and behavioral problems, to have difficulty getting along with their peers, and to get in trouble with the police."

Boys who don't have fathers to teach them what it means to be a man adopt the "aggression and swagger of boys who must prove their manhood all by themselves," and they often prove it by committing violent crimes.

Girls—desperate for male approval—are getting pregnant.

Meanwhile, the number of unwed mothers is increasing.

Earlier this month, the National Center for Health Statistics reported that the over-all birth rate to unmarried women has grown by more than 50 per cent since 1980, with 1.2 million babies born to unwed mothers in the U.S. in 1992. In Canada, the rate has also doubled in the same period, with more than one-quarter of Canadian babies now born to unwed mothers.

Blankenhorn attributes this to a shift in our values.

"I think it has to do with a cultural shift to a much more individualistic, me-centred society in which increasingly we believe that our main responsibility is to ourselves," he says. "Larger moral purposes such as marriage, family and community tend to recede and take second place."

Source: Kenton Robinson, "Does father figure? Do children really need their fathers?" Copyright 1995, *Hartford Courant*. Reprinted with permission.

Unit Six

SOCIAL INEQUALITY
Introduction: Causes and Consequences of Social Inequality

◆ ◆ ◆

What is inequality? What are various aspects of unequal distribution of scarce resources? Why are some people rich and others poor? Are rich people born rich or is their wealth as a result of their motivation and hard work? Are rich people healthier than poor people? Do the rich control the government and political apparatus more than the poor? Answers to these questions are provided in this and subsequent chapters and are part of understanding the nature, causes, and consequences of unequal distribution of education, wealth, power, and prestige.

One way to answer these questions is to present a classic view of this subject by Kingsley Davis and Wilbert Moore (1945). According to them, the main **functional necessity** for every society is to motivate and place individuals in the social structure. That is to say, for Davis and Moore, a society must induce its members to perform the duties of various positions in the social structure.

A society must concern itself with motivation at two different levels:

1. Instill in individuals the desire to fill certain positions in society.
2. Once in these positions, these individuals should have the desire to perform the duties attached to them.

However, some positions are more desirable, others require special talents or training, and still others are functionally more important for the society than others. Therefore, the question is how to ensure that important social duties are performed with diligence. Davis and

Moore's answer is differential rewards. A society must have some types of rewards that help to induce members performing important jobs and must have some way of distributing these rewards according to the importance of these positions. There are various rewards that a society can use in order to ensure that essential services are performed. These include:

1. Material rewards: the things that contribute to sustenance and comfort.
2. Recreational rewards: the things that contribute to humour and diversion.
3. Symbolic rewards: the things that contribute to self-respect and ego expansion.

Therefore, according to Davis and Moore, social inequality is an unconsciously evolved device by which societies ensure that the most important positions are conscientiously filled by the most qualified persons, who are in turn rewarded according to their contribution to society. According to this understanding, every society, no matter how simple or complex, must differentiate people in terms of both prestige and esteem, and must therefore possess a certain amount of institutionalized inequality. But how should we distribute rewards? What positions should get more rewards, and hence have the highest rank in the system of inequality? Davis and Moore respond that most rewards should be given to positions that have the greatest functional importance for the society, require the greatest training or talent and are most **scarce** in terms of finding people who can fill these positions.

Davis and Moore stated that a person's qualifications can come about through inherent capacity, talent, and training. Therefore, if the required skills are scarce (because of rarity of talent or the costliness of training), the position must have an attractive reward attached to it so that it draws the necessary skills in competition with other positions. This means, in effect, that the position must be high in the social scale—must command great prestige, high salary, ample leisure, and the like.

Many critics have questioned this explanation of inequality. Among these, Melvin M. Tumin (1953) is well known. First, Tumin agreed that social inequality is present everywhere in society. However, he questioned whether it is inevitable and positively functional to society. He asked the following questions: What does it mean to be "functionally important," or how do we know which position has "survival value" for the social structure? In order to answer these questions we need to identify and calculate functionality and know what is the minimum versus maximum survival requirement of a society. For example, although an engineer is functionally important to society, so too is the unskilled worker without whom engineers could not do the work. Similarly, is a mother less functional to the survival of the society than a doctor? Can a society exist without children being born and raised?

Second, Tumin also questioned whether only a limited number of individuals in any society have the talents or can be trained to have the skills appropriate for the more functionally important positions. The problem here is that not all talents are recognized in a society. In fact, the existence of inequality may make it more difficult to recognize and realize such talents. For example, access to education depends upon the wealth of one's parents, and when wealth is differentially distributed, large segments of the population are likely to be deprived of the chance to even *discover* their talents. Moreover, the unequal distribution of rewards in one generation tends to result in the unequal distribution of motivation in the succeeding generation. Parents pass their wealth and knowledge to their children, who in turn benefit from such resources. There is some noticeable tendency for upper-class to restrict further access to their privileged positions, once they have sufficient power to enforce such restrictions. For example, they may limit access to upper-class clubs, which are sources of job networks and within-class marriages. Therefore, the upper class tends to limit the opportunity for upward mobility of individuals from lower classes.

Accordingly, stratification systems are *inherently antagonistic* and not functional to the development of equality of opportunity and realization of talents.

Third, Tumin questioned whether the allocation of differential rewards in scarce and desired goods and services is the only or the most efficient way of recruiting appropriate talent to these positions. There are other motivational schemes that may be more efficient and adequate. People may work for the "joy of work," "instinct for workmanship," "intrinsic work satisfaction" or "social duty."

Finally, the argument that higher rewards should be given to those who sacrifice money and time in order to train themselves is more of a justification of inequality by the powerful than an explanation of inequality. For example, in Canada, children of the privileged class sacrifice little since the education system is largely subsidized by the taxpayers. Even if we accept that there is such a sacrifice, it is not often the individuals who undergo the sacrifice but their parents. There is ample evidence that shows that privileged parents are better able to help their children attain higher education than are less-privileged parents (see debate).

As another example, the debate in this section shows the importance of parents' social standing for their children's access to scarce resources. As we know, one of the main reasons that students continue with their education past high school is because they want to get a degree relevant to a well-paying job. But how does one know what is a good education? In fact, is entry into higher education a matter of students' choice, or rather, is it prescribed through their class or origin? Do children of upper classes have a higher likelihood of enrolling in colleges or universities, acquiring a degree, and obtaining a good job than those of the lower classes? Answers to these questions have preoccupied sociologists and policy-makers for a long time.

Anisef, Ashbury, and Turrittin attempted to provide answers to such questions in 1974 by evaluating students who first responded to survey questions when in grade 12 in Ontario and were the subjects of the survey for 14 years, ending in 1988. The researchers' primary interest was whether types of schooling (university or college) make a difference in occupational attainment. Their finding was consistent with what was expected: that university graduates do better than college graduates (see also box insert). Anisef, Ashbury, and Turrittin also found that parents' socioeconomic status had a strong influence on their children's own socioeconomic status. Therefore, type of educational system and social-class background both are important for the chance of success in the labour market. Upper-class children are more likely to go to university and get a good job. Anisef et al. also argued that type of education (i.e., university versus college degrees) is more important than numbers of years pursuing an education.

Anisef, Ashbury, and Turrittin's research is criticized by Guppy. Guppy does not disagree with the importance of parents' social class or even with the role of university compared to college in improving students' access to higher income and resources. His disagreement is primarily with Anisef et al.'s discussion that *type* of education is more important than *years* of education. Guppy argued that type and years of education are, in fact, correlated. Accordingly, those who go to university are more likely to have higher numbers of years of education (since they generally can) than those who go to college (since they generally cannot). That is, one can basically allocate two years of studying for a college degree, but four years are necessary for an undergraduate university degree. Therefore, Anisef et al.'s conclusion could be spurious. A **spurious relationship** is when we state that B causes C, when in fact both B and C are caused by A, making the original causal argument spurious. The reason for Anisef et al.'s emphasis on the effect of type of education rather than on education itself on income is the result of the structural differences between the two education systems and not type or years of education. Another problem with Anisef et al.'s research is their argument that the effect of education on income is limited up to the time one gets a job. They argue that "once a person has entered the labour market, education has done its job." Guppy states that this is incorrect, too. The reason Anisef et al. found that education has no effect after entering the labour market was because they controlled for its effect by analyzing college and university graduates differently. That is, their empirical model, by definition, takes into account the education effect and thus fails to show education's lifelong effect. Other research has shown that education effect is a life-long process and is one of the best predictors of occupational attainment.

The proceeding discussion suggests that Davis and Moore were correct in saying that talent and skill as measured by education is important for access to higher resources such as income. However, critics are also correct in arguing that parental social class is important for students' access to resources. In fact, critics argue that education effect itself is due to parental class effect.

Thus, Guppy suggested that education's (as a substitute for talent, motivation, and skill) effect on income is spurious in the sense that upper-class children get better education because of their social class and thereafter higher income.

Tumin's critique of Davis and Moore is rooted in a Marxian argument that sees inequality in class positions as a fundamental source of other inequalities. According to Marx, in order to live we need to eat, and in order to eat we need to produce. Therefore, those who control the production process also control other aspects of life, such as the distribution of rewards. For example, capitalists own the means of production, such as factories, technology, and land. They decide who to hire, for how long, and in what capacity, as well as what to produce, how to produce it, and in what quantity. In contrast, workers, not having any ownership of means of production, are forced to sell their labour power to the capitalists for wages that allow them to maintain a minimum level of subsistence. Marxists argue that the difference in wages paid to the workers and the income received by the capitalists through selling the products produced by the workers constitutes **surplus value,** and is called **exploitation.** Therefore, the more the workers produce, the richer capitalists become, while the workers remain at the subsistence level (see Table 6.1, which shows an expanding wealth gap in Canada). That is to say, for Marxists, the difference in income or rewards among people is a function of class relations and has little to do with motivation and hard work.

Moreover, Marxists point to the importance of class relations in producing alienating environments for human beings. Recall that Marx started from a truism that in order to live we must eat and in order to eat we must produce. Therefore, production of human needs and wants is the first historical social act that also fundamentally differentiated humans and animals. True, animals produce too, but animals produce instinctively and for their immediate use. Humans produce universally, for many generations to come, and they produce creatively. In the process of production, human beings use their labour power, their creativity, to modify nature. The outcome of their creativity is their product (i.e., the object). However, humans may lose control of their creativity or their object of creation. Marx argued that once they lose control over their product in terms of how and when to produce it, or if their product is taken away from them, humans become alienated from their labour power, their creativity, their humanity, their species-being.

According to Marx, there are four types of **alienation:**

1. Alienation from the *products* of workers' labour: Under capitalism, workers sell their labour power for wages. As a result, they do not have control over their product, the purpose for which it is created, how it is disposed of, its quantity or quality, and its content. Capitalist production depends on the extent to which it creates profit for the capitalist, not for the needs and desires of workers. Workers are only entitled to their predetermined wages. Capitalists can ensure that workers produce more by introducing new technology. However, though workers' productivity increases and profit for the capitalist increases, the workers' wages do not increase. Whatever profit is created as a result of their work goes to the capitalist. Therefore, the more the workers produce, the more profit is created, and the richer the capitalists become, while the workers become relatively poor.

2. Alienation from the *work process:* Since workers have sold their labour power, they also do not have control over the organization of work—the manner in which the work is organized, divided, and allocated—and what tools or machineries are used. Employers have the power to decide whether or not work will be performed and can deny workers the realization of their human potential and creativity.

3. Alienation from *self:* Marx views work as a medium of self-expression, self-development, and creativity. But work has become a means for physical survival; it has become a means to an end. Workers sell their labour power for money in order to buy with money what they need to satisfy their physical needs. Thus, work takes on an instrumental meaning: a means to an end, not an end in itself. Again, in this process, humans are estranged from their humanity. It is not a surprise that people use the expression "Thank God It's Friday" so cheerfully. Only in one or two days in the week do they do what they want for themselves and not for others.

4. Alienation from *one another:* People are placed in different hierarchical positions. Some are employers, others are workers, and so on. This produces different interests and is a source of social conflict. The consequence is that people of different classes do not interact or intermarry.

We notice that the sources of alienation are not in the person but in the social structure. Rinehart (1987) distinguishes three sources of alienation.

1. The institution of private property ensures concentration of wealth in the hands of a few. However, there is a large group of people who have nothing to sell or exchange in the market except for their labour power. The first group, who own the means of production, decides what and how things are to be produced, and how work is to be organized. The second group, who does not own the means of production, similarly does not have control over the process or organization of work. Therefore, the first group tends to alienate the second group from work, its process and products.

2. Market is another source of alienation. Under a market situation, decisions are made based on prices and profits. The calculation of pecuniary gains overrides other human considerations. For example, in order to increase profit, employers may need to ensure a higher shelf life for a product. This means that in its creation, the product will have preservatives that could be harmful to human beings. Therefore, the market tends to produce an alienating environment whereby workers become unemployed. Similarly, the law of demand and supply limits the workers and capitalists alike to be able to decide on what to be produced. For example, it may be that there is more demand for military equipment than baby food. If so, profitability of producing guns will direct investment away from baby foods to the military industry.

3. **Division of labour** also produces alienation in that it separates individuals into skill groups or specialization levels. Mental labour is separated from manual labour, and conception of work is separated from its execution. Work becomes more fragmented, repetitive, and mindless.

Marx's views on inequality, however, have not gone unchallenged. For example, Max Weber objected to Marx's emphasis on property relations as the only axis of class relations. Weber defined **class** as numbers of people who share similar opportunities for acquiring material goods in the market. For him, marketable skills in addition to property relations are important determinants of class. He also distinguished status from class. **Status** refers to the relative prestige of an individual and the negative and positive perception by others. Variation in status can be determined by people's evaluation of education, occupation, ethnicity or race, and gender or sex, among other things. Thus, people may value some types of education or occupation more than others. For example, persons operating locomotives, or supervisors in machining occupations often have a higher income than

Table 6.1   Median and Share of Total Net Worth

| All Family Units | Median Net Worth | | | Share of Total Net Worth | | |
	1984	1999	% change	1984	1999	Difference
Deciles						
1st	−1,824	−5,700	−85	−0.5	−0.06	−0.1
2nd	674	101	−12.2	0.1	0	−0.1
3rd	6,743	5,920	6.2	0.5	0.4	−0.2
4th	21,380	22,700	9	1.7	1.3	−0.4
5th	45,365	49,580	3	3.5	2.8	−0.7
6th	72,155	81,466	12.9	5.6	4.7	−1
7th	104,764	129,000	23.1	8.2	7.4	−0.8
8th	147,751	192,500	30.3	11.5	11	−0.6
9th	222,861	299,373	34.3	17.5	17.4	−0.2
10th	464,376	628,100	35.3	51.8	55.7	3.9

Source: Statistics Canada, *The Evolution of Wealth Inequality in Canada,* 1984–1999, Tables 4 and 5, No. 11F009 and No. 187.

teachers, yet the former have lower social status. Similarly, ethnic or racial or gender groups are valued differently in various societies. Women tend to have lower paying jobs whereas men have better paying jobs (see Table 6.2). Another dimension of inequality, according to Weber, is power. **Power** is the ability to influence the behaviour of others despite their opposition. The more power one has, the more one is able to put his or her wishes into practice at the expense of others. In general, Marx emphasized economic relations, whereas Weber had a more multidimensional view of social classes.

owned by the top 50 percent of the population, and less than 6 percent of the wealth is owned by the bottom 50 percent of the population. Why are some people wealthy and others not?

Table 6.2 highlights occupations that are mainly occupied by males and those that are mainly occupied by females. It shows that higher paying jobs and blue-collar jobs are mainly occupied by males. In contrast, clerical and sale occupations or "pink-collar" low-paying jobs are mainly occupied by females. Why do men and women end up in different types of jobs?

TABLE TALK

Table 6.1 shows the median net worth of Canadians. **Median** is the middle point. It is the point at which half of people have a net worth above it and the other half below it. The table reveals that 10 percent of the population have a negative net worth and that their situation has deteriorated—they are more in debt. In contrast, the 10 percent of people own over 50 percent of the wealth, and this has increased between 1984 and 1999. To put it differently, over 94 percent of the wealth in Canada is

QUESTIONS

♦ ♦ ♦

1. What has been important for your educational achievement: your motivation or your parents' socioeconomic positions? Explain why?
2. Are all or most of your friends from a similar socio-economic background? What do you think are the implications of your friends' class background on your success in the past or future?
3. If you were to suggest a practical policy to the prime minister that could reduce inequalities in

Table 6.2   Gender Distribution by Occupation

	Males	Females
Male Occupations		
Heavy equipment operators	97.8	2.2
Construction	96.8	3.2
Forestry, mining and oil	93.1	6.9
Primary production labourers	82.9	17.1
Protective services	81.6	18.4
Professional occupations	61.5	38.5
Senior management	75.3	24.7
Machine operators	70.7	29.3
Female Occupations		
Secretaries	2.1	97.9
Registered nurses and supervisors	5.9	94.1
Child care and home support	6.4	93.6
Assistant occupations in health	13.3	86.7
Cashiers	14.1	85.9
Food and beverage services	22.6	77.4
Clerical	27.3	72.7
Administrative and regulatory	27.4	72.6
Retail sales and clerks	39.9	60.1

Source: Statistics Canada, Census 2001.

Canada, what would that policy be? Why do you think that the policy would have an effect in reducing inequalities?

4. Do we need to motivate people by giving them more money in order to make them work harder? Are there other ways of ensuring that people's needs are met?

5. Why do some students decide to enroll in university instead of college or college instead of university?

6. In your opinion, do employers value the number of years of education or do they value type of education? Do employers value a certain field of study?

7. Is there a difference in cultural values of individuals from different social classes? If yes, in what ways? How do these values affect one's occupational placement?

8. What is surplus value? How is it created?

9. List some occupations that you think result in an alienating environment? Why do you think these occupations are more alienating than others?

Differential Effects of University and Community College Education on Occupational Status Attainment in Ontario

Paul Anisef
York University

Fredrick D. Ashbury
York University

Anton H. Turrittin
York University

◆ ◆ ◆

INTRODUCTION

◆ ◆ ◆

Numerous studies document how the "number of years" of schooling significantly affect adult socio-economic status attainment (Hunter, 1988). However, few researchers have focused on the impact of "type of post-secondary institution" on occupational status outcomes (Turrittin, Anisef, and MacKinnon, 1982; Monk-Turner, 1988). Key exceptions have been the recent studies in the United States by Dougherty (1987) and by Monk-Turner (1988). There are important differences, Monk-Turner believes, between community colleges and universities that scaling years of schooling clouds. "Community colleges do not just offer two years of a college education," Monk-Turner declares, "rather they offer a different kind of education. There are significant qualitative differences between community college and four year college institutions" (1988: 148).

Both Dougherty and Monk-Turner find that graduates of community colleges do less well in terms of average occupational status and average earnings relative to four-year college graduates (the equivalent of universities in Canada). Both authors note the large increase in community college enrollments in the U.S. in the last 30 years, and both authors recognize the role that community colleges play in offering another path for social mobility, especially for youth from working-class and minority backgrounds. We are invited to consider, therefore, that attending a community college impacts on individuals' occupational status outcomes differently than undertaking a course of study at university. Such "differences" frame the research problem, that is, the anticipation of significant status attainment outcomes differ across the community colleges and universities of Ontario.

We contend that these differences are related to the stratification in Ontario, and reflect the impact of secondary school stratification as well as an increasing degree of internal stratification among post-secondary institutions. . . . Breton appropriately emphasizes that an adolescent's views about class of destination can be explained as much,

From Paul Anisef, Fredrick D. Ashbury, and Anton H. Turrittin, "Differential effects of university and community college education on occupational status attainment in Ontario," *Canadian Journal of Sociology* 17(1) 1992, pp. 69–83.

if not more, by a high school's internal stratification system (e.g., organization of curriculum into programs of study) as by class of origin (1970: 17). Porter, Porter, and Blishen, in a subsequent analysis, support this view and suggest that, despite gains that many underprivileged children make, the structure of educational inequality is reproduced from generation to generation as those from different backgrounds are prepared for their respective stations and callings (1982: 315). This reproduction of inequality extends to the post-secondary level and a substantial body of research has "consistently replicated the finding that over the course of this century students from families of higher socio-economic status are more likely than their less privileged peers to enter post-secondary education, especially university" (Guppy and Pendakur, 1989: 50).

It is common knowledge that Canada's post-secondary education expanded dramatically after 1960. While the expansion of universities is often noted, there ought to be equal awareness concerning the growth of community colleges in the same period. In fact, from the early 1960s to the middle 1980s, the portion of students enrolled in non-university post-secondary institutions rose from 30 percent to just over 40 percent of all post-secondary enrollments. . . . The community colleges are especially interesting institutions because, by adopting a multi-purpose curriculum with an emphasis on an "open" admissions policy, community colleges have attracted a much wider cross-section of society, in socio-economic terms, compared to universities (Dennison, 1984: 142). Thus, colleges have been viewed as a major democratizing force equalizing educational opportunities and helping to flatten occupational stratification (Fortin, 1987).

The expansion of Canadian post-secondary education did lead to increases in the diversification of institutions at this level and increases in the absolute chances of university and community college attendance for all segments of society. However, the reproduction of inequalities has been sustained by stratification among universities and colleges. While community colleges have provided new opportunities for working-class youth, universities, despite their enrollment growth, have remained the preserve of the middle and upper middle classes. . . .

RESEARCH PROBLEM, DATA, AND METHODS

◆ ◆ ◆

Our primary objective is to measure the impact of post-secondary type of education on occupational status attainment. Much of the status attainment and stratification liter-

ature has led us to hypothesize greater occupational status returns, on the average, for university than for community college or other vocational post-secondary graduates. This analysis will identify the influence of type of post-secondary institution first entered on current career outcomes as measured by the Blishen occupational status index. . . .

A full accounting of the impact of post-secondary institution on occupational attainment is beyond the scope of this paper. To do so would require a theorizing of the links between social background factors of individuals and groups; individual agency; the internal stratification of elementary, intermediate, and secondary school systems; the internal stratification of universities, colleges, and other post-secondary institutions; employer behaviour; and features of the labour market. With respect to background factors, for example, it is widely known that socio-economic status, gender, ethnicity, and rural-urban residence have played key roles at every stage of the educational process ultimately leading to entry into the labour force.

We recognize the salience that some authors (Hunter, 1988) have given to both years of schooling and type of educational certification (degree or diploma) as measures of educational attainment. In the American literature on higher education, there is a debate as to whether years of education or type of educational institution attended is more significant in understanding the occupational attainment process (Dougherty, 1987; Monk-Turner, 1988). If our Ontario data base had encompassed many generations of respondents, employment of years of education would have been an appropriate measure of educational attainment. With recent cohorts of Ontario population, years of education is not meaningful; youth populations cluster at the last years of education offered by the main educational institutions, the high schools, community colleges, and universities.

While it would have been desirable to have developed a years of education variable for our data, we can do so only by returning to our respondents. A years of education variable is actually quite difficult to construct given the significant numbers that now engage in part-time education, start one degree but then change to another, attend other types of post-secondary educational schools, etc. Standard questions such as "How many years of schooling have you completed altogether?" when coded in terms of whole years, simply ask respondents to estimate a year level without giving the researcher the control over the act of data reduction that goes into a respondent providing a codable answer. Our regression analysis and occupational analysis both lead to the conclusion that type of educational institution is critical for analyses of occupational status attainment process.

The initial survey of the educational and occupational intentions of grade 12 Ontario students was based on a random sample of 99 secondary schools selected from across Ontario (Anisef, 1975: Appendix 3) of which 97 agreed to participate. Ultimately, 2,555 students were surveyed during the spring of 1973 (response rate of 86.6 percent). Two subsequent phases of the research consisted of follow-up telephone interviews conducted in the fall of 1973 and 1974. In the 1979 Phase Four, 1,522 persons or 59.6 percent of the original Phase One sample were contacted again; at this time respondents were approximately 23 years of age.

In the summer of 1987 (Phase Five), 14 years after the initial study, the relocation of Phase Four respondents was initiated and completed in the summer of 1988. Of the 1,522 persons in Phase Four, the researchers were successful in relocating 1,222 respondents, 80.3 percent of the Phase Four and 47.8 percent of the original Phase One sample. These individuals were briefly interviewed by telephone. It should be stressed that the purpose of this telephone interview was to relocate respondents and to obtain only a few new pieces of data. Because of the limited nature of this follow-up (a full-scale follow-up study is intended in the future), our present occupational information was similarly limited to a few questions.

Phase Five respondents, at the time of the telephone interview, were about 32 or 33 years of age. Those respondents that did not enter post-secondary education after leaving high school would have been 15 years into careers by 1988. Those that chose to enter a community college or university program would have been at least 10 years into their careers by 1988. In 1979, 36 percent of respondents had no further post-secondary education, 24 percent had attended community college, and 36 percent had attended university. By 1988, the proportion with only high school education had dropped to 31 percent, 27 percent had now attended or obtained a community college certificate, and almost 40 percent now had university and/or professional courses or degrees. That is to say, since the summer of 1979, 23 percent of respondents obtained some form of further education. Of the respondents with additional education after 1979, both men and women had similar patterns of further educa-

Table 1   Means for Variables in the Regression Models

Variable	University			College			Combined Group		
	Mean	Std Dev	Cases	Mean	Std Dev	Cases	Mean	Std Dev	Cases
GENDER	.494	.501	387	.590	.493	251	.531	.499	638
SES	.85	.226	375	−.029	.205	239	.041	.225	614
STRATA	2.530	1.109	387	2.896	1.098	251	2.674	1.118	638
FAMSIZE	3.523	1.379	386	3.816	1.504	250	3.638	1.436	636
PROG	.915	.280	386	.664	.473	247	.817	.387	633
HSGPA	.640	.481	381	.390	.489	249	.541	.499	630
FAMENC	2.871	1.149	387	2.717	1.178	251	2.810	1.162	638
NONFAMENC	2.527	1.097	387	2.462	1.078	251	2.502	1.089	638
SCA	.076	.111	387	−.005	.131	250	.044	.126	637
LOE	59.546	14.259	313	50.057	13.260	211	55.725	14.615	524
LEE	2.757	.526	325	2.087	.625	207	2.496	.654	532
BLISHEN79	53.434	12.058	235	49.596	9.548	198	51.679	11.135	433
PSTYPE88			387			253	.395	.489	640
SEXED88	5.974	2.002	387	4.769	1.479	251	.625	.836	638
BLISHEN88	60.255	10.099	336	52.120	10.631	222	57.019	11.048	558

Missing data were treated using the pairwise technique available in SPSSX.

tion, except that fewer women went on to higher professional degrees than men. Approximately 69 percent of Phase Five respondents were married at the time of the follow-up interview, and 59 percent had at least one child.

DATA ANALYSIS

◆ ◆ ◆

Using our fifteen variables we developed a regression model for all post-secondary graduates (combined group) that explained 37.2 percent of the variance (adjusted value) and demonstrated that type of educational institution (PSTYPE88) was statistically significant in explaining current occupational status attainment. To further under-

stand the impact of type of institution, we developed separate regression models for university and college of applied arts and technology (CAAT) graduates. The mean values and standard deviations for all of these regressions are shown in Table 1. The unstandardized and standardized coefficients, statistical significance, and variance explained for each of the three regressions are shown in Table 2.[1]

Differences between university and college students are evident with respect to the means of our variables in Table 1. Compared to students graduating from CAATS, university students on average have higher socio-economic status, are more frequently from large urban centres, are from smaller families, are disproportionately from academic programs in high school, receive stronger

Table 2   Multiple Regression with Current Occupation as Dependent Variable for University Graduates, College Graduates, and the Combined Group

Variable	University graduates[1]			College graduates			Combined group		
	B	beta	Var exp	B	beta	Var exp	B	beta	Var exp
GENDER[2]	−1.422	−.071	.021	1.896	.088	.007	−1.665	.075	.007
SES	5.081*	.114	.026	5.726	.110	.026	4.795**	.098	.052
STRATA	−.658	−.072	.019	−.156	.016	.004	−.426	.043	.021
FAMSIZE	.888*	.121	.000	−.583	−.082	.004	.261	.034	.001
PROG[2]	−3.046	−.084	.000	−3.441**	−.153	.001	−2.945**	.103	.007
HSGPA[2]	.123	.006	.014	.838	.039	.012	.326	.015	.028
FAMENC	.750	.085	.010	−.476	−.053	.000	.271	.028	.003
NONFAMENC	−.176	−.019	.000	.381	.039	.002	.125	.012	.001
SCA	4.937	.054	.015	2.070	.025	.012	4.484	.051	.021
LOE	.052	.074	.016	.088	.109	.038	.073**	.097	.035
LEE	−.495	−.026	.001	1.632	.096	.004	.521	.031	.009
PSTYPE88[2]							−10.779***	−.477	.035
SEXED88							3.728*	.282	.013
BLISHEN79[2]	.421***	.502	.214	.510***	.458	.188	.434***	.437	.165
CONSTANT	35.451***			23.063***			32.989***		
CONSTANT[3]	59.261***			54.449***					
ADJUSTED R[2]		.290***			.242***			.372***	

1. Includes those persons with post-graduate and professional degrees beyond university graduation.

2. Dummy variables with 0 = omitted category and 1 = present category. See Note 3 for details.

3. Value of constants when independent variables are transformed by their total sample mean values (see text for further explanation).

* = p < .10, ** = p < .05, *** = p < .01

family and non-family encouragement for pursuing post-secondary education, have more positive self-concepts of ability, and have higher educational and occupational expectations in high school. Higher Blishen scores are attached to first occupations of university graduates compared with CAAT graduates, with the difference being even greater for current occupations. In short, a reward for university attainment is a higher status occupation.

It will be noted in Table 2 that the intercepts indicate whether type of post-secondary institution is consequential for current occupational status. Before running each regression, the mean for the relevant variable for the combined group was subtracted from each variable's value. In effect, this procedure permits us to ask whether university or college graduation results in different occupational status attainment outcomes for the average post-secondary graduate. When the calculations are performed, a five-point Blishen score difference between university and college graduates emerges in favour of university graduates (as shown in the next to the last line of Table 2), this difference being statistically significant.

With respect to the separate regressions for university and college graduates in Table 2, only first job (BLISHEN79) is statistically significant at .01 level in both models. This finding is supported in other research (Boyd, et al., 1985). Once a person has entered the labour market, education has done its job.

When all post-secondary graduates are combined, we have a much larger sample with greater diversity of values on all variables. As the last two columns in Table 2 show, the regression model associated with the combined group yields five variables that are significantly related to current occupational status. These are socio-economic status, program in high school, level of occupational expectation, educational attainment, and first job. The negative sign for educational attainment indicates that, relative to university graduates, college students obtain lower current occupational status, holding all other variables constant.

In keeping with the importance of noting gender differences, the lack of statistical significance for gender when regressions are run separately for university and college graduates should not be construed to mean that gender exerts little impact on educational attainment and occupational opportunity. . . . It is common knowledge that the use of occupational status Blishen scores disguises important differences by gender in labour market locations (Turrittin, Anisef, and MacKinnon, 1982). This has the result of showing women obtaining jobs of equal status to men's jobs when in fact many women are headed into female job ghettos with restricted income and

mobility chances. . . . This effect is shown in Table 3. This table clearly suggests that women and men university and community college graduates head for very different kinds of occupations in the labour market.

DISCUSSION

◆ ◆ ◆

There is controversy concerning whether educational institutions promote social mobility and reduce social status disparities, or whether educational institutions are part of the sorting process that maintains social stratification. . . . With regard to community colleges in the U.S., Dougherty characterizes this debate as one between a functionalist view of the community college, and what he calls the class-reproduction school. The functionalist view sees the community college as serving society by "providing social mobility and teaching the technical skills needed by a complex industrial economy" (Dougherty, 1987: 86). Dougherty cites Medsker (1960: 4) who indicates that the two-year college "is perhaps the most effective democratizing agent in higher education." By contrast, class-reproduction critics believe that community colleges are simply another element in the class-based tracking system reproducing class structure by sorting and sifting young people into educational institutions and subsequent job levels where job status and income are closely related to type of education received and the class background of students (Bowles and Gintis, 1976; Karabel, 1972).

Each of these viewpoints has a certain validity but, at base, they are looking at quite different features of society. A functionalist perspective focuses on mobility and training effects of education for individuals. A class-reproduction perspective examines distributional aspects, in particular how inequalities in the world of work (where income and status are produced) become linked to education and family.

Because community college education does result in occupations with higher prestige scores compared to parent's occupations, students graduating from community colleges may well perceive that they have attained social mobility as a result of their education. Still, our data strongly suggest that universities and colleges are, in fact, doing the jobs that it is generally agreed they are mandated by society to do. Universities prepare youth for high status occupations in the managerial, professional, and white-collar sectors of the occupational structure. The major component of such education is a general education with only a few programs being fairly job specific

Table 3   Current Occupational Distributions by Educational Attainment and Gender

Occupational Category	University Graduates*		Community College Graduates		Total Number	Percent Community College Graduates
	Number	Percent Women	Number	Percent Women		
Engineering professionals	20	0.0	1	0.0	21	4.8
Other professions	64	40.6	6	83.3	70	8.6
School teachers/college teachers	35	74.3	4	100.0	39	10.3
Managers/managerial	52	42.3	11	63.6	63	17.5
Business occupations—financial	32	25.0	10	30.0	42	23.8
Computer programming and related	15	66.7	5	60.0	20	25.0
Law enforcement occupations	6	16.7	2	0.0	8	25.0
Radio/journalism	7	14.3	3	0.0	10	30.0
Farmers/farm workers	3	0.0	2	0.0	5	40.0
Miscellaneous occupations	18	5.6	16	81.3	34	47.1
Salespersons	10	10.0	10	0.0	20	50.0
Self-employment	15	40.0	15	53.3	30	50.0
Secretarial and clerical	20	80.0	25	96.0	45	55.6
Other health occupations	8	100.0	20	90.0	28	71.4
Nursing	9	100.0	29	96.6	38	76.3
Supervisors/forepersons	3	66.7	11	27.3	14	78.6
Skilled trades and technicians	7	0.0	34	2.9	41	82.9
Semi-skilled/unskilled blue collar	1	0.0	12	8.3	13	92.3
Totals	335	43.9	216	54.6	551	39.2

Note: Table excludes respondents where occupation is not known, housewives not in the labour force, and students.

*Includes those with further graduate and professional education.

(engineering at the undergraduate level, and professional education after university graduation). By contrast, the CAAT system is designed for specific occupational training with only some general education. Designed for short-term vocational education as a terminal stream (not linked, in Ontario, to further post-secondary education such as transfer to university), students from community colleges were to enter specific jobs.

That universities and colleges place graduates in different segments of the labour force would not reinforce social stratification and social inequality if the labour market itself was not already stratified by status, gender, and wealth. Group competition in the labour market uses the kinds of certificates generated by educational institutions to restrict opportunity and enhance position. Describing this process in any detail is beyond the scope of this paper. The process is captured in recent theorizing called "closure theory" which draws both from conflict theory and the writings of Max Weber (see Parkin, 1979; Collins, 1979; Murphy, 1984). Collins in particular argues that increasing general levels of education have resulted in rising demands for specific kinds of education by both employers and occupational groups, the former to minimize training costs and obtain certain kinds of individuals, and the latter to protect and enhance position in the labour market associated with status and income. We hypothesize that, while more and more young people in Ontario have obtained post-secondary education, the labour market itself has "adjusted" by the increasing use of certification leading to exclusion, this process resulting in graded occupational outcomes of status matching the new range of educational status outcomes in place of the old narrower range of no or some high school, high school graduation, and university.

The use of credentialism, increasingly prevalent in the Canadian labour market, is supported by professional associations and employed as a mechanism for screening out certain kinds of candidates for positions. This increased emphasis on credentialism parallels the diversification of post-secondary education and the former may well serve to maintain internal stratification among Canadian universities and colleges, particularly with reference to occupational status returns. Increased democratization of post-secondary institutions should ordinarily signal increased social mobility opportunities for working-class college students. However, educational credentialism hampers rather than facilitates the career opportunities of college students. While university students are able to pursue advanced training beyond the baccalaureate degree, post-diploma programs are a relatively small component of the Ontario community college system. This means that credentialism acts as a form of discrimination for college graduates, artificially constraining their career advancement relative to university graduates. Our findings show that the spread in average occupational status (Blishen) points between university and college graduates increases with length of time in the labour market, a spread favourable to university graduates.

Several observations are noteworthy regarding our findings. That status of first occupation correlates highly with current occupational status is a finding common to much mobility research. . . . We hypothesize that, even over long periods of time, people's occupational status scores are not likely to alter substantially. Those that enter lower status occupations are not likely to experience prospects that enhance mobility (unless these jobs are temporary and held by highly qualified persons). Those that enter higher status occupations are not likely to make large moves, especially within the ten year time frame of this study, that would result in substantial increases in occupational status scores. Our data show that university graduates gained on average about seven Blishen score points between first and current job, whereas CAAT graduates gained on average less than three Blishen points.

Our findings apply only to Ontario university and CAAT graduates and are not broken down by field of study or occupational fields entered by graduates. Educational credentialism may affect career advancement but vary across different occupational fields. More research is needed regarding the effects of credentialism and the perception of its influence. In addition, while we have shown that institutional variation at the post-secondary level contributes to our understanding of occupational status attainment, a further disaggregation may be warranted. Lennards (1988) argues that universities themselves should be further differentiated into three types: those which focus on mainly undergraduate teaching, those which develop graduate teaching and research activities but which focus, in the main, on the teaching component, and those which focus on graduate training and research. . . . If this conceptualization is warranted, as we believe it to be, then the effects of type of post-secondary education can be more effectively understood.

Undoubtedly a greater emphasis needs to be given to the dimension of gender in understanding the influence of type of post-secondary institution on occupational attainment. Early American status attainment research neglected women; Canadian mobility research has not made that mistake (Boyd et al., 1985). Significantly, Canadian scholars have been strong critics of status attainment for inadequately theorizing the role of gender (Fox, 1989). Important new theorizing regarding women and work ought to now bring greater adequacy and sophistication to longitudinal studies linking education and work with respect to gender and other group statuses (Fox, 1989; Armstrong and Armstrong, 1990).

Our findings pertain to Ontario, and research of a similar sort is needed in other regions of Canada to confirm or modify the patterns we have established in the Ontario context. The particularities of "type" of post-secondary education in different parts of Canada are worthy of further investigation. As in the U.S., compared to universities, Ontario community colleges recruit different kinds of students, provide a limited general education, strongly focus on vocational training, and typically place graduates in different kinds of occupations. Our research findings support the claim of Monk-Turner and others (Monk-Turner, 1988; Dougherty, 1987) that, with the differentiation and diversification of post-secondary education, we need to examine the quality of education received as well as to examine additional aspects such as internal institutional stratification and the dimensions of gender and other group differences. What we have here are post-secondary educational institutions that recruit particular populations which are not passive recipients of educational programs, but which take part in selection in ways that often affirm traditional and differential gender and class expectations regarding education and occupational goals. This creates some social and occupational mobility both upward and downward. Differences in recruitment and outcomes in the educational system become amplified by the inequalities in job rewards (income, status, power, etc.) which are already embedded in the occupational structure.

The purpose of this paper has been to document the effects of type of post-secondary education on occupational status attainment where previous Canadian research has focused almost exclusively on university education. We propose that this analysis lends itself to a discussion of the effects of credentialism. Institutional differentiation, therefore, is an important factor which must be considered and developed in any research on occupational status attainment.

---

1. The operational definitions of variables utilized in our regression models are as follows. Gender: Gender is coded as 0 = male and 1 = female. SES: Socio-economic status is based on a factor analysis of five 1973 variables including mother's education, father's education, parent's total income, father's occupation (Blishen score), and mother's occupation (Blishen score). This is a continuous variable with values ranging from a low of −0.470 to a high of 0.640. STRATA: Urban/rural school is an ordinal variable which pertains to region of Ontario in which the respondent's high school was located. Values are 1 = Metro Toronto, 2 = other large cities, 3 = smaller cities, and 4 = small towns and rural areas. FAMSIZE: Family size is an interval variable which refers to the number of members of the family in which the respondent was raised, as reported in 1973. PROG: Program in high school as reported in 1979, is coded 0 = commercial/technical/vocational, and 1 = academic. HSGPA: High school grades, is an ordinal variable which reflects respondents' grades or marks in grade 11, as reported in 1973. Values are: 0 = 69 percent or lower, and 1 = 70 percent or more. FAMENC: Family encouragement is a continuous variable referring to family encouragement for continuing education taken from a factor analysis of questions 3a to 3h in the 1973 survey. The range of scores is from a low of 3.659 to a high of 1.969. NONFAMENC: Non-family encouragement is a continuous variable referring to non-family encouragement (by teachers and guidance counsellors, for example) for continuing education taken from a factor analysis of questions 3a to 3h in the 1973 survey. The range of scores is from a low of 4.234 to a high of 3.149. SCA: Self-concept of ability is a continuous variable referring to self-concept of ability to pursue higher education based on a factor analysis of questions 20 to 26 on the 1973 survey. The range is from a low score of −0.505 to a high of 0.335. LOE: Occupational expectation is a Blishen score based on the 1973 survey. Respondents were asked to indicate the job he/she expected to end up doing. LEE: Educational expectation is based on educational plans for the fall 1974 coded as 1 = no postsecondary, 2 = community college, and 3 = university. PSTYPE79: Educational attainment reported in 1979 is coded as 1 = university degree (undergraduate, graduate, postgraduate, or professional degree); 2 = community college, 3 = both university and CAAT, and 4 = no postsecondary. BLISHEN79: Occupational attainment in 1979 is the Blishen score of the respondent's 1979 occupation. PSTYPE88: Educational attainment by 1987-88, as determined in the follow-up telephone survey of respondents, is coded as in PSTYPE79 above, except that further graduate or professional education received a score of 1. This variable was recoded to be 0 = university graduate (and including graduate and professional education), and 1 = community college certificate or diploma. SEXED88: Interaction variable formed as the product of Gender and PSTYPE88. BLISHEN88: Occupational attainment 87/88 is based on the Blishen score.

Commentary and Debate/ Commentaire et débat

Does School Matter: An Invited Comment on Anisef, Ashbury, and Turrittin's "Differential Effects of University and Community College Education on Occupational Status Attainment in Ontario"

Neil Guppy
University of British Columbia

◆ ◆ ◆

Does where you go to school matter? Anisef, Ashbury, and Turrittin (hereafter AAT) argue that it does. They show that university graduates do better than college graduates in attaining high status jobs. That is hardly surprising. Statistics Canada annually publishes tables showing the different incomes of women and men who have attained various educational levels (see e.g., Bellamy and Guppy, 1991: 164).

What makes AAT's paper important is their attempt to explain how education links to paid work. They first suggest that others have erred by concentrating on *years of schooling* rather than on *type of schooling*. They then show that type of schooling (community college versus university) makes a difference to a person's occupational attainment, net of factors like social origin, expectations, first job, and sex. Finally they argue that their central finding can be understood to result from credentialing processes.

For ease of presentation, specificity, and brevity, I will develop my remarks in four successive points.

1. *Type* versus *year*: AAT claim that "attending a community college impacts on individuals' occupational status outcomes differently than undertaking a course of study at university." They attribute this status difference to type of schooling. SES differences could, however, just as easily be attributed to years of schooling since college and university graduates differ on both type and years of schooling. Without a proper methodological design to control for possible spurious effects, a sound interpretation of their results is impossible (comparisons of type versus amount of schooling have been reported by Leiper and Hunter, 1990 and Monk-Turner, 1985, among others).

There is merit in observing that others ignore type of schooling and fasten on years of education. But reversing the process by ignoring amount of schooling

From Neil Guppy, "Does school matter: An invited comment on Anisef, Ashbury, and Turrittin's 'Different effects of university and community college education on occupational status attainment in Ontario,'" *Canadian Journal of Sociology* 17(1) 1992, pp. 85–88.

and focusing only on type of schooling strikes me as equally blinkered. AAT also overstate the case that type of schooling has been neglected. While status attainment researchers focus mainly on years of education, the credentials associated with education streams have not been forgotten. Boyd (1982: 10) interprets her results as showing that "formal schooling has certification properties which qualify or disqualify people from certain kinds of occupations." Furthermore, Jones (1985: 101–61) has a lengthy discussion of the education and occupation link, where schooling is treated as a set of discrete educational types.

2. *Credentials:* AAT claim their results show that "credentialism is becoming increasingly important in the Canadian labour market." This is directly opposite to the view of Hunter (1988: 763) who argues that "strict credentialist arguments do not obviously apply to Canada." Although Hunter's paper is cited, his findings are conveniently ignored.

Exactly how credentialism and type of schooling are equated by AAT is not clear. They provide, at best, only a loose association between type of schooling and credentialism. It is hardly surprising, for example, that nurses trained in colleges have different SES scores than nurses trained in universities. The content of their training differs, their years of training differ, and their certificates differ. AAT imply that it is the type of ticket or diploma, the credential, that matters, not the content of schooling. They may be correct. However, the relevant studies must contrast credentialist and non-credentialist accounts of the general link between education and work. While credentialism plays down the content of education, research on educational outcomes has recently grown (see e.g., Evers and Gilbert, 1992). Non-credentialist explanations, such as human capital theory or market signalling, cannot be ignored. The balance of evidence with which I am familiar, using a comparative design, favours non-credentialist explanations, especially market signalling.

3. *Education's half-life:* AAT claim that "once a person has entered the labour market, education has done its job." This runs counter to most other research. Education is one of the best predictors of life chances, especially occupational attainment. Indeed AAT's data contradict their own conclusion since the gist of their paper is to show that type of schooling makes a difference to occupational SES. The confusion occurs when AAT interpret the results of separate regression models for college versus university graduates. Only first job is statistically significant in both models, but of course education is held constant in each and so education cannot have any lasting effect. It is not that "education has done its job," but that education is constrained from having any effect by their statistical analysis.

Although AAT cite Boyd et al. (1985) to support their claim that only first job affects current occupational SES, AAT's conclusion runs counter to the "principal findings" reported in Boyd et al. (1985: 516) where it is claimed that "educational level has a persistent association with occupational status at career stages beyond entry into the labour force." Education has a long half-life and contrary to AAT's claim, their own data show as much.

4. *Measuring type of education:* As AAT correctly note, the measurement of years of schooling is increasingly difficult as part-time enrollments increase, stopping out escalates, and rates of "parking" or "warehousing" change. However, it is equally the case that the measurement of type of schooling is difficult. First, is college versus university the best way to differentiate within higher education? Differences by field of study might be as, or even more, revealing (in their combined model, AAT show that high school curricular track has an effect on current occupational SES). Second, is there homogeneity within both the college and university sectors? Ryerson is often held up as somewhat anomalous in the Ontario system (AAT's comments on Lennard's [1988] ideas are important here too). Third, how should researchers cope with people holding both college and university certificates, especially in the case of "reverse transfers" (university then college)? Fourth, given the high rates of attrition in the post-secondary system (Gilbert, 1991), how are non-completers to be handled?

Effectively AAT handle measurement problems by excluding everyone except those who have completed either a college or university programme (but not both). People with only some college or university experience are excluded. Furthermore, the difference between college and university is taken as an indicator of "the quality as well as the quantity of post-secondary education." The implication of this is not clear, both in terms of measurement and conceptualization.

Conclusion: AAT ask an important question. Schools are not alike and we need to incorporate that differentiation into our thinking about the education-occupation link. It is also important, however, to consider competing theoretical explanations about the processes underlying this link, and to use these different explanatory models in designing and analyzing our research.

University Education Is Worth the Money

Michael Citrome

But Quebec Wrong to Cut Bursaries. Tuition-Fee Increase Would Be Better Way to Give More Funding to Universities

You've seen the scary numbers: rising tuition rates, skyrocketing student debt. Yet a university education remains one of the few real bargains in our society. You can't afford not to get one.

Statistics saying the average Canadian university student will graduate with $23,000 in debt and that Canada's 2002–03 tuition bill was $3.8 billion, up 10 percent from the previous year, are making students (and parents) wonder whether university is really worth the expense.

But those statistics are misleading, and often pushed by people with a vested interest in making you insecure about the cost of education: student associations hell-bent on cutting tuition rates and/or investment companies out to sell you Registered Education Savings Plans.

Instead of getting people to save for their children's educations, they might lead lower-income families to steer their kids away from university, and/or push debt-averse young people right into the workforce.

That's unfortunate because statistically, a university degree will make you richer, and also will make your career more secure.

The claim that the average Canadian university student graduates with $23,000 in debt would be pretty scary—if it were accurate. In fact, that number applies only to the 55 percent of university students who use student loans, a caveat that frequently goes unmentioned.

And don't pay any attention to those aggregate figures that include all students and put the so-called average debt at around $12,000. That's hogwash. Student debt figures reflect a very real divide between haves and have-nots. Either you borrow or you don't.

Which is why the Quebec Liberal government's decision to turn $103 million of bursaries, which don't have to be paid back, into loans, which do, is particularly vexing. It affects only the have-nots, while the haves happily let mom and dad write tuition cheques.

A better solution would have been to scrap Quebec's eight-year-old tuition freeze, which has made universities poorer as the amount they collect in real dollars shrinks year-to-year with the rising cost of living.

A proportional increase in bursaries would offset rising tuition for the neediest students, while richer ones would still benefit from the lowest tuition rates in Canada, but at a price more sustainable for the universities.

But what about the more than half of students who graduate with that average of $23,000 in debt? Well, when you think about it, $23,000 doesn't seem so bad when you consider that, according to Statistics Canada, a university graduate can expect to earn $1 million more over the course of a lifetime, than someone with only a high school diploma. And the unemployment rate for university graduates is about half that of high-school graduates.

A $1-million return for a $23,000 investment? Sounds too good to pass up. Even if the first few years out of school are a struggle because of loan repayments, it's a very worthwhile investment in the long run.

Too much emphasis is placed on graduating from university debt-free. Taking time off from school to earn money only keeps you in school longer, so your career will be shorter and you'll earn less in the long run.

But why did the total amount that Canadians spend on tuition jump by more than 10 percent in one year? It seems that despite rising costs, university educations are more popular than ever. Enrollment has been steadily rising since the late 1990s, so the total amount of money Canadians spend on tuition is going up because more people are paying tuition. Enrollment is actually rising faster than tuition, maybe even in spite of it.

And as long as more people are seeking post-secondary education, more of our money is going to go to paying tuition. And it's money well spent.

Michael Citrome is a journalist and student. His youth-finance column New Money runs Saturdays in the *Gazette*'s Montreal Works section.

Source: Michael Citrome, "University education is worth the money," *The Gazette*, Montreal, Sept. 17, 2004, p. A21. Reprinted with permission of the author.

Rise and Fall of the Middle Class

Cristobal Young

In *The Wealth of Nations*, free market hero Adam Smith wrote, "wherever there is great property, there is great inequality. For one very rich man, there must be at least five hundred poor." The "invisible hand" of the market was efficient, Smith argued, but obviously not all that fair. It was not until the end of the Second World War that things really changed. A middle class rose from the ranks of industrial workers, along with growing professional occupations.

Jobs were plentiful. New legislation offered unprecedented protection for working people. Trade unions flourished. Workers had the leverage to demand fair wages.

The quality of public education improved dramatically, and post-secondary schooling was subsidized—allowing widespread access to education for the first time. Unemployment Insurance was established, and later, public health care and pensions.

The income, security, and living standards of this new class bridged the chasm between the privileged elite and the impoverished masses.

But over the years, the political and economic forces that created the middle class have reversed and the 19th century class divisions are once more taking root.

Inequality in the U.S. is now greater than at any time since the Second World War. The progress of half a century was wiped out in a right-wing revolution and a binge of corporate and government downsizing.

In New York City, for example, the degree of inequality is now roughly the same as in Guatemala.

Of course, while the U.S. is the richest nation in the world, it has always cherished a belief in "individual responsibility." The wealth has never trickled down that far.

What has happened to Canada's middle class in this time of political and economic upheaval? Michael Wolfson, a top researcher at Stats Canada, set out to tackle the question.

Since the late 1960s, the market-based income (before tax and transfer payments) of Canadian families has changed dramatically. In 1967, about 40 percent of families earned mid-level incomes. By 1994, the middle had fallen to only 25 percent of families.

The decline of the middle class was a very gradual ebb until the 1980s. But the fundamental economic restructuring, and particularly the last recession, rocked our society—eroding the foundations of social equity.

Two hundred years ago, Adam Smith argued that the primary role of government was to protect the riches hoarded by a nation's elite. "The affluence of the rich," Smith wrote, "excites the indignation of the poor. . . . Both driven by want, and prompted by envy," the poor seek to "invade his (the elite's) possessions."

"It is only under the shelter of the civil magistrate," says Smith, "that the owner of valuable property . . . can sleep a single night in security."

"The acquisition of valuable and extensive property," Smith believed, "requires the establishment of civil government."

That was the late 18th century. Today, the role of government is not to protect the elite, but the middle class. While the free market is increasingly marked with disparity, the distribution of total, after-tax family income has not changed much. What has brought stability amid change is government tax and transfer payments.

The social safety net has largely protected Canadians from the soaring poverty of the free market. As market incomes (especially wages) drop, government has made up the difference—more or less. And those few with growing incomes have been taxed back into the middle.

Wolfson's study shows that the middle class—after tax and social transfers—is larger than the free market has ever produced, at about 45 percent of Canadian families. And it's almost unchanged in more than 20 years.

The free market is increasingly incapable of delivering the social and economic justice Canadians have come to expect. And on the battle cry of "less government," the institutions that uphold social equity are under attack.

Social programs, a progressive tax system, and the regulation of corporate profit-making—these policies and levers give us the ability to mold our economic world into something we believe in and cherish. And it is slipping away.

Canada is creeping back to a Smithian era, where in his words, "the affluence of the few supposes the indigence of the many."

And as the layers of government created to protect the middle class are vilified and stripped away, we are increasingly left with a Smithian government—a government that exists largely to shelter Canada's elites from the society they created.

Cristobal Young is a researcher at the Greater Victoria Child and Youth Advocacy Society.

Source: Cristobal Young, "Rise and fall of the middle class," *Times-Colonist*, May 21, 1997, p. 1. Reprinted with permission of Dr. Cristobal Young, Department of Sociology, Princeton University.

Unit Seven

EDUCATION
Introduction: Education and Students' Response

◆ ◆ ◆

Every individual is exposed to some type of education, and almost all people are exposed to formal education (see Figure 7.1). Education is one of the fundamental institutions that shapes our awareness of the world and helps ensure we have more opportunities in the labour market. How and why does education shape our awareness, knowledge, and labour market opportunities? Does education ensure upward opportunities or does it reproduce existing inequalities? Is there anything in the educational curriculum that helps one group succeed more than another group? These are the types of questions that will be addressed in this chapter.

Formally, educational institutions adhere to the principle of social justice. Basically, all people are given equal opportunity to develop their talents, regardless of their class, gender, or race/ethnicity. Informally, educational institutions tend to foster **sponsored mobility,** allowing some groups more opportunities and access than other groups.

According to the equal-opportunity model, the educational system ensures that individuals acquire the necessary skills that are used for the labour market selection, based on individual merits (motivation, talent, grades, degrees, etc.). On the other hand, Marxists argue that education is an institution that reproduces inequality, ensuring that upper- and middle-class children end up in upper- and middle-class jobs, whereas working- and lower-class children end up in working- and lower-class jobs. For Marxists, the educational system primarily ensures that working-class children possess the

necessary skills and are psychologically prepared for manual and physical jobs in the capitalist labour market. This process of reproduction of the lower classes is due to the fact that:

- Lower- and working-class children are less likely to afford higher education.
- The educational curriculum is incompatible with these children's class culture.

Consequently, lower- and working-class children drop out of school or end up with lower educational qualifications and therefore lower paying jobs. In contrast, middle- and upper-class children end up with higher educational qualifications and occupational positions because they can both afford it and because the educational curriculum is compatible with their class culture.

How does the educational **curriculum** affect the reproduction of social classes?

According to Bourdieu, social classes differ in their "cultural capital." **Cultural capital** refers to the ensemble of high-status culture and cultivated dispositions that manifest themselves in such things as appreciation of higher education and the best schools, attendance in museums, art galleries, theatres and concerts, appreciation of classical music and knowledge of composers, and strong language and literary skills. Such values, attitudes, and behaviours learned in the family mediate the relationship between class background and education. Upper classes have at their disposal a large share of cultural capital and are able to cultivate this capital better than other classes. Moreover, the cultural capital of middle and upper classes matches closely with the school curriculum. According to Bourdieu, "the educational system reproduces all the more perfectly the structure of distribution of cultural capital among classes . . . in that the culture which it transmits is closer to the dominant culture and that the mode of inculcation to which it has recourse is less removed from the mode of inculcation practiced by the family" (Bourdieu, 1977: 493).

What is in the school curriculum that might match middle- and upper-class culture? Richer (1982), a Canadian sociologist, pointed to educational values such as **universalism** and neutrality, an ethic of inter-individual competition, an emphasis on materialism and work rather than on play, and a submission of self to authority. These values are compatible with middle-class values, such as deferred gratification, concern for interindividual competition, tendency toward goal orientation, and reliance on verbal over physical skills. Richer's research revealed that lower- and working-class children differ from middle- and upper-class children wherein the former are less likely to be achievement, future, and competitively oriented or to emphasize symbolic rewards, whereas the latter are more likely to be oriented toward these attributes. These differences, he argued, result in different educational outcomes by social classes.

As an example, let us say your professor has asked you to write a paper on communism. You are given one month to complete this task. You will be penalized substantially if you fail to hand in your assignment on time (sound familiar?). Now, consider the potential experience of two hypothetical students. According to the differences in class culture stated above, we expect that a middle- or upper-class student, who tends to be more analytical and goal-oriented, will look at the problem as a discrete, self-contained entity and isolate it from other issues. This student will emphasize the goal of finishing the project on time by reviewing a few articles on communism as well as providing an example, such as the Russian experience with communism. Having focused on the goal, this student will hand in the assignment at the end of the month and on time.

Now, let us consider the example of a student whose working-class culture tends to be relational and mean oriented. This type of student will be more interested in the exercise in and of itself, rather than in the goal of finishing the project on time in order to receive a good mark. This student might read several articles on Marx's views on communism, then on Lenin's views, and so on. After reading various scholars' views, this student might take the example of Russia and then evaluate whether it differs from that of China, then Cuba, and so on. By the time the student is halfway through the project, the deadline has approached and the student is already developing a grade deficit or penalty of being late. Therefore, from these examples you will notice that interconnected and relational learning may be incompatible with the well-defined time–space division prevalent in schooling. If that is the case, then students whose value system is congruent with the "hidden curriculum" of schools would do better than their counterparts.

Therefore, if middle- and upper-class cultures are compatible with the hidden educational curriculum, whereas lower- and working-class cultures are incompatible, we would expect that the latter would have lower educational attainment than the former. Evidence on importance of class background on educational attainment is presented in Table 7.1. This table shows a clear advantage for children having fathers and mothers with a higher education and occupation. That is, parents with higher socioeconomic status are able to ensure their offspring will have higher educational opportunities. Other evidence with different data and different years also consistently showed that parental socioeconomic position is strongly related to children's educational attainment (Nakhaie and Curtis, 1998; Nakhaie, 2000). However, you should have noticed that despite the link, the evidence does not tell us directly whether educational inequality is due to parental wealth and ability to afford higher education or to the correspondence of class culture and school curriculum. Nevertheless, given that parental occupation represents affordability and parental education represents "credentialized cultural capital" (Bourdieu, 1977), we can state that both factors are important for the offspring's educational attainment. Parents with higher occupations provide the economic resources as well as ensuring the internalization of cultural values necessary for the success of their children. The higher the educational attainment of children, the higher their income (see Table 7.2). Therefore, the upper social classes reproduce themselves, first through higher education for their offspring and then indirectly in wealth, income, or other resources.

The educational institution, however, has other functions in addition to preparing individuals for the job market or reproducing social classes. It offers students access to the World Wide Web (see Table 7.3) and also helps shape their ideas and consciousness. The debate that you have read in the section on culture evaluated whether education ensures support for the status quo and the social system, and if so, whether there is a difference in ideological orientation by type of education.

Education can also be studied in terms of how it can develop a consumerist culture wherein students are oriented toward grades and may even cheat in order to secure such grades. The debate that follows discusses the consumerist culture of (higher) education. Delucchi and Smith argue that universities and colleges operate on the basis of the **postmodern** logics of **performativity.** It is not what professors teach and students learn that is important. Rather, the question that is predominant in these institutions is what education is good for? Thus, language, reason, and science are not the mechanisms of arriving at truth as modernists believed. Postmodernists argue that these mechanisms are part of a series of discourses socially and contextually created, none of which offers superior truth claims. Consequently, student consumerism dictates what and how courses are taught in educational institutions. For example, students are obsessed with grades, and faculty are acquiescent to such demands by inflating grades in order to ensure higher course evaluations.

In response to this discussion, Eisenberg does not dispute these suggestions; instead, he argues that the source of consumerism is not postmodernism; rather, it is educators' changing pedagogy and shifting classroom demographics that are the sources. For example, there has been a shift in classroom pedagogy, wherein the focus now is to encourage reflexive and critical thinking, meaningful experiences, and relevant information. The change in pedagogy creates classroom situations that are distinctive from the traditional approach of authoritarian teaching. This produces students who tend to critically evaluate their experience and thus demand specific types of education relevant to their present and future interests.

TABLE TALK

◆ ◆ ◆

Figure 7.1 shows a continual increase in school attendance from 1976 to 2001, particularly for females. Why is female school attendance higher than that of males?

Table 7.1 shows educational attendance of males and females by their class background. It reveals that the higher education and occupation of parents, the more likely that their offspring will acquire a university degree. Moreover, father's education and occupation tend to be more important than that of the mother's, particularly for male children. Why does class matter for educational attainment of offspring?

Table 7.2 shows the role of education for income: the higher the education, the higher the income. However, the influence of education on income is substantially higher for males than for females. Why?

Table 7.3 shows that socioeconomic status also influences access and use of the Internet: the higher the education and income of the household, the higher the use of the Internet. Do you think that access to the Internet at home is important for individual social mobility today?

Figure 7.1   School Attendance for 16 to 24 Age Group

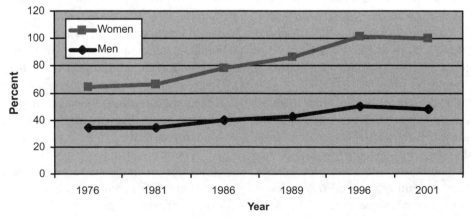

Source: Statistics Canada, Catalogue No. 75-001-XIE.

Table 7.1   Educational Attainment by Parental Education and Gender (25 Years of Age and Over)

	Males Less than Diploma	Males Post-secondary	University	Females Less than Diploma	Females Post-secondary	University
Father's Education						
University Degree	13.6	27.2	59.2	12.5	37.4	50.1
Some Postsecondary	27.8	41.3	30.8	26.9	42.8	30.3
Secondary	39.6	33.1	27.4	37.5	42.2	20.3
Elementary	64.1	23.6	12.4	63.6	26.3	10.1
Mother's Education						
University Degree	14.1	31.5	54.3	15.9	35.2	48.9
Some Postsecondary	29.1	36.6	34.3	23.1	44.9	32.1
Secondary	37.8	36.1	26.1	39.2	40.8	20.1
Elementary	65.7	21.5	12.8	68.1	23.6	8.3
Father's Occupation						
Professional/Managerial	21.4	26.3	52.3	20.7	35.4	43.9
White Collar	40.1	32.2	27.7	38.6	39.3	22.1
Blue Collar	57.1	30.3	12.6	60.1	29.1	20.8
Farm	68.2	21.6	10.1	64.6	27.1	8.3
Other	57.5	30.8	11.7	54.9	35.3	9.8
Mother's Occupation						
Professional/Managerial	13.1	33.2	53.6	23.2	35.9	40.9
White Collar	36.7	36.9	26.3	36.6	37.5	25.9
Blue Collar	53.4	35.1	11.5	60.9	27.5	11.6
Farm	50.1	40.8	9.1	59.6	31.6	8.8
Other	55.9	36.6	17.5	57.1	30.6	12.3

Source: Statistics Canada, General Social Survey, 1995.

Table 7.2   Average Income by Levels of Education and Sex

	Males	Females	F/M
Less than High School	24,242	14,973	0.62
High School or Some Postsecondary	30,885	19,880	0.64
Trade Certificate or Diploma	37,711	21,650	0.57
College Certificate or Diploma	41,404	26,435	0.64
University Degree or Higher	60,822	36,716	0.60

Source: Census of Canada, 2001.

QUESTIONS

1. Do you agree or disagree that consumerism has become a key aspect of higher education? Explain your answer?
2. Do you think students are more likely to cheat now than in the past? Why or why not?
3. If you were to evaluate your professors, would your mark in the course affect your evaluation? Explain your answer.

Table 7.3   Household Internet Use by Sociodemographic
            Characteristics

	1999 %	2000 %	2001 %	2002 %	2003 %
All households	28.7	40.1	48.7	51.4	54.5
Education of head of household					
Less than high school	9.6	16.1	22.8	24.3	25.5
High school or college	29.6	42.8	51.3	54	57.6
University degree	52.4	65.1	74.2	75.9	78.7
Household income					
Lowest quartile	10.9	16.5	22.6	25.1	26.7
Second quartile	18	31.2	40	39.9	44.6
Third quartile	32.4	47.4	56.4	62.3	64.7
Highest quartile	53.5	65.4	75.8	78.4	81.9

Source: Statistics Canada, CANSIM, Tables: 358-0003, 358-004, 358-005, and 358-0017.

4. Do you agree or disagree that the majority of students perceive postsecondary education as a means to an end, rather than an end in itself? Explain your answer.
5. Do you think that there is such a thing as a hidden curriculum in schools? Explain your answer and provide examples.
6. Do you think that class culture is an important source of students' success in school? Why or why not?

A Postmodern Explanation of Student Consumerism in Higher Education

Michael Delucchi
University of Hawaii-West Oahu

William L. Smith
Georgia Southern University

◆ ◆ ◆

Recent issues of *Teaching Sociology* have featured essays imploring instructors to acknowledge and to exercise control over the authority inherent in the teaching role. Gary Long and Elise Lake (1996) contend that "ethical teaching" requires honesty about the socially structured differences between professors and students. The authors also suggest that a customer-service approach to the student-professor relationship undermines effective pedagogy. In a similar vein, Jodi O'Brien and Judith Howard (1996) state that "a widespread reluctance to assume the cloak of authority is the root dilemma underlying many of the ills that beset contemporary higher education, including the decline of respect for the profession in general, [and] the perpetuation of a culture of complaint and cynicism" (p. 327).

We are receptive to the above observations and believe that maintaining clear distinctions between student and instructor roles need not lead to faculty elitism (Long and Lake, 1996; O'Brien and Howard, 1996). We do not advocate that instructors become indifferent to their students, but we do assert that educating students is more important than coddling them and treating them as customers (Weiss, 1982). However, recent work in the humanities and social sciences (Bloland, 1995; Crook et al., 1992; Zemsky, 1993) leads us to believe that student consumerism is a product of a new historical era—postmodernism—and not easily amenable to "ethical teaching" or the use of "responsible authority." Consequently, we maintain sociologists can most appreciate the pedagogical challenges associated with student consumerism, grades as a biasing factor in teaching evaluations (Feldman, 1996), cheating (Sloss, 1995) and grade obsession (Wiesenfeld, 1996) by examining the implications of postmodernism on higher education.

The term "postmodern" appears with increasing frequency in the titles of presentations at professional meetings, but few of the discussions address directly the impact of the modern/postmodern divide as it pertains to teaching undergraduates. Clayton Dumont (1995: 307) argues that thinking traditions, such as postmodernism, can assist sociologists in understanding the cultural nature of their epistemologies. The paucity of teaching faculty's general engagement with the postmodern is surprising, because the postmodern era continues to have an impact on the way in which students approach their education. Perhaps nowhere are the characteristics of postmodernism more apparent than among undergraduate attitudes toward their education.

In this paper we employ the concepts of "performativity" (Crook et al., 1992) and "implosion of boundaries" (Baudrillard, 1983), two essential components of postmodernism, to illuminate student consumerism and its challenges to collegiate pedagogy. . . .

THE MODERN/POSTMODERN DISTINCTION
◆ ◆ ◆

. . . The modernist perspective maintains that language, reason, and science (i.e., the scientific method) are the

From Michael Delucchi and William L. Smith, "A postmodern explanation of student consumerism in higher education," *Teaching Sociology*, Vol. 25, 1997, pp. 322–327. Reprinted by permission of the authors and the American Sociological Association.

foremost mechanisms for arriving at truth. Modernism asserts that language describes and serves as a reliable means of accessing reality. Through scientific inquiry, modernists claim to be progressing toward true knowledge of the universe and to be acquiring knowledge important for problem solving in society. With its emphasis on reason and the rational unfolding of history, modernism equates change with progress, which is defined as increasing control over nature and society (Bloland, 1995).

Postmodernism can be viewed as a perspective or as a new historical era. . . . In either case, the major thrust of postmodernism is to attack modernist assumptions about language, reality, and science. For postmodernists, language is not a path to truth or a method for describing reality, but simply a series of discourses socially created in varying contexts, none of which offer superior truth claims. Science is not viewed as a value-free form of knowledge, but as a discourse created within a political context where power struggles occur for the control of its meaning (Lyotard, 1984). Therefore, postmodernism as a perspective challenges the most basic assumptions of the European Enlightenment, the foundation, upon which much of higher education depends.

POSTMODERNISM AND HIGHER EDUCATION

◆ ◆ ◆

Colleges and universities are intended to be places of intellectual freedom where all views are debated and subjected to critical scrutiny. Allan Bloom's (1987) controversial work laments that this approach to knowledge is losing legitimacy in higher education. In the postmodern era, there is danger in the collapse of the distinction between knowledge inside the university and outside, so that certain kinds of knowledge—once the monopoly of higher education—are now shared with institutions outside the academy.

Implosion means that the boundary between a simulation and reality disappears, that is, implodes, and the basis for determining "the real" is gone (Baudrillard, 1983). For example, Geyer (1993: 511) argues that colleges and universities are losing their legitimacy to television entertainment, news and documentary spectacles, as well as radio talk shows, which "have developed a power commensurate with university education." These media compete with the rationality and disciplinary standards upon which much of higher education curricula are based. The collapse of boundaries between the inside and outside of the academy delegitimates the belief in professors as experts, particularly as ultimate authorities on the subjects they teach.

American consumer culture is most disruptive to undergraduate education. In the postmodern world, "performativity" is the most powerful criterion for determining worth, replacing agreed upon, rational, modernist criteria for merit. Postmodernists describe performativity as "the capacity to deliver outputs at the lowest cost, [which] replaces truth as the yardstick of knowledge" (Crook et al., 1992: 31). In other words, efficiency and effectiveness become the exclusive criteria for judging knowledge and its worth in society and within the academy.

Gary Long and Elise Lake (1996) contend that an undue emphasis on customer service in higher education inverts the professor-student relationship by vesting authority in students as consumers. "Consumerism can undermine the concept of merit by contributing to the pernicious idea that students are customers, to be served only in ways they find pleasing" (Long and Lake, 1996: 111). Under such conditions, professors may be reluctant to hold students to exacting standards of performance and those who resist grade inflation may be unfairly penalized (Park, 1996). Support for this claim is found in work by Robert Powell (1977), who conducted an experiment in which an instructor varied his grading criteria from stringent to moderate to lenient in five sections of the same course. Powell (1977: 197) reports that the instructor received higher evaluations when students were required to do less work, received higher grades, and learned less. Few institutions of higher education are immune from this phenomenon although it is one of the dirty little secrets we deny publicly.

Students' evaluations of faculty members measure a variety of factors such as personality and expressiveness, which may or may not be related to learning, but are salient criteria to student consumers. Penny Wright, Ray Whittington, and G.E. Whittenburg (1984: 8) report that over 90 percent of the variance in students' ratings of faculty members can be attributed to the instructor's personality. In a postmodern academic environment of increasing relativism and consumerism, some faculty members begin to pander to the allure of students as consumers. For example, Baker and Copp (1997) conclude that college students negatively evaluate professors who fail to provide the customer-service traits (e.g., understanding, concern, friendliness, sensitivity, and support) that they expect from faculty members. Consequently, faculty members may become more concerned with their popularity (or being "liked") than providing students with rigorous course work, especially when promotion and tenure are linked to the results of students' evaluations. Their identity as "Professor" becomes tied to how likable they are to their students (Weiss, 1982).

Louis Goldman (1990) states, "Most students are interested in getting good grades; those instructors who give students high grades and communicate to them that they are learning well usually are rewarded with high ratings. Quid pro quo" (p. B2). Are students' evaluations of faculty members influenced by the grades students receive in a course? Several researchers have concluded that grades cannot be dismissed as a biasing factor in teaching evaluations (Feldman, 1976, 1996; Marsh, 1984; Powell, 1977; Wright et al., 1984). For example, W. Robert Kennedy (1975) found that students receiving either an A or B as an actual grade in a course gave significantly higher evaluations to the instructor than those receiving a C or D. More recently, Richard J. Gigliotti and Foster S. Buchtel (1990: 348) studied 691 students enrolled in 38 courses and 16 disciplines and concluded that grades influenced teaching evaluations. However, based on an extensive review of empirical studies Feldman (1996: 6) suggests that part of the positive correlation between grades and evaluation of instructors is due to a "validity effect" and some part of the association might be due to a spurious factor that has been labeled as a "student characteristic effect." Nevertheless, while the extent to which students use evaluations to "reward" or "punish" teachers based on the grade they received remains unresolved, according to Feldman (1996), "almost all of the available research does show a small or even modest positive association between grades and evaluation" (p. 6).

Scholars in a variety of disciplines, including sociology, psychology, and economics have reported on the escalating problem of cheating in college courses (Bunn et al., 1992; Davis et al., 1992; Sloss, 1995). In a study of 476 students enrolled in a microeconomics course, over 80 percent reported they had witnessed cheating and 50 percent indicated they have cheated themselves. Most of these students (over 70%) did not consider cheating a problem (Bunn et al., 1992: 199–201). The researchers conclude that the cavalier attitude toward cheating is reinforced by the belief among students that cheating can raise grade point averages, thereby enhancing their competitiveness in the job market upon graduation (Bunn et al., 1992: 198).

Theodore Wagenaar (1995) describes successful teaching as "more than effective in-class teaching behaviors; it is what students learn" (p. 67). Unfortunately, research indicates that students preoccupied with their grade point average (GPA), practice a system of learning that emphasizes making a good grade at the expense of deeper, critical analytic learning (Rabow and Hernandez, 1988). . . .

Much of what students want to consume that higher education has supplied in the past is either in the process of erosion, for example, high culture, or can be supplied by other sources (vocational education, or the World Wide Web). As Robert Zemsky (1993) writes, "Students today want technical knowledge, useful knowledge, labor-related knowledge in convenient, digestible packages" (p. 17). In a postmodern world, the role of a traditional liberal arts education is devalued, because consumer culture questions the assumption that liberal arts knowledge is relevant knowledge. Consistent with the phenomenon of performativity, the rhetoric of accountability in higher education promotes a customer-service relationship between students and faculty members. When colleges and universities cater to student consumerism, it is inevitable that some faculty members will succumb to its demands.

CONCLUSIONS
◆ ◆ ◆

Postmodernism's terms and assumptions have entered sociology and other social sciences over the past two decades. Postmodern perspectives are significant in their potential to account for the extensive changes in our society as we move from a production to a consumption society. An important consequence of postmodernism is that as the boundary between higher education and the market collapses, few (if any) academics are unaffected by student consumerism.

Long and Lake (1996) and O'Brien and Howard (1996) implore faculty members to make explicit the authority of expertise and inequalities inherent in the student-professor relationship. Wilbert McKeachie's (1978) delineation of teacher's roles (the teacher as expert, formal authority, socializing agent, facilitator, ego ideal, and person) bolsters these recommendations. However, the question remains: Will clear articulation of the responsibilities associated with these roles enhance teaching in a consumer culture? We are skeptical. The postmodern world is replete with ambiguity and contradiction. We now teach in a context in which the standard categories of modernism fail to account for (that is, to explain and make predictable) the conditions we face in the classroom.

Postmodernism makes us aware of the destabilization and uncertainty that confronts our students. A postmodern perspective is pertinent to the teaching of sociology because it involves a salient critique of modernism, the foundation upon which much of our training and scholarship has rested. Consequently, reasserting the belief in professors as experts and authorities on the subjects they teach is unlikely to stem the tide of pedagogical challenges that accompanies student consumerism.

Some academics view postmodernism as a regressive intellectual movement that seeks to dismantle the progress associated with the Enlightenment. Others see postmodernism as the basis for the creation of autonomous discourse groups that respond to their own vocabularies and sets of values in a freer, more open academy. Herein lies the tension between the two. The modernist orientation is to resolve problems, while the postmodern perspective identifies contradictions in discourses and attempts to maintain that essential tension (Bloland 1995: 551).

In critiquing modernism, postmodernism challenges the legitimacy of what higher education purports to be doing. An important consequence of postmodern thought is that few of us in academia are unaffected by the arguments that challenge our epistemology and in turn our approach to pedagogy. If we embrace postmodernism as a critique that applies to both modernists and to critics of modernism, dialogue becomes possible. The image of relativism hangs over all of our disciplines. Therefore, we must begin to engage our colleagues and students in dialogue, even as we recognize that the tension between modernist orientations and postmodern perspectives will not be easily resolved.

Education and the Marketplace: Conflicting Arenas? Response to "A Postmodern Explanation of Student Consumerism in Higher Education"

Anne F. Eisenberg
University of Iowa

◆ ◆ ◆

Educators express their concerns about the changing dynamics of college classrooms in a number of different forums, from sessions held at professional meetings to articles in disciplinary journals to discussions conducted on the Internet among members of various academic disciplines. In "A Postmodern Explanation of Student Consumerism in Higher Education" (hereafter noted as "Consumerism"), the authors provide a framework, or perspective, with which to understand such changes and they encourage educators to use such an understanding in their "approach to pedagogy" (p. 326). The framework contends that society has evolved into a new era, moving from a modern to a postmodern period resulting in a "student consumerism" that drastically affects classroom expectations, behaviors, and outcomes for students and educators alike.

"Consumerism" presents a compelling case encouraging educators to use a postmodern sensibility to inform their pedagogy, based on two underlying assumptions key to the utility of this approach. First, the authors seem to assume that educators are passive recipients of socially changed, and charged, classroom situations. Second, they present student consumerism as a new phenomenon representative of the postmodern era and as a negative influence on the classroom environment. I suggest that examining these two assumptions leads us to challenge the adequacy of the proposed approach. Specifically, I contend that the two assumptions are inaccurate representations of higher education and that it is possible to

have a more sociologically informed understanding of our changing classroom dynamics.

In this response, I address each assumption and conclude that the problems encountered in classrooms, such as students' obsession with grades, faculty members pandering to the interests of students, and assignment of student grades affecting course evaluations, are the result of two interacting social forces—educators' changing pedagogy and shifting classroom demographics—rather than a "postmodern" shift in society. More to the point, changing classroom dynamics reflect the fact that while our pedagogical approaches as educators (agents of education) have changed, neither our own nor students' expectations have changed to reflect such a shift.

Additionally, students entering our classrooms are more diverse than in previous decades where the majority of students were most likely white and middle-class. Today a large number of ethnic, racial, and religious minorities are enrolling in college and are, in many cases, the first members of their families working for a college degree. This impacts higher education in two distinct ways. First, educators (who are most likely white and middle-class) have a limited understanding of their students' backgrounds, experiences, and training. Second, the new students in our classrooms have no clear expectations concerning classroom behavior and possible outcomes of such experiences. Finally, I discuss the implications of the proposed alternative explanation for changing classroom dynamics.

From Anne F. Eisenberg, "Education and the marketplace: conflicting arenas?" *Teaching Sociology*, Vol. 25, 1997, pp. 328–332. Reprinted by permission of the authors and the American Sociological Association.

NEL

121

ASSUMPTIONS RECONSIDERED

◆ ◆ ◆

In "Consumerism," the first assumption implies that educators are passive recipients of changing classroom environments. This assumption can be traced to the general view held by most writers concerning the goals of higher education as a social institution and educators as its agents. These perceived goals include educating the masses and schools as an arena "where all views are debated and subjected to critical scrutiny" (p. 323). Some writers have identified a liberal arts education as the avenue for achieving these goals (Anderson, 1992; Smith, 1990). For example, the Association of American Colleges views the "basic ingredients of a liberal arts education [to include]: (1) inquiry, abstract logical thinking, critical analysis; (2) literacy (writing, reading, speaking, listening); (3) understanding numerical data; . . . (5) science; . . . and study in depth" (Wagenaar, 1993: 352).

Educators help maintain stable social structures through traditional pedagogical practices, such as the "banking method" of teaching that ensures the protection of knowledge and the experts responsible for such knowledge (Freire, 1993; Hooks, 1994; Scheper-Hughes, 1992). According to contemporary "radicals," this approach to education views students as empty human vessels into which authoritative experts deposit knowledge and information. The banking method results in classroom situations where students passively receive information and form relationships with educators that are clearly based on subordination. Classroom dynamics consist of one-way dialogues with educators in positions of power who act as the experts, shaping every aspect of the "learning" environment.

In contrast to the banking method, recent pedagogical discussions reflect educators' interest in changing their teaching styles. The purpose of such changes is to gain different outcomes for their students, such as critical and reflexive thinking, meaningful experiences, and relevant information (Applegee, 1996; Long, 1995; O'Brien and Howard, 1996; Stoecker et al., 1993; Thompson and Tyagi, 1993; Weast, 1996). Some writers focus on specific philosophies to direct their teaching methods, including: critical, liberatory, and feminist pedagogies (Freire, 1993; Hooks, 1994). Whether guided by a particular philosophy or specific student outcomes, this change in pedagogical directions creates classroom situations distinctly different from the traditional approach to education.

While the banking method results in a quiet and disciplined classroom where the only speaker is the instructor and interactions are limited, teaching methods associated with new pedagogical directions encourage student action and participation in the learning process. This results in classrooms where students work in groups, participate in their own learning process by determining course topics, and select the assignments to complete for successful completion of the course. Applebee (1996) calls this "knowledge in action" and envisions learning as an experiential and participatory process, similar to Freire and hooks. In other words, students are vocal and active participants in the classroom setting. Rather than the instructor's voice resounding in the quiet of a lecture hall, educators' new pedagogical directions lead to multivocal classrooms. These classrooms may be chaotic at times as students are encouraged to challenge authoritative knowledge structures.

The above discussion demonstrates that rather than serving as passive recipients of changing classroom environments, educators act as the catalysts of such change. Educators' changing pedagogical philosophies seek a more liberatory process of learning and more critical outcomes for their students. These new philosophies may result in classrooms in which the subordinate/superordinate relationships between students and teachers have been transformed into teacher-as-student/student-as-teacher relationships (Freire, 1993). The validity of the first assumption underscoring a postmodern approach to pedagogy is thus questionable.

The second assumption implicit in "Consumerism" is student consumerism resulting from a postmodern mentality and having a negative influence on the classroom environment. The authors of "Consumerism" contend that a consequence of student consumerism is faculty members behaving like performers to retain student interest, grade inflation due to student complaints, and excessive cheating among students. Specifically, they posit that the postmodern environment results in "increasing relativism and consumerism, [where] some faculty members begin to pander to the allure of students as consumers" (p. 324). In turn, consumerism makes "performativity" the criterion by which educators are evaluated since it is their ability to attract as many students as possible and keep them from being disgruntled.

There are two important aspects to the second assumption implicit in "Consumerism"—students in a modern era were more interested in being educated and the same type of students operate with a consumer mentality in today's "postmodern" classroom. Specifically, the modern student was less likely to be focused on the "bottom line" of education and therefore less likely to engage in behavior antithetical to the goals of higher education (as opposed to the postmodern student). Additionally, the authors imply that the composition of students in the classroom is comparable over time allowing them to compare the behavior of students in the modern era with those in the postmodern era.

The history of modern public education in America highlights the role of such institutions in training and creating the populace into a work force necessary for mass production in industries such as steel and automotive. Higher education tended to be reserved for members of the white, middle-class who expected to gain the skills and graces necessary to retain their place in society. In other words, educators were responsible for producing a literate work force and were held accountable for their actions. There are examples throughout the history of American education where educators were fired or schools closed because they failed to meet public needs. In other words, education has always been a "consumer" item in America. While the "consumers" were the industrial magnates of the late nineteenth and early twentieth centuries, the consumers today are the people who are responsible for bearing the majority of the cost of education today—the family and individual students.

The second aspect to "student consumerism" is clearly understanding the student population. While higher education used to be reserved for the white, middle-class, today a greater percentage of students are more likely to be women and minorities—ethnic, racial, and economic. Additionally, a greater number of students are the first in their families to attend college. This means that students entering college today do not have the same backgrounds, experiences, and expectations as previous generations or as their instructors. The majority of educators in higher education are white and middle-class, resulting in a gap in our understanding of the students in our classrooms.

In other words, rather than an essential shift in society to a postmodern perspective leading to tense, awkward, and uncomfortable classroom situations, an actual measurable social change is occurring in higher education. Consumerism is no longer represented solely by corporate entities but now includes families and students carrying the financial burden of higher education. Additionally, the changing demographics of students results in educators with little or no understanding of the social and cultural experiences of these students.

SUMMARY

◆ ◆ ◆

While I agree with the authors of "Consumerism" that the classroom environment is changing, I am hesitant to attribute such changes to shifting historical and social eras. Rather, I suggest that educators are agents of some change as they seek to engage students in the learning process. Conflict and friction arise when both educators' and students' expectations concerning classroom behavior and outcomes have not adjusted to the shift in pedagogical philosophy and associated techniques. Additionally, changing student populations result in educators who do not necessarily understand the goals, hopes, and expectations of this new generation. The basis of a solution consists of educators more actively learning about their students, integrating such knowledge into their teaching strategies, and creating realistic expectations both for students and themselves. Our new approaches to teaching encourage meeting the needs of students, but we must first discover and understand their needs and expectations. We cannot predict the outcome of our new teaching approaches without first understanding the population with whom we interact.

Guest Editorial: Big Marks on Campus: Grade Inflation a Major Concern

From the editorial desk of The Ottawa Citizen.

Grade inflation is the dirty little secret of North American academe. Two years ago, Harvard University professor Harvey Mansfield showed his "contempt" for Harvard's practice of inflating grades—more than half its undergraduate students enjoyed A− or A grades—by issuing two sets of marks to those taking his political philosophy course: an "official" grade for the public record and a "private" one that reflected his real assessment of their work.

Since Mansfield's "experiment," there's been numerous reports of U.S. universities indulging "upward grade homogenization," as a Yale University official described it. And now, it seems, Canadian universities are equally guilty.

A CanWest survey of undergraduate grading patterns at two dozen universities shows that in the past decade, marks have been creeping up in all but a few disciplines. Similarly, a study by two University of Windsor professors, who compared first-year university grades at Ontario universities from 1974 to 1994, found "significant" grade inflation. So are students smarter today than they were 20 or 30 years ago?

Not likely, considering that while grades were inflating, the scores from scholastic assessment tests were in decline.

So what's going on?

The most comprehensive explanation involves a conjunction of phenomena—everything from higher education and the willingness of administrators to link funding to business-oriented measures of performance costs to an entitlement culture in which everyone must be esteemed, and a "grade-grubbing" attitude among students who regard their university years as merely a way-station on the career path.

Leon Craig, who's taught political science at the University of Alberta for 31 years, says that in too many cases, students expect higher grades because they're paying a lot of money for their education, teachers give those grades because it helps their careers, and administrators accept the practice because it makes the university look good and helps them raise money.

Phil Azzie, a lecturer at the University of Ottawa, has a similar view. He says he gets a lot more students fishing for higher grades. "They seem to regard high marks as the payback for the cost of their education."

Whatever the reason, grade inflation corrupts the education system, morally and intellectually. Even something as seemingly innocuous as teacher evaluations can be corruptive. Students naturally tend to give a higher evaluation to professors who give them higher grades. Faculties with large pools of satisfied students have a better chance of acquiring a greater share of limited funding resources. Thus, everybody—students, professors, administrators and governments—has a vested interest in inflating grades.

The consequences are insidious. If you can no longer distinguish the average student from the great, everyone is diminished. Universities that indulge in grade inflation are telling even those who excel that their degrees are without substantive value. Such a practice corrodes the reputation of Canada's universities. In the long run, that's bad for everyone.

Source: "Big marks on campus: grade inflation a major concern," *The Ottawa Citizen*, Editorial Desk, 24 April 2003, p. A16. Reprinted with permission of The *Ottawa Citizen*.

Cheating

Sarah Schmidt

It's not for everyone: UBC study finds emotionally cold, impulsive thrill-seekers are more likely to cheat.

Students who are emotionally cold, manipulative, and impulsive thrill-seekers are most likely to cheat at university—more so than their narcissistic, Machiavellian or perfectionist classmates, a new Canadian study has found.

A team of researchers at the University of British Columbia set out to determine which, if any, personality traits are good predictors of cheating. The "intriguing but somewhat disturbing" conclusions about the personality type known as subclinical psychopathy raise tough ethical considerations for school officials, the researchers say in the forthcoming edition of *Contemporary Educational Psychology*.

"The fact that cheating is just one in their history of antisocial behaviours suggests that subclinical psychopaths top the 'most likely to be expelled' list. Yet, early diagnosis and surveillance of such individuals raises a host of practical and ethical controversies," the report states.

"For example, it seems unlikely that school boards and university senates would approve of mass pre-screening of students for psychopathy. Any attempt to determine probability-of-expulsion in advance suggests an unsavoury 'guilty until proven innocent' approach toward the students."

The study, carried out at UBC by psychology Prof. Delroy Paulhus and graduate students Craig Nathanson and Kevin Williams, involved 770 undergraduate students enrolled in three introductory psychology classes.

The students were notified their instructor would be watching for cheating on the five multiple-choice exams, using cheating detection software. To corroborate the results, the research team cross-referenced those identified by the software as potential cheaters with seating charts. In each case, the pairs or clusters of students turned out to be seated in immediate proximity to each other.

Of the 770 students, 291 completed a comprehensive battery of personality measures. Personality traits in the so-called "Dark Triad"—narcissist, Machiavellian, and subclinical psychopathic—were the best predictors of cheating.

Of the three dark personalities, subclinical psychopathy—characterized by cold emotion, interpersonal manipulation, impulsive thrill-seeking and a tendency to engage in antisocial behaviour—was the strongest predictor.

The researchers had assumed perfectionists—characterized by a drive to produce work that often conforms to unrealistic standards—would also have a propensity to cheat, but the study did not show this personality type to be a good predictor of cheating.

The team found other personality traits—agreeableness, extraversion, conscientiousness, emotional stability and openness to experience—were equally poor predictors of cheating.

There were no significant differences in cheating between the sexes, ethnicities or academic majors.

Since students with poorer scholastic competence have more motivation to cheat, the researchers conducted a second study to confirm the personality predictors held up even after controlling for scholastic competence.

The researchers replicated the pattern associations between personality and cheating in a separate study of 250 students enrolled in two second-year undergraduate classes. Of these students, 150 also completed the battery of personality, ability and prior-knowledge tests.

After controlling for both ability and prior academic knowledge, subclinical psychopathy again emerged as the strongest predictor.

This combination spells bad news for instructors trying to stamp out cheating in their classrooms, Paulhus said in an interview.

"Teachers have to go out of their way with prevention measures because you're not really going to talk people out of those personalities [and] you're not going to make less able students as able as their competition."

TELLTALE SIGNS

◆ ◆ ◆

It's not always easy to spot students who are likely to be expelled for cheating. A few pointers:

- Personality traits in the so-called "Dark Triad"—narcissist, Machiavellian, and subclinical psychopathic—are the best predictors.

Continued

- Subclinical psychopathy—characterized by cold emotion, interpersonal manipulation, impulsive thrill-seeking and a tendency to engage in anti-social behaviour—is the strongest predictor.
- Perfectionists, characterized by a drive to produce work that often conforms to unrealistic standards, would also have a propensity to cheat, but the study did not show this personality type to be a good predictor of cheating.

- Other traits such as agreeableness, extroversion, conscientiousness, emotional stability and openness to experience, are also poor predictors of cheating.
- There were no significant differences in cheating between the sexes, ethnicities or academic majors.

Source: Sarah Schmidt, "Study identifies which type of student most likely to cheat," *National Post,* June 24, 2005, p. A17. Material reprinted with the express permission of CANWEST NEWS SERVICE, a CanWest Partnership.

Unit Eight

RACE AND ETHNIC RELATIONS
Introduction: Power Elites and Ethnoracial Relations

◆ ◆ ◆

Canada is a society composed of diverse ethnic and racial groups (see Table 8.1). Some of these groups have more power, privilege, and access to resources than others (see Table 8.2). John Porter (1965), one of the most famous Canadian sociologists, identified three broad groups in terms of power and privileges in Canada. First are the **charter groups** (English and French) whose rights are enshrined in the Canadian constitution. Among the charter groups, the British have more power and privilege than the French. The British control key economic and political institutions in Canada. They have also implemented policies that aim at assimilation of French into the Anglo-Saxon way of life and culture (i.e., assimilate them to the dominant culture). When we look at Canadian history, we notice that from the time of the conquest of New France to the present, the French have been subject to various policies of conformity to Anglo-Saxon domination. However, in the past and recent times, Quebeckers have been able to resist British domination. For example, Quebeckers enacted Bill 101 (the language bill), thus limiting and even reversing previous language loss (i.e., reversing the process whereby the proportion of people speaking French was decreasing and those speaking English was increasing). In addition, the **Quiet Revolution** (i.e., the process of increasing urbanization, industrialization, and bureaucratization in Quebec) resulted in an improvement in the standard of living in Quebec. This "revolution" was important in that it helped expand a new Francophone middle class and organized labour whose political loyalty and economic

interests rested with Quebec and not with Canada. Therefore, it is not surprising that, in recent times, French earnings have become more comparable to those of the British. Together, the British and French constitute more than half of the Canadian population (see Table 8.1).

Porter called the second broad group the **entrance groups**. These are noncharter first, second or third generation immigrants from Europe and elsewhere. Generally, in terms of power and privilege, Europeans are more similar to the charter groups than other entrance groups. However, some Europeans (e.g., Spanish, Greek, or most of East Europeans) have lower status and privilege than Northern and Western Europeans and charter groups. In contrast, the other entrance groups who are bioculturally different from Europeans experience significant negative stereotype, prejudice, and discrimination. These groups are broadly identified as visible minorities. On average, they have higher education but lower paying occupation, income, and status (see Table 8.2).

Porter called the third group the **treaty groups**. These include Aboriginals who have signed treaties with the government. Of course, some Aboriginals do not have such treaties. Among all groups in Canada, Aboriginals have substantially lower education, occupation, income, and status. They have poor housing and health, and higher mortality and suicide rates than all other groups in Canada.

The charter and entrance groups are each composed of more than one ethnic or racial group. An ethnic group is made of people with common ancestry and a common sense of belonging to that ancestry. Some ethnic groups have higher **ethnic identity** than others. A sense of identity is formed because of a common culture, shared history, territory, religion, and charismatic leadership (e.g., French in Quebec share a Catholic religion, a shared history often defined in relation to the British, and various charismatic leaders who have championed the Québécois cause). Possession of key institutions (e.g., education) is also important for ethnic identity formation.

Ethnicity is different from race. Historically, race is defined genotypically (genetic makeup) and phenotypically (physical attributes such as skin colour). However, sociologists have come to the conclusion that the term "race" is not a useful scientific concept. The reason for this has to do with the fact that:

- There are few biological differences between groups identified as "races."
- There are more similarities between "races" than differences.
- There have been significant intermarriages and immigration in human history. Interracial marriages and immigration have wiped out "pure races," if there was such a thing to begin with.
- There is no evidence that biological makeup attributed to race can explain human attitudes, knowledge, and behaviour.

As an example, scientists recently discovered a tiny genetic mutation that could explain the first appearance of white skin in humans. Their work suggests that the skin-whitening mutation occurred by chance in a single individual after the first human exodus from Africa. This person apparently became the first ancestor of the "white race." They found out that this skin-whitening mutation involved a change of just one letter of DNA code out of 3.1 billion letters in the human genome that makes a human being (*The Washington Post,* December 17, 2005). This finding should make us critical of attributing any significance to "racial" differences.

The above considerations do not mean that there is no correlation between the phenotypical makeup of individuals (e.g., skin colour) and certain ideas and behaviours. But that such a correlation exists does not mean causality. Take the example of Canadian Aboriginals. Evidence suggests that they are significantly more likely to be found in prison than whites. At first we may explain this by their "race." However, ask yourself the following questions: Is their rate of incarceration a function of their race or a racist justice system that has criminalized their way of life, of officers who have targeted Aboriginal people, and of judges who have issued

harsher sentences against Aboriginals compared to whites? Furthermore, is the higher rate of incarceration a function of their "race" or their poverty, which was produced through colonization of their way of life? Finally, if biology is a determinant, why is it that some members of a "racial" group commit crime and others do not? Do they not all have the same biological makeup? Questions such as these should make us think twice when attributing a group's higher rate of incarceration to their "race," or considering race as a useful concept in explaining human behaviours. So if it is not race, what accounts for differences and inequalities between groups? Explanations include present and past discrimination and racism, stereotypes, prejudice, cultural differences, institutional closures, and structural limitations.

Stereotype refers to an exaggerated and one-sided view about a group. Stereotype is basically a picture in one's head that tends to minimize internal differences of a group and maximize the group's similarities. Therefore, stereotypes are often based on perceptions rather than factual information about a group. Stereotypes can be positive, such as when a group is seen as "hard workers" or "smart," or stereotypes can be negative, such as when a group is seen as "drunks" or "criminal." Such perceptions may have a kernel of truth, but this does not mean that all members of a group are either smart or criminal. A stereotypical perception can result in prejudice, discrimination, and opportunity obstacles for a group.

Prejudice is often a biased attitude based on an unfavourable attitude toward a group. It is a type of rigid judgment that informs and shapes one's perception of others. Once prejudicial attitudes are formed, they result in inflexible generalizations about the group. When you see a visible minority and ask the person, "Where are you from?" you may be asking the question based on a prejudicial attitude that tends to view all visible minorities as foreigners, ignoring that many have been born in Canada. This example suggests that prejudice is based on erroneous generalizations and inaccurate information.

Prejudice is an attitude whereas **discrimination** is a behaviour. The latter means unequal treatment of groups based on negative prejudice and stereotypes. Discrimination involves practices that limit development of full potential and opportunities for members of racial minorities. For example, discrimination occurs in the circumstance where a black and a white person with similar qualifications apply for the same job and only the white person is offered the position. In a 1985 Toronto study, Henry and Ginzberg (1985) asked job applicants with similar resumés to apply for the same job. They found that the chance of white applicants being offered the job was three times higher than that of black applicants. In some cases, a black applicant without an accent was offered an interview, but once there, he was informed that the job had been taken. Soon after, a white applicant arrived and was offered the same job. Researchers concluded that there exists substantial racial discrimination affecting the mobility of members of racial minorities.

When prejudice or discrimination is directed against ethnic or racial minorities, it is also called **racism**. Racism has three interrelated aspects to it. First, there is belief that biologically distinct races exist. Second, there is a belief that races are organized hierarchically. Third, there is a belief that this hierarchy is based on the superiority of one race and the inferiority of the other race(s) (Potvin, 2000). Racism can occur at the individual level and includes racial slurs, jokes, name calling and mistreatment of individuals considered biologically inferior. Racism can also occur at the institutional level. **Institutional racism** or **systemic racism** refers to rules, regulations, and policies that systematically produce differential treatment of specific ethnoracial groups. Below are a few examples of institutional racism in Canadian history (see Anderson and Frideres, 1985):

- Cultural and physical genocides: Canadian Aboriginals have been subject to physical and cultural annihilation. For example, blankets of the Aboriginals were infected with diseases that whites had become immune to, resulting in many Aboriginal deaths. Similarly, Aboriginals' way of life was criminalized in Canada.
- The Chinese head tax: At the turn of the 20th century the Chinese were forced to pay $500 tax for being Chinese.
- Oriental Exclusion Act: From 1925 to 1947, Orientals were barred from coming to Canada.
- Internment of Italian and Japanese: During World War II, Italians and Japanese were placed in internment camps for fear of collaboration with the enemy. Germans were excluded from internment.
- Immigration policies: Early immigration policies defined visible minorities as undesirable groups and restricted immigrants' family formation and unification. European immigrants were given preference.

In recent years overt racism has been declining and has been replaced with a type of racism called **democratic racism** (Henry et al., 2000). This form of racism makes two conflicting sets of values congruent. On the one hand, there is a dominant view that cherishes equality and justice. On the other hand, prejudice and discrimination are tolerated by blaming the victim for not having "acceptable" credentials, "being a poor fit," or "being unable to adapt" to the Canadian ways of life. For example, people may no longer say that blacks are inferior. Rather, some tend to say that blacks are disadvantaged because of their lack of effort. Thus if blacks have lower status and power than whites, this difference is perceived to be due to black's assumed lower work ethic rather than their experiences of prejudice and discrimination. Given the assumption of equal opportunity, it is believed that if blacks work hard they can succeed similar to whites in Canada. The tendency in democratic type of racism is to promote equality of opportunities without acknowledgment of past discriminations that have limited equality of conditions.

Broadly speaking, ethnoracial inequality can be explained by:
- Cultural attributes and individual characteristics of the group. For example, Nagler (1972, 1975) argued that Aboriginals are more present oriented, do not have a work ethic, and have a different conception of time than non-Aboriginals. Similarly, Herrnstein (1990) argued that blacks and whites have different characteristics. He suggested that blacks have lower intelligence as measured by aptitude tests and are less motivated than whites. According to these researchers, these differences in attributes, traits, and cultural values tend to explain the extent of inequalities between ethnoracial groups. Their argument is rooted in an understanding that the industrial labour market is competitive, and individuals are allocated to the best positions based on their motivation, qualification, and skills. Therefore, they conclude that either minorities are doomed to remain at the bottom of social inequality due to their traits and attributes, or they should change their cultural values and become similar to dominant white groups with respect to motivation and work ethic in order to advance in industrial societies.
- **Institutional barriers.** According to Porter (1965), Canadian history is rooted in immigration and conquest. Consequently, the British, as the conquerors, have institutionalized avenues of upward mobility based on their own cultural values, norms, laws, attitudes, behaviours, language, and institutions.

Therefore, the conquered and the newly arrived, particularly those who are bioculturally different from the British, have been subject to their institutional power. Dominant groups possess a much larger share of cultural and social networks and thus are better able to reproduce themselves through their children. On the other hand, immigrants' and visible minorities' cultural value systems and social networks are undermined due to the ability of the British (and French) in privileging their own institutions and value system.

- **Colonization** process. Frideres (1988) argued that white colonizers have destroyed Aboriginals' social and cultural systems and have subjected Aboriginals to economic and political dependence. In the process the colonizers have ensured that Aboriginals have lower education, higher poverty, and more health problems. Finally, they have used these inequities as justification of their own racial superiority and thus have further exploited Aboriginal resources.

- **Split labour market.** Bonacich (1972, 1976) argued that due to certain historical events (slavery, immigration, immigrants' poor organization, etc.), the labour market has been divided based on race and ethnicity, wherein one group gets paid less than the other despite their similarity in efficiency and productivity. This division is beneficial to the capitalists who search for cheap labour but is a source of conflict among the working class themselves. The less organized and often unfamiliar with the labour market ethnoracial minorities may strike a bad bargain and work for less pay. The more organized (white) workers see these cheaply paid workers (ethnoracial minority) as a source of problem, because these workers tend to lower the wages and are therefore competition. This often gives rise to what is known as working-class racism: The working class direct their anger toward minorities through racist slurs, insults, and hate crime, and so on. In Canada, Bolaria and Li (1988) similarly have attributed ethnoracial inequalities and development of racism to capitalists' continual search for docile and cheap labour.

- **Intersection model.** Feminists of colour, such as bell hooks (1984) and Patricia Hill Collins (1990), have brought to our attention the fact that there are simultaneous effects of racism, sexism, and class exploitation as interconnecting systems of privilege and domination. They suggest that gender is racialized, race is gendered, and both are subject to class-related domination. Therefore, they suggest that the interaction of race, class, and gender produce distinct forms of oppression that are not captured by any of these individually (see Stasiulis, 1999).

As discussed above, according to John Porter, individuals from various ethnic groups have access to different resources and are evaluated differently. Porter's view of Canada has been the subject of substantial discussion and controversies. In the debate that follows, Ogmundson and McLaughlin provide evidence that for each category of elites (business, political, media, labour, etc.), the British proportion has declined from 1935 onward, and that of the French and other ethnic groups have increased. Therefore, according to these researchers, British domination is a thing of the past, and there is a tendency toward a decline of British power and privileges. Nakhaie questions such generalization on the grounds that Ogmundson and McLaughlin fail to take into account the changes in the ethnic composition of the Canadian population. That is, when we take into account the declining population of the British and the increasing proportion of other ethnic groups, the evidence suggests that the British have maintained their elite domination, particularly among the directors of the largest economic corporations. Nevertheless, there has been a modest increase in the French and other ethnic group representation among the elites. However, this increase has not been at the expense of the British, but it is more likely that the French and other groups have established parallel institutions of upward mobility.

TABLE TALK
◆ ◆ ◆

Table 8.1 shows the distribution of ethnic groups in Canada. It reveals that the British and French are not as numerically dominant in Canada as they were in the past. This is due to the fact that in recent censuses, Canadians were allowed and encouraged to select "Canadian" as their ethnic group. Most British and French respondents choose this option. The "Canadian" group amounts to 36.8% of the single origin population. The table also shows that visible minorities are now a major numerical group, with 18.6% of single origin response category. Do you think that the Canadian government has played a role in constructing new racial groups (i.e., visible minority) in Canada? If so, how?

Table 8.1   Distribution of Single and Multiple Ethnoracial
Origins in Canada

Ethnic Origin	Single %	Multiple %	Single and Multiple %
British Isles origins	14.4	30.2	23.5
French origins	5.9	15.1	11.1
Québécois	0.4	0.1	0.2
Canadian	36.8	20.4	27.6
Other North American origins	0.2	1.0	0.6
Western European origins	6.1	11.1	8.9
Northern European origins	0.9	3.3	2.3
Eastern European origins	4.8	6.8	5.9
Southern European origins	7.6	3.9	5.5
Other European origins	1.1	0.7	0.9
Oceania origins	0.1	0.2	0.1
Subtotal	78.3	92.8	86.6
Caribbean origins	1.8	0.7	1.2
Latin, Central and South Americans	0.8	0.4	0.6
African origins	1.0	0.5	0.7
Arab origins	1.3	0.5	0.8
West Asian origins	0.9	0.2	0.5
South Asian origins	4.4	0.7	2.3
East and Southeast Asian origins	8.4	1.1	4.2
Subtotal	18.6	4.1	10.3
Aboriginal origins	3.1	3.1	3.1
	3.1	3.1	3.1
Total	100	100	100

Source: Statistics Canada, Census 2001.

Table 8.2 displays the average income of Canadians working the full year and full time. It shows that some of the groups identified as visible minority earn substantially less than others, even if they were born in Canada (e.g., Aboriginals, South Asians, blacks, and Filipinos). Although the extent of ethnoracial earning inequalities are substantial in Canada, the largest of these inequalities are among immigrants, wherein visible minorities earn substantially less than nonvisible minorities. However, some of the nonvisible minority groups are not doing that well either (e.g., Greeks). Why do you think there is more of an ethnoracial income gap among immigrants than native-born Canadians?

Table 8.3 shows the level of comfort Canadians have with four targeted ethnoracial groups. There are three ways of reading this table. First, most Canadians are comfortable having a boss, a teacher, or marrying a person, who is Aboriginal, Asian, or black. The comfort question ranges from 1 to 4, with 1 being very comfortable and 4 very uncomfortable. Since the average score is just under 2, then Canadians generally express comfort with these groups. However, they do not express being very comfortable. This suggests some level of prejudice and discrimination. The second way of reading the table is to evaluate variations. On average, the level of comfort is lower when supporting marriage of a relative like a sister or daughter to visible minorities. Third, there are variations by groups involved and the group that may be prejudicial. For example, Muslims are subject to the most discomfort than others. On the other hand, the group identifying itself as "Canadian," tends to be somewhat less tolerant than others. French are most uncomfortable with Muslims than others, and so on. Why do you think Muslims tend to be viewed more negatively? Do you think that 9/11 is somewhat responsible for intolerance toward this group? Why?

QUESTIONS

1. Do you think that minorities are portrayed negatively in the media? If yes, is there evidence that things are changing?
2. What are your views on Canadian multiculturalism?
3. Was there anything in this chapter that changed your views on visible minorities or the way they have been treated in Canada? If yes, what was it?

Table 8.2   Average Earnings of Ethnoracial Groups in Canada

(Working, Full Time, Full Year, Age 25-65)

	Total Population	Native-Born	Immigrants
Aboriginals	$25,918	$25,912	$26,629
Latin American	$28,517	$35,882	$28,224
Korean	$30,609	$36,604	$30,211
South Asian	$29,251	$35,383	$29,093
Filipino	$29,832	$36,264	$29,593
Black	$31,800	$34,130	$31,495
West Asian	$34,334	$42,236	$33,887
Vietnamese	$32,466	$34,058	$32,444
Arab	$36,625	$41,819	$36,050
Chinese	$35,566	$46,941	$34,303
East Indian	$35,881	$39,675	$35,618
Southeast Asian	$39,641	$51,490	$33,367
Canadian	$37,184	$37,170	$38,816
Portuguese	$36,460	$35,952	$36,614
Polish	$40,454	$45,737	$37,558
Hungarian	$39,697	$40,822	$38,331
Balkan	$40,230	$47,146	$37,284
French	$40,891	$40,867	$41,250
Greek	$36,005	$38,749	$33,548
German	$41,667	$41,370	$42,729
Dutch	$42,787	$42,595	$43,184
Ukrainian	$41,940	$42,190	$39,500
Italian	$43,034	$43,976	$41,606
British	$45,211	$44,186	$48,827
Jewish	$61,309	$66,295	$52,597
Other European	$41,010	$41,558	$40,434
Others	$40,518	$40,351	$42,239
Total	$39,568	$40,031	$37,884

Source: Statistics Canada, Census of Canada (PUMF), 2001.

Table 8.3   Canadians' Average Perception of Comfort with Visible Minorities

Do you feel comfortable:
if your boss is someone who is:

	Black	Aboriginal	Asian	Muslim
British	1.60	1.65	1.69	1.75
French	1.65	1.76	1.67	2.05
European	1.61	1.72	1.63	1.81
Canadian	1.89	1.91	1.91	2.12
Visible	1.79	1.64	1.64	1.82
Other	1.63	1.76	1.67	1.70
Total	1.66	1.73	1.70	1.87
N	628	628	628	628

If a teacher in your local school was someone who is:

	Black	Aboriginal	Asian	Muslim
British	1.58	1.61	1.65	1.76
French	1.62	1.62	1.63	1.94
European	1.59	1.66	1.57	1.90
Canadian	1.69	1.69	1.70	1.90
Visible	1.73	1.79	1.85	1.85
Other	1.52	1.77	1.58	1.69
Total	1.60	1.66	1.64	1.84
N	619	619	619	619

if your relative like your sister or daughter was going to marry someone who is:

	Black	Aboriginal	Asian	Muslim
British	1.71	1.79	1.73	2.06
French	1.79	1.82	1.83	2.29
European	1.86	1.79	1.82	2.23
Canadian	1.90	1.99	1.91	2.27
Visible	2.02	1.96	1.78	2.06
Other	1.86	1.84	1.76	1.97
Total	1.82	1.84	1.80	2.16
N	617	617	617	617

1 = very comfortable, 4 = very uncomfortable.

Visible = Chinese, East Indian, Filipino, Aboriginal.

Source: CRIC-*Globe and Mail* Survey, June 2003.

4. Do you think that once in Canada, minorities should abandon their way of life and assimilate into Canadian society?

5. Do you think that Canadian society provides opportunities for minorities to assimilate?

6. Do you think ethnic communities continue to influence the attitudes and behaviours of their members?

7. Why do you think racial and ethnic inequality persists in Canada today?

8. Table 8.1 shows different levels of earnings by ethnoracial groups. What do you think explains these differences?

Trends in the Ethnic Origins of Canadian Elites: The Decline of the BRITS?

R. Ogmundson
University of Victoria

J. McLaughlin
University of Victoria

◆ ◆ ◆

The conventional wisdom concerning ethnicity in Canada has been dominated by the imagery of *The Vertical Mosaic* published in 1965 by John Porter. This conventional wisdom maintains that Canada is characterized by pronounced ethnic stratification especially at the level of elites which are thought to be dominated overwhelmingly by those of British origin.

Subsequent research at the level of the general population, some of it done by Porter, has generally indicated that overall ethnic stratification in Canada is minimal and is declining. The findings indicate that those of British origin no longer enjoy an especially favoured position. . . .

If ethnic stratification has decreased at the mass level, the question naturally arises as to whether it has waned at the elite level as well. Appointments such as those of Schreyer, a German Catholic, and Hnatyshyn, a Ukrainian, to the post of Governor-General might lead us to believe that it has. Furthermore, it might seem probable that the evolving ethnic composition of the general population would eventually—though perhaps only in a generation or two—be reflected at the highest levels of our society and that some initial indications of this trend may already be evident.

Conversely, however, virtually all historical and international experience tells us that any inequalities found in a stratification system are typically most pronounced at the level of elites (Putnam, 1976). This has been found to be true even when the more powerful ethnic group is in a numerical minority. Thus, notwithstanding diminished ethnic stratification at the mass level, it is possible that an entrenched British upper class continues to dominate the key decision-making positions at the elite level of Canadian society. It cannot be assumed, without investigation, that a decline in the role of the British has actually taken place. This paper explores that question.

THE LITERATURE

◆ ◆ ◆

The imagery of the 'vertical mosaic' at the elite level begins with Porter's studies of seven elites at a variety of times ranging from 1940 to 1961. These were the political elite, the public service elite, the mass media elite, the intellectual elite, the religious elite, the labour elite and the business elite. Four of the seven (labour, media, intellectual, and religious) were analysed separately as predominantly anglophone and predominantly francophone elites. The national elites and the anglophone elites were then found to be dominated by those of British origin. It is this finding which seems to have indelibly impressed itself on the intellectual consciousness of Canada.

Only four of the seven elites, the political (1961–73), public service (1973), business (1972) and media (1972) have been studied again by scholars consciously attempt-

From R. Ogmundson and J. McLaughlin, "Trends in the ethnic origins of Canadian elites: the decline of the BRITS?" *Canadian Review of Sociology and Anthropology*, Vol. 29, No. 2, May 1992, pp. 227–242. Reprinted with permission of the Canadian Sociology and Anthropology Association.

Table I   Trends in the Ethnic Origins of a Political Elite

	1940–60(a)	1961–73(b)	1974–87(c)
	%	%	%
British	75.1	67.1	58.6
French	21.7	24.2	23.6
Other	3.2	7.5	16.3
Unknown	—	1.2	1.5
N =	157	161	203

Sources:

(a) The political elite includes all those who, between 1940 and 1960, were federal cabinet ministers; all provincial premiers; all justices of the Supreme Court of Canada; presidents of the Exchequer Court; and the provincial chief justices (Porter, 1965: 604). On the ethnic origins data, see Porter, 1965: 389, and Olsen, 1980: 22.

(b) A replication of Porter, see Olsen, 1980: 127. Missing data were additionally calculated and added to the table by James McLaughlin.

(c) The third column includes all supreme court justices, federal cabinet ministers, provincial premiers, and provincial chief justices over the years 1974–87. This elite omits the presidents of the Exchequer Court (now Federal Court), a very small group. Information was drawn from the *Canadian Parliamentary Guide* and the *Canadian Almanac and Directory*, various years. It should be noted that ethnic origin is measured differently in each of these studies.

ing to work in the Porter tradition. Unfortunately, the replications were not precise. Hence, even in these cases, inferences about trends can only be made with caution. Furthermore, even the most recent of these attempted replications is now almost 20 years old.

Subsequent research in other traditions has been done at a variety of times and places on a variety of elites utilizing different definitions of elites and different measures of ethnic origin. However, to our knowledge, no systematic overall examination of trends in the ethnic origins of Canadian elites has been reported since the publication of *The Vertical Mosaic* in 1965. The 1977 study done at York University (Williams, 1989) would come the closest but the definition of elite is radically different.

DATA AND METHODS
◆ ◆ ◆

Porter's original data are used as a benchmark. Subsequent findings, notably those of Clement (1975) and Olsen (1980), are employed to help reveal trends. In most cases, new data on the ethnic origins of the elites in question will also be reported. Relevant observations in the literature will be discussed as well.

FINDINGS

Let us begin with the political elite (1940–60), which Porter defined as including both legislative and judicial figures. Olsen's replication (1961–73) indicated a decline of those of British ancestry from 75.1 to 67.1 percent. Our approximate replication for the years 1974–87 indicates a further decline to 58.6 percent (see Table I). Further confirmation of this trend is provided by data on the ethnic origins of federal and provincial cabinet ministers since 1935. Here the British proportion declines from 73.7 percent of federal cabinet ministers in 1935 to 51.3 percent in 1985. For provincial cabinet ministers, the proportion falls from 85.2 percent in 1935 to 57.5 percent in 1985 (see Table II). Examination of the ethnic origins of Members of Parliament indicates a similar trend from 59.6 percent British in 1965 to 52.1 percent in 1985 (see Table III).

More specific study of the political elite over this time period confirms the impression given by these numbers. Few would deny that much of the post-1965 era was largely dominated by Pierre Trudeau and his French Canadian colleagues such as Marchand, Lalonde, and Chrétien. Similarly, the growing importance of the provinces, especially Quebec, during this time period has also emphasized the centrality of the French Canadian role in Canadian politics. What the Trudeau era did for French Canadians may have almost been matched by what the Mulroney era has done for 'third ethnics,' in which names like Mazankowski, Paproski, Epp, Jellinek, and Hnatyshyn have become prominent. In the judiciary, a Jewish Canadian, Bora Laskin, was probably the leading jurist of his generation.

In the case of the public service/bureaucratic elite, the findings are similar. Once again, the data reported by Olsen (1980: 78) indicate a decline of participation in the elite by those of British origin from 84 percent in 1953 to 65 per cent in 1973. Further confirmation of this trend is provided by data on the ethnic origins of federal and provincial deputy ministers since 1935. Here the British proportion declines from 93.8 percent of federal deputy ministers in 1935 to 47.8 percent in 1985. For provincial deputy ministers, the proportion falls from 86.7 percent in 1935 to 62.7 percent in 1985 (see Table II, bottom panel). Similar patterns are found in the case of the military elite (1965-75-85), and in the Supreme Court (1965-75-85) (see Table III). This confirms the trend noted by political scientists Van Loon and Whittington (1976: 326). More recently, Campbell and Szablowski (1979) have reported similar findings. Indeed, they found that: ". . . central agents' socioeconomic backgrounds resemble

Table II   Trends in the Ethnic Origins of Federal and Provincial Cabinet Ministers and Deputy Ministers (or Equivalent), 1935 to 1985

	1935	1945	1955	1965	1975	1985
Cabinet Ministers(a)						
Federal						
British	73.7	68.4	65.0	57.7	58.6	51.3
French	15.8	31.6	35.0	42.3	34.5	23.1
Other	5.3	—	—	—	6.9	25.6
Unknown	5.3	—	—	—	—	—
Column N=	19	19	20	26	29	39
Provincial						
British	85.2	70.2	70.6	72.5	62.8	57.5
French	12.3	22.6	18.5	16.2	18.6	21.2
Other	2.5	3.6	7.6	9.2	16.5	18.9
Unknown	—	—	3.4	2.1	2.1	2.4
Column N=	81	84	119	142	188	212
Deputy Ministers(b)						
Federal						
British	93.8	86.7	72.2	58.8	54.5	47.8
French	—	6.7	22.2	23.5	13.6	34.8
Other	6.2	—	5.6	17.6	31.8	17.4
Unknown	—	6.7	—	—	—	—
Column N=	16	15	18	17	22	23
Provincial						
British	86.7	75.3	81.7	71.9	70.0	62.7
French	12.0	15.3	12.5	18.0	14.7	12.4
Other	1.2	7.1	5.0	7.0	14.1	21.5
Unknown	—	2.4	0.8	3.1	1.2	3.4
Column N=	83	85	120	128	170	177

Source: (a) *Canadian Parliamentary Guide*, various years.
(b) *Canadian Almanac and Directory*, various years.

those of the general populace much more closely than do the backgrounds of bureaucratic elites in other advantaged liberal democracies for which we have comparable data" (1979: 165).

In the case of the mass media, Porter separated the anglophone and francophone organizations. The francophone media were found to be controlled by independent francophones, while the anglophone media were found to be controlled by upper class British families. Unfortunately, however, Porter did not report percentages of ethnic origins in the manner adopted for other elites. He did, however, give the impression of overwhelming (99%-?) British dominance of the anglophone media in 1961. Clement (1975), in a somewhat differently defined elite, found a reduction in the British proportion to 81.9 percent by 1972 (but see Baldwin, 1977a; 1977b; and Clement, 1977). More recently, an analysis of the ancestry of the directors of newspaper chains in 1980 found that 69.1 percent were of British origin. Though the three elites discussed here are comparable only in a crude sense, the data would seem to indicate that the role of individuals of British origin in the media elite may well have been decreasing over time.

More comparable data were collected for the broadcast media elites, and here a clear trend is apparent. If one looks at the ethnic origins of commissioners, directors and executive officers of the CRTC, CBC, CTV, and Global networks in 1975, 1985 and 1989, one finds that the proportion of British origin drops from 60.3 percent in 1975 to 49.4 percent in 1989 (see Table IV).

In the case of the intellectual elite, Porter selected the more 'ideological' sections of the Royal Society. In 1961 he studied both Section I (French language and civilization) and Section II (English language and civilization). He found the first to be overwhelmingly dominated by those of French origin and the second to be overwhelmingly dominated by those of British origin. Our examination in 1987 of Section I indicates that it continues to be dominated by those of French origin (94.1%) while Section II shows a decline in those of British origin from 92 to 72.3 percent (the 1987 data come from the Royal Society calendar for that year). Perhaps it is significant that the francophone section remained highly exclusive. As Porter (1970: 166) himself notes, his choice of the Royal Society as an elite in the educational system has been subject to some criticism. However, other categories which might well have been designated as educational elites—university presidents and ministers/deputy ministers of education—display a similar pattern. The British component falls from 75.8 percent in 1965 to 58.8 percent in 1985 (see Table III).

In the case of the religious elite, Porter provided information which seemed to indicate that the Anglican church was totally dominated by those of British origin, most of

Table III   Trends in the Ethnic Origins of Members of Parliament (Federal), Supreme Court, Military Elite, Broadcast Media Elite, Educational Elite, and Labour Elite—1965 to 1985

Members of	1965	1975	1985	Members of	1965	1975	1985
Parliament (a)				**Education (b,c)**			
British	59.6	53.4	52.1	British	75.8%	71.9%	58.8%
French	25.0	29.5	24.5	French	11.3	10.9	13.2
Other	15.4	14.8	21.3	Other	9.7	14.0	23.5
Unknown	3.1	2.3	2.5	Unknown	3.2	3.2	4.4
Column N=	260	264	282	Column N=	62	64	68
Supreme Court (a)				**Labour (d)**			
British	77.8	55.6	44.2	British	72.4	50.0	58.8
French	22.2	22.2	33.3	French	17.2	25.0	35.3
Other	—	22.2	22.2	Other	6.9	25.0	5.9
Unknown	—	—	—	Unknown	3.4	—	—
Column N=	9	9	9	Column N=	29	24	17
Military (b)							
British	64.8	64.7	58.6				
French	24.1	17.6	20.7				
Other	7.4	11.8	13.8				
Unknown	3.7	5.9	6.9				
Column N=	54	34	29				

Source:
(a) *Canadian Parliamentary Guide*, various years.
(b) *Canadian Almanac and Directory*, various years.
(c) *Corpus Almanac & Canadian Sourcebook* (Sova, 1988), all university presidents; and Ministers of Education and Deputy Ministers (from b above).
(d) *Directory of Labour Organization in Canada*, various years, President of National Unions or Canadian Vice-Presidents of International Unions. Largest unions only (in 1965 and 1975 one international, with no Canadian director, excluded).

these from the United Kingdom itself, while the Catholic Church elite was predominantly French Canadian (57.9%) in 1952. Data on the Anglican church elite in 1987 indicate only slightly reduced predominance by those of British origin (93.5%) (but see Nock, 1979; 1981). So far as the Catholic church is concerned, our findings indicate that, by 1982, the French Canadian role has declined (57.9 to 43.9%) while the role of 'third ethnics' has increased from 0.0 to 12.3 percent. This is the one case so far in which the British component actually increased (see Table V).

In the case of the labour elite, Porter again divided his study into a mainly anglophone labour elite and an

Table IV   Trends in the Ethnic Origins of a Broadcast Media Elite—1975, 1985, and 1989

	Broadcast Elite (a)		
	1975	1985	1989
British	60.3	55.7	49.4
French	17.2	26.1	21.2
Other	13.8	10.2	24.7
Unknown	8.7	8.0	4.7
N=	58	88	85

(a) See text for elite definition.
Source: Financial Post Delivery of Directors, various years.

Table V   Trends in the Ethnic Origins of the Elites of the
Catholic and Anglican Churches(a)

Catholic (b)	*1952(d)*	*1982(e)*
British	35.7%	42.1%
French	58.9	43.9
Other	5.4	12.3
Unknown	—	1.8
N=	56	57
Anglican(c)	*1952*	*1987*
British	99.9(?)	93.5%
French	—(?)	—
Other	—(?)	3.2
Unknown	—	3.2
N=	26	31

(a) The Catholic and Anglican church elites are made up here of all bishops, archbishops, and cardinals residing and holding office in Canada (see Porter, 1965: 514–5).

(b) Catholic officials in 1982 were obtained from the *Catholic Institutional Guide* (Joncas, 1983).

(c) Anglican officials in 1987 were taken from the 1987–88 *Crockford's Clerical Dictionary* (Crockford, 1988).

(d) The figures for 1952 are drawn from Porter, 1965: 515–7.

(e) The years 1982 and 1987 were chosen because they were the most recent years for which data were available.

Table VI   Trends in the Ethnic Origins of Various Business Elites

	1951(a)	*1972(b)*	*1977(c)*	*1985(d)*
British	92.3%	86.2%	77.9%	67.8%
French	6.7	8.4	7.9	14.8
Other	1.0	5.4	14.3	14.8
Unknown	—	—	—	2.7
N=	760	775	142	264

It must be emphasized that these elites have been chosen in very different manners and are not comparable in any rigorous sense.

(a) This elite is drawn mainly from the directors of firms with 500 or more employees. See Porter, 1965: 223; Appendix II. For the ethnic origins data, see Porter, 1965: 286. Also Clement, 1975: 232.

(b) See Clement, 1975: 128, 232. This elite is drawn mainly from directors of 'dominant' corporations. '. . . a corporation was defined as dominant if it had assets of greater than $250 million and income of over $50 million . . .' (p. 128).

(c) See Williams, 1989: 73, 74, 76. This 'large business' elite included 'chief executive officers of the largest Canadian corporations in key areas of the economy' (p. 74).

(d) This elite consists of the directors of the 20 largest Canadian companies by total assets as listed in the *Financial Post Survey of Industrials* (Pattison, 1985).

overwhelmingly francophone one. In the case of the more national, mainly anglophone group, he found that about 69.4 percent were of British origin; 14.6 percent of French origin; and 16 percent of 'third ethnic' origin, whereas virtually all of the francophone elite were of French origin. We were unable to replicate Porter's procedures but did find that if one looks at leadership of major unions in Canada the British proportion falls from 72.4 percent in 1965 to 58.8 percent in 1985 (see Table III). However, this was one case in which there was no clear increase in 'third ethnic' proportions.

Finally, there is the case of the business elite. Porter (1965) found virtually complete domination by those of British origin (92.3%) in 1951. Clement (1975), in a somewhat differently defined elite, found a slight reduction in the British proportion to 86.2 percent by 1972. Williams (1989), in another somewhat differently defined business elite, reports a further reduction in the British proportion to 77.9 percent by 1977. An analysis of the origins of the directors of the 20 largest Canadian companies in 1985, as ranked by total assets, indicates a further decline to 67.8 percent British origins (see Table VI).

FINAL COMMENTS

The overall contour of the findings indicates that the days of domination of Canadian elites by those of British ancestry are coming to a close, and that the original imagery of the 'vertical mosaic' needs revision. This finding indicates that the changes at the mass level earlier reported by Porter and many others now seem to be reaching the highest levels of our society.

Assuming that the findings reported here stand up under scrutiny, a number of interesting thoughts present themselves. This overall picture may obscure important variations in the relevance of ethnic origins by region, institution, and generation. A given ethnic origin could be a major advantage in one situation, irrelevant in another, and a distinct handicap in a third. Furthermore, one cannot help but note the fact that a remarkably high proportion of the 'third ethnics' are, in fact, of Jewish origin. Their aggregate success in expanding the size of the 'other' category may obscure difficulties still experienced by individuals with names like Eymundsen, Pajekowski, Taglianetti, and Singh.

Nonetheless, the findings also encourage the pleasant thought that the sociological anomalies that characterize the Canadian case may be unusual openness and a high degree of social justice rather than the reverse. As Taylor (1991) notes in his discussion of the apparent reduction of racism in Canadian immigration policy, such anomalies are sufficiently rare as to demand study.

Possibly, the findings are best understood as indicating a 'circulation of elites.' Perhaps, another implica-

tion of these findings is that liberal capitalist democracy has once again demonstrated a capacity for meaningful social change. Porter would presumably be pleased (Porter, 1979; Rich, forthcoming).

Vertical Mosaic among the Elites: The New Imagery Revisited

M. Reza Nakhaie

Queen's University

◆ ◆ ◆

. . . This paper demonstrates that Ogmundson and McLaughlin's (1992) conclusions are misleading because they ignore changes in the ethnic composition of the Canadian population. This is an important omission, given the Canadian population dynamic in which the British share of the total population has continually declined and that of the "third" ethnic group has increased. The shift in the ethnic composition of the Canadian population has been particularly drastic since the Immigration Acts of 1967 and 1976. . . .

The Vertical Mosaic (Porter, 1965) has become the single most influential book published in Canada since World War II. By 1974, more than 70,000 copies had been sold (Rich, 1976: 14). Porter himself received the MacIver Award in 1966 for an outstanding contribution to the social sciences. . . . Nevertheless, many scholars have come to criticize him for his measurement of elites, his indiscriminate use of statistical data and his biased interpretations. Rich (15) suggested that the book was "distorted" and a "caricature" of Canadian society. Later, he called the vertical mosaic image of Canada a "myth" (1991: 419). Tepperman (1975: 156) argued that "it is patently false that ethnicity and social class are interchangeable in Canada." Berkowitz (1984: 252) called Porter and Clement "good" journalists but "bad" sociologists. Brym (Brym and Fox, 1989: 99, 112) also questioned the *Vertical Mosaic* imagery as being "seriously deficient."

Perhaps the most persistent and systematic criticism has come from Ogmundson (1990; 1992; 1993) and Ogmundson and McLaughlin (1992, 1994). In his 1990 article, Ogmundson argued that Porter was biased in his selection of the elites and that Clement failed to replicate

Porter's selection methodology; thus, "it is impossible to infer trends over time with any confidence" (see also Hunter, 1976: 126). He argued that Clement and Olsen used quite different measures of ethnic origin, and therefore that Canadian elites couldn't be compared between periods (170–71). In addition, measures of ethnic origin by last name over-estimate British origins because many of the "other" ethnic groups have Anglicized their names. Finally, he argued that missing cases are likely to refer to those of the third ethnic groups and, by excluding them from the analysis, Clement and Porter under-estimated the "other" ethnic origins' representation in the elites (see also Ogmundson, 1993). He concluded that the traditional imagery is "obsolete" (1990: 165) and should be "abandoned" (1993: 383). In his subsequent paper, which was a reply to Clement (1990), Ogmundson (1992: 314) presented a measured critique and suggested that his earlier paper was intended to "bring . . . back in" the critical observations of the mid-1970s against Porter and Clement. He emphasized that "Canadian elites are becoming *less exclusive*" (emphasis in original).

Rich suggested that Ogmundson's (1990) paper delivered "the coup de grace to the myth that institutional elites in Canada have been exceptionally exclusive in terms of their social origins" (1991: 419). However, it was Ogmundson and McLaughlin's (1992) paper that aimed to deliver the final blow to the prevailing Canadian academic consciousness. . . .

Porter, Clement and Olsen have argued that, according to the dominant "meritocratic" ideological assumption, the assignment of social tasks should be based on ability and talent, and that social characteristics

From M. Reza Nakhaie, "Vertical mosaic among the elites: the new imagery revisited," *Canadian Review of Sociology and Anthropology,* Vol. 34, No. 1, Feb. 1997, pp. 1–24. Reprinted with permission of the Canadian Sociology and Anthropology Association.

such as ethnicity should not be impediments to achieving positions at the top of institutional hierarchies because social justice demands the equalization of opportunities to compete for the privileged positions (see also Parkin, 1971: 13). However, contrary to this ideology, if it is found that ethnicity is an important factor for recruitment to elite positions, then inequality of opportunity and not "meritocracy" should be considered as the hallmark of the society (Porter, 1965: 265, 217; Clement, 1975a: 2, 7). In this regard, they have shown that there is little randomness in the representation of the ethnic groups at the elite level and that, in fact, elites tend to be exclusive by establishing patterns of selection—patterns of preference based on the attitudes and values of those already at the top, "because the selection of successors is one of the prerogatives of power" (Porter, 1965: 265; Clement, 1975a: 250; Michels, 1962: 34). Thus, these scholars have argued that the established patterns of selection and access to elite positions demonstrate inequality of opportunity, which reproduces the dominant ethnic group at the highest level of power and privileges, pointing to class continuity for this group. This type of reproduction does not mean that there is no mobility: "Rather it means that there is sufficient continuity to maintain class institutions" (Porter, 1965: 285n; Clement, 1975b: 50; Olsen, 1980: 82).

In contrast, Ogmundson and McLaughlin have suggested the "end of the British dominance," the "abandoning" of the vertical mosaic imagery, and thus implied equality of access to elite positions because *they did not standardize the proportion of each ethnic group in the elite to that of their respective general population.* It is not that they were unaware of this methodology. In fact, Ogmundson and McLaughlin argue that "it is tempting . . . to make a systematic comparison between elite ethnic origins and the census reports on ethnic origins of the general population for various decades." They leave this task aside, though, because it "is beyond the scope of the . . . paper" (1992: 230). But why? Weren't the focus and scope of the paper a revision and re-evaluation of Porter's, Clement's and Olsen's empirical analyses and theory? . . .

DATA AND METHODS

◆ ◆ ◆

To standardize the ethnic groups' elite participation across time, the conventional Index of Dissimilarity is calculated (a measure first introduced by Clement [1975a: 234, Table 35]). This index represents the ratio of the ethnic proportion in the elite to the corresponding proportion of the Canadian population in the census. A figure above 1.00 denotes over-representation and a figure below 1.00 suggests under-representation.

We calculated five indices of dissimilarity for each elite category. The first index is based on the general population. This is the index that is directly comparable to that of Porter, Clement and Olsen. The second index is based on the population of ethnic groups over 35 years of age, the third for those between 35 and 65, the fourth for males between 35 and 64 years of age, and the fifth for Canadian-born males. Indices two to four are based on the reality that elites are not selected from the younger population . . . and that some elites are constrained by mandatory retirement. The fourth index is also based on the fact that women are still rarely found among the elites. Clement (1975a: 266n; see also 191, 332) wrote that "women are probably the most under-represented social type in the economic elite. Of the total of 946 persons holding elite positions, only 6 or .6 percent of the total are women." Williams (1989: 72) surveyed 588 elites in 1977 and showed that only 17 were women, mainly in the local political arena. In 1990, Clement (184n) wrote that according to the *Financial Post* (June 5, 1989: 35), "only 7 of the 1,169 chief executive officers in the 1990 *Directory of Directors* are women." The final index is based on the expectation that those who are born in Canada have a better chance for the inheritance of ownership, a higher access to networks for occupational mobility, and often a superior command of the official languages than immigrants. . . . In addition, we constructed an index for the Québec-born French males, based on the expectation that the French-Canadians in Québec may have a higher chance of elite recruitment than French-Canadians outside Québec (Clement, 1975a: 236). . . .

FINDINGS

◆ ◆ ◆

The ethnic composition of the Canadian population from 1931 to 1986 is assembled in Table 1, apparently for the first time. Clearly, the British proportion of the population continually declined and that of other groups (and to a lesser extent the French) increased from 1931 to 1986. This trend persisted, whether we use the total population or the age- and sex-specific portions of the total population. The largest decline for the British and increase for "other" ethnic groups was registered in the 35–64 age group. In contrast, the smallest decline for the British population is among the Canadian-born males, followed by

Table 1   Percent Distribution of Canadian Ethnic Groups, 1931–1986

Year	1931	1941	1951	1961	1971	1981	1986
Total Population							
British	54.5	49.7	47.9	44.4	45.0	43.7	35.2
French	26.7	30.3	30.8	30.7	28.9	29.1	33.9
Others	18.8	20.0	21.3	24.9	26.1	27.2	30.8
Population 35+							
British	59.5	56.5	53.5	48.8	47.1	42.7	37.2
French	22.7	24.3	25.2	26.0	26.3	26.3	31.9
Others	17.8	19.2	21.3	25.2	26.6	31.0	30.9
Population 35–64							
British	58.9	55.1	51.3	47.2	44.3	40.8	34.6
French	23.2	24.5	26.3	27.4	26.4	27.3	33.3
Others	17.9	20.3	22.4	25.4	29.3	31.9	32.1
Population 35–64 Males							
British	56.1	53.3	50.2	46.4	43.5	40.1	34.4
French	22.0	23.7	25.6	26.8	25.9	26.8	32.5
Others	21.9	23.0	24.2	26.8	30.6	33.1	33.1
Population Canadian-born Males							
British	50.2	48.5	47.8	45.8	47.6	42.3	38.0
French	35.3	36.0	36.0	36.3	34.1	31.3	40.4
Others	14.5	15.5	16.2	19.9	18.3	26.4	21.6
Québec French	28.3	28.4	28.0	28.1	26.6	24.8	33.3

Sources: Census of Canada, 1931, 1941, 1951, 1961, 1971, 1981 and 1986.

*Ethnic groups in 1981 and 1986 are based on the single-ethnic-origin responses.

**1981 population is based on Census Metropolitan Areas and Census Agglomerations of 50,000 population and greater.

***1986 population is based on 20% sample data.

that of the total population. The smallest increase for the "other" ethnic groups, as expected, is among the Canadian-born males. Overall, the French portion of the total population has slightly increased from 1931 to 1986, but among the Canadian- and Québec-borns their population has been basically stable. Excluding the question of nativity, it seems that Porter, Clement and Olsen actually used a conservative index to show British dominance among the elites.

Tables 2 through 6 present the indices for various elites based on the percentages provided by Ogmundson and McLaughlin (1992) and the census population reported above. These tables all indicate a vertical ethnic mosaic at the elite level as demonstrated previously by Porter, Clement and Olsen.

We start with the ethnic representation in the most dominant institution in the Canadian capitalist structure (Table 2). The dominant positions in this institution include the board of directors, which makes the most important decisions "about the expansion of the economy, its direction, scope and level of technology. With these decisions they determine rates of employment and the types of occupation that will exist in . . . [Canadian] society" (Clement, 1975a: 24). Table 2 shows that, from 1951 to 1985, British elites dominated the economic arena, or what Clement has called the "big bourgeoisie"

Table 2   Index of Ethnic Representation in the Business Elite, 1951–1985

Elite year	1951[a]	1972[b]	1977[c]	1985[d]
Census year*	1951	1971	1981	1986
British				
1. Total population	1.93	1.92	1.79	1.98
2. Population aged 35+	1.72	1.83	1.83	1.87
3. Population aged 35–64	1.80	1.95	1.92	2.01
4. Male pop. aged 35–64	1.84	1.98	1.94	2.02
5. Can.-born male	1.93	1.81	1.85	1.83
French				
1. Total population	0.22	0.29	0.26	0.45
2. Population aged 35+	0.26	0.32	0.29	0.48
3. Population aged 35–64	0.25	0.32	0.28	0.46
4. Male pop. aged 35–64	0.26	0.32	0.29	0.47
5. Can.-born male	0.19	0.25	0.25	0.38
6. Québec-born male	0.24	0.32	0.31	0.46
Others				
1. Total population	0.05	0.21	0.52	0.49
2. Population aged 35+	0.05	0.20	0.45	0.49
3. Population aged 35–64	0.06	0.18	0.44	0.47
4. Male pop. aged 35–64	0.05	0.18	0.43	0.46
5. Can.-born male	0.07	0.29	0.53	0.70
N =	760	775	142	257
Unknown	—	—	—	7

Sources: Notes and proportion of ethnic groups in the elites are based on Ogmundson and McLaughlin (1992: 235).

a. This elite is drawn mainly from the directors of firms with 500 or more employees (see Porter, 1965: 223 and Appendix II; Clement, 1975a: 232).

b. This elite is drawn mainly from directors of "dominant" corporations with assets of greater than $250 million and income of over $50 million (see Clement, 1975a: 128, 232).

c. This elite included chief executives of the largest Canadian corporations in key areas of the economy (see Williams, 1989: 73–75).

d. This elite included the directors of the 20 largest Canadian corporations by total assets, as listed in the *Financial Post Survey of Industries* (see Pattison, 1985).

*The Index represents the ratio of the ethnic proportion in the elite to the corresponding proportion of the Canadian population for the closest census time. A figure above 1.00 denotes over-representation and a figure below 1.00 suggests under-representation (see Clement, 1975a: 234, Table 35).

(1975a: 6). In fact, using the more stringent indices, the British increased their economic elite participation from 1.84 in 1951 to 2.02 in 1985. Understandably, the index of British representation among the business elites shows a slight sign of decline if compared to the Canadian-born population. As noted above, however, this index fails to take into account the foreign-born members of the economic elites in the numerator. Consistent with Clement (1975a: 234), French and "other" ethnic groups registered gains among the economic elites in this period but were still under-represented relative to their populations. Thus, in 1985, French and "others" were almost equally under-represented in relation to their populations, while the British were over-represented. In other words, to reach an ethnic economic elite parity in more recent years, French and "other" ethnic groups would have had to double their economic elite participation and the British to decrease it by half. The Canadian-born male index, however, shows a lower elite representation for the French than for "other" ethnic groups. In general, with respect to inequalities that stem from the concentration of economic power, there has been little (if any) decline in the British index of elite representation in the boardrooms of the major Canadian corporations. French and other ethnic groups have improved their elite representation, but the process of change over the last 35 years seems to be slow.

Table 3 illustrates the index of ethnic representation in the political elite for the period 1940 to 1987. The index, based on the general population, shows a slight decline for the British in this elite category, and more so for the index based on the Canadian-born population; the other stringent indices, however, point to the stability or increase of British political elite representation. Here, the image is again very close to the conventional picture in which French and "others" are under-represented and the British are over-represented. The indices for the British stood around 1.50, for the French around 0.80, and for "other" ethnic origins, below 0.60. Again, the exception is in the flawed index based on the male Canadian- and/or Québec-born French. Nevertheless, the image is still a vertical one.

The image in Table 4 is basically the same as Table 3. British stability among the federal and provincial cabinet elites, as well as among deputy ministers (but see the Canadian-born index), supports the traditional imagery; so do the junior positions of the French and "others." This table, however, has two distinctive features. First, the change in French participation among cabinet ministers is more pronounced than French representation in the polit-

Table 3   Index of Ethnic Representation in the Political Elite, 1940–1987

Elite year	1940–1960[a]	1960–1973[b]	1974–1987[c]
Census year	1941–1961	1961–1971	1971–1986
British			
1.	1.60	1.79	1.48
2.	1.43	1.67	1.41
3.	1.47	1.74	1.51
4.	1.51	1.78	1.53
5.	1.60	1.71	1.32
French			
1.	0.71	0.82	0.76
2.	0.86	0.94	0.82
3.	0.83	0.85	0.80
4.	0.79	0.93	0.82
5.	0.60	0.70	0.73
6.	0.77	0.90	0.93
Others			
1.	0.14	0.30	0.58
2.	0.14	0.29	0.57
3.	0.14	0.28	0.54
4.	0.13	0.26	0.52
5.	0.19	0.42	0.74
N =	157	159	200
Unknown	—	—	3

Sources: See Table 2 (see also Ogmundson and McLaughlin, 1992: 230).

a. Includes all those who were federal cabinet ministers, all provincial premiers, all justices of the Supreme Court of Canada, presidents of the Exchequer Court and the provincial chief justices (see Porter, 1965: 604).

b. As above (see Olsen, 1980: 127).

c. All Supreme Court justices, federal cabinet ministers, provincial premiers and provincial chief justices for the years 1974–1987.

*The percentage of ethnic groups are calculated at the mean level of the two years.

ical elites in general. For a brief moment in 50 years of politics (1945), they reached their true share of the cabinet ministers, without being under-represented relative to their population, a pattern that is negated once we control for place of birth both in Canada and in Québec. Second, the "other" ethnic groups gained more "elite" representa-

tion in the lower ranks of the deputy ministers than the cabinet ministers, particularly if they were born in Canada. Thus, by 1985, the British scored around 1.50 for both cabinet and deputy ministers, the French scored slightly better than 0.80 among the cabinet ministers and below 0.60 among the deputy ministers, while "other" ethnic origins scored just over 0.50 among the cabinet ministers and around 0.70 among the deputy ministers.

Table 5 presents the indices for ethnic representation for members of parliament, and for military, education and labour elites. The conventional imagery and the stability of British dominance are more apparent among the first two types of elite than the last two. Although the vertical ethnic mosaic imagery is intact, there are some indications that British elite participation in education and labour, as a proportion of their population, has declined, and that that of the non-British has increased. Interestingly, the highest gain among the labour elite is for the French. By 1985, the French, with a score of about 1.30, and the British, with a score of about 1.40, were both over-represented, while "others," with a score of around 0.20, were under-represented. The French were, nevertheless, still the junior partner here. This table also shows that being Canadian-born is generally inconsequential to the British but slightly more beneficial to the French and "other" ethnic groups.

Finally, Table 6 illustrates once again the traditional vertical ethnic mosaic imagery, this time for media elites. The British dominance, with a score of around 1.50 in the broadcast elites, is clear. The French, with a score of just under 0.70, are for the first time not even a junior partner. By 1989, they are replaced by "other" ethnic groups, with a score of over 0.80, in second place. The Canadian place of birth was particularly beneficial to the "third" ethnic groups' elite media representation in 1975 and 1985.

CONCLUSION AND DISCUSSION

A correct conclusion from the data provided by Ogmundson and McLaughlin (1992) is *not* to "abandon" the traditional imagery at the *elite level*, or even to suggest a noticeable decline in British participation among the elites as a proportion of their population. Such a conclusion points to the "verisimilitude" of the data. The more accurate conclusion—and this is consistent with Clement (1975a: 234; 1975b: 46)—is that British elite participation and dominance have basically been stable and that,

Table 4   Index of Ethnic Representation among Federal and Provincial Cabinet Ministers and Deputy Ministers, 1935–1985

Elite year	1935	1945	1955	1965	1975	1985
Census year	1931	1941	1951	1961	1971	1981
Provincial and Federal Cabinet Ministers						
British						
1.	1.55	1.44	1.50	1.61	1.41	1.38
2.	1.42	1.27	1.34	1.46	1.35	1.41
3.	1.44	1.30	1.40	1.51	1.43	1.47
4.	1.51	1.35	1.43	1.54	1.46	1.50
5.	1.69	1.48	1.50	1.56	1.33	1.42
French						
1.	0.50	0.83	0.70	0.67	0.73	0.79
2.	0.58	1.04	0.85	0.79	0.80	0.87
3.	0.57	1.03	0.82	0.75	0.80	0.84
4.	0.60	1.06	0.84	0.77	0.81	0.85
5.	0.38	0.70	0.60	0.57	0.67	0.73
6.	0.47	0.89	0.77	0.73	0.79	0.92
Others						
1.	0.11	0.15	0.31	0.32	0.59	0.62
2.	0.11	0.16	0.31	0.31	0.58	0.54
3.	0.11	0.15	0.30	0.31	0.53	0.53
4.	0.09	0.13	0.28	0.29	0.51	0.51
5.	0.14	0.19	0.41	0.44	0.85	0.64
N =	34	33	38	43	41	62
Unknown	1	1	—	—	—	—
Federal and Provincial Deputy Ministers						
British						
1.	1.61	1.60	1.69	1.63	1.58	1.44
2.	1.48	1.40	1.51	1.48	1.46	1.47
3.	1.49	1.44	1.58	1.53	1.55	1.54
4.	1.57	1.49	1.61	1.56	1.58	1.57
5.	1.75	1.64	1.69	1.58	1.45	1.49
French						
1.	0.38	0.47	0.45	0.62	0.51	0.46
2.	0.44	0.59	0.55	0.74	0.56	0.59

Continued

Table 4   Index of Ethnic Representation among Federal and Provincial Cabinet Ministers and Deputy Ministers, 1935–1985 *Continued*

Elite year	1935	1945	1955	1965	1975	1985
Census year	1931	1941	1951	1961	1971	1981
			Federal and Provincial Deputy Ministers			
French *Continued*						
3.	0.44	0.59	0.53	0.72	0.56	0.57
4.	0.46	0.63	0.57	0.72	0.57	0.58
5.	0.29	0.40	0.39	0.53	0.43	0.49
6.	0.36	0.51	0.50	0.68	0.55	0.62
Others						
1.	0.11	0.31	0.24	0.34	0.62	0.79
2.	0.11	0.32	0.24	0.34	0.61	0.70
3.	0.11	0.31	0.23	0.33	0.56	0.68
4.	0.09	0.27	0.21	0.32	0.53	0.65
5.	0.14	0.40	0.31	0.43	0.89	0.87
N =	164	167	234	263	352	378
Unknown	—	2	5	7	6	11

Sources: See Table 2 (see also Ogmundson and McLaughlin, 1992: 231). For cabinet ministers: *Canadian Parliamentary Guide*; for deputy ministers: *Canadian Almanac and Directory.*

Table 5   Index of Ethnic Representation in the Various Elites, 1965–1985

Elite year	1965	1975	1985	1965	1975	1985
Census year	1961	1971	1981	1961	1971	1981
		Members of Parliament[a]			*Military Elites*[b]	
British						
1.	1.34	1.21	1.22	1.52	1.53	1.44
2.	1.22	1.16	1.25	1.38	1.46	1.47
3.	1.26	1.23	1.31	1.42	1.55	1.54
4.	1.28	1.25	1.33	1.45	1.58	1.57
5.	1.30	1.15	1.26	1.47	1.44	1.49
French						
1.	0.81	1.04	0.86	0.81	0.65	0.76
2.	0.96	1.15	0.95	0.96	0.71	0.84
3.	0.91	1.14	0.92	0.91	0.71	0.81
4.	0.93	1.17	0.97	0.93	0.72	0.83
5.	0.69	0.88	0.80	0.69	0.55	0.71
6.	0.89	1.13	1.01	0.89	0.70	0.89

Continued

Table 5   Index of Ethnic Representation in the Various Elites, 1965–1985 *Continued*

Elite year	1965	1975	1985	1965	1975	1985
Census year	1961	1971	1981	1961	1971	1981
		Members of Parliament[a]			Military Elites[b]	
Others						
1.	0.62	0.58	0.78	0.31	0.48	0.54
2.	0.61	0.57	0.70	0.30	0.47	0.48
3.	0.61	0.51	0.68	0.30	0.43	0.46
4.	0.57	0.49	0.65	0.29	0.41	0.45
5.	0.77	0.82	0.82	0.39	0.68	0.56
N =	268	262	276	51	32	27
Unknown	8	2	6	3	2	2
		Education Elites[b,c]			Labour Elites[d]	
British						
1.	1.76	1.65	1.41	1.70	1.11	1.34
2.	1.60	1.57	1.44	1.54	1.06	1.38
3.	1.66	1.67	1.51	1.59	1.13	1.44
4.	1.69	1.70	1.53	1.62	1.15	1.47
5.	1.71	1.56	1.49	1.63	1.05	1.39
French						
1.	0.38	0.39	0.47	0.58	0.86	1.21
2.	0.45	0.43	0.52	0.69	0.95	1.34
3.	0.43	0.43	0.51	0.65	0.95	1.29
4.	0.44	0.44	0.51	0.67	0.96	1.32
5.	0.32	0.33	0.44	0.49	0.73	1.13
6.	0.42	0.42	0.56	0.63	0.94	1.42
Others						
1.	0.40	0.56	0.90	0.28	0.96	0.32
2.	0.40	0.54	0.79	0.28	0.94	0.19
3.	0.39	0.49	0.77	0.28	0.85	0.18
4.	0.37	0.47	0.74	0.26	0.82	0.18
5.	0.50	0.79	0.93	0.36	1.36	0.22
N =	60	62	65	28	24	17
Unknown	2	2	3	2	—	—

Sources: See Table 2 (see also Ogmundson and McLaughlin, 1992: 232).

a. *Canadian Parliamentary Guide.*

b. *Canadian Almanac and Directory.*

c. *Corpus Almanac & Canadian Sourcebook* (Sova, 1988), all university presidents; and ministers of education and deputy ministers (from b above).

d. *Directory of Labour Organization in Canada.* President of national unions or Canadian vice-president of international union. Largest unions only (in 1965 and 1975); one international, with no Canadian directors excluded.

Table 6 Index of Ethnic Representation in the Media Elite, 1975–1989 (Broadcast Elite)[a]

Elite year	1975	1985	1989
Census year	1971	1981	1986
British			
1.	1.47	1.38	1.47
2.	1.39	1.42	1.39
3.	1.49	1.48	1.50
4.	1.52	1.51	1.50
5.	1.39	1.43	1.36
French			
1.	0.65	0.98	0.65
2.	0.72	1.08	0.69
3.	0.71	1.04	0.66
4.	0.73	1.06	0.68
5.	0.55	0.91	0.55
6.	0.71	1.14	0.67
Others			
1.	0.58	0.41	0.84
2.	0.57	0.36	0.83
3.	0.51	0.35	0.80
4.	0.49	0.33	0.78
5.	0.82	0.42	1.20
N =	53	81	81
Unknown	5	7	4

Sources: See Table 2 (see also Ogmundson and McLaughlin, 1992: 234).
[a]Based on *Financial Post Directory of Directors*.

consistent with Porter (1965: 285n), there is a clear ethnic vertical mosaic among the Canadian elites. The findings presented here also echo conclusions reached by Olsen (1980: 82). For the bureaucratic elite, he found some marginal change in the position of French and "other" ethnic groups since the time of the Porter study, which points to a "more open, more heterogeneous and probably more meritocratic, than the old" elite. But, he continues, the "overall pattern is one of the marked persistence of ethnic preferences in recruitment." Similarly, we have shown that there is a clear pattern of preference for recruitment to elite positions for people of British origin.

On the other hand, consistent with the traditional imagery as well as with the views held by Brym and Fox (1989: 112), Hunter (1986), Berkowitz (1984), Rich (1991), Ogmundson (1990; 1992; 1993), and Ogmundson and McLaughlin (1992; 1994), the French and "other" ethnic groups have increased their elite participation. However, since the decline of the British in elite positions has equalled their relative decline in the Canadian population, one can conclude that the increase in the French and "other" ethnic group elite participation has not necessarily been at the expense of the British. To put it somewhat differently, there has been an absolute decline in the British elite position but, relative to their population, there has been little, if any, decline. The French and "other" ethnic groups, on the other hand, have increased their elite participation in both absolute and relative terms. . . .

On a conceptual level, Ogmundson and McLaughlin (1992: 237) relied only on the changes in the proportion of ethnic groups among the elites and ignored the ethnic composition of the population. Therefore, they suggested that their findings indicate a "circulation of elites." This is a doubtful conclusion. In Pareto's words, the British "foxes" still dominate Canadian power structures and the French and "other" ethnic "lions" are still subordinate (see Pareto's *Treatise* in Lopreato, 1965).

Even if we accept Ogmundson and McLaughlin's data based on the percent distribution of ethnic elites, the British proportion of elites never fell below the 50 percent level except in one case—the broadcast media elites in 1989, at 49.4 percent. Assuming that, at the elite levels, decisions are made collectively and democratically, the balance of power is still overwhelmingly in favour of the British. This is because the French and "other" ethnic groups do not share a similar type of ethnic consciousness, a fact which causes disunity among the non-British; the "other" groups are further divided among themselves by ethnic origin, with little ethnic consciousness. In fact, research has shown that members of "other" ethnic groups frequently lose their "ethnicity" in Canada (see Reitz, 1985; Isajiw, 1990; Breton, et al., 1990).

The findings presented here on the extent of continuity of ethnic homogeneity in elite positions show that it seems to be rooted in Canadian history, which is built on conquest and immigration (Clement, 1975a: 231). The conquerors have institutionalized avenues of upward mobility, understandably based on their own preferred values, attitudes and behaviours, thus limiting the access of the conquered and the newly arrived to positions of power. Those who dominate the boardrooms of the major Canadian institutions make decisions and establish rules of recruitment based on the cultural values of their own British ethnic affiliation and "preferred" social background. The conquered and the newly arrived, on the other hand, have established "parallel" social networks and institutions for upward mobility that for the most part are distinct from what is available to the British (see Clement 1975a: 239; Breton, 1978). Similarly, since earlier British dominance among Canadian institutions has established the frame of reference for future incumbents, one of the requirements of becoming a member of elite institutions is perhaps now to be "non-ethnic" (see Clement 1975b: 50; Williams, 1989: 83; Berkowitz, 1980; Kanter, 1977). As Porter (1965: 218) has shown, the process of "like recruiting" is widespread in all of the dominant Canadian institutions.

In sum, these changing positions over 50 years can be judged in two ways. They may indicate the extent to which the British have kept their elite over-representation intact, or they may suggest a substantial intrusion of other cultural elements (see Porter, 1965: 64).

The findings, however, do not support Ogmundson and McLaughlin's (1992: 237) conclusions that "the days of domination of Canadian elites by those of British ancestry are coming to a close" and that the original imagery of "vertical mosaic" at the *elite level* needs revision. What prevails in Canada is a British ruling class that has had and still has effective instrumental control in each category of elites, and that has structurally dominated, and continues to dominate, the basic institutions of society *despite* a rapidly declining share of the general population. The inequality of access to elite positions remains the hallmark of Canadian society, and the new "balance" of the population, into a third each of British, French and "other," is *not* reflected in the positions of power. Nevertheless, there are strong indications that, in recent years, the French and "other" ethnic groups' access to elite positions has increased compared to their share of the general population.

Race, Income Splits Toronto, Study Warns; 'Huge' Inequality Shown in Survey of Census Figures

Elaine Carey

Toronto is rapidly becoming segregated along racial, ethnic, social and economic lines, warns a new study commissioned by the city.

There are "huge inequalities" in income, employment, education and rates of poverty among ethno-racial groups, says the study by York University professor Michael Ornstein, obtained by *The Star*.

In many visible minority groups, more than half the families are living below the Statistics Canada low-income line while in other white, European and British-origin groups, the rate is less than 10 percent.

Unemployment rates vary from less than 6 percent among Europeans to more than 40 percent in some black groups and child poverty rates range from less than 10 percent to more than 60 percent.

The differences are almost all tied to race. Almost every one of the poorest groups is a visible minority, says the analysis of 1996 census data.

"The more visible you are the more difficulties you have," said Ornstein, director of York University's Institute for Social Research. "It's clear the groups that are worst off are black."

Ornstein looked at each ethnic-racial group's levels of income, education, and employment. He also analyzed earnings and family incomes and considered how long people had lived in Canada.

Ethiopians, Ghanaians, Afghans and Somalis are the most severely disadvantaged, with poverty rates ranging from 52.2 to 70 percent. They are trapped in low-wage jobs, even though most have a high school education.

A second very large group live in "severe disadvantage," with high unemployment, low-skill jobs, low education and high rates of school drop-outs. They include Vietnamese, Iranians, Tamils and Sri Lankans.

A third group suffering "significant disadvantage," with poverty rates around 50 percent, includes aboriginals, Central Americans, Jamaicans, West Indians and people with multiple South Asian heritage.

More than half the children from four areas of the world live in poverty. That includes 41,560 African, black and Caribbean children; 10,805 Arab and West Asian children; 10,325 Latin American children; and 23,060 South Asian children.

"Among the very poorest people, things have gone drastically wrong," Ornstein said in an interview. "Things have gotten worse in a really scary way. The levels of poverty are such that children don't have enough to eat."

While new immigrants are among the worst off, "this is not primarily a settlement problem in the sense that you can say 'All newcomers face this,'" he said.

"There's clearly a very big race dimension to it and it doesn't disappear over time. These things are really built into our social structure.

"Black groups as a whole don't have as high incomes as their education suggests," he said. "We are seeing a significant amount of job discrimination against black people in particular and to a lesser extent, South Asians."

Coming to Canada as a refugee also creates long-term disadvantage, he said. Many of the Africans, Afghanis and Vietnamese who came here as refugees more than a decade ago are still poorly off.

The report shows "overwhelming evidence of widespread discrimination against members of many of Toronto's ethno-racial communities, particularly those from the black community," said Tim Rees, director of the city's access and equity office. "There are huge disparities in the life experience and life chances of different communities in Toronto.

"If we are to feel pride that Toronto is home to the world, we cannot at the same time tolerate the reality that many communities within our midst are living worlds apart," he said in an interview.

"The report was distributed to every member of council last week but there are no plans to discuss it or act on it at council," Rees said. The old city of Toronto's access and equity committee was disbanded when the new city was amalgamated in 1998 and there is no longer a committee dedicated to dealing with race issues.

"I think these statistics hit you in the face," Rees said. "Poverty is based on race to a disturbing level. We can't afford to ignore that. We need to address it in a far more provocative fashion."

The report will filter out to various city departments and "hopefully will be used as a basis for policy development and priorities," he said.

Continued

Ornstein, who analyzed the same data from the 1991 census for the city, said the new study shows the income gap in Toronto is widening.

"There's a bigger difference in pay between the best and worst jobs and when that happens, somebody's got to be a loser," he said.

But there are "critical things" that need to be done to change that, he said. "The minimum wage is relatively low and people who are working on it can't lead a decent life especially if they have children."

The social welfare cuts in 1996 have had a "devastating effect on people who are the worst off," he said. Toronto also faces "an incredible housing crisis."

All three are policies of the provincial government and "it's the province that has to act," he said.

Source: Elaine Carey, "Race, income splits Toronto, study warns," *Toronto Star,* July 7, 2000, p. A01. Reprinted with permission—Torstar Syndication Services.

Unit Nine

HEALTH AND ILLNESS
Introduction: Neoliberalism and Health Inequalities

◆◆◆

A fundamental source of identity and pride in Canada is its unique health-care system. Canadians cherish their health-care system and use it as a source of demarcation between themselves and the United States. The Canadian health system is based on government's responsibility in providing comprehensive, accessible, and universal health care for all Canadians. Does this mean that there is no health inequality in Canada? Do all Canadians benefit from the health-care system equally? If we were to look at Aboriginal Canadians' health situation, our immediate answer would be negative. Aboriginals have more than twice the **infant mortality rate** and death rate of the general population. Their **life expectancy** is about 30 years lower and their suicide rate is about three times higher (six times higher for the 15–24 age group) than the general population. Their major causes of death, in addition to motor vehicle accidents, drowning, and fire, are diseases of the circulatory and respiratory system, cancer, suicide, and chronic conditions (e.g., tuberculosis and diabetes) (see Frideres, 1994).

Why do Aboriginals have more health conditions than others? Four possible explanations of health conditions are lifestyle, environment, health-care system, and biological makeup. Lack of a proper diet, heavy smoking, and alcohol consumption, as well as lack of physical activity are examples of lifestyles that are related to an individual's health and well-being. According to the lifestyle explanation, Aboriginals are responsible for their own health conditions. They need to exercise, change their diet, not smoke, and moderate

their drinking level. However, we should also remember that Aboriginals are more likely to live in areas that are a substantial distance from the major metropolitans, and they have the lowest socioeconomic status in the country. This means that they have limited access to health services, prescription drugs, and the barest of material necessities (e.g., heat, food, and clothing). They also have less knowledge about healthy lifestyles, such as nutritious diets. Aboriginal people living in rural areas are also exposed to hazardous environments. Various industrial and resource development projects have polluted water and disrupted fish and game stock, resulting in environmental pollution in Native communities. For example, the amount of mercury in the blood of Aboriginal residents of the White Dog and Grassy Narrows Reserves in Ontario is 40 to 150 times higher than among average Canadians. Native communities in Cluff Lake and St. Regis in Saskatchewan and Serpent River in Ontario have been subject to uranium pollution, acid discharge, and fluoride pollution, respectively (Frideres, 1994).

Another explanation related to lifestyle that tends to emphasize individual responsibility views health conditions as being related to social relations (known as **social capital**). Those who are socially connected, have mutual contacts and support, and trust others tend to be healthier than their counterparts. According to Putnam (2000), the more integrated that individuals are in the community, the less likely they are to experience colds, heart attacks, strokes, cancer, depression, and premature death of all sorts. In fact, he stated that "social capital appears to be a complement if not a substitute for Prozac, sleeping pills, anti-acids, vitamin C and other drugs we buy at the corner pharmacy" (2000: 288). Social capital (social ties and supports) helps individuals access medical information, resources such as a ride to the doctor's office, clinic, and hospital, or emotional types of support. However, we should note that access to social capital varies by socioeconomic status. The social capital available to lower classes is less useful for improvement of health than the social capital available to upper social classes. For example, lower classes have less access to appropriate health information and resources needed for improvement of health. In other words, although lifestyle and social relations are important sources of health conditions, they, themselves, tend to be consequences of the environment, social structure, and social policies.

As alluded above, research tends to show a strong relationship between structured inequality and health conditions (see Tables 9.1 and 9.2). Generally, people are healthier if they have higher or at least adequate incomes, are from higher educational and occupational groups, and have proper housing and enough food to eat (Dave-Smith et al., 1998). Those with lower education and income tend to be less happy with their health and have more stress, higher blood pressure, and higher cholesterol than those with higher education and income. Lower income neighbourhoods also have higher rates of circulatory diseases, cancers, injuries, and suicide (Federal Report on the Health of Canadians, 1996).

Wigle and Mao (1980) showed that the differences in life expectancy between the highest and lowest median household income quintiles are 6.2 years for males and 2.9 years for females. Humphries and Doorslaer (2000) showed that those with higher income have better self-assessed and functional health. As well, poor housing affects physical and mental health through location, type, and structure of housing, lack of amenities and privacy, overcrowding, dampness, mould, air pollution, and inadequate heating. These forces, in turn, result in an increased exposure to risk factors such as stress, smoking, drinking, cross-infection, and eating "for comfort" (Cole-Hamilton and Lang, 1986; Wilkinson, 1997).

In addition to social class, environment, and ethnoracial origin, gender also differentiates the healthy and less healthy. Often, the types of health conditions experienced by men and women differ—cardiac arrest and breast cancer, respectively. Women experience more health problems in old age because they live longer.

Also, some of women's health problems are due to their higher poverty rate compared to men. Finally, Rosenberg and Wilson (2000) showed that males at the upper income level tend to have more chronic conditions than women.

Let us take another example related to gender. Women experience anorexia (i.e., eating disorder) substantially more than men. In fact, anorexia is often associated with women. Susan Bordo (1993) pointed to the fact that certain cultural currents play important roles in the development of anorexia. She identified three axes as cultural sources of anorexia where they grip and repress the "body." However, historically, the female body has been significantly more subject to cultural grip and manipulation than the male body. These three axes include:

- The **dualist axis.** Human existence is divided into two realms or substances: the bodily or the material versus the mental or spiritual. In our culture, the bodily or material part confronts us as an alien, as the other, not-me, not-self. The body is experienced as the prison or confinement that the soul, will, or mind needs and struggles to escape. The body is presented as the enemy. It is a source of distraction by its requirement of food, lust, fear, and fancies. The body fights against our will to control it or to subdue its spontaneities. Thus, anorectics try to control their body, to prevent it from becoming fat, by controlling its appetite, hunger, and desire. For the anorectic, the body is thus experienced as alien, an outsider, with the soul or will being trapped within it. As one woman described it: "I feel caught in my body," "I am a prisoner in my body."

- The control axis. Anorectics try to control their alien body and be its master. They push their body to the limit—they exercise, cycle, run, and so on, before they collapse. They push themselves to the extreme and try to overcome all physical obstacles in pursuit of becoming slender and being in control of the body. They enjoy the thrill of being in total charge of the shape of their body. They attempt to sculpture the body into a work of art. They continuously watch themselves in the mirror, check their abs and muscles, and flex their legs, working hard to sweat until, as one woman said, "I really feel like a woman." They experience pleasure in controlling their own body in a world where "people no longer feel they can control events outside themselves . . . but they can control the food they eat and how far they can run."

- The gender/power axis. Bordo also noted that the tyranny of slenderness is not gender neutral, pointing out that over 90 percent of anorectics are women. The media is filled with images of slender models. As well, slenderness has become a dominant desire among school girls in colleges and universities and among working girls. Women's weight has become a focal issue, pushing them to lose weight, to trim the "Big Butt," and to control, as one anorectic stated, the "dictator who dominates me," "a little man who objects when I eat." The anorectic's dictator, the other self, is always male. Many anorectics, Bordo reported, wanted to be a boy when they were children, or their father wanted to have a boy and was disappointed to get a girl, "less than a boy."

Bordo, therefore, showed how the anorectic body has been subject to the cultural gaze that has attempted to train it, torture it, and force it to carry out specific tasks. By highlighting the importance of the power of culture and the importance of gender inequity, Bordo shifted the argument from a biomedical explanation of anorexia to that of a social explanation.

We end the discussion of health and illness by paying attention to the importance of social policies, and then we introduce our debate. The Canadian health-care system has been a major focus of debate between those who adhere to a **neoliberal** market economy as against those who believe in social justice, egalitarianism, and health care as a fundamental human right. Neoliberals would want to minimize state intervention in the market. During recent decades, major concerns have arisen over the increasing costs and the capacity of the health-care system to accommodate the growing populations. Concerns over escalating costs have encouraged a shift in the Canadian government's responsibility from providing comprehensive, accessible, and universal health care to one of fiscal responsibility, accountability, and efficiency. This shift, waged by conservative think tanks such as the C.D. Howe and Fraser Institutes, meant cutbacks to and decentralization of health care as well as the development of a new paradigm where more responsibility for health care is placed on community and informal support: the family, the neighbourhood, churches, and individuals (see Chappell, 1997; Forget, 2002). The implication is that government policies have shifted from the notion of universal health care to that of individual responsibility, social cohesion, and social-support types of explanation.

Earlier in this chapter, Wilkinson had argued that in advanced capitalist countries, higher income inequality leads to lowered social cohesion, which in turn produces poorer health status. In the debate that follows, Coburn paid attention to the social context of income inequality and argued that there is an affinity between neoliberalism (exemplified by the recent government policies), income inequality, and lowered social cohesion. Neoliberalism produces both higher income inequality and lowered social cohesion. This is due to the fact neoliberalism has undermined the welfare state (governments' responsibility of taking care of the population in need). Neoliberalism has a direct effect on both health and social cohesion. Therefore, Coburn focuses on the causes of income inequalities and not just its consequence (health problems). Such focus in turn helps us understand the causal pathways involved in inequality–health status relationships. Wilkinson agrees with the importance of the social, political, and economic context of socioeconomic status or income inequality and health. However, for him, the central issue is the degree to which health is affected by welfare-state policies other than those directly concerned with income inequalities. He insists that relative deprivation affects health independent of welfare policies.

TABLE TALK

◆ ◆ ◆

Table 9.1 displays average health problems of Canadians by income quintiles (each quintile is 20% of the population). It shows that the more income a person has, the less likely it is that this person has chronic health problems or depression, and the person is less likely to smoke and is more likely to do physical exercise. Table 9.2 shows that number of chronic health problems and involvement in early sexual intercourse is also higher among those who were in need of the basic necessities of life, such as food. Do you think that government should make health services available to all who need it, or should the government ensure that people take care of themselves, without universal health care?

Table 9.1   Canadian Health by Income Quintiles

| | Income Quintiles | | | | | |
	Lowest	2	3	4	Highest	Total
Number of chronic conditions	1.9	2.0	1.7	1.4	1.2	1.5
Depression scale: short-form score	1.1	0.8	0.6	0.5	0.4	0.6
Positive self-perceived health	3.1	3.2	3.5	3.8	4.0	3.6
Physical activity more than 15 minutes (# per month)	21.1	19.6	20.8	23.6	26.6	23.1
Number of years of smoking (current daily smokers)	25.3	25.6	24.9	23.0	22.5	24.0

Source: Canadian Community Health Survey, 2001.

Table 9.2   Average Number of Chronic Health Conditions
and Age at First Sexual Intercourse

	Number of Chronic Health Conditions	Age at First Sexual Intercourse
Food Conditions		
Household did not run out of money to buy food	1.3	18.1
Household ran out of money to buy food	1.8	17.0
Always had enough food	1.6	17.2
Sometimes had enough food	1.9	16.9
Often did not have enough food	2.5	17.0
Received food from a charity	2.1	16.8

Source: Statistics Canada, National Population Health Survey, 1996/97.

QUESTIONS

1. What do you think is the most important cause of health problems? Why?
2. Do you think that inequality causes health problems, or do you think that poor health causes inequality? Why?
3. Do you think that an attack on the welfare state is also an attack on social cohesion? If so, why?
4. Currently in Canada, there is a heated debate about public or private health care. What insights can be drawn from the articles in relation to this debate?
5. Why are some people healthy and others not?
6. What do you think are the major sources of health conditions for Aboriginals? Why?
7. Why is it that some ethnoracial groups have more health problems than others?

Income Inequality, Social Cohesion and the Health Status of Populations: The Role of Neo-Liberalism

David Coburn

University of Toronto

◆ ◆ ◆

INTRODUCTION

◆ ◆ ◆

. . . It has long been known that there are historically persistent inverse relationships between SES [socioeconomic status] and health status within nations. In most developed countries health inequalities have not decreased despite rising national wealth (as measured by increasing GNP per capita) and improvements in longevity. Recently attention has turned to analysis of the relationships between levels of inequality and longevity amongst the economically advanced nations rather than only within them. In his interesting and provocative book, *Unhealthy Societies: The Afflictions of Inequality* (1996), a central writer in the area, Richard Wilkinson, proposes that, after certain absolute levels of GNP per capita are attained (about US$5000), the major determinant of differing levels of health status amongst nations lies in their degree of income inequality. In the developed nations, controlling for such factors as GNP/cap, the greater a nation's income inequality—the poorer the average national health status. That is, it is inequality rather than wealth that is important for health. . . .

A focus on absolute levels of income as determinants of health does not explain why some 'rich' countries show lower levels of health than do some poorer, but more egalitarian, countries. It has also been frequently pointed out that within countries, there are differences in health status across the SES gradient. That is, it is not simply those at the low end of the SES continuum that are the issue. Even SES groups quite high in income and SES show poorer health than those immediately above them. Attention has thus turned to the more indirect influence of psycho-social factors on health status rather than simply the direct and immediate effects of material life circumstances. If indeed relative status is related to health up and down the SES hierarchy, then it is likely that psycho-social factors, and not only absolute material conditions are a major influence on health (Wilkinson, 1997a).

Though the psycho-social channels relating inequality to health status within countries are numerous and rather general, many observers argue that those lower in SES show lowered self-esteem, lack of control, more harmful emotional reactions to life events, higher stress or the like. Attempting to explain between country differences Wilkinson, Kawachi and others (Kawachi and Kennedy, 1997; Kawachi et al., 1997; Wilkinson, 1996) have drawn on the work of Putnam (1993) to argue that social cohesion/trust is one of the main mechanisms linking the national degree of income inequality with health. Putnam had contended that northern Italy was more socially and economically successful than southern Italy because the north had developed greater 'social capital' that is, more extensive social networks and greater social 'trust' than had the south. Drawing on these findings, the 'inequality' theorists argue, with some supporting evidence, that higher income inequality produces lowered social cohesion/lower trust which in turn produces lowered health status. It is also implied that between country differences are explained by the fact that elongated status hierarchies exacerbate the status effects noted within countries. Thus, there is a, more or less linear, income inequality-social cohesion/trust/esteem, etc., health status linkage. . . .

BACKGROUND

◆ ◆ ◆

As a number of analysts note almost all the attention within the SES-health status tradition has been devoted to attempts to explain why and how SES is related to health (Bartley et al., 1998; Daly et al., 1998; Popay et al., 1998). There has been an overwhelming tendency to focus on the possible social/psycho-biological mechanisms through which social factors might be tied to health rather than on examination of the basic social causes of inequality and health. With only a few exceptions . . . there has been a startling lack of attention to the social/political/economic context of SES or income inequality—health status relationships. It is striking that in various summaries of the literature relating SES to various negative outcomes, and in those proposing or studying various measures to 'prevent' these negative outcomes, the possible causes of inequalities are seldom, if ever, mentioned. For example, a good deal of attention is now centered on low income children in the belief that enriching their environments will help prevent health or other difficulties later in life. Seldom, however, is there any discussion of the causes of SES differences themselves

The neglect of putative 'causes' is justified on the basis that we should focus our research attention on something we can actually do something about (Syme, 1998). SES or income inequalities are, apparently, viewed as beyond the reach of reform activities.

In broadening the discussion about the determinants of health Wilkinson contends that Income Inequality produces social disorganization (or lowered social cohesion) which leads to lower average national health status. He is, however, somewhat equivocal about the nature of the causal pathways involving income inequality and social cohesion. In places he suggests that it is possible that social cohesion produces lowered income inequality or that there is some form of reciprocal relationship between the two. That is, a highly cohesive community might 'not permit' high levels of income inequality. Wilkinson also suggests that income inequality may directly produce both lowered social cohesion and lowered longevity, i.e., social cohesion might not be the mediator between income inequality and health status. In a number of places

Wilkinson and particularly Kawachi and colleagues also imply that markets are at the source of the income inequality problem even though there are obviously differences amongst 'market societies'. Other writers point to the importance of welfare state measures or a version of social capital (referring to the social infrastructure) as possibly underlying either social cohesion or as a major link between income inequality and longevity (Daly et al., 1998; Davey Smith, 1996; Kawachi and Kennedy, 1997; Kawachi et al., 1997).

Here, I extend the discussions linking income inequality and health by arguing that, rather than income inequality producing lowered social cohesion/trust leading to lowered health status, neo-liberalism (market dominance) produces *both* higher income inequality and lower social cohesion (a proposition suggested by Muntaner and Lynch, 1999) and, presumably, either lowered health status or a health status which is not as high as it might otherwise have been. Neo-liberalism has this effect partly through its undermining of (particular types of) welfare state. Discussion of this thesis, while focused on the income inequality-health status international literature, also has implications for the more widespread and substantial evidence of within country SES—health status relationships. It also draws in analyses of the 'rise and fall' of the welfare state as well as the presumed class causes and consequences of such a sequence and thus broadens and contextualizes the topic. . . .

In asserting a particular affinity between neo-liberalism, inequality and lowered social cohesiveness I point out:

1. that 'ideal-typical' neo-liberal tenets are congruent with the production of, or at least acceptance of, greater socio-economic inequalities (and that selective examples support that contention); and,

2. that there are striking parallels between 'ideal' or pure neo-liberal ideology or tenets and factors related to, or constituent of, social disorganization/lowered trust;

3. that neo-liberalism and economic globalization are associated with the decline of the welfare state. This decline is one of the causes both of increased inequality and lowered social cohesion. . . .

GENERAL TENETS OF NEO-LIBERALISM

◆ ◆ ◆

I assume that neo-liberalism refers to the dominance of markets and the market model. Though composed of a complex combination of characteristics the basic assumptions of neo-liberalism, the 'philosophy' of the new right are:

1. that markets are the best and most efficient allocators of resources in production and distribution;
2. that societies are composed of autonomous individuals (producers and consumers) motivated chiefly or entirely by material or economic considerations;
3. that competition is the major market vehicle for innovations.

Neo-liberalism is distinguished from neo-conservatism by the fact that the latter contains a particular social component supportive of traditional family values, particular religious traditions etc. and not only a 'free-enterprise' economic doctrine.

The essence of neo-liberalism, its pure form, is a more or less thoroughgoing adherence, in rhetoric if not in practice, to the virtues of a market economy, and, by extension, a market-oriented society. While some neo-liberals appear to assume that one can construct any kind of 'society' on any kind of economy, the position taken here is that the economy, the state and civil society are, in fact, inextricably interrelated.

THE RELATIONSHIP BETWEEN NEO-LIBERAL DOCTRINES AND INEQUALITY

◆ ◆ ◆

Neo-liberals, I contend, are not particularly concerned about inequality or regard it either as a positive virtue or as inevitable or necessary. That is, if 'the market' is the best or most efficient allocator of goods and resources neo-liberals are inclined to accept whatever markets bring. Certainly, political parties which espouse neo-liberal principles have been the mainspring behind attacks on the Keynesian Welfare State (KWS), whose functions included, not only the correction of market fluctuations but also the amelioration of market-produced inequalities. The welfare state, in the neo-liberal view, interferes with the 'normal' functioning of the market. Neo-liberals oppose any form of 'intervention' in markets because they feel that such intervention damages the operation of 'the invisible hand' which most efficiently aligns production, consumption and distribution (while they at the same time deny that markets themselves are 'structured' by state action).

Neo-liberals contend not only that market inequalities are the necessary by-product of a well-functioning economy but that these inequalities are 'just' because what one puts into the market one gets out. That is, the invisible hand doctrine implies some reasonable relation-ship between one's activities and subsequent 'rewards'. Moreover, as noted, there is a resistance to 'correcting' market produced inequalities through various welfare state measures, since these are assumed to lead to 'market distortions'. State actions then are not only inefficient but may also be unethical (while some feel markets are 'ethical,' e.g., Hendrickson, 1996, others radically disagree see McMurtry, 1998). . . .

Neo-Liberalism, the Welfare State and Inequality

The contemporary rise of neo-liberalism and of inequality following the 1970s is historically tied to the decline of the welfare state. While markets produce inequalities these may be 'prevented' (through labor market policies) or ameliorated (through social welfare measures or the 'decommodification' of education, health and welfare). Decommodification meant that access to social resources was not completely determined by market criteria (i.e., income or wealth) or by power in the market (the ability of some groups to bargain for 'private' welfare benefits— see Esping-Andersen, 1999). Both health, through the effects of the welfare state on the social determinants of health, and health care, through various forms of national health care systems, are tied to the fate of 'the welfare state'. Any consideration of the social determinants of health would have to take account of welfare state dynamics. Whether or not the effects of welfare state measures are direct and material or indirect and psycho-social is a matter of dispute. Nevertheless, as Popay et al. (1998), Bartley et al. (1998) and Daly et al. (1998) and others note there may be critical periods of the life cycle in which the 'buffering' effects of the 'social wage' or of social policies generally are crucially important. Daly et al. even contend that: "political units that tolerate a high degree of income inequality are less likely to support the human, physical, cultural, civic, and health resources needed to maximize the health of their populations" (Daly et al., 1998, p. 319). Bartley et al. (1997, p. 1195) feel that the welfare state has both material and psychosocial effects "by preventing dramatic falls in living standards and by a wider effect on the degree to which citizens experience a sense of control of their lives." Redistributive policies are important materially and psycho-socially. George Davey Smith (1996, p. 988) contends that: "Cross nationally, higher levels of both social expenditure and taxation as a proportion of gross domestic product are associated with longer life expectancy, lower maternal mortality, and a smaller proportion of low birthweight deliveries" (see also Kaplan et al., 1996; Kennedy et al., 1996). There are thus many suggestions that 'the welfare state' provided the material base for a more cohesive society and/or more or less directly influences health status.

Neo-liberals opposed or only reluctantly accepted the Post-World War II establishment of the major attributes of the KWS as expressed in various pension, social insurance, health care, labor market or welfare measures involving government actions. Nevertheless, the example of the KWS was used to argue that capitalism had 'solved' one of its major problems through ameliorating the inequalities produced by market mechanisms. Whereas, in the 19th century, inequality had been viewed as legitimate or perhaps inevitable, within the KWS issues of inequality seemed no longer a major concern, first, because through the notion of 'social citizenship' inequalities in the market were ameliorated and, second, because fluctuations of 'boom and bust' were reduced by Keynesian counter-cyclical economic policies (demand stimulation in times of downturn; restriction of demand in times of boom).

Most welfare state analysts attribute the formation of welfare state measures, directly or indirectly to some form of working class pressure or, in more complex formulations, to various class coalitions and class strength. . . . Ross and Trachte (1990) and others have implied a lessened resistance to working class pressures for welfare state measures from dominant classes in an era of monopoly capital because of divisions within capital between the competitive and monopoly sectors. The KWS, however, is not a unitary phenomenon. As Esping-Andersen (1990, 1999) has indicated, there are various 'types' of welfare state of which the ones involving the least state action, and the greatest dominance of market-related solutions were the liberal welfare states of the Anglo-American nations (as opposed to social democratic or corporate welfare states developed elsewhere). In fact, it can be argued that the liberal welfare states did do the least to either prevent (particularly because of the absence of labor-market policies) or to rectify (through social welfare and health care) the depredations of the capitalist marketplace and the inequalities it tended to produce. Within liberal welfare states social policies were most generally designed to supplement market provision, to reflect participation in the market, or generally, to be targeted or 'means-tested' rather than universal in application. That is, these measures are less 'decommodifying' (Korpi and Palme, 1998).

Most recently, given globalization, in which finance, and, to a lesser extent, industrial, capital has escaped from national controls while labor has not, has come a return to neo-liberal doctrines. . . . Economic globalization was aided by neo-liberals and neo-liberalism benefited from economic globalization. Hence a 'restructuring' of society, including markets and the welfare state. In a global era it is claimed that higher degrees of inequality are inevitable or that inequalities are an inescapable adjunct to economic growth or to the 'realities' of international competition. Inequality is also viewed as a key motivational factor aiding a productive economy i.e., through lowering the costs of (some) labor. Any measures to alter market-produced motivations simply deform the operation of markets and, furthermore, are unjust or at least inefficient. Inequality, then, is more to be welcomed or at least accepted than it is to be prevented or ameliorated by state or other forms of welfare (see Kenworthy [1998] for a summary and rebuttal of many of these arguments). . . .

Redistributive policies in the less neo-liberal states have been important in reducing inequalities. . . . Welfare states did tend to do what they were supposed to do. Inequalities are thus, more or less directly related to the class structure because class pressure tends to reduce the degree to which markets predominate.

The most recent evidence from the United States, Britain, Australia, Canada, New Zealand and the OECD countries generally, indicates that neo-liberalism in action, while obviously a far from perfect neo-liberalism, is associated with (more or less) rapidly increasing inequality. The U.S. and the UK, but also Canada and Australia, show much higher inequality than do such countries as Switzerland, Germany or the Netherlands who, in turn, show higher inequality than do the Scandinavian countries. . . . It is not that inequalities did not exist before recent neo-liberal regimes or doctrines, simply that inequality was and is, exacerbated under neo-liberalism. . . .

Arguably then markets produce income inequalities, and neo-liberalism opposes measures to redistribute income resources—therefore the proposition: *the more market-oriented or neo-liberal the regime the greater the income inequality*. . . .

THE RELATIONSHIP BETWEEN NEO-LIBERALISM AND SOCIAL COHESION/TRUST

◆ ◆ ◆

A strong argument can be made that neo-liberal doctrines are antithetical to social cohesion or to social 'trust'. The image of society which neo-liberalism carries with it is that of voluntaristic 'possessive individualism'. . . . The most appropriate relationship is that embodied in contracts reflecting varied material self-interests. In the neo-liberal view, societies are not more than the sum of their parts. As Margaret Thatcher asserted, there is no such thing as 'society' only individuals or families. Whereas in previous liberal theory the state is viewed as at least partially representative of the 'general interests of society', in the neo-liberal perspective the state should have as small a role as possible. Not much is said by many neo-liberals, however, about how markets themselves are constructed or about corporate monopolies or oligopolies although thoroughgoing neo-liberals, i.e., libertarians (utopian capitalists) claim to want to break up such market hindrances. . . .

Given the absence of a broader sense of community, neo-liberals advocate individualistic market based 'solutions' to problems. Thus, 'gated' communities and private security guards as a response to crime, private health insurance as a response to the increased health needs of an aging population. There is an emphasis on private versus public transportation, private versus public schooling, private versus public health care (see Reich, 1991). Reducing the size of government means reducing government expenditures. Neo-liberals strongly favor lower taxes (see Raphael, 1999). Given the use of government revenues to redistribute income then lower taxes imply increased inequality but also connote a privatizing or individualizing of societal risks and opportunities. Even given obvious societal 'inefficiencies' as, for example, in the U.S. health care system, neo-liberals prefer private to public expenditures (Drache and Sullivan, 1999).

The absence of any concept of 'the social' in neo-liberalism is related to neo-liberal views which imply the universalizing of market characteristics to all areas of human existence. Even 'the self' comes to be viewed in terms of its market use. In an 'enterprise culture' the self is seen in terms of 'its' usefulness on the market as an instrument for 'economic' advancement. Social development or even 'social capital' becomes individual 'human capital'. The importance of those aspects of 'social capital', aspects of the social environment which benefit everyone, are downplayed or ignored. . . . Society is thus reduced to a collection of individuals in which the whole is viewed simply as the sum of the individual voluntary actions— social structure disappears.

Privatization and the lack of (noncontractual) connections amongst citizens, implies a generalized increase in scepticism or distrust towards one's fellows. If everyone is legitimately seeking their own economic self-interest, as neo-liberalism implies, then there is reason for widespread

suspicion of the motives and intentions of others rather than 'trust'. There might be an increasing emphasis on self-aggrandizement at the expense of collective goals, an increasing contempt for public institutions and a lack of support for those organizations through which collective notions are expressed, maintained or reproduced.

Furthermore, since markets are efficient (and just) allocators of rewards, then economic or 'social' problems are attributed to individual failings. If markets give people what they deserve there is likely to be an increase in individual blame and an inclination to punish rather than help others. Thus, recipients of social welfare measures are 'welfare bums'. As Sennett and Cobb indicate there are many relatively nonvisible 'injuries of class' (Sennett and Cobb, 1973).

While it has been asserted that neo-liberalism produces a lowered sense of community it might also be argued that the rise of neo-liberalism is itself a signifier of the decline of more widespread feelings of social solidarity. The political rise of neo-liberalism is freighted with a more individualistic view of society and, perhaps, itself reflects a decline in the notion of 'we are all in the same boat'. Not only do neo-liberal policies undermine the social infrastructure underlying social cohesion but neo-liberal movements themselves are partial causes of the decline of a sense of social cohesion.

Thus the proposition: *The more market-oriented the society, the higher the social fragmentation and the lower the social cohesion and trust.*

NEO-LIBERALISM, INCOME INEQUALITY AND SOCIAL COHESION/TRUST

◆ ◆ ◆

Bringing the two major areas noted above together leads to our general hypothesis that neo-liberalism produces *both* higher levels of inequality *and* lower levels of social cohesion (cf. Muntaner and Lynch, 1999). Rather than an inequality—social cohesion—health status sequence neo-liberalism produces both inequality and social fragmentation which may, if Wilkinson and others are right, have negative consequences in lowered health status.

DISCUSSION

◆ ◆ ◆

The model which emerges based on this argument is thus that economic globalization is accompanied by and produces changes in the balance of class power. The decline of working class power in the face of a resurgent business class is marked by the domination of neo-liberal ideology and policies, by attacks on the welfare state, and by a dominance of employer interests in the market. The decline of the power of workers to bargain for benefits within markets (Esping-Andersen, 1999), or to politically force decommodification through state welfare measures, produces higher income inequality and lowered social cohesion and, directly and indirectly, lowered health status. International differences in health status can thus be traced to different national class structures, national institutions and different national degrees of 'marketization' within common international pressures. . . .

Inequality is not a necessary condition produced by extra-human forces. Degrees of inequality are clearly influenced by international, national and local political policies which are amenable to change. We can either ignore these processes or seek to understand and begin to change them.

Deeper Than "Neoliberalism."
A Reply to David Coburn

Richard G. Wilkinson
University of Sussex

◆ ◆ ◆

Coburn criticises what he calls the "startling lack of attention to the social/political/economic context of SES or income inequality—health status relationships". But in Britain during the Thatcher period, when income differences widened so dramatically, there was never any doubt as to the political responsibility. Even those who thought governments only partially to blame for the adverse trends were in no doubt about their failure to take effective countermeasures. When Coburn criticises the research effort saying, "Health matters have for too long been viewed as somehow separate from the societies in which they are, in fact, embedded", and goes on to say that he "hopes to bring the social back in", it sounds like a voice from the past. He says "income inequalities are, apparently, viewed as beyond the reach of reform activities", but research has focused on them precisely because they are *inescapably* affected by government policies. Indeed, a recent Rowntree report says that it would cost only about 1% of GDP to bring all incomes in Britain up to the EU poverty line of half average income (Howarth, Kenway, Palmer & Miorelli, 1999). Because a crucial part of the problem has always been political will, the best tactic has seemed to be to demonstrate the high health and social costs of poverty and inequality.

Coburn argues that it is not so much income inequality that creates low social cohesion and poor health, but "neoliberalism" which creates all three: that is the "politics" which we supposedly leave out of the picture. He believes that the health impact of the "decline of the welfare state" is central. However, changes in taxes and benefits are probably not in contention here: while they are an important determinant of income distribution. . . , Coburn would presumably also include them in the welfare state provision which neoliberal governments have cut. The central issue is then how much health is affected by welfare state policies other than those directly concerned with income maintenance and redistribution. The main working hypothesis has been that income distribution affects population health by changing the burden of relative deprivation on health so that wider income differences will tend to be associated with steeper social gradients in health. . . . There is widespread agreement that relative deprivation affects health. . . . The weakness of saying, as Coburn does, that the problem is neoliberalism rather than increased relative deprivation, is that it merely limits the theory to a historically specific instance: widening income differences seem likely to be damaging, almost whatever their source.

Without the recent widening of health inequalities it is reasonable to assume that national standards of health would have increased more rapidly. But the difficulty of attributing the deterioration of, or slower improvement in, death rates among the least well off to the public provision of health services, education and housing, rather than to the additional burden of relative deprivation, is that we are dealing with what are usually rather marginal changes in the provision of factors which are anyway probably not among the most powerful influences on population health. Take health services as an example. With the exception of the USA, the developed countries almost all retained close to universal health care coverage during the 1980s and '90s. Yet universal medical care coexists with large health inequalities. This is because the beneficial effects of medical care on case-fatality rates are overpowered by socioeconomic factors which continue to cause huge differences in the incidence rates of most of the important causes of death. Given the two, three or four-fold differences in the incidence of life threatening conditions in different social classes, it is extremely implausible that the two, three or fourfold differences in mortality are attributable to relatively small differences in treatment. Indeed, in Britain (one of the few places where data were available at the time) health inequalities widened substantially even during the post-war period when the National Health Service and much of the rest of the "Keynesian Welfare State" was set up. Widening health inequalities are clearly not confined to the most obviously neoliberal Reagan–Thatcher period but have occurred throughout much of the second half of the 20th century. . . .

The relation between income inequality and health involves not only the effects of changes in the burden of low social status but, perhaps rather less obviously, also the effects of poor social affiliations. The data suggests that where income differences are wider, there is a strong tendency for levels of trust and strength of community life to be lower (Kawachi et al., 1997; Putnam et al., 1993) and for rates of violence, homicide and hostility to be higher (Hsieh and Pugh, 1993; Williams et al., 1995). The remarkably strong correlations suggest that there is a "culture of inequality" marked by a more hostile and less hospitable social environment (Wilkinson, 1999a, b).

If wider income differences are divisive and accompanied by a deterioration in the quality of the social environment, it would be remarkable if health was not affected. Low social status and social affiliations are—at least in terms of population attributable risks—two of the most powerful determinants of population health. They have both been repeatedly associated with two or even threefold differences in mortality and morbidity (Berkman, 1995). Almost any measure of social affiliation is a good predictor of health, and it seems likely that most would be closely associated with each other. Although we used to assume that the direct effects of poorer material circumstances accounted for the social gradient in health, it now looks as if a major part of the association between low social status and poorer health springs from the experience of low social status or subordination itself. This interpretation is strongly supported both by the importance of relative income. . ., and by the work on the physiological effects of social status among non-human primates—including experiments in which social status was manipulated while diet and the environment were held constant, so leaving little scope for anything other than psychosocial explanations. . . . This interpretation also fits well with the increasing success of psychosocial factors in explaining health inequalities.

The powerful biological effects of psychosocial pathways to disease seem to hinge primarily on the effects of chronic physiological arousal, which appears to have widespread health effects analogous to more rapid ageing (Sapolsky, 1998). It looks as if social sources of anxiety and arousal may be among the most potent. Elsewhere I have discussed the evidence that we remain acutely sensitive and attentive to issues to do with friendship and rejection, low social status, feelings of inferiority and not being respected as equals. . . . As social beings, we come to know ourselves partly reflexively—through each other's eyes. Among the most salient general dimensions of the social environment which we monitor carefully are issues to do with friendship and rejection, superiority and inferiority. If these are important sources of anxiety, then perhaps we have the makings of a plausible explanation of why these aspects of the social environment are such powerful health risk factors. . . The probability that the explanations are to be found in this direction is increased by what we are learning of the importance to later health of early emotional development. . . . Issues to do with security and insecurity and the development of stress responses provide the common ground.

Returning for a moment to the other link between social status and friendship, we need to know not only why they have important effects on health, but why the quality of social relations deteriorates as the social hierarchy becomes more unequal and hierarchical. The most plausible explanation is surely that dominance and social affiliation are two sides of the same coin. Dominance hierarchies are based on power, coercion and access to resources regardless of the needs of others, whereas friendship is based on reciprocity, sharing, mutuality and a recognition of others needs. These are the two fundamentally different bases on which human beings can associate: either on the basis of power or on the basis of social obligations and mutuality. In this sense friendship is the opposite of dominance, and inequality is inimical to friendship.

Underlying this is the enduring problem of potential competition for access to resources. Indeed, Gilbert has suggested that what human and animal dominance hierarchies have in common is that they are—as terms like "pecking order" suggest—about power to hold, or gain access to, resources (Gilbert, 1992). In contrast, the gift is a symbol of friendship because it states, in the clearest possible terms, that the giver and receiver are not in competition for resources. Food sharing similarly symbolises that the participants do not compete with each other for the basic necessities of life. These issues go so deep because the potential for conflict with members of one's own species—who have all the same needs—is so great. But among humans the stakes are particularly high. Not only can we be each other's most feared rivals for everything from food and shelter to sexual partners and jobs, but other people also have the potential to be the greatest source of support, care, assistance, love and learning. Usually among animal species the best which can be hoped for is that devices, such as territorial segregation, will keep the peace. But for humans, other people can be the best or the worst: there is not just the problem of avoiding conflict, there is also the possibility of gaining the enormous benefits of membership of the cooperative group. This means that the nature of social relations has always been crucially important to welfare—even in terms of basic material welfare: hence the egalitarianism, gift exchange and food sharing which seem to have characterised the hunting and gathering societies which have dominated at least 90% of human existence. In effect, coping with the social environment has been every bit as taxing as the material environment in human development, and this is why such intensely social risk factors as social affiliation, low social status and emotional devel-

opment early in life, have been identified by modern epidemiology as key influences on population health in developed societies.

Putnam contrasts the "horizontal", or egalitarian, dimension of society which fosters a stronger community life, with the "vertical" dimension (patron/client relations up and down the social hierarchy) which is inimical to closer community relations (Putnam et al., 1993). Trower, Gilbert and Sherling (1990) referred to these two bases of social organisation as "agonistic" and "hedonic". It appears that what income inequality is picking up on is the extent to which social interaction is structured according to hierarchical relations of dominance and subordination or on the basis of a greater mutuality between social equals. And just as the more unequal societies have higher rates of violence, hostility and homicide, and lower levels of trust and community involvement, so they are likely to generate more social anxiety and chronic stress. In an important sense these distinctions are also the basis of social class in that classes are groups of people supposedly bound together by greater equity, yet separated from each other by socioeconomic inequality.

Inequality the Real Threat to Health Care

Dennis Raphael

The greatest threat to the health of Canadians is increasing economic inequality—the degree to which wealth is being concentrated in the hands of the few as opposed to being equitably distributed across the population.

Canada has long been an unequal nation, but the past decade has seen significant increases in economic inequality. And Ontario has been leading the way with policies designed to take from the poor and middle-class and give to the wealthy. How are economic inequality and health related and what are the consequences of this relationship?

Numerous studies have found that people live longer and healthier in nations with equitable wealth distribution. Within nations, economic inequality is also related to health. Unequal U.S. cities and states have higher death and illness rates. Inequality is also associated with state and city levels of unemployment, incarceration, homicide, low birth weight, smoking, income assistance, use of food stamps, and disability.

In Canada we have been spared many of the problems seen in the U.S. and one explanation for this appears in a recent study by Statistics Canada staff: Income is distributed much more fairly in Canadian cities and provinces than in the U.S. But these data were from the 1991 census and we know that economic inequality in Canada has since increased.

Researchers estimate that years of life lost in Canada due to differences in wealth are close to years lost to major killers such as cancer and heart disease.

Economic inequality influences the health of Canadians in three ways:

Economic inequality creates poverty and people living in poverty suffer from a range of health problems. Additionally, poverty has consequences in terms of performance in school, use of the health-care system, and quality of attained employment. Poverty's effects on health are direct, related to absolute material deprivation, and indirect, involving psychological reactions to relative deprivation.

Second, there is increasing evidence that economically unequal societies, in addition to having higher levels of poverty, provide fewer services and weaker social safety nets, adding to the difficulties of those living in poverty. And the poverty rate has been growing in Canada as services have been decreasing. This is especially true in Ontario.

The third way economic inequality affects health is through weakening social cohesion. Citizens who differ in economic resources become distanced from each other and lose common commitments to civic institutions. This estrangement, when combined with the weakening of communal social structures, leads to social disintegration. Symptoms of disintegration include increasing levels of sickness and premature death, accident rates and crime, and declines in civil commitment and participation.

Health status has been declining in Canada as economic inequality has increased.

Recently published studies show widening regional inequality in Manitoba, premature morbidity rates and increased incidence of low birth-weight babies in Ontario. On a broad level, scores on a Social Health Index developed by the Canadian government have been declining since the mid-1980s even as Gross Domestic Product has increased. The Index is based on measures of infant mortality, child abuse, child poverty, teen suicides, drug abuse, high school dropout, unemployment, average weekly earnings, persons 65 or over in poverty, out-of-pocket health expenses, alcohol-related fatalities, being on social assistance, access to affordable housing, and the gap between rich and poor.

Additionally, in Canada—especially in Ontario—there are signs of civil decay. There are record levels of poverty and homelessness and 37 percent of Toronto children now live in poverty, an increase of 66 percent since 1989.

Decreasing percentages of Canadians turn out to vote in federal elections, decreasing from 75 percent in 1984 to 67 percent in 1997; in Ontario the figures are 76 percent and 66 percent respectively.

Health Canada and many provincial health documents recognize income and wealth as determinants of health. Forty key publications on economic inequality and health are now available in *The Society and Population Health Reader, Volume I: Income Inequality and Health*, published by the New York–based New Press. The volumes *Health and Wealth and The Widening Gap* provide the latest Canadian and British data, respectively.

Given what we know, why has this issue received so little attention in Canada? Elected officials understandably ignore the growing gap between rich and poor, because as one writer has noted, the gap has not

Continued

been preordained by extraterrestrial beings, but created by the policies of governments.

The reason for neglect of this issue by medical and health reporters—given the number of recent studies and reports on economic inequality and its influence on health—is less clear.

Canadians have taken for granted a country where peace, order, and good government were its guiding values. These values are threatened by increasing economic inequality. Canadians have also defined their nation in terms of its health-care system. The sustainability of this system is jeopardized by the health effects of increasing economic inequality.

Public discussion of the degree of economic inequality in Canada and means of halting its increase appears timely, for the observations of American observer Peter Montague are now relevant for Canada:

"In the U.S., government policies of the past 20 years have promoted, encouraged and celebrated inequality. These are choices that we, as a society, have made. Now one half of our society is afraid of the other half, and the gap between us is expanding. Our health is not the only thing in danger. They that sow the wind shall reap the whirlwind."

Source: Dennis Raphael "Inequality the real threat to health care," *Toronto Star,* March 7, 2000, p. 1. Reprinted by permission of Dr. Dennis Raphael, School of Health Policy and Management, York University.

Unit Ten

POLITY
Introduction: State, Civic Engagement, and Politics

◆ ◆ ◆

What are the various functions of state institutions (government)? Who controls them? What is the extent of involvement of the general public in the decision-making process of state institutions? Before answering these questions we should distinguish the political system from civil society. The latter includes domestic affairs regulated by individuals (such as housing, learning, reading newspapers, listening to the radio, watching TV, going to religious places, and other voluntary activities). The former involves the federal, provincial, and municipal governments, and executive, judiciary, and military institutions.

A **pluralist** view of the state system suggests that it is made up of a great variety of people and interest groups that help ensure that everyone gets a fair and representative voice in its management and decision-making process. According to this view, the government acts as an arbitrator that helps mediate diverse interests and relationships. Accordingly, rules, regulations, and laws are legislated without bias toward any group. They are based on consensus, the main purpose of which is to ensure balance and justice. Therefore, pluralists argue that the state and its various institutions are representative of all members of the society, most of which are elected to office in a free and democratic society. Elected individuals have, in turn, power over the general public. However, such power is limited to rules and regulations that are legitimated. The pluralist explanation of power is rooted in Max Weber's view of domination.

For Weber, the most stable forms of social relationships are those that are subjectively legitimated. For

example, the state has legitimate monopoly over the organized use of force within a given territory. Professors and universities have legitimate monopoly over students' future through their assignment of grades and granting of degrees. Weber was, therefore, not speaking about power but about authority. **Power** refers to one's ability to influence others and reach a goal even against opposition from those who are subject to power. However, because of the inherent opposition, Weber argued that an institution or society organized through the use of power is not stable. Societies are more stable if those who are subject to power obey commands because they are legitimated (i.e., **authority**).

Weber referred to legitimated power as domination, and he distinguished three types of domination or authority:

1. Traditional authority is based upon the belief in the "sanctity" of age-old rules and sanctions. For example, in small rural communities, elders have authority. Similarly, parents have authority over children.

2. Legal–rational authority is based on impersonal norms that have been rationally established. Therefore, those who are subject to authority obey a command because it has been constructed based on impersonal rules and regulations. The person issuing the command is also subject to these impersonal norms and rules. There are many examples of legal–rational forms of authority in modern bureaucracies. For example, professors assign a grade based on rules established by the university and stipulated in the course outline. Therefore, they cannot assign a grade based on whether they like or

dislike a student's race, sex, and so on. Similarly, judges can pass a verdict only based on laws legislated by the parliament. They cannot judge based on the sex or race of a person.

3. Charismatic authority refers to a certain quality of an individual personality, by virtue of which the person is considered extraordinary, with supernatural, superhuman, exceptional powers, or qualities. Persons with charismatic authority reject the past and are often revolutionary. Vladimir Lenin during the Russian Revolution, Martin Luther King during the Civil Rights Movement, Ayatollah Khomeini during the Iranian revolution, and Trudeau-mania during late 1960s in Canada are all examples of charismatic leaders.

In contrast to pluralists, Marxists argue that the state is either an instrument of the ruling class (the most powerful groups, particularly the corporate elites), or acts on their behest. There are two types of Marxist explanations of state:

1. Instrumentalists focus on the linkage between individuals occupying key state positions and upper classes. For example, Panitch (1977) noted that the list of the Board of Directors of the Grand Trunk Railway read like a list of the Fathers of Confederation. Examples, such as John A. Macdonald as the president of Manufacturers Life Assurance Company, and John Galtas an executive of the British American Land Company, point to the link between business and state bureaucracy. Similarly, Porter's (1965) and Clement's (1975) analyses of the class background of officials in control of state bureaucracies revealed a strong link between the two. In more recent times, Guppy et al.'s (1987) study of members of the parliament from the 1960s to the 1980s revealed the accuracy of the "law of increasing disproportion." They revealed that political candidates tend to come disproportionately from higher social classes, elected officials are even more likely to come from upper classes, and cabinet ministers are yet more likely to come from among those of high socioeconomic origins. Guppy et al. also showed that over 48 percent of candidates and 54 percent of elected representatives were business owners and self-employed professionals. Moreover, over 60 percent of the cabinet ministers were business or executive people and lawyers. They concluded that the privileged economic elites and the modern parliamentarians absolutely belong together.

2. Structural-Marxists pay attention to the activities of the state that correspond to the interests of the capitalist class. They focus on state functions that tend to help with **capital accumulation, coercion, and legitimization.** According to Panitch (1977), the Canadian state has been involved in providing favourable climates for capitalist economic growth, ensured availability of cheap labour through immigration, and investment in the infrastructure, which is useful to capitalists, but they may not want to invest in it because they may see it as risky or unprofitable. State policies all help to accumulate capital for capitalists. Moreover, the Canadian state has helped capitalists by using coercive force in order to ensure stability and profit maximization. Examples include suppression of the Riel Rebellion in Manitoba, employment of troops against strikers in Winnipeg in 1919, use of the War Measures Act in Quebec, and various back-to-work legislations. Finally, the Canadian state has enacted policies and legislations that aim to integrate lower classes into the system, giving them the semblance of power but without substance. These policies may include such things as redistributive taxation, the right to strike, union protection, anticombine legislation, and so on. However, Panitch suggests that the Canadian state has not fully developed its legitimization function. For example, although Canada has a Charter of Rights and Freedoms, it also has given the parliamentarians the power to override such rights if they have reason to do so.

The general conclusion by Marxists is that the class interests of corporate elites and the larger group of the capitalist class are translated into major state policies. One may wonder, however, if perhaps state policies coincide with the capitalist class interests because state officials want to be re-elected and want to keep their jobs (Brym, 1993). In order for state officials to maximize their supporting vote, they may enact policies that help social stability, economic growth, and capital accumulation. Such policies are welcomed by all people, though capitalists may benefit more from them.

This brings us to the question of whether Canadians vote along their class or other affiliations. Marxists again suggest that people vote according to their economic interests and ideological orientation related to those interests. Pluralists believe that class is one among many sources of political alignment, such as religion, ethnicity, and region. A study by Nakhaie (1992) of the votes in three elections (1979, 1980, and 1984) revealed that, in general, the importance of these forces varies by political parties. The New Democratic Party (NDP) appears to be the party of unionized workers, unskilled labourers, farmers, nonreligious individuals, those with nondominant religious denomination, and those from British Columbia. The Liberal party appears to be the party of Catholics, French Canadians, high and low ranking managers, professionals, and people from Quebec and Ontario.

The Conservative party tends to get support from the large and small **bourgeoisie,** those with some college and university education, Protestants, Anglophones, Western residents, and those in sale occupations (Nakhaie, 1992). However, given changes in the political system, such party alignment may have also changed since 1984. For example, the emergence of the Bloc Québécois in federal politics means that most of the Liberal support in Quebec has shifted toward support of the Bloc (for a snapshot of political participation by age groups, see Table 10.1).

It is obvious that informed political participation is the foundation of democracy. However, in Canada, turnout steadily declined, from 75 percent in the 1984 election to 61 percent in the 2000 election. The voter turnout in 2004 was 60.9 percent and slightly increased to 63.9 percent in the 2006 federal election. The declining turnout in Canada and elsewhere can be viewed as a decline in a nation's political health. Therefore, it is not surprising that political scientists have been preoccupied with the source of this decline and ways in which it can be reversed.

In the debate that follows, scholars attempt to explain why people vote (or do not vote). Earlier, Milner (2001) pointed to the importance of "civic literacy," as measured by newspaper readership, for voting. Milner's (2001) multination study revealed a significant relationship between both illiteracy rate and daily newspaper readership with the tendency to vote at municipal elections. This is an important consideration for political scientists, since the democratic process is argued to be effective if voters are knowledgeable and informed. However, Pattie and Johnston's analysis showed that such a relationship was insignificant when appropriate controls were included in the model. That is to say, newspaper readership was an important factor for voting, but increased readership did not show more voting.

Nakhaie used Canadian data and showed that media consumption substantially contributed to voting. However, he argued that the meaning of civic literacy should be expanded to include knowledge of important social issues and not just reading the newspaper. People read the press for a variety of reasons. It is the attentiveness to current affairs in newspaper readership or other media information that seems to be important to voter turnout. The "civic literacy" argument points to the importance of citizens' knowledge of the political environment. Such individuals are well informed about the government and political issues, and they follow political news consistently. However, reading a newspaper does not mean that one reads the news or pays attention to politics. One might read only the sports or entertainment sections of the newspaper, not paying attention to current affairs at all. The effect of news attentiveness, as confirmed in Nakhaie's study, is also testimony to the rational and informed participation of voters. The health of democratic societies is based not just on voters' participation but, more importantly, is predicated on substantial information. Attentiveness to news and current affairs ensures such information (also see Nakhaie, 2006).

TABLE TALK

◆ ◆ ◆

Figure 10.1 shows percentage of eligible voters who turned out to vote from 1867 to 2004.

Except for 1898 when only 44 percent participated in federal elections, about 70 percent of Canadians have continuously voted in each election until 1997, after which turnout declined to 60.9 percent in 2004. Why has there been a recent decline in electoral participation?

Table 10.1 shows percentage of each age group who participate in politics. Basically, younger generations are least likely and older generations are more likely to vote and to pay attention to news and current affairs. For example, 32.6 percent of those under 24 years of age and over 80 percent of those over 45 years of age voted in the 2000 federal election. Older age groups are more than twice as likely as younger age groups to pay attention to news and current affairs. However, younger age groups are generally similar to if not more involved than older age groups in terms of other civic engagements, such

Figure 10.1   Voting Turnout in Canada, 1867–2004

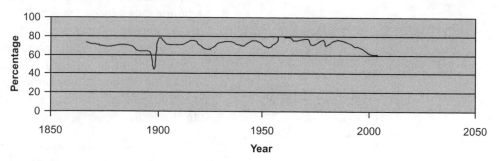

Source: Elections Canada, Voter Turnout at Federal Elections and Referendums, 1867–2004. (URL http://www.elections.ca/content.asp?section=pas&dir=&document=turnout&lang=e&textonly=false)

Table 10.1   Political and Civic Participation of Canadians by Age Groups

| | Age Group of the Respondent | | | | | | | |
	15–24	*25–34*	*35–44*	*45–54*	*55–64*	*65–74*	*75+*	*Total*
Voted in the last federal election	32.6	57.8	71.1	80.3	86.1	89.4	88.6	72.3
Voted in the last provincial election	35.2	55.1	69.3	79.1	85.2	88.7	87.4	71.1
Voted in the last municipal or local election	24.9	39.8	55.7	65.3	73.9	79.0	77.5	58.5
Past Year:								
Searched for information on political issues	34.5	29.1	23.6	24.5	23.6	19.1	12.6	24.8
Volunteered for political party	2.3	2.2	2.6	3.4	5.2	4.8	2.7	3.2
Contacted newspaper/politician	7.8	11.4	13.9	16.0	16.9	14.7	8.5	13.1
Signed a petition	28.7	30.8	31.9	31.3	28.1	20.1	12.6	28.0
Boycotted a product/chose product	18.6	25.6	23.2	23.0	18.7	9.7	5.2	19.6
Attended a public meeting	16.9	19.6	25.1	26.0	25.6	23.7	15.4	22.4
Spoke out at a public meeting	26.6	33.5	38.3	42.8	41.4	40.4	32.2	37.8
Participated in a demonstration or march	10.8	7.3	6.2	6.1	5.3	2.3	0.8	6.0
Frequency of following news and current affairs:								
Daily	37.7	55.7	67.1	76.3	85.0	89.2	89.1	69.5
Several times each week	36.0	27.8	20.9	15.2	9.0	5.8	5.7	18.7
Several times each month	11.6	7.3	5.3	3.1	1.6	1.3	1.5	4.9
Rarely or never	14.6	9.2	6.7	5.4	4.3	3.6	3.8	7.0

Source: Statistics Canada, General Social Survey, 2003.

as signing petitions, boycotting products, or participating in demonstrations. Except for participating in demonstrations or marches, there is a tendency for younger age groups to be more passively involved than the older groups, who seem to be more actively involved. Why do you think that the younger generation is least likely to vote or pay attention to current affairs?

QUESTIONS

1. Which social groups in Canada do you think are represented more in the political decision making? Why?
2. Do you agree with a Marxist or a pluralist view of the Canadian state? Why?
3. Have you ever voted in an election? Why, or why not?
4. What role do you think religion, education, ethnicity, or socioeconomic status plays in the political party one votes for?
5. Why do you think that voting turnout is so low in Canada, the United States, and Britain?
6. Do you think media literacy is important for voting? Which type of media play an important role? Why?
7. What suggestions do you have that might increase voter turnout?

Civic Literacy and Falling Electoral Turnout: The United Kingdom 1992–1997

C. J. Pattie
University of Sheffield

R. J. Johnston
University of Bristol

◆ ◆ ◆

Canadian general elections have been marked by rapidly declining public participation. The decline in turnout since the 1980s has been apparently inexorable, down from 75 per cent in the 1984 and 1988 contests to just under 70 per cent in 1993, 67 per cent in 1997, and just 61 per cent in the 2000 contest. . . .

Canada's experience, while striking, may be part of a wider trend. Many established democracies have seen (sometimes dramatic) falls in electoral turnout (Gray and Caul, 2000). For instance, in the United States, only around 50 per cent of the adult population voted in the 2000 presidential election, compared to turnouts of around 62 per cent in the 1950s (though some have argued this may be a measurement artefact rather than a real decline: for example, McDonald and Popkin, 2001). And in the United Kingdom only 59 per cent of electors bothered to vote in the 2001 general election, down 11 percentage points since the previous general election in 1997 (itself a postwar low turnout, down nearly seven percentage points from the relatively high 78 per cent participation rate in the 1992 contest).

Declining citizen involvement in a basic part of modern democracy is a widespread problem. But how are we to account for it, and, more importantly, how can it be countered? How are citizens to be brought back to the polling booth? In this article, we consider one novel and important recent suggestion: Henry Milner's "civic literacy" approach (Milner, 2001a, 2001b, 2002). Can we expect increased civic literacy to deliver more widespread electoral participation?

CIVIC LITERACY AND ELECTORAL PARTICIPATION

◆ ◆ ◆

. . . Milner's intriguing argument concerns the ability of citizens to access and assimilate political information. And this has potential consequences for electoral participation. He asks, "can we expect people who do not keep up with political events to vote?" (Milner, 2001a: 3). Within this, civic literacy refers to citizens' knowledge of their political environment. "Civic literates," if we can coin such a term, are well informed about their country's government (and, perhaps also, about the international scene), follow political developments and participate actively in political life (even if only to the extent of voting regularly). By contrast, "civic illiterates" have only limited knowledge, make little or no attempt to keep up with events, and are disengaged from the political scene.

To a large extent, Milner argues, levels of civic literacy in a society reflect the educational success or failure

From C. J. Pattie and R. J. Johnston, "Civic Literacy and Falling Electoral Turnout: The United Kingdom 1992–1997," *Canadian Journal of Political Science*, Vol 36:3, July/August, pp. 579–599.

of that society and, in particular, its literacy levels (in the conventional sense of reading competence). Widespread literacy is claimed to be an important contributor to strong civic literacy, since it affords members of the public ready access to a wide range of information sources, particularly those offered by the print media. . . . In a cross-national analysis of Western democracies, Milner demonstrates clear correlations between national functional illiteracy and levels of political knowledge and participation. The higher the level of functional illiteracy in a country, the lower the level of political knowledge there; the greater the reliance on TV for information and entertainment, the lower the turnout at elections.

Canada emerges poorly from Milner's analysis. Despite the quality of the Canadian elite education system, the country (like the U.S. and the UK) scores relatively high on levels of functional illiteracy, and low on levels of political knowledge. Newspaper circulation, meanwhile, is relatively low: Canada ranks 16th out of the 18 developed nations studied by Milner. Television dependency, by contrast, is high. In Milner's terms, then, the conditions are set for relatively low levels of civic literacy in Canada. Falling turnout in Canadian elections would seem to be a consequence of a decline in political knowledge among the Canadian public, therefore, and the latter, in its turn, a result of the relative weakness of Canadian civic literacy.

A key implication of the analysis is that political knowledge must be increased in order to improve turnout. To achieve this, Milner argues, it is necessary to improve adult literacy skills in order to enable all citizens to follow politics closely. And, more than this, the newspaper-reading habit is seen as a crucial element in fostering civic literacy. For Milner, this is "the most important single aspect . . . of promoting civic literacy" (Milner, 2001a: 23). Turn Canada into a nation of avid newspaper readers, and not only will levels of political knowledge rise across the population, but the decline in turnout should also be reversed.

A NEWSPRINT PANACEA?

◆ ◆ ◆

But is enhanced civic literacy quite the panacea that Milner seems to suggest? To some extent, we are reminded of the well-known paradox of education and turnout. Cross-sectional analyses of political participation suggest that, other things being equal, the more highly educated in society are more likely to vote (and get involved in other sorts of political activity) than are those

with few or no formal educational qualifications (Verba et al., 1995). The apparent conclusion from the cross-sectional analyses seems clear: if you want to boost turnout nationally, get a larger proportion of the population through high school and university. But cross-temporal studies suggest this is not the case. Over time, turnout has declined in a number of countries *despite* improving levels of educational attainment: more Americans were high school and college graduates in 2000 than in 1952, but turnout was lower. The cross-sectional relationship does not necessarily translate into a cross-temporal one. Improving educational attainment does not improve electoral turnout (Franklin, 1999; Gray and Caul, 2000). Not only that, but not all newspaper reading is devoted to current affairs: people read the press for a variety of other reasons, for instance, to follow their favourite sport. What people read in the press is at least as important as the fact that they read the papers at all. Will increasing newspaper readership (assuming this can be achieved) be any different? We cannot take the result for granted.

Furthermore, even if a cross-sectional and cross-temporal relationship were to be established between, say, newspaper readership and voting, the direction of causation is still not absolutely clear. It is conceivable that, far from newspaper readership raising political knowledge and encouraging turnout, the causal chain may run in the opposite direction. Electors who have decided they will vote may then feel they need information on which to base their electoral choice and so start reading the press, the opposite causal direction to that implicit in Milner's argument. There may, in fact, be a process of mutual feedback, with newspaper readership encouraging turnout, and turnout encouraging further reading, and so on in a "virtuous circle" (Norris, 2000). Untangling the causal mechanisms is unlikely to be easy.

Even within Milner's own analysis there are some signs that "civic literacy" might not be a panacea—or even a partial cure—for low turnout. Turnout in Quebec has been higher than in most other provinces. Even in 2000, 64 per cent of Quebeckers went to the polls, higher than the national average of 61 per cent. Only Prince Edward Island (73 per cent) and New Brunswick (68 per cent) had higher turnouts. But, as Milner himself points out: "As for literacy, civic and otherwise, Quebecers read fewer newspapers and watch more television than Canadians as a whole. . . . In the IALS [*International Adult Literary Survey*] prose comprehension test, a very high 28 percent of Quebecers were functionally illiterate (level 1) compared to 20 per cent for the rest of the country" (Milner, 2001a: 27). On the face of it, from a civic literacy perspective we might expect turnout to be lower than average in Quebec. But in fact we see the opposite.

And, of course, what the "civic literates" get from their newspaper reading may not encourage their interest in politics and the political system. Much press (and other) media coverage of politics and politicians presents them in an unfavourable light. The outcome of reading such negative material may be to encourage a distrust of politicians and politics and discourage voter turnout. This was certainly the case in the UK between 1992 and 1997; one of the dominant themes of that Parliament was sleaze of corrupt and unseemly behaviour by a number of MPs (mainly Conservatives). These were stories hardly likely to encourage a greater engagement with the political and electoral systems unless the reader was thereby encouraged to become involved in order to "clean up" politics (which was a substantial part of Labour's claims in the 1997 election campaign). . . .

PANACEA OR MIRAGE?

◆ ◆ ◆

Milner's analysis rests on aggregate data, gathered at the national level. As such, it carries a risk of committing an ecological fallacy. Just because there is an aggregate relationship between civic literacy and turnout does not mean that there must also be a relationship at the level of individual voters. We therefore concentrate in what follows on the analysis of individual voters. Following Milner's injunction concerning the importance of the press in developing civic literacy, we focus on newspaper readership. In particular, to which extent do individual voters have the newspaper reading "habit": are they regular paper readers, do they look at the press occasionally or do they ignore the print media altogether?

The data are drawn from the 1997 British Election Study (BES) cross-section data and from the 1992–1997 British Election Panel Study (BEPS), which followed the same group of voters over a five-year period. These data were selected for two reasons. First, there are important similarities between the Canadian and the British cases. Like Canada, Britain has experienced rapid falls in electoral turnout: the 1997 election had, at the time, the lowest turnout of any postwar election (Heath, 2000; Heath and Taylor, 1999; Pattie and Johnston, 2001). British and Canadian elections are both conducted on the basis of single-member constituencies with plurality voting. And, as measured by the IALS, levels of functional illiteracy in both countries are broadly similar (in fact,

the UK scores worse on this measure than does Canada). Where they differ is on newspaper circulation, which is around twice as high in the UK as in Canada.

Second, the BES and BEPS data contain a wide range of information regarding individuals' political knowledge, participation, voting and media use, two aspects of which make them particularly useful for this study. Vote verification exercises have been conducted in all British Election Studies since 1987: we know the actual turnout, as well as the self-reported turnout, for both surveys (Swaddle and Heath, 1989; Burden, 2000; Bernstein et al., 2001). And both surveys ask in some detail about newspaper reading habits: which papers are read, how often and so on. And, through the panel study, we have information on changing press reading habits, since respondents were asked the same questions in 1992 and 1997. . . .

NEWSPAPER READERSHIP, CIVIC LITERACY AND TURNOUT IN BRITAIN IN 1997: A CROSS-SECTIONAL LOOK

◆ ◆ ◆

. . . Respondents to the 1997 BES were asked whether they regularly read a daily morning newspaper and those who did were further asked how often they read a newspaper. The responses reveal an electorate roughly split in half (Table 1): just over one half of all respondents read a paper most days of the week (and 43 per cent claimed to read a paper every day), while 41 per cent said they were not regular newspaper readers. This probably overestimates the proportion that never read the press since it

Table 1   Frequency of Newspaper Readership, Political Knowledge, and Turnout, 1997

I read the newspaper	Frequency %	Average political knowledge score	Voting % 1997
Every day	42.9	4.37	83.6
4 or 5 days a week	8.9	4.22	80.5
2 or 3 days a week	6.3	3.96	73.9
1 day a week or less	0.9	4.48	94.7
Never	40.9	3.75	77.6
N	2,903	2,861	2,250

Source: 1997 British Election Study cross-section.

includes those who are occasional readers, but it does indicate that a very large minority of the adult population do not have the newspaper "habit."

Milner suggests a relationship between newspaper readership and political knowledge, and there is certainly evidence for this in the British data. Political knowledge was measured in the BES through a short quiz. Respondents were offered a series of factual statements about British politics, and asked which were true and which false. . . . Political knowledge was related to frequency of newspaper readership (Table 1). . . .

Similarly, for electoral turnout in 1997, those who read the press regularly were much more likely to vote than those who seldom or never read newspapers (Table 1). While 84 per cent of those who read a paper daily voted (and remember we are looking here at verified actual turnout, not at self-reported voting), only 78 per cent of those who seldom or never read a paper turned out. . . .

These results are consistent with the "civic literacy" argument. But one obvious objection is that we have not adequately controlled for other independent factors that are known to be related to the turnout decision. For instance, much of the literature reports that age, social class and education are related to electoral participation. . . . We can take these into account through a multivariate analysis.

Our first model contains just one independent variable: frequency of newspaper readership (Table 2, column 1). . . . As we have already seen, frequency of newspaper reading was related to individual electoral participation in 1997. But, interestingly, the most frequent newspaper readers were the only group whose probability of turning out differed significantly from that of the least frequent paper readers. Other things being equal, those who read a paper every day were 1.4 times more likely to vote in the election than were those who never read a paper. That said, as indicated by the model diagnostics, frequency of newspaper readership was not able to account for much of the variation in turnout: the pseudo-R^2 value is only 0.01.

Much of the conventional literature on turnout argues that electoral participation is related to various socio-economic factors (Pattie and Johnston, 1998). Adding controls for the "usual suspects" of individual age, class and education improved the overall fit of the model significantly (Table 2, column 2). As conventional wisdom would suggest, older voters were more likely to vote than were the young, and those with lesser educational qualifications were less likely to vote than those with more. More important for our analysis here, these extra controls

do not explain away the relationship between newspaper reading habits and turnout. The most frequent readers are still more likely to vote than those who read the press less frequently.

Socio-economic factors are not the only ones which might affect electoral participation, however. Political factors, too, can have an influence (Heath and Taylor, 1999; Johnston and Pattie, 2001; Pattie and Johnston, 2001). Rational voters should be more likely to participate if the election is closely fought than if the result is a near certainty (one extra vote in a landslide is unlikely to make a difference). Nor are they likely to vote if they see little real difference between the main rivals for government (why waste effort by voting for more of the same?), or if they do not feel the result is important. We have therefore added further controls for respondents' perceptions of the difference between Labour and Conservatives at the 1997 election, for feelings of efficacy (measured by responses to two questions: whether respondents agreed with a statement to the effect that it did not matter which party was in power in Westminster, things would go on much as before; and whether they agreed with a claim that "people like me" had little influence on government decisions), and for their self-reported interest in the outcome of the election. Unfortunately, we do not have measures, in the 1997 BES, of their perceptions of the closeness—or not, as Labour was widely expected to win in 1997—of the competition. These controls do make a difference to our conclusions regarding civic literacy (Table 2, column 3). Not surprisingly, of course, those who are not interested in the result of the election are much less likely to vote than those who are very interested. But with the inclusion of the political variables, the "civic literacy" relationship ceases to be significant. Civic literacy (at least as measured by whether members of the electorate are regular daily newspaper readers) does not add to our understanding of electoral participation over and above the conventional socio-political model.

To some extent, it could be argued that civic literacy, interest in the election result, and perceptions of the gap between the main parties are all related. It would seem sensible to suspect that those who read the press regularly have a clearer idea of where the parties stand, and a keener interest in the outcome of a poll than those who never consult a newspaper. If this is true, then civic literacy might still have an indirect effect on electoral participation. We therefore correlated frequency of newspaper readership against our "political" measures. There was indeed a statistically significant relationship in the expected direction between newspaper readership and caring who won the

Table 2　Frequency of Newspaper Readership and Electoral Turnout, 1997: Logistic Regression

	Voted, 1997		
	1	2	3
Frequency of newspaper readership (comparison = never read paper)			
Every day	0.37[a]	0.31[b]	0.25
4 or 5 days a week	0.10	0.11	−0.00
2 or 3 days a week	−0.30	−.27	−0.31
1 day a week or less	0.85	0.68	0.61
Respondent's age		0.02[a]	0.02[a]
Respondent's gender (comparison = female)			
Male		0.14	0.15
Respondent's social class (comparison = salariat)			
Routine non-manual		−0.26	−0.22
Petty bourgeoisie		−0.40	−0.28
Foreman & supervisors		0.27	0.34
Working class		−0.48[b]	−0.32
Respondent's education level (comparison = university degree)			
Higher education below degree		0.03	0.06
School qualifications		−0.16	−0.06
Other qualifications		−0.31	0.09
No qualifications		−0.45	−0.34
Perceived difference between Conservative and Labour, 1997 (comparison = great difference)			
Some difference			0.18
Not much difference			−0.09
The party in power does not matter, 1997 (comparison = agree)			
Neither agree or disagree			0.28
Disagree			0.04
People like me have no say in government actions, 1997 (comparison = agree)			
Neither agree or disagree			−0.00
Disagree			0.25
Cared who won election (comparison = cared a good deal)			
Did not care much			−0.18[a]
Constant	1.63	0.90	0.80
Initial—2 log likelihood	1609.06	1609.06	1609.06

Continued

Table 2   Frequency of Newspaper Readership and Electoral Turnout, 1997: Logistic Regression *Continued*

| | Voted, 1997 | | |
	1	2	3
Model improvement	11.54	49.42	128.44
Significance	0.02	0.00	0.00
% Correctly classified	82.9	82.9	83.0
Nagelkerke R^2	0.01	0.05	0.12
N	1761	1761	1761

[a] significant at p 0.01.

[b] significant at p 0.05.

[2] verified turnout.

Source: 1997 British Election Study cross-section.

election (Table 4a). Some 45 per cent of those who cared a great deal about the outcome of the election read a paper every day, for instance, compared to 37 per cent of those who were not interested in the result. (The relative proportions are virtually reversed at the other end of the readership scale: 39 per cent of those who cared a great deal never read a paper, compared to 47 per cent of those who did not care.) The politically interested were slightly more likely to read newspapers frequently than were the uninterested. But the relationship was very weak: in a bivariate regression model (not reported here) civic literacy accounted for only about 0.001 per cent of the variation in interest in the election outcome. Similarly, there is a significant relationship between civic literacy and feelings of personal efficacy. Those who felt they could have some influence were more likely to be frequent newspaper readers than were those who felt they had little influence (Table 4d). But, once again, a regression analysis (not reported here) reveals the underlying relationship is weak, with an R^2 of just 0.01 per cent. And there was no relationship between readership and either perceptions of differences between the parties or of the difference changing a party of government might make (Table 4b and 4c). If there is an indirect effect of civic literacy on turnout, therefore, it is a very weak one.

But even if we were willing to accept such an apparently tenuous indirect effect, however, what would we make of it? The problem, as so often in social sciences, is one of establishing causal direction. Advocates of the civic literacy perspective would argue that getting the newspaper habit fosters interest in politics by exposing the reader to more information. From this perspective, the disappearance of a significant relationship between newspaper reading and turnout when interest in the result of

the election is taken into account is just what one would expect. Interest in the outcome could be seen as an intervening variable between newspaper reading and voting. But causation might equally plausibly run in quite the opposite direction. It could be that the first key step is to get electors interested in politics again: if they are interested, this argument would go, they will seek out more information, and hence will read newspapers more often. From this alternative perspective, interest in the election outcome is an antecedent variable, and the apparent relationship between newspaper readership and voting picked up in the earlier models is just a consequence of a poorly specified original model.

The results in Tables 2 and 3 can be interpreted in two quite different ways. Either the civic literacy argument does have a role to play in accounting for election turnout (if interest in the result is an intervening variable), or it does not (if interest in the result is the antecedent). The best we can say so far is that individual-level cross-sectional data produce results that are not wholly inconsistent with the civic literacy perspective—though they do not provide particularly strong support. But we cannot be more decisive than this. With cross-sectional data, unfortunately, we can do little more to untangle the problem, since we have no knowledge of what happened first.

BUILDING A CROSS-TEMPORAL PERSPECTIVE

◆ ◆ ◆

Ideally, the way forward would be to conduct some sort of experimental study, raising newspaper readership among a random group of individuals while holding it constant among a control group. Such a research design lies beyond

Table 3 Frequency of Newspaper Readership (Continuous) and Electoral Turnout, 1997: Logistic Regression

| | Voted, 1997 | | |
	1	2	3
Frequency of paper readership	0.04	0.03	0.01
Respondent's age		0.02[a]	0.02[a]
Respondent's gender (comparison = female)			
Male		0.12	0.12
Respondent's social class (comparison = salariat)			
Routine non-manual		−0.27	−0.22
Petty bourgeoisie		−0.42	−0.30
Foremen & supervisors		0.30	0.35
Working class		−0.47[b]	−0.32
Respondent's education level (comparison = university degree)			
Higher education below degree		0.05	0.09
School qualifications		−0.12	−0.03
Other qualifications		−0.35	0.04
No qualifications		−0.42	−0.32
Perceived difference between Conservative and Labour, 1997 (comparison = great difference)			
Some difference			0.17
Not much difference			−0.08
The party in power does not matter, 1997 (comparison = agree)			
Neither agree or disagree			0.27
Disagree			0.04
People like me have no say in government actions, 1997 (comparison = agree)			
Neither agree or disagree			−0.00
Disagree			0.24
Cared who won election (comparison = cared a good deal)			
Did not care much			−1.19[a]
Constant	1.56	0.74	0.67
Initial—2 log likelihood	1609.06	1609.06	1609.06
Model improvement	0.73	42.27	122.60
Significance	0.40	0.00	0.00
% Correctly classified	82.9	82.9	82.9
Nagelkerke R^2	0.00	0.04	0.11
N	1761	1761	1761

[a] significant at p 0.01.

[b] significant at p 0.05.

[2] verified turnout.

Source: 1997 British Election Study cross-section.

Table 4   Newspaper Readership and Perceptions of the Political Context, 1997

	a) Cared who won		b) Perceived Con-Lab difference		
Frequency of newspaper reading	A great deal %	Not very much %	Great difference %	Some difference %	No difference %
Every day	44.8	37.1	45.3	41.7	43.7
4 or 5 days a week	9.2	8.2	8.3	9.2	9.1
2 or 3 days a week	6.2	6.7	5.5	7.0	6.3
1 day a week or less	0.9	1.0	1.1	0.9	0.9
Never	38.9	47.0	39.9	41.2	40.0
N	2186	706	943	1222	668
χ^2 (p)	16.75	(0.002)	4.35	(0.825)	

	c) The party in power does not matter			d) People like me have no say in govt.		
Frequency of newspaper reading	Agree %	Neither %	Disagree %	Agree %	Neither %	Disagree %
Every day	44.3	44.1	42.2	46.5	40.3	39.4
4 or 5 days a week	8.8	8.6	10.3	7.9	9.7	12.2
2 or 3 days a week	5.4	7.3	6.2	5.0	8.7	6.2
1 day a week or less	1.0	0.3	1.2	0.8	1.0	1.2
Never	40.5	39.7	40.1	39.8	40.3	41.0
N	1075	395	945	1401	484	515
χ^2 (p)	6.39	(0.604)		22.65	(0.004)	

Source: 1997 British Election Study cross-section.

our resources, even were it technically feasible. However, panel survey data provide a partial alternative. The 1992–1997 BEPS followed a group of respondents between the two elections who were asked about their newspaper reading habits in 1992 and again in 1997: the same question was used as in the 1997 cross-section discussed above. This allows us to construct a measure of change in frequency of newspaper reading over the life of a Parliament. A majority of the population was stable in its newspaper reading habits over time: 60 per cent gave the same answer to the question "how often do you read your paper" in 1992 and in 1997 (Table 5). Of course, "stability" here includes both those who always read a paper every day and those who never read a paper. Of more interest to us, however, is the substantial minority of BEPS respondents whose engagement with the press changed between 1992 and 1997: fully 20 per cent of the sample became more frequent newspaper readers, while just over 15 per cent read a paper less frequently at the later, than at the earlier, election.

Recalling that one of Milner's key suggestions for raising turnout is boosting newspaper reading, it is the 35 per cent of "changers" who are most of interest to us here. Our BEPS data do not allow us to assess directly the impact of an externally sponsored strategy of boosting newspaper readership. However, our knowledge of individuals' self-induced changes in reading habits does give us a sort of natural experiment within which to assess the potential utility of actions to encourage newspaper reading. If the "civic literacy" argument is correct, then change in newspaper reading habits should be reflected in change in chances of turning out. Those who become more frequent newspaper readers between elections should also be more likely to turn out in the subsequent election than those who read the press less often at the end than at the beginning of the inter-election period.

Once again, we investigate the impact of newspaper reading using logistic regression. Our dependent variable is still individual turnout in 1997, coded as before (with

Table 5   Changing Frequency of Newspaper Readership, 1992–1997

	%
Read papers less often in 1997 than in 1992	20.4
No change in frequency of newspaper reading	64.0
Read papers more often in 1997 than in 1992	15.6
N	1378

Source: 1992–1997 British Election Panel Study.

one important difference, however: for cost reasons, no vote verification was carried out on the final wave of the 1992–1997 BEPS, so we have to rely here on self-reported turnout). The key independent variable here is the measure of change in newspaper reading habits described in Table 5. If the civic literacy model is correct, we would expect a positive relationship between changing readership habits and turnout: those who become more frequent readers should be more likely to vote than those who lose the regular newspaper habit. The change in frequency measure is entered as a categorical variable in a logistic regression model (those whose newspaper reading declined in frequency between 1992 and 1997 are the comparison group), with self-reported turnout at the 1997 election as the dependent (Table 6, column 1). Our first model assesses the civic literacy case alone. We do not find the expected positive relationship. Crucially for the civic literacy account, there is no significant difference in turnout between those who became less frequent newspaper readers over the inter-election period, and those who became more frequent readers.

As discussed above, however, turnout is also influenced by social and political factors. We take these into account using the controls introduced in Table 2. Together, they constitute an alternative, socio-political explanation for turnout which is assessed in the second and third columns of Table 6: overall, the socio-political model performs as expected. Older electors are more likely to vote than the young, while working-class electors and those with no educational qualifications are less likely to do so than members of the middle-class salariat and the university-educated. And those who felt that a change in party of government would make little difference, who felt their own views were unlikely to be taken into account by government, or who did not care about the result of the election were much less likely to vote in 1997 than were individuals in the respective comparison groups.

But the "change in newspaper reading" coefficients remain insignificant in each model. It would seem that civic literacy has nothing to add to the more conventional socio-political explanation of electoral participation. Those who had taken to reading the press more often were no more likely to turn out at a general election than were those whose reading habits had stayed constant, or who had become less frequent readers.

As before, we have re-estimated our model using different specifications of changing newspaper readership habits and also controlling for socio-political factors (Table 7). Model 1 uses the three-point index of change in newspaper reading habits employed in Table 6, but fitted as a continuous, not a categorical, variable. Models 2 and 3 focus on readership habits in 1997, controlling for readership habits in 1992. Model 2 fits both 1997 and 1992 readership habits as continuous variables. as before, the readership variables are coded from 1 (daily readership) to 5 (never read a paper). Model 3 uses the same variables, but entered as categorical variables and with the "never read a paper" group as the comparison in each case. Models 4 and 5 use an extended version of the "change in readership frequency" scale. By subtracting the 5-point 1992 readership frequency measure from the equivalent 1997 measure, we obtain a 9-point change in readership scale, where -4 represents someone who was a daily newspaper reader in 1992 but who never read a paper by 1997, 0 represents no change, and $+4$ represents an individual who never read a paper in 1992, but who read one each day in 1997. Model 4 fits this 9-point scale as a continuous variable, and Model 5 fits it as a categorical variable, with the group of individuals who went from daily newspaper readership in 1992 to never reading a paper in 1997 as the comparison group.

None of the alternative model specifications provide any evidence of a "civic literacy" effect, however. In no case are any of the coefficients significant. No matter how we measure it, the changing pattern of newspaper readership does not affect electoral turnout.

Of course, it may be that change in newspaper readership is related to some or all of the "political" variables (difference between Conservative and Labour; effect of changing party of government; personal efficacy; and caring who won the election), and hence changes in civic literacy have an indirect effect on turnout. To assess this, we correlated the change in readership frequency measure against each of the socio-political measures. (Table 8 gives the relevant chi-square and p-values.) There is little evidence in the panel study data of indirect civic literacy

Table 6   Changing Newspaper Readership and Turnout at the 1997 General Election: Logistic Regressions

	Voted, 1997		
	1	*2*	*3*
Change in readership 1992–97 (comparison = read papers less often)			
Read with same frequency	0.17	0.09	−0.01
Read more often	0.22	0.11	−0.01
Respondent's age		0.03[a]	0.03[a]
Respondent's gender (comparison = female)			
Male		−0.32	−0.37
Respondent's social class (comparison = salariat)			
Routine non-manual		0.19	0.13
Petty bourgeoisie		−1.11[a]	−0.88[b]
Foremen & supervisors		−0.28	−0.69
Working class		−0.58[b]	−0.55
Respondent's education level (comparison = university degree)			
Higher education below degree		−0.94	−0.94
School qualifications		−0.89	−0.77
Other qualifications		−2.22[a]	−2.19[b]
No qualifications		−1.58[a]	−1.47[a]
Perceived difference between Conservative and Labour, 1997 (comparison = great difference)			
Some difference			−0.42
Not much difference			−0.44
Does it make a difference who wins the election 1997 (comparison = quite a lot of difference)			
Some			−0.61[b]
Not very much			−1.10[a]
People like me have no say in government actions, 1997 (comparison = agree)			
Neither agree or disagree			0.20
Disagree			0.50[b]
Cared who won election, 1997 (comparison = cared a good deal)			
Did not care much			−1.46[a]
Constant	1.98	0.79	0.10
Initial—2 log likelihood	941.72	941.72	941.72
Model improvement	0.77	68.93	195.66
Significance	0.68	0.00	0.00

Continued

Table 6   Changing Newspaper Readership and Turnout at the 1997 General Election: Logistic Regressions *Continued*

	Voted, 1997		
	1	*2*	*3*
% Correctly classified	88.0	88.0	88.8
Nagelkerke R²	0.00	0.10	0.27
N	1281	1281	1281

[a] significant at p 0.01.
[b] significant at p 0.05.
[2] self-reported turnout.
Source: 1992–1997 British Election Study cross-section.

Table 7   Alternative Specifications for Changing Newspaper Readership and Turnout at the 1997 General Election: Logistic Regressions

	Voted, 1997				
	1	*2*	*3*	*4*	*5*
Change in paper readership (3 point)	−0.01				
Frequency of paper readership 1997		−0.09			
Frequency of paper readership 1992		0.02			
Frequency of paper readership 1997 (comparison = never read paper)					
Every day			0.36		
4 or 5 days a week			0.15		
2 or 3 days a week			0.01		
1 day a week or less			1.14		
Frequency of paper readership 1997 (comparison = never read paper)					
Every day			0.02		
4 or 5 days a week			−0.38		
2 or 3 days a week			0.19		
1 day a week or less			5.59		
Change in paper readership (9 point)				0.06	
Change in frequency of newspaper readership 1992–1997 (comparison = -4: daily 1992–never 1997)					
−3					2.07
−2					0.32
−1					0.76
Same					0.42
1					0.09
2					0.61
3					1.51
4: never 1992–daily 1997					1.39

Continued

	Voted, 1997				
	1	*2*	*3*	*4*	*5*
Respondent's age	0.03[a]	0.03[a]	0.03[a]	0.03[a]	0.03[a]
Respondent's gender (comparison = female)					
Male	−0.37	−.040	−0.38	−0.36	−0.35
Respondent's social class (comparison = salariat)					
Routine non-manual	0.13	0.11	0.15	0.12	0.11
Petty bourgeoisie	−0.88[b]	−0.87[b]	−0.90[b]	−0.88[b]	−0.90
Foreman & supervisors	−0.68	−0.71	−0.71	−0.69	−0.71
Working class	−0.55	−0.54	−0.56	−0.54	−0.58[b]
Respondent's education level (comparison = university degree)					
Higher education below degree	−0.94	−0.92	−0.94	−0.93	−0.96
School qualifications	−0.77	−0.77	−0.84	−0.76	−0.76
Other qualifications	−2.19[b]	−2.10[b]	−2.10[b]	−2.16[b]	−2.14[b]
No qualifications	−1.47[a]	−1.48[a]	−1.56[a]	−1.47[a]	−1.49[a]
Perceived difference between Conservative and Labour, 1997 (comparison = great difference)					
Some difference	−0.42	−0.41	−0.39	−0.43	−0.44
Not much difference	−.04	−0.44	−0.47	−0.45	−0.48
Does it make a difference who wins the election 1997 (comparison = quite a lot of difference)					
Some	−0.61[b]	−0.60[b]	−0.57[b]	−0.60[b]	−0.64[a]
Not very much	−1.10[a]	−1.11[a]	−1.19[a]	−1.11[a]	−1.08[a]
People like me have no say in government actions, 1997 (comparison = agree)					
Neither agree or disagree	0.20	0.22	0.17	0.22	0.19
Disagree	0.50[b]	0.51[b]	0.48	0.51[b]	0.49
Cared who won election, 1997 (comparison = cared a good deal)					
Did not care much	−1.46[a]	−1.43[a]	−1.46[a]	−1.44[a]	−1.44[a]
Constant	0.10	0.35	1.47	0.11	0.27
Initial—2 log likelihood	941.73	941.73	941.73	941.73	941.73
Model improvement	195.66	197.87	207.04	196.52	205.91
Significance	0.00	0.00	0.00	0.00	0.00
% Correctly classified	88.8	88.8	89.3	89.0	89.3
Nagelkerke R^2	0.27	0.28	0.29	0.27	0.29
N	1282	1282	1282	1283	1281

[a] significant at p 0.01.

[b] significant at p 0.05.

[2] self-reported turnout.

Source: 1992–1997 British Election Study cross-section.

Table 8   Newspaper Reading and Interest in the Campaign: Chi Squares

	Chi square values		
	:Hari.' v 1I		I"
	Change in readership frequency 1992-1997		Paper reading frequency 1997
	3 point	9 point	
Care who won 1997	3.26 (0.20)	8.46 (0.39)	5.20 (.027) 271
Con-Lab difference 1997	1.29 (0.86)	9.47 (0.89)	16.31 (0.04)
Make a difference who wins 1997	10.94 (0.30)	23.73 (0.10)	7.50 (0.48)
People like me have no say 1997	4.48 (0.34)	8.32 (0.94)	8.22 (0.41)

Numbers in parentheses are p-values.
Source: 1992–1997 British Election Panel Study.

effects. Only two of the twelve relationships tested are significant. There is a significant relationship between the 3-point change in readership frequency scale and perceptions of whether it makes a difference who wins the election. And there is also a relationship between frequency of newspaper readership in 1997 and perceptions of the difference between the Conservatives and Labour. However, neither relationship is quite what the civic literacy model would lead us to expect. So, for instance, 16 per cent of those who in 1997 felt who won an election would make a great deal of difference had become more frequent newspaper readers between 1992 and 1997. But so had 19 per cent of those who felt that a change of governing party would not make very much difference. And while 52 per cent of those panel respondents who felt there was a great difference between the Conservatives and Labour in 1997 read a paper each day in the election year, so did an almost identical 51 per cent of those who saw no real dif-

ference between the parties. At best enhanced civic literacy here is sending out confusing signals. At worst, it makes little or no difference to turnout.

CONCLUSIONS

The results reported here are disappointing for one of the key recommendations of the "civic literacy" remedy for declining turnout. They suggest that newspaper readership, like education, is related to voter turnout cross-sectionally but not cross-temporally. While cross-sectional data show frequency of newspaper reading is related to individual turnout, our results suggest this evaporates when we add controls for socio-economic position and political evaluations, raising a classic chicken-and-egg problem: what comes first? Interest in politics or civic literacy? Our attempts to get around this by using panel data also demonstrate that changing newspaper reading patterns have little or no bearing on electoral participation. Even when we find some signs of a "civic-literacy effect," the statistical evidence is relatively weak, the substantive effect is small and adding socio-economic controls makes it evaporate.

The poor performance of civic literacy in encouraging individual voters to participate is disappointing. The analyses reported here strongly suggest that the main factors underlying electoral participation (and changes in participation) remain, in part, sociological (older voters, middle-class voters and well-educated voters are the most likely to cast a ballot). But this cannot be the whole story. As numerous cross-temporal studies have demonstrated, turnout falls even as the electorate ages and becomes more middle-class and better educated. The other part of the story, we think, is political. Analyses of British elections belie the Impression of Inexorable decline in electoral turnout (Pattie and Johnston, 2001). Rather, what seems to underlie participation rates is politics. Turnout rises when the election result is perceived to be hard to predict, and it falls when the outcome seems a foregone conclusion.

Newspaper Readership and Federal Electoral Participation in Canada

M. Reza Nakhaie
University of Windsor

◆ ◆ ◆

Political scientists agree that informed political participation is the foundation of democracy. It empowers the citizen and ensures checks on and balance of the authority and power of the state and other entities. Turning out to vote is the most common and easily measured form of citizen political participation in a democracy. In fact, all sides of the ideological spectrum agree that voting is the symbolic essence of the democratic government and responsible citizenship. It is an indication of a nation's political health (Mishler, 1979; Miller 1980). Voter turnout is so fundamental that political scientists have been alarmed by the nonvoting of a large segment of the population. Some have referred to low turnout as a "crisis" (Norris, 1999: 257) or "sickness" (Johnston, 2001: 4) of electoral democracies. In Canada, turnout steadily declined from 75 percent in the 1984 election to 61 percent in the 2000 election. The most recent election in Canada, 2006, showed a small increase in turnout (63.9 percent). The decline in turnout is not specific to Canada. A similar trend is also apparent in other countries, such as the U.S. and UK (Howe and Northrup, 2000; Blais et al., 2002; Pattie and Johnston, 2003).

Previous research highlighted the importance of the socioeconomic makeup of the voters, generational differences in voting, legal restrictions on voting, and political contexts of elections (Miller, 1992; Pattie and Johnston, 1998; Lyons and Alexander, 2000; Blais et al., 2004). Less attention was given to the importance of civic engagements such as reading newspapers and following political issues and current affairs. Putnam (2000: 218) argued that newspaper readership is a "mark of substantial civic engagement." For him, newspaper readership was one of the "hallmarks" of successful Italian regions (1995: 66). Similarly, Milner (2001) pointed to the importance of

"civic literacy," as measured by newspaper readership. Milner's (2001) multination study revealed significant relationships between both illiteracy rates and daily newspaper readership with tendency to vote at the Municipal elections. This is an important consideration for political scientists, since the democratic process is argued to be effective if voters are knowledgeable and informed. Newspaper readership enables citizens to access political information and to act based on such information. Newspapers tend to inform individuals about their governments, political platforms, and thus enable them to effectively participate in the political process. However, further analysis by Pattie and Johnston (2003) showed that such a relationship was small and then became statistically insignificant when appropriate controls were included in the model. Their study of the 1997 British election showed that 83.6 percent of those who read newspapers on a daily basis voted in this election compared to 94.7 percent of those who read the paper once a week or less and 77.6 percent of those who never read newspapers. However, once they included other variables that have previously been shown to affect turnout in the logistic regression model (socioeconomic, sociodemographics and political factors), newspaper readership did not influence the voting process any more.

In this paper, I suggest that Pattie and Johnston's finding on a lack of "civic literacy" effect is due to their measure, "frequency of newspaper readership." People read the press for a variety of reasons. Some may not pay attention to current affairs which is the underlying theme of civic literacy. It is the attentiveness to news and current affairs in newspaper readership that can be important to turnout. The "civic literacy" argument points to the importance of citizens' knowledge of the political environment. Such individuals are well informed about the government and political issues

From "Newspaper Readership and Federal Electoral Participation in Canada" by M. Reza Nakhaie, *Sociology and Anthropology*, University of Windsor.

and follow political news consistently. However, to read the newspaper does not mean that one reads news or pays attention to politics. It is possible that one might read only the sports or entertainment section of the newspaper, not paying attention to news and current affairs.

Moreover, their study was based on the UK data. It is important to ascertain whether their results can be generalized to other countries. For this purpose, I will use the General Social Survey (Cycle 17) that studied, among other things, turnout for the 2000 Canadian Federal Election. Finally, consistent with Pattie and Johnston's study, I will control for the effects of the "usual suspects" or those variables that are shown to be related to turnout. Education, social class, and income have been standard predictors of turnout (Heath et al., 1991; Heckelman, 1997; Saxena, 2003). Individuals of higher socioeconomic status are more likely to have a stake in the political system, to be gate keepers and opinion leaders, and to influence the system. For example, education is both a measure of socioeconomic status and very important for political decision making. It is related to literacy and political knowledge, both of which are highly related to voting (Verba et al., 1995; Pattie and Johnston, 2001). Higher education increases one's capacity to understand complex political issues (Strait, 1990). It increases political awareness and information, contributes to an appreciation of the relevance of political decisions, and encourages civic responsibility. The general wisdom is that those with higher education, better jobs, and more income have a higher propensity to vote than their counterparts (see Pattie and Johnston, 1998, 2001, 2003; Howe and Northrup, 2000).

In Canada, it has been said that regionalism is one of the pre-eminent facts of Canadian politics (Mishler, 1979). Provinces differ in economic development, wealth, power, and other resources, which in turn affect the stock of social capital and political participation. Evidence also suggests that elder individuals are more likely to vote than younger ones. Similarly, women are somewhat less likely to vote than men, though the difference may have been eroded (Mishler, 1979; Miller, 1992; Howe and Northrup, 2000; Blais et al., 2002, 2004; Pammett and LeDuc, 2003; Saxena, 2003; Blais et al., 2004).

DATA

The data source is the Cycle 17 of the General Social Survey: Social Engagement (2003), Public Use Microdata File, administered by Statistics Canada. The final sample for this analysis includes 23,347 individuals who were eligible to vote in the election.

MEASUREMENT

◆ ◆ ◆

Respondents were asked: Did you vote in the last "federal," election? Each individual's response was coded into yes=1 and no=0. As well, an index of political behaviour was constructed based on sum of respondents past year's involvement in the following activities: searched for information on political issues; volunteered for a political party; expressed views by contacting newspaper/politician; signed petition; boycotted a product/chose a product for ethical reasons; attended a public meeting; spoke out at a public meeting; participated in a demonstration or march; or, was a member/participant in a political party/group.

Civic engagement was measured by attentiveness to the news and current affairs. This variable is indicative of voters' level of (political and/or social) sophistication. It provides the necessary social and political knowledge to make an informed decision and thus is the link between social capital and voting (Milner, 2001). The focus is on how often citizens pay attention to news and current affairs and not so much what type of current affairs they pay attention to. Certain types of news, such as political corruption, may, in fact, increase the sense of distrust and reduce voting. Respondents were asked the frequency to which they "follow news and current affairs." Then they were asked about the media source for this. Those who said that they use newspapers were given the following choices: rarely or never = 1, several times each month = 2, several times each week = 3, and daily = 4. Other individuals included those who paid attention to news and current affairs but used other media sources.

Education was coded into: less that high school = (reference category), graduated from high school diploma, college degree, and university degree. Social classes included those who work for themselves and have more than ten employees (large bourgeoisie), or ten or less employees (small bourgeoisie), or no employees (petty bourgeoisie), those who work for others (workers = reference category), and others outside the labour force. Personal income included 12 categories, from no income to $100,000 and more. Regions included: Atlantic, Quebec, Ontario (reference category), Prairies, and BC. Gender included male with female as the reference category. Marital status included married, with others as the reference category. Age was made of 14 categories, starting at 18 to 19 years of age and ending at 85 years of age and over. Finally, respondents were asked to state their level of confidence in federal parliament. This variable had four categories (no confidence at all = 1, not very much confidence= 2, quite a lot confidence = 3, and a great deal of confidence = 4).

ANALYSIS WITHOUT CONTROLS

◆ ◆ ◆

Table 1 shows the percentage of respondents voting in the 2000 federal elections and their average level of polit-

Table 1   Newspaper Readership, Political Participation and Electoral Turnout

	Political Participation Index		Voted in the 2000 Federal Election	
	Mean	N	Yes	No
How frequently do you follow news and current affairs?				
Media Source = newspaper			%	%
Rarely or never	2.65	74	52.7	47.3
Several times each month	2.94	117	52.5	47.5
Several times each week	3.01	599	63.6	36.4
Daily	3.48	3313	80.8	19.2
Other Media Sources	2.95	1340	65.4	34.6
DK, NA	2.15	13	50.8	49.2
Total	3.27	5456	72.3	27.7

Political Participation Index = sum of:

Past year: searched for information on political issue

Past year: volunteered for political party

Past year: expressed view by contacting newspaper/politician

Past year: signed a petition

Past year: boycotted a product/chose product for ethical reasons

Past year: attended a public meeting

Past year: spoke out at a public meeting

Past year: participated in a demonstration or march

Past year: member/participant in political party/group

Source: Statistics Canada, General Social Survey, Cycle 17.

ical participation for each level of attention to news and current affairs in newspapers. It shows that, as attention to news and current affairs in newspapers increases, so do electoral and political participation. The average political participation index for those who never or rarely read newspapers is 2.65 compared to 3.48 for those who read the paper on a daily basis. Similarly, whereas only 52.7 percent of respondents who never or rarely read newspaper voted, 80.8 percent of those who read the paper on a daily basis voted in the 2000 Federal election. In sum, there is a clear relationship between reading newspapers and paying attention to news and current affairs and participation in electoral and political processes.

ANALYSIS WITH CONTROL

◆ ◆ ◆

Table 2 shows the logistic regression results for relationships between the various measures and voter turnout. These estimates (B coefficients) present us with the differences in the log odds on voting for those in a category compared to the reference category for each predictor. Since the log odds may have little intuitive meaning, the exponentiated coefficients are also presented (Exp (B)). The exponential of a coefficient is the factor by which the unlogged odds on vote are multiplied for one unit of change in the predictor variable (e.g., gender). For interval and ratio variables, one needs to exponentiate the coefficient and then take it to the power of the desired category. If the exponential value is more than 1, then the relevant category has a higher effect on voting than the reference category. In contrast, if the exponential is less than 1, then the relevant category has a lower effect on voting than the reference category. Results are presented in four models in order to evaluate the relationship between newspaper readership and voting as we take into account the effect of other variables in successive models.

Model 1 shows that the exponential value for those who paid attention to news and current affairs by reading newspapers on a daily basis is 3.779 and positive. This means that they are about 3.8 times more likely to vote in the election than those who never or rarely read the paper (reference category). Model 2 shows that this exponential declined to 2.586. This suggests that some of the original relationship between daily newspaper readership and voting was due to respondents' age, gender, marital status, and region of residence. For example, elderly individuals tend to read the paper more and vote more. Thus, when Model 2 takes the age effect (and that of region, marital status, and gender) into consideration, the daily newspaper readership effect declined. This effect declined again when socioeconomic variables were taken into account in Model 3. Again, the more educated and higher classes were more likely to read the paper and/or vote. Therefore, taking their effect into account (as well as those of age, gender, marital status, and region), diminished the daily newspaper readership's effect on voting. Now, the turnout tendency for those who pay attention to news and current

Table 2   Logistic Regression of Electoral Turnout on Predictors

	B Model	Exp(B) 1	B Model	Exp(B) 2	B Model	Exp(B) 3	B Model	Exp(B) 4
Newspaper Readership								
Daily	1.330	3.779[a]	0.950	2.586[a]	0.753	2.124[a]	0.609	1.838[a]
Weekly	0.449	1.567[a]	0.610	1.840[a]	0.477	1.612[a]	0.349	1.418[b]
Monthly	−0.006	0.994	0.214	1.239	0.107	1.113	−0.093	0.911
Other Sources	0.528	1.695[a]	0.309	1.362[a]	0.232	1.261[c]	0.124	1.132
Age			0.235	1.265[a]	0.264	1.302[a]	0.275	1.316[a]
Male			−0.041	0.960	−0.179	0.836[a]	−0.201	0.818[a]
Married			0.497	1.643[a]	0.440	1.552[a]	0.467	1.595[a]
Atlantic			0.458	1.582[a]	0.570	1.768[a]	0.502	1.652[a]
Quebec			0.749	2.116[a]	0.851	2.341[a]	0.812	2.252[a]
West			0.117	1.124[c]	0.166	1.181[a]	0.140	1.150[b]
BC			−0.195	0.823[a]	−0.167	0.846[b]	-0.157	0.854[b]
University Graduate					0.632	1.881[a]	0.706	2.026[a]
College Graduate					0.562	1.754[a]	0.578	1.782[a]
High School Degree					0.356	1.428[a]	0.377	1.458[a]
Bourgeoisie more than 10 employees					0.491	1.633	0.507	1.661
Bourgeoisie 10 or less employees					−0.209	0.812[c]	-0.209	0.811[c]
Petty bourgeoisie					−0.067	0.935	−0.098	0.907
Others					−0.191	0.826[a]	−0.159	0.853[a]
Income					0.093	1.098[a]	0.087	1.091[a]
Confidence in Federal Parliament							0.055	1.056[c]
Constant	0.108	1.114	−1.814	0.163[a]	−2.793	0.061[a]	−2.746	0.064[a]
N	23347		23313		23128		20408	
Initial—2 log likelihood	26556		23573		22800		19407	
Nagelkerke R Squared	0.057		0.221		0.251		0.252	

Reference Categories: newspaper = does not read newspaper; gender = female; marital status = not married; region = Ontario; education = less than high school

Social class = workers.

a Significant at p .001.

b Significant at p .01.

c Significant at p .05.

affairs by reading newspapers is 2.124 times of those who never or rarely read the paper. Finally, Model 4 takes the effect of the political factor (confidence in federal parliament), too. In this model, the daily newspaper effect declined to 1.838 times of those who do not read the paper at all. Nevertheless, this exponential value is statistically significant. This suggests that despite holding the effect of all other variables constant (or into account), newspaper readership has a significant effect on voting turnout.

Among sociodemographic and socioeconomic predictors, older individuals, females, those living in Quebec, university graduates, those with higher income, and those with more confidence in federal parliament are more likely to participate in the electoral process than their counterparts.

In sum, this study showed that "Carriers of creed" (Tocqueville, 1945), who are the engines of the democratic system, are more likely to be politically informed and engaged in the civic society. They tend to have a sense of social responsibility and political participation. Thus, the civic responsibility of being abreast of current affairs is also fundamentally important for an informed and rational voting process. This is consistent with Milner's argument on the importance of civic responsibility. It does not support Pattie and Johnston's (2003) UK study. The effect of news attentiveness is also testimony to the rational and informed participation of voters. The health of democratic societies is based not only on voters' participation but, more importantly, on substantial information. Attentiveness to current affairs ensures such information.

Canada, unlike Australia, Belgium, and Greece, does not have a system of compulsory voting. Therefore, in order to deal with declining turnout, various other policy suggestions are made. These include having a fixed date for elections rather than allowing the government in power to hold an election whenever it wishes (within five years of office), increasing the power of parliamentary committees, ensuring regular referenda on major policy issues, or making individual votes more important by giving the parties with more votes more seats. Although these are important considerations, this paper suggests that instilling norms of civic responsibilities also has the expected effect of an increase in turnout. Therefore, it may be important to instill such norms early on by ensuring that schools encourage students to pay attention to news and current affairs and/or make available free copies of newspapers to students. Such efforts will nurture a new generation of aware and active citizens who may be able to reverse the tide of declining turnout.

Civics Class Key to Voting

Henry Milner

For those concerned with declining voter turnout, the first winter election in a quarter century should send shivers up your spines.

If the historically low viewership of the first round of debates was any indication, there is little doubt that the record low turnout of 61 per cent in the 2004 election will be surpassed. But the fundamental cause of declining turnout—apathy among young voters—will remain long after the winter snows are gone.

The recent steady drop in turnout, from 75 per cent in 1988 to 61 per cent in 2004, has been due largely to the fact the generation that reached adulthood during this period has not developed the habit of voting anywhere near the level of previous generations.

To simplify, among Canadians under 30, more than 60 per cent do not vote, as opposed to only about 25 per cent of those over 30. With the generation of "political dropouts" gradually replacing habitual voters, overall turnout can be expected to continue to decline.

While a similar tendency can be found in other countries, the generation gap appears greatest in Canada—greater even than Great Britain, the only comparable country where overall turnout dropped as abruptly as in Canada. And, it appears, even more than elsewhere, abstention by young Canadians is a result of inattentiveness to and thus ignorance of politics, rather than a rejection of existing parties or candidates.

In work published by the Institute for Research on Public Policy, I explore the causes of this, and what, if anything, might be done.

Young Canadians do well on cross-national tests of educational performance, but when it comes to the basic political knowledge, they are found wanting.

The result is inevitable: as the authors of the 2004 Canadian Election Study put it: "It is hard to cast an informed ballot if you do not know who the potential prime ministers are or what their parties are promising."

The classroom is the crucial arena. For young people to develop the habit of keeping up with political events after leaving school, a key policy choice concerns promoting attentiveness to political information through civic education. Courses should address students as soon-to-be voters, and their content must reflect this.

Fixed election dates (which have been adopted by British Columbia and, more recently, Ontario) would help as well, allowing civics teachers to plan course content accordingly. Election dates in Canada are typically known only months—if not weeks—before they are called, which leaves far too little time to plan public events, seminars, mock elections and other tools with a proven track record of boosting youth turnout.

It is no accident that the May 2005 student mock election in British Columbia (for which the date was known well in advance) achieved better results than a similar exercise prior to the June 2004 federal election.

As far as content is concerned, students must be given opportunities to engage political realities. Developing the habit of reading newspapers remains important. But we need to break through the negative image of individual politicians inevitably produced by the partisan clash in the media which puts politicians on the defensive ensuring that they appear inauthentic and "turn off" young, unsophisticated potential voters.

The best way to do so is to bring the political parties into the classroom. A good part of this can be done virtually, through full use of the channels of communication, electronic and otherwise that best fit the reading, listening and viewing habits of the emerging generation. But it also needs to be physical.

Can we imagine politicians at different levels being systematically invited to civics classes? Obviously, it would have to be done on a fair and representative basis, ideally complementing a proportional form of elections in which small parties—which often have distinct principle-based positions on different issues—have a fair chance of having democratically elected, and therefore legitimate, spokespersons to represent them. Such representativeness would make the entire political system more legitimate in the eyes of the young people.

But would it raise overall turnout? Given the replacement of high-voting by low-voting generations taking place, nothing short of compulsory voting could be counted upon to do so in the short term. But we can be sure that such measures will make the number of political drop-outs lower than it would otherwise be by fostering political knowledge and participation among those whose home and external environments are poor in political information.

And these days, with the credibility of politicians so low, we cannot afford to disregard any measure that could rebuild confidence in those at the centre of our democratic institutions.

Henry Milner is a Visiting Fellow at the Institute for Research on Public Policy. His studies, "Are Young Canadians Becoming Political Dropouts? A Comparative Perspective" and "Fixing Canada's Unfixed Election Dates: A 'Political Season' to Reduce the Democratic Deficit," are available at: http://www.irpp.org.

Source: Henry Milner, "Civics class key to voting," *Calgary Herald*, January 3, 2006, p. A8. Reprinted with permission of the author.

Unit Eleven

THEORY
Introduction: Modern Theorists Meet
Their Post-Modern Critics

♦♦♦

One sociological task is to develop a wide-ranging system of ideas or tentative and general explanations about social relations. These general explanations are called theories. Humans have always been involved in the development of some form of explanation about their social world. However, the history of modern sociological theories in the West started with the Age of Reason or **enlightenment** and changes that took place during the seventeenth and eighteenth century. Zeitlin (2001) identified six social conditions that helped the emergence of the enlightenment:

1. **Political Revolutions** (e.g., French revolution): These revolutions resulted in disorder and a breakdown of traditions. Scholars, therefore, were challenged to explain order and disorder, stability, and change that occurred after these revolutions.

2. **Industrial Revolution:** This revolution was associated with technological advancements and development of large industries and bureaucracies. These changes were the impetus for migration of people from farms to urban centres for the purpose of finding employment in large industries. Scholars became concerned with the disruption of traditional social relations as well as the conditions of the working class in the urban centres.

3. **Rise of Socialism:** People working in harsh urban and industrial environments and experiencing poverty and exploitation searched for an alternative way of life. Similarly, scholars sought to develop a social

system with more equality in ownership of the means of production (i.e., machineries, tools, and factories).

4. **Urbanization:** People were uprooted from their village communities and entered the big cities, which had problems such as overcrowding, pollution, noise, traffic, crime, among others. These issues became part of the new research agenda and discussion of scholars.

5. **Religious Transformations:** The various changes, as stated previously, affected people's views on life and the afterworld. One such fundamental religious transformation was the emergence of Protestantism, which entailed a distinctive world view as compared to Catholicism. Karl Marx, Max Weber, and Emile Durkheim all wrote about the role of religion in relation to social stability and change.

6. **Growth of Science:** New scientific methods of analyzing the world and its elements, as well as their explanation, emerged. The natural sciences, such as chemistry, physics, and biology, enjoyed substantial status. Sociology also adopted the methods of the natural sciences.

In sum, these transformations were intimately related to the development of enlightenment as a period of remarkable intellectual development, where philosophers and social thinkers challenged traditional ways of life and helped produce grand, general, and abstract systems of ideas derived from the real world and aimed at changing that world. It was reasoned that the natural world was dominated by natural laws and that the goal of scientists was to discover these laws in order to use them to change the world for the better. Enlightenment scholars used the methods of the natural sciences and applied them to the social world to help them discover social laws governing human behaviours (see Zeitlin, 2001).

In our discipline, Auguste Comte (1798–1857) is well known because he coined the term "**sociology.**" At first, he called this new science "social physics" but later changed it to sociology. His understanding of sociology is indebted to his intellectual mentor, Claude Henri de Saint-Simon (1760–1825), who had a major and lasting influence on Comte's life and work. However, the two men quarrelled over Saint-Simon's insistence that society needed immediate reform by the industrialists and bankers. Comte, on the other hand, believed that theoretical work should take precedence over reform activities. Nevertheless, Comte heavily borrowed from Saint-Simon in developing his understanding of social change and social order.

Comte argued that evolution of human society has paralleled the evolution of the individual mind. All individuals pass through three stages of development: affective, cognitive, and active. In the affective stage, individuals are governed by biologically innate propensities (e.g., instincts of preservation, drive for food and shelter, sexual instinct, instinct of pride and vanity, and instinct of attachment and veneration). In the cognitive stage, contemplation, mediation, and deductive and inductive reasoning are important sources of human conduct. Finally, in the active stage, courage in undertaking, prudence in execution, and firmness in accomplishment become important.

Comte also argued that just as individuals tend to be devoted believers in childhood, critical metaphysicians in adolescence, and natural philosophers in adulthood, so has human society in its growth traversed these three major stages. Each branch of human knowledge has passed successively through three different theoretical conditions. For Comte, every successive stage in the evolution of the human mind necessarily grew out of the preceding one. Moreover, he stated that these stages correspond to the stages in the development of social organization, of types of social order, of types of social units, and of the material conditions of human life. Below are Comte's three stages of development in human society:

1. **Theological stage:** In this stage, humans explain events through the will and actions of humanlike gods, spirits, demons, and other supernatural beings. In other words, the human mind, seeking the essential nature of beings—the first and final causes of all effects—supposes all phenomena to be produced by the immediate action of supernatural beings. At the upper end of this stage, priests manage the society and military men rule it. This meant the emergence of hierarchies and specialization of those people whose task was knowledge and power. Comte used examples of Egyptian, Greek, and Roman **polytheism** as the most developed societies in this stage.

2. **Metaphysical stage:** This was basically a transitional stage between the first and third stage. Events were understood in terms of innate essence or original causes. The intellectual focus was on critique of theistic doctrines and emphasis on free intellectual inquiry in order to organize the social world based on its inherent natural causes. This stage, which corresponds roughly to the Middle Ages, was under the sway of churchmen and lawyers. The state also arose into social prominence at this time.

3. **Scientific** or **positive stage:** In this stage, science became the major force of knowledge and the search for absolute notions, and the origin and destination of the universe. The causes of the phenomena were abandoned. Scholars applied themselves to the study of observable scientific relationships and their laws. This stage was governed by industrial administrators and scientific moral guides. The whole human race became the operative social units.

Although Comte insisted on the importance of intellectual knowledge for social development, he included other causes of change and development. He argued that population increase is a major source of social progress, and the increase in **division of labour** is a powerful impellent of social evolution. In addition, he saw that the seed of social order was sown in the family. For Comte, the true social unit is the family. It is within the family that the elementary, egotistical propensities are curbed and harnessed to social purposes.

Comte conceived society by analogy with a biological organism. He noticed that though a biological organism has material boundaries, (e.g., human skin) human society does not have boundaries and cannot be kept by physical means, but only by spiritual ties. Three of the most important sources of these ties are language, religion, and division of labour. Language is the vessel in which the thoughts of preceding generations and the culture of the ancestors are stored. Without common language humans could never have attained solidarity and consensus; no social order would have been possible. Moreover, religion furnishes the unifying principle, the common ground without which individual differences would tear society apart. It allows humans to overcome their egotistic propensities and ensue social order. In fact, Comte saw religion as an indispensable source of legitimization of governments. No temporal power could endure without the support of spiritual power. Lastly, division of labour links humans to their fellows. Therefore, it contributes to human solidarity by creating functional interdependency among individuals, or human organisms (see Zeitlin, 2001; Ashley and Ornstein, 1998; Turner et al., 1998).

Besides Comte, many other classical philosophers and social scientists have contributed to the development of sociology. However, the intellectual contributions of Marx, Weber, and Durkheim have had a lasting influence. Each of these sociologists became important because they shaped a theoretical paradigm, or school of thought. What follows is a discussion of key aspects of these three classical social theorists based on their own work and those of contemporary sociologists. Because we have discussed some of their concepts and arguments in previous chapters, here we continue with the issues raised by Comte (social change and social order).

Karl Marx's (1818–1883) writings are extensive and include more than 40 volumes, some of which are philosophical and others political. Marx divided human societies into modes of production. In each mode of production, human activity and the relationship between them is organized differently. Five great modes of production include primitive communism, slavery, Asiatic mode of production and feudalism, capitalism, and advanced communism. The first and the fifth modes of production (primitive and advanced communism) are classless societies, whereas the three in the middle (slavery, feudalism, and capitalism) are class societies.

Under primitive communism, land and resources were plentiful and the population small. Therefore, there was no need for private ownership of land or resources. However, as population increased and division of labour expanded, people started to produce more, and **surplus products** appeared (i.e., production outpaced consumption). The accumulated surplus product was passed from one generation to the next. Moreover, as population increased, tribes came into contact with one another. This resulted in wars between tribes over scarce resources. The victorious tribe confiscated the wealth of the defeated tribe and enslaved its members. These slaves at first belonged to the victorious tribe as a group and not to a specific individual. However, with increasing wars, specialized armies and leaders were created. These leaders slowly started to confiscate the wealth and appropriate the slaves for themselves and thus established hierarchies and the class system. Those who had wealth and slaves became the dominant group, while the slaves and propertyless became the subordinate groups. Therefore, the first class society emerged. For Marx, **class** is defined in terms of individuals' relationship to the organization of production. Those who own and control key elements of production (i.e., slaves, land, tools, etc.) constitute the dominant class (slave owners), and those who do not own the means of production constitute the subordinate class (slaves).

Under the slavemode of production, there was no distinction between the work needed for survival of the producers and the extra work (**surplus labour**) that was appropriated by the slave owners. Whatever the slaves produced belonged to the masters. Even the children of slaves belonged to the masters. Masters could do whatever they wished with the slaves, their families, and their belongings. Masters provided some means of subsistence (e.g., food) to slaves because they did not want to lose their "tools of production." Slaves were considered a fixed part of the means of production. They did not have any formal or legal freedom; they were simply considered "talking animals." However, since slaves did not have any legal existence, there was also no compulsion for them to work. Therefore, masters used force in order to make slaves work and produce more. As can be seen, slavery was an inefficient mode of production. To ensure that slaves worked and did not escape, masters needed to hire many other people to oversee them. Nevertheless, many slaves escaped or worked less.

Marx argued that numerous factors resulted in the emergence of **feudalism**. Among these factors were the continual wars between tribes and communities. These wars resulted in many free peasants asking large landowners for protection, and the landowners, in turn, received the peasants' land rights, in exchange for this protection. These peasants became bonded serfs. Similarly, kings granted certain nobles large parcels of lands and subjects in exchange for the nobles' loyalty to the king against rivals. Finally, the defeat of peasants in wars meant that many of the new nobles and lords acquired large amounts of land belonging to the defeated peasants, and the peasants themselves became serfs. **Serfs** were a group of people who worked on the landlord's land and kept a share of the output for themselves. For example, serfs might have produced and kept one-third of the product for themselves and gave the remaining two-thirds to the landlord. In this case, one-third of the output was considered the serfs' **necessary labour** for their own survival, with two-thirds surplus labour given to the landlord. Surplus labour or surplus product was either paid as rent, in cash, or in kind to the landlord, or as tax to the king for use of the land.

It is evident that serfs had more control over the means of production than slaves. Serfs were able to buy oxen or a parcel of land if they worked hard. In addition, they were not bought and sold individually as were slaves. However, if the landlord sold the land, serfs were also included in the bargain; they were sold along with the land. Therefore, serfs had limited freedom. Slaves were put to work by force, whereas serfs had to work because of tradition and legal pressures. Finally, although feudalism was more efficient to the landlord than slavery was to the slave owners, the former had problems too. There was little motivation for serfs to work beyond the minimum. Their experience was that whatever they produced, a large share went to the landlord or to the king. This inequity diminished their incentives to work. Moreover, as cities and industries emerged, many serfs escaped the lords' domain and went to work in the cities.

The third and final class-based society for Marx was capitalism and the **capitalist** mode of production. Capitalism is based on the process that separates direct producers (serfs, small farmers, etc.) from their means of production. This separation occurred when serfs and peasants who had some control over or owned the means of production lost this control or ownership and became workers. Marx's reasons for this change are multifaceted. We already discussed the tendency of serfs to escape to the cities, looking for work. Similarly, various economic crises resulted in free peasants borrowing against their land in order to buy consumer goods and tools of production, leaving them unable to pay their debt, and hence they lost their land. They became landless peasants searching for jobs in the cities. Development of money relations in rural areas meant that peasants produced for the market and thus increased their dependency on the market, which subjected them to market crisis and fluctuations. Looking at the classic case of England, Marx pointed to the importance of state policies such as the **Enclosure Act** in forcing many peasants off their land, which was intended for sheep-grazing for the expanding wool-based industries.

Under capitalism, workers are not bonded to the land. In fact, there is no legal pressure for workers to work. But work they must. Not having any ownership of means of production to exchange in the market for their basic needs forces workers to sell what they do own, which is their labour power (their ability, creativity, etc.). Therefore, workers have formal freedom in that they are free to sell their labour power to whomever they wish, but they must sell it in order to survive. This means that they are under economic pressure to work and produce.

What is important here is that workers do not necessarily think that they are exploited in the way that slaves or serfs were. Slaves gave all their production to their master, and the serfs gave a portion of their work or product. Both slaves and serfs were able to observe and conceptualize the fact that they were exploited by their master or lord. Workers got paid for their work, so on the surface there was no clear exploitation that workers could point to. Marx, however, went deeper and argued that the form of exploitation that workers encounter is more serious because it is disguised as wages paid for work performed. The fact is, Marx pointed out, that workers produce more than they get paid for. This is true for several reasons:

- Modern factories enable workers to produce considerably more than is necessary to cover the cost of their subsistence (i.e., their wages). Whatever the workers produce over and above their wage is surplus product and is appropriated by the capitalist as profit.
- By lengthening the workday or using two or three shifts, employers make sure that workers produce more per day, which minimizes the cost of production.
- By reducing wages or creating competition among workers (for example through racial or gender divisions), workers are paid less but produce the same or more.
- By speeding up the process of production through rationalizing the organization of work (e.g., assembly line production, computer use, etc.) and introducing new machinery, employers ensure that workers produce more during the same period of time.

These sources of exploitation are some of the reasons that workers experience alienation or become involved in work stoppage, sabotage, and rebellions. According to Marx, these problems will shake the foundation of capitalist society and result in a new stage in human history. Once the capitalist system is overthrown, socialism emerges, where private property is eliminated and workers have control over the process of production. Once private property is eliminated, there will be no need for the state or government because the state exists in order to serve the interests of the dominant classes over those of the subordinate classes. If there is no private property, there are no classes and no need for the state or government. This introduces the advanced communist stage. At the communist stage, people work according to their ability and take from the society according to their needs. This also means there is no need for the market since people only produce and consume what they need. This is possible because of the expansion of technology, machinery, and robots, which can do most of the necessary work. People can become, to paraphrase Marx, hunters in the morning, fishers in the afternoon, and philosophers at night. The division of labour would also disappear since people would then be multifaceted producers. This marks the end of alienation and the beginning of communism.

Max Weber's (1864–1920) work can be viewed as an intense debate with Marx and Marxists. Whereas Marx offered a theory of capitalism, Weber developed a theory of the process of rationalization and through that an explanation of capitalist development. For Weber, the principle characteristic of modern society is **rationalization,** which is expressed by a widening of the sphere of relation to goals. He was interested in explaining why institutions of society are becoming more rational in the West, but not in the East. By institutional rationalism, he meant formal rationality (i.e., a concern for the actors making choices of means and ends). But these choices are made in reference to universally applied rules, regulations, and laws. These rules, regulations, and laws are, in turn, derived from large-scale organizations and structures (e.g., bureaucracies). According to Weber, **bureaucracy** is a typical example of rationalization. This type of rationality is also called "purposively rational" conduct. Here, an individual's rationality assesses the probable results of a given act in terms of the calculation of means to an end. In securing a given objective, a number of alternative means of reaching that end usually exist. The individual, faced with these alternatives, weighs the relative effectiveness of each of the possible means of attaining the end and the consequence of securing it for other goals that the individual holds. Thus, one can apply the rational application of scientific knowledge to any activity. In modern days, you can see this in fast-food restaurants such as McDonald's, where both the customers and the workers are led to seek the most rational means to ends. McDonald's restaurants epitomize the rational means by which a worker can dispense and customers can obtain food quickly and efficiently (see Ritzer, 1992).

However, Weber's main concern, as was Marx's, was the nature of capitalist enterprise and the specific characteristics of Western capitalism. Their similarity of interest and Weber's continuous debate with Marx's arguments resulted in some scholars indicating that Weber's whole life was concentrated on a dialogue with Marx's ghost.

Both Marx and Weber stated that the starting point for development of capitalism is around the 16th century. However, they differed in what was most important for such an historical transformation. Weber sought his explanation in differences in religions of the Western and Eastern world and the importance of the Protestant **Reformation** for the development of capitalism in the West. Therefore, Weber searched for a religious explanation of this transformation whereas Marx was mainly interested in economic forces.

Weber saw religion as an attempt by people to find an explanation for the suffering they experienced in the world. Thus, for him, religion developed out of a need to explain inconsistencies in society that separated reality from an ideal existence. Weber noticed that the answers to these inconsistencies were of two kinds:

1. **Other-worldly mystics** (associated with Eastern Religions, Buddhism, Hinduism) view salvation as being achieved through the separation of one's self from body. Mystics reject the world that people can perceive with the fine senses as illusionary. Individuals are encouraged to escape from pain and suffering through mental detachment from the world.

2. **Inner-worldly ascetics** (e.g., Protestantism) agree that most problems stem from physical involvement in the world, but they suggest a different solution. They argue that it is not the world that causes suffering but the doubt and temptation that lie within each individual. Therefore, ascetics suggest that the world and body can be mastered and disciplined so that doubt and temptation can be defeated. Thus, the inner-worldly ascetics escape suffering by living in the world in a disciplined manner.

Now that we are familiar with Weber's classification of world religions, we can discuss his famous book: *The Protestant Ethic and the Spirit of Capitalism*. In this book, Weber focused on the attitude of economic individualism, which helped break down traditional feudalism. Weber opened the book by stating a certain statistical fact: Modern European business leaders and owners of capital, as well as skilled labourers and technically and commercially trained personnel of modern enterprises, were overwhelmingly Protestant. This was also the case in the early 16th century, where the early centres of capitalist development were strongly Protestant. In order to explain the correlation between Protestantism and capitalism, Weber analysed the content of Protestant beliefs and assessed their influence on the actions of believers and their economic activities.

He argued that traditional workers worked as much as necessary in order to earn and meet their usual needs. In contrast, modern workers seek more and more money, even after making enough for their usual needs. Moreover, they do not spend this extra money for luxurious consumptions. Therefore, he concluded that the spirit of modern capitalism is characterized by a unique devotion to earn wealth and to avoid using the earned income for personal enjoyment. He related this capitalist spirit to the **Protestant ethic** and argued that Protestants are concerned with the idea of a "**calling.**" Weber further noticed that the concept of a calling came into being only at the time of the Reformation. According to Protestants, the calling of an individual is to glorify God through the conduct of day-to-day life.

Weber took the example of John Calvin (1509–1564), a French theologian, in order to make his point and highlighted three major aspects of Calvinist teaching:

1. "God does not exist for men, but men for the sake of God." Therefore, humans must glorify Him on earth.
2. Humans are unable to know the divine truth. Only God knows.
3. All humans are predestined and their actions cannot influence the divine judgment.

Thus, believing in predestination meant that humans, priests, or laypersons could not intercede with God to produce their salvation (notice the difference with Catholicism where priests can gran absolution). Two conclusions were derived from this:

1. Individuals should consider themselves as one of the chosen. Any doubt signifies imperfect faith and therefore lack of grace.
2. The most appropriate means to develop and maintain the necessary self-confidence that individuals are one of the chosen is through intense world activity.

Thus, for Calvinists, the performance of hard work became regarded as a "sign" of election—not a method of salvation. Hard work was a method of eliminating doubts in salvation. Consequently, believers saw labour as the highest positive ethical salvation.

Weber also argued that according to Calvinism, accumulation of wealth as an enticement to idle luxury was unacceptable. Calvinists instead reinvested the wealth acquired through hard work because material profit acquired through the pursuit of duty in a calling was highly recommended. As a result, if individuals worked hard and succeeded in their calling, they would interpret their success as a sign of salvation. They would ask themselves rhetorically: "Would God let me succeed in my calling if I was not one of the chosen? Since I succeeded, I must have been one of the chosen."

Therefore, hard and diligent work was useful for believers in several ways. First, it kept individuals busy, preventing them from thinking about their suffering in this world and their faith in the next world. Second, it helped them succeed in the work they were doing, allowing them to become rich. Finally, since they were not able to spend their newly acquired wealth for self-consumption, they reinvested it in business activities. Therefore, a new breed of psychologically motivated entrepreneurs, or what is also known as capitalists, was formed. Weber, therefore, concluded that the origin of the capitalist spirit is found in the Calvinist religious ethic. He argued that there is an "elective affinity" between Calvinism and the economic ethics of modern capitalist activity (see Giddens, 1971; Zeitlin, 2001).

Emile Durkheim (1858–1917), like Marx and Weber, was interested in the emergence of modern society and the decline of traditional feudal societies. Durkheim viewed society as an integrated unit that in some sense is comparable to that of a living organism. However, Durkheim, like Auguste Comte, argued that the animal organism is governed mechanically whereas human society is bound together by that of ideas. This meant that society has its own specific properties that are separable from those of its individual members.

In his famous book, *The Division of Labour in Society* (1964 [1933]), Durkheim wanted to find out how and why society is possible. In order to answer these questions he first distinguished between traditional and modern societies. He noticed that modern and traditional societies are different with regard to the kind of social solidarity that governs them. Traditional societies are based on **mechanical solidarity,** which is based on resemblance of parts. That is, individuals differ from one another as little as possible. They feel the same emotions, cherish the same values, and hold the same things sacred. Therefore, society is stable because of a lack of individual differentiation. In traditional societies, every individual is a microcosm of the whole. This means that there exists a **collective conscience,** or a body of beliefs and sentiments that are common to all members of the society. For example, crime is viewed as an act that violates those sentiments that are universally approved and adhered to by members of the society. Therefore, any crime committed against a person is viewed as a crime against all because it violates the community's sentiments. Therefore, in this type of society, laws tend to be repressive and criminals are punished severely. The goal of punishment is to protect and reaffirm the collective conscience.

In contrast, modern societies are based on **organic solidarity,** where consensus results because of differentiation. Everyone is free to believe, to act, and to desire according to their own preferences. However, they are dependent on each other for survival due to a high division of labour. Therefore, solidarity stems not from a common belief or sentiment, but from functional interdependence in the division of labour. All individuals are dependent on each other for their contribution to the survival of the society. For example, the carpenter needs the plumber, who needs the police, who in turn needs the teacher, who needs the students.

According to Durkheim, this type of society tends to be governed by restitutive or cooperative laws. The purpose of punishment when a misdeed is committed is to restore things to the previous state, or to organize cooperation among the individuals. The point is not to punish but to re-establish the state of things as it should have been in accordance with justice. For example, a person who has not settled his or her debt must pay it. Crime is no longer viewed as being committed against the society but against a specific individual.

Durkheim argued that the development of society is correlated with the progressive displacement of the repressive by restitutive laws. The higher the level of social development, the greater the relative proportion of restitutive laws compared to repressive laws. Social development itself is a function of increasing differentiation and division of labour. The causes of social division of labour and differentiation in a population are due to the **material** (the number of individuals in a given space) and moral (the intensity of communication between individuals) density of the population. As population increases, people are more likely to become closer and to communicate with each other. This ensures shared knowledge of skills and abilities, which in turn allows the expansion of division of labour. With differentiation, people need each other for survival. This is called functional interdependency of parts. Therefore, Durkheim's general law is that division of labour in society varies in direct ratio with the volume and density of the population.

However, as division of labour increases, so does individualism, which means that the pervasiveness of the collective conscience in society declines too. But if the collective conscience declines, why is society still possible? Why does it not break down? Durkheim argued that individualism actually strengthens another element of the collective conscience: the cult of individual, or the focus upon worth and dignity of the individual, rather than the collective. That is, the expansion of division of labour creates an entire system of rights and duties that link modern individuals in durable ways. These rights and duties slowly become formal laws, with systematic codification. Thus, in a society with a high division of labour, each individual contributes to the survival of society, and individuals interact in accordance with their obligations to others and to society as a whole. This dependency and obligation become the moral glue, rules, and regulations that bind the self-sufficient units together. Therefore, the growing individualism is positive, even necessary, as long as it does not destroy both morality and social solidarity (see Giddens, 1971).

The destructive source of this morality is exemplified in anomic and forced divisions of labour. When there are genuine regulations that guide the interactions between people, there is no problem of division of labour, as people recognize one another's obligations and contributions. For example, when there is **equality of opportunity,** individuals can occupy appropriate social positions based on their ability and skills. However, if there is moral deregulation or normlessness, anomic division of labour develops. This produces lawlessness and economic crisis. For example, when there is extreme inequity in wealth, or poverty, principles that tend to justify moral regulations disappear, and people become unhappy, resulting in conflict and social problems. Similarly, if rules are unjust, forced division of labour develops. This is when self-interest becomes the guiding principle of powerful people, preventing others from a just position in society that is appropriate to their level of skills and abilities. This, again, compromises social solidarity, which could result in conflict.

Durkheim suggested that under both anomic and forced division of labour, the state should manage problems by generating appropriate moral and just regulations or laws, ensuring fair play, moral responsibility, and mutual obligations (see Grabb, 1990).

POSTMODERN THEORIES

◆ ◆ ◆

What is common to Marx, Weber, and Durkheim is their attempt to develop general, grand theories of society rooted in their understanding of historical development. **Postmodern** theories call these general theories **meta narratives** and consider them questionable. Postmodern theorists have a strong antipathy toward the suggestion that there is an overall pattern in history. They argue that human meanings, human subjects, and their history are all socially constructed and are culturally specific. There is no essential human being, human subject, or even a unified human consciousness. Society is far more fragmented than we are told to believe. In fact, postmodernists go so far as to argue that humans are mere images of an image that does not have a base in reality. Humans are simulations, similar to Data, an android in the TV series "Star Trek," who are made after an image of an image of human beings, despite substantial plurality of human life. Simply stated, postmodernists argue that philosophers, social scientists, and other scientists are involved in "language games" and that their language game is one among many; none better than the other.

It is this debate on grand theories that is included in this text. The project of modernity, rooted in the enlightenment, was to study social institutions, develop a unified and grand theory of humanity, and help improve human conditions through managed social change (emancipation of humanity). David Cheal used examples from Canadian and international studies and argued that this project is untenable. Relying on Lyotard's writings, Cheal argued that scientific knowledge is based on language games where one group (legislators, editors, etc.) tends to delegitimate certain knowledge and legitimate others (i.e., **paralogy**). It is this continuous process of delegitimation and legitimation that by definition makes grand theories impossible to achieve. If we cannot achieve or agree upon a general theory of society, he suggests, we cannot emancipate or liberate humanity.

According to Bonnie Fox, Cheal's criticism of knowledge as discursive and subjective is untenable. In order to make this assertion Cheal must use some form of empirical evidence to be able to substantiate his assertion. Yet, use of empirical evidence would question his assertion that knowledge is discursive, or is based on a set of ideas that are agreed upon. Fox also questioned the assumption that there is no essential self as argued by postmodernists. By asserting that subjectivity (and therefore self) is a social construct, postmodernists falsely separate biology from nature and present an overdetermined conception of self. Finally, Fox questioned Cheal's view on the power of feminists to hinder or close the debate in sociology. According to Fox, feminists are not a major force in sociology, and even if they were, male sociologists do not pay much attention to their writings.

QUESTIONS

◆ ◆ ◆

1. What are the key explanations of social change according to Marx, Weber, and Durkheim?
2. How does Durkheim differ from Comte in his explanation of social change and social order?
3. How important is "theory" in sociology?
4. Do you agree with Cheal's argument that the problem facing sociology today is that of "polycentric closure" caused by the increasing social diversity of sociologists? Why, or why not?
5. Why is Cheal's assertion problematic, especially in relation to his discussion of feminist sociologists?
6. Based on the articles, what is your understanding of postmodernism? Why has it had such a dramatic and controversial impact on the social sciences?
7. Is there an essential self? Is there a fixed and coherent essence to individuals?
8. Alternatively, is there not a fixed individual self? Are all individuals socially constructed and are they constantly being reconstructed? Discuss.
9. Are scientists and sociologists involved in language games? If so, how?
10. What is (was) the modernity project?
11. Has science failed to improve human conditions?

Authority and Incredulity: Sociology between Modernism and Post-Modernism

David Cheal

University of Winnipeg

◆ ◆ ◆

INTRODUCTION

◆ ◆ ◆

Recent debates among philosophers and literary critics about concepts of modernity and post-modernity are currently reshaping understandings of the social sciences in a wide-ranging international dialogue. . . . Anglo-Canadian sociology has until now remained largely detached from these discussions. . . . The issues raised by post-modernism are not without relevance for understanding the lines along which sociology in English-speaking Canada is developing. Ideas introduced in the modernism/postmodernism debate help to focus attention upon emerging issues in Canadian sociology, such as the sociology of culture and feminist epistemology.

The general issue to be taken up in this paper can be framed as the reflexive interpretation of sociological knowledge, considered as an aspect of contemporary culture. . . . The concept of culture refers to ideas which are capable of being communicated and learned. Knowledge is that dimension of culture that is concerned with competent intersubjective significance. . . . As competent discourse, knowledge is shaped by the pragmatic strategies of symbol manipulation that are employed in achieving and demonstrating competence. . . . When these strategies are part of an organized and self-conscious world of knowledge production, they give rise to *epistemological practices*. . . . Science is one such world. Scientific knowledge is the kind of discourse that a community of scientists judges to be rational in relation to a set of explicit rules for the verification and falsification of ideas.

There are, no doubt, many epistemological practices in the social sciences which could usefully be discussed. The particular practices to be examined here are consequences of theoretical pluralism. In discussions of pluralism in sociology the relationship between theoretical approaches is often problematized as a struggle between truth and falsehood, between correct interpretation and error, between science and myth (Brym and Fox, 1989). . . . As Habermas (1981: 6) reminds us, "One can certainly not conjure up by magic the compelling beliefs which command authority." Arguably, the most important issues at stake in sociology today involve the search for compelling beliefs. . . . These issues deserve our attention at this time, whether we choose to call our time modern or post-modern.

MODERN KNOWLEDGE

◆ ◆ ◆

Modernity is a *project,* in which the goal of *progress* is thought to be achieved through the *managed* transformation of social institutions. The project of modernity dominated the classical formulations of sociology as a discipline. . . . According to Anthony Giddens, the very existence of sociology is "bound up with the 'project of modernity'" (1987: 26): That is because the historical origins of sociology lie in "the coming of modernity," which is to say in the dissolution of the traditional world and the consolidation of the modern (Giddens, 1987: 15). In Giddens's view, contemporary sociology remains faithful to its origins in three related respects. Firstly, Giddens claims that the subject matter of sociology is "the social world brought about by the advent of modernity"

From David Cheal, "Authority and incredulity: Sociology between modernism and post-modernism," *Canadian Journal of Sociology* 15(2) 1990, pp. 129–147.

(Giddens, 1987: vii–viii). By this he means that the substantive core of sociology is the study of those institutions, such as the nation-state, that were created by and which in turn have created the continuous transformation of social life. Secondly, Giddens maintains that the "'ambition of sociology' continues to be to improve the human condition, through the practical governance of social change" (1987: 17). Thirdly, Giddens holds that the "idea of achieving a unified theoretical language for sociology is . . . more or less convergent with the first springs of development of the discipline" (1987: 29). . . .

These three themes—namely, the study of institutionalized transformation, the social direction of social change, and the program of an integrated foundation for social knowledge—are closely related in sociological theory. . . . These themes are linked by the belief that modern societies are different from traditional societies, since modern institutions offer the promise that human existence can be improved. It is the particular responsibility of the sociologist to recognize and to support those social movements which seek to ensure that the changes brought about by modern institutions are indeed progressive. In order to do this, a universal intellectual foundation is necessary. This is to facilitate comprehensive models for the description of change, which may be used to determine the extent of its beneficial consequences throughout society, and ultimately the world.

This neatly interlocking set of ideas has had a powerful influence upon sociology, which is still felt today in positive interpretations of nationalism. . . . However, it is a form of sociological discourse that only makes sense from within the larger discourse of modernity. . . . Since modernity is "merely" an historic option and not an historical necessity the modernist complex in sociology aptly described by Giddens is open to question.

POST-MODERN KNOWLEDGE

◆ ◆ ◆

It is no longer possible to take for granted the idea that the modern world is capable of producing endless human progress leading inexorably into an ever more glorious future (Vattimo, 1988: 4–11). Rather, such historicist claims, which are exemplified by the Marxist model of progress through class struggle, now appear reflexively as merely one manifestation of a questionable culture of modernity. The most serious questioning of modernist assumptions has come from the post-modernist theorists, such as Jean-François Lyotard (1984).

Lyotard claims that science was until recently legitimated by programs for the emancipation of humanity and for the unity of all knowledge (i.e., the second and third points in Giddens's definition of sociology outlined above). He believes that these two "grand narratives" have now lost all grounds for credibility and cannot be revived in their classical forms. Lyotard questions the presumptions of modernist thought, because of failures in its programs for emancipation (e.g., Marxism) and because of the fragmentation of science.

The claims of the post-modernists are controversial, and they have provoked a considerable critical response. Some of the deepest concerns about post-modernism are held by theorists on the left, who believe that Marxist meta-narratives about revolutionary agents of emancipation from capitalism still retain much of their validity at the end of the twentieth century. . . . Left modernism's faith in its own progressiveness crucially depends upon the belief that it is the wave of the future. It cannot, therefore, possibly conceive of its own eclipsing. In defence of their claim to occupy the future, left modernists have sometimes tried to define post-modernism as merely a current expression of conservative social formations (Habermas, 1981: 13; Sangren, 1988: 418). However, there is enough of value to be learned from post-modernism to suggest that such a point of view is oversimplified, and post-modernism cannot be so easily dismissed. . . . We shall see below that post-modern ideas about the connections between knowledge, power, and discourse have recently been given a radical thrust within feminism.

Turning now from meta-narratives of emancipation to meta-narratives of unified knowledge, Lyotard points out that the speculative unity of knowledge envisaged in positivistic epistemology is broken. Furthermore, he does not believe that Habermas's ideal of knowledge, as agreement arrived at through non-distorted reciprocal communication, is attainable in practice. That is because scientists would first have to agree on the rules of discourse by which agreement on scientific problems is to be achieved, and because they would also have to agree that the ultimate goal of dialogue is consensus. Lyotard maintains that Habermas's faith in agreement is unrealistic on both counts (Lyotard, 1984: 65–66). As Lyotard puts it, in contemporary science: "There are many different language games—a heterogeneity of elements. They only give rise to institutions in patches—local determinism" (Lyotard, 1984: xxiv).

This does not mean that totalizing accounts of a supposedly unifying social scientific paradigm no longer exist. Narratives of paradigmatic expansion can still be found in several social science language games, including the structural analysis of networks. . . . However, the fact remains that these days any particular claim to the truth is merely one alternative among several such possibilities. As a result, no one paradigm ever becomes *the* paradigm, and the predictable consequence of paradigmatic "revolutions" is merely a constant circulation of concepts. . . . Subjectively, Lyotard claims, the failure of paradigmatic revolutions to deliver on their promise of unification has resulted in a widespread "incredulity toward meta narratives." He therefore claims that the only viable legitimation for scientific knowledge today is paralogy, that is, the ceaseless creation of the new in unexpected forms of reasoning which breach established rules (Lyotard, 1984: xxv).

If there is any one theme which links the various interests in post-modernism, it is purely pluralism (McKinney, 1986; Hassan, 1987: 167–87; Bauman, 1988a: 225–26). It is thought that there are multiple meanings in social life, and in social theory, that define multiple realities. . . . [Lyotard] claims that the status of knowledge is altered when science enters the post-modern condition of pluralization. Each item of knowledge is no longer a piece that has a place (or should have a place) within a cumulative body of knowledge. Instead, it is an element in the *continuous production of conceptual pluralism.* Lyotard's invocation of a new term—the post-modern—to describe this condition is important. It suggests that we should no longer join the modernists in describing pluralism as a crisis, that is to say as an *event* which might be overcome by superior technique. Instead, we are encouraged to see apparent chaos as an ongoing *state,* within which the possibilities for all future knowledge will be determined (Bauman, 1988b).

Lyotard is, of course, not the only one to make the point that theoretical pluralism may be the normal, and even the desirable, condition in the human sciences rather than a temporary aberration. . . . What makes Lyotard's work fruitful is his insight that the dilemmas created by a pluralistic science are not only cognitive problems, but they are also problems of authority. The contingencies created by the existence of a plurality of theories appear to us as individuals primarily as the question of what to believe. Collectively, however, this uncertainty takes the form of the question of whose beliefs will be accepted by others.

Lyotard (1984: 8) observes that the status of knowledge as science is decided by "legislators," for example, journal editors, reviewers, session organizers for conferences, seminar leaders, etc. Legislators prescribe the conditions under which statements are accepted into the discourse of the scientific community. Their gatekeeping for the scientific community is a social role, and the authority of the legislators depends upon the social processes by which their decisions are authorized. The nature of scientific knowledge therefore ultimately depends upon the legitimacy of the legislators, whose appointments and actions are judged to be in accordance with a set of principles that constitute the scientific community. However, the consequence of paradigmatic pluralism is that such legitimation is precarious, since there exists not one set of principles but many.

DELEGITIMATION
◆ ◆ ◆

Science, Lyotard points out, is an unstable activity because by legitimating itself science throws its own unstated assumptions open to critical reflection (1984: 38–39). The result, he observes, is "a process of delegitimation fueled by the demand for legitimation" (Lyotard, 1984: 39). This process is full of contradictions and dangers.

Delegitimation consists of attacks upon institutions and persons, whose purpose is to discredit the procedures for the legitimation of legislators, as well as to deauthorize particular legislators for their failure to act in accordance with correct principles. Both tactics are widely practiced in sociology today. In fact, degradation ceremonies are such frequent performances that they have become commonplace and pass almost unrecognized, as normalized science. [Three] examples of delegitimation performances will be described here, in order to provide some empirical data for the discussion that follows.

In a recent letter to the editor of *Society/Société,* Barry Wellman (1989) complains that the Canadian Sociology and Anthropology Association is not a professional organization. In support of his complaint Wellman alleges that there is poor "quality control" in the selection of conference session organizers and participants. As a result, he claims, the legislators for the discipline include individuals who lack certified preparation for their role. In addition, Professor Wellman decries a "lack of opportunity for senior colleagues to participate in an advisory role." The unfortunate consequence, apparently, is that "wise counsel from established scholars" is lost to Canadian sociology. . . .

[A second] illustration of delegitimation in sociology is to be found in the work of Dorothy Smith. Here we move to a higher, and more abstract, level of critique. Smith's broad delegitimation of most sociological institutions is exemplified in her demand that women should engage in "the repudiation of the professional, the expert, the already authoritative tones of the discipline, the science, the formal tradition, and . . . return to the seriously engaged and very difficult enterprise of discovering how to begin from ourselves" (Smith, 1979: 144). Smith's attack is launched from the base of a carefully argued position that women are everywhere systematically discriminated against, and that the privileged status of male speakers includes the social sciences, most of whose practitioners have been men (Smith, 1974; 1975). Smith believes that men in the social sciences have not understood women's lives, and perhaps they have misunderstood their own lives too. This is because the work that women perform, for men in their capacities as wives, secretaries, and assistants makes possible a suppression of consciousness of routine matters among men, who are thereby limited to understanding the world in abstract and scientific terms. That is not the case for women, she argues, whose social location enables them to see the world in ways that are *both* abstract and scientific *and* material and local. The standpoint of women is therefore judged to be superior to that of men. But "women's standpoint locates a subject in the fundamental 'item' of the twofold basis of knowing the world. The organization which divides the two becomes visible from this base. It is not visible from within other" (Smith, 1979: 169).

[A third] illustration of sociological delegitimation to be considered here concerns the selectivity practiced by Canadian nationalists in presentations of what counts as Canadian sociology. Jackson has been most explicit about the positive side of this selectivity. He notes that "the very act of selecting particular paradigms from a broad range of possibilities is a political act . . . to favour certain paradigms over others is to further legitimize currently-established ways and to legitimize those emerging on the scene" (Jackson, 1985: 617). On the negative side, approaches such as symbolic interactionism and exchange theory have been delegitimated as being largely irrelevant to Canadian concerns. Brym, for example, has acknowledged that he excluded "the considerable body of purely micro-sociological research that has been conducted in English Canada" from his review of Anglo-Canadian sociology (Brym and Fox, 1989: 2). This exclusion is justified, he states, because: "In my view, such work is Canadian only in an incidental sense and is properly thought of as contributing more to a substantive field . . . than to the study of a certain geographical area . . . sociological research that does not tell us something about how and why Canada is significantly different from, and significantly similar to, other societies has not been reviewed

here" (Brym and Fox, 1989: 2). Micro-sociology, it seems, is delegitimated for failing to contribute to Canadian sociology insofar as it is presumed not to address questions of Canadian identity vis-à-vis the United States. Whether or not this is the kind of thing that Lyotard had in mind, it is certainly striking confirmation of his claim that knowledge today is atomized into heterogeneous networks of language games (1984: 17).

POST-MODERN SCIENCE: PARALOGY OR POLYCENTRIC CLOSURE?

◆ ◆ ◆

Under present conditions of plural language games, Lyotard's prescriptions for post-modern science are potentially of great significance. In Lyotard's opinion, post-modern science has given up searching for total knowledge of a system—any system. Instead it embraces empirical discontinuities and paradoxes, which often translate into conflicts between opposed interpretations and models. Once it is accepted that there is no determinate solution to certain kinds of problems, a variety of possible solutions may be tolerated, and indeed encouraged, as alternative descriptions of the objects to be investigated. . . . As Lyotard puts it, post-modern knowledge "refines our sensitivity to differences and reinforces our ability to tolerate the incommensurable. Its principle is not the expert's homology, but the inventor's paralogy" (Lyotard, 1984: xxv).

Lyotard (1984: 61) emphasizes that locally determined innovation is not in itself paralogy, although that is part of it. Paralogy, he claims, is a move "in the pragmatics of knowledge." . . . It is the dual process of delegitimating old knowledge, and legitimating the new, within a dialogic scientific "game." More than that, Lyotard's description of this process assumes that the game of science is always open to new solutions and to new players, and that the possibilities for new knowledge are therefore boundless. This is an idealized description, that rests upon a concept of science as a uniform field. Studies in the sociology of sociology, on the other hand, indicate that Lyotard's description of the principle of openness in science must be qualified by accounts of the social processes of professional and political closure that are at work everywhere (Murphy, 1983).

It is necessary to add to Lyotard's account of science here by noting that scientists in their roles as legislators are in fact decision makers. The social forces that constrain participation in academic language games are not only external to science, but they also penetrate it. They are mediated by scholars and scientists themselves in their struggles for scholarly recognition (Murphy, 1983: 658). In the social sciences many legislators do identify with totalities, such as "Canada" (Brym), or "women" (Smith), on whose behalf they claim to speak. Some totalities, such as "the profession," seem likely to serve as bases for attempts to reinstate the project of a unified sociology. Other totalities, such as "women's standpoint," are unifying in their internal reference, but are divisive in their external reference. They have been important influences pushing sociology in the post-modern direction of theoretical pluralism. . . . The latter development is especially interesting, because it is now evident that pluralizing totalities do not end in consensus *or* in paralogy.

Paralogy is one of two epistemological practices that can be detected in post-modern sociology. The other is *polycentric closure*. Paralogy and polycentric closure have quite different implications for the future of post-modern knowledge. Which of them predominates must have a considerable effect upon both the form and the content of sociology. . . .

Brym and Smith legitimate particular fields of sociological research (Canadian studies and women's studies), through delegitimating alternative approaches that make competing claims for attention. This is, in Lyotard's phrase, "delegitimation fueled by the demand for legitimation." Lyotard (1984: 39) expected that widespread delegitimation would result in the loosening and flattening of the established hierarchies of science, accompanied by the erosion of disciplinary boundaries, the crossing of intellectual borders, and a state of constant flux in the relations between different fields of enquiry. To a remarkable extent this has been achieved within Canadian studies, and most especially in women's studies. But contrary to what we might have expected, new barriers were erected at the same time between these fields and the surrounding matrix of social scientific discourse. This practice of polycentric closure consists of marking out particular territories within which certain kinds of work (e.g., micro-sociology, and studies of women conducted by men) are unwanted. The result is a mosaic of bounded discourses.

The dilemmas of polycentric closure as a post-modern epistemological practice have been felt more acutely by feminists than by nationalists (though see Brym, 1989). That is because the nation-state is one of the great totalizing institutions of modernity, whose borders are coterminous with what needs to be known for administrative purposes. Women, on the other hand, have generally existed as a marginalized Other in all forms of modernization. Their knowledge has been felt to be of little use to the centres of power in modern institutions. Therefore, the ambiguities and contradictions of a social science that oscillates between power and autonomy, between totalizing and relativizing, between authority and incredulity, between closure and openness, are more visible today in feminist theories of knowledge than they are in any other area. . . .

The feminist project of the emancipation of women requires a compelling narrative which describes what women are and what men are, how and in what ways men and women are different, and why men are a problem for women. In order to pursue this project successfully it has been found necessary to engage in the deconstruction of beliefs contained in resistant cultures, that are variously described as androcentric, misogynistic, patriarchal, phallocentric, etc. (Weedon, 1987). These deconstructions have often employed post-modern theories that see all knowledge as socially constructed within particular discourses, and they typically delegitimate claims to truth as concealed claims for male power. . . . However, such deconstructions cannot stop at "man," but inevitably extend to the category "woman" and thus to woman's standpoint (Fraser and Nicholson, 1988). They therefore end by casting doubt upon the naturalness of concepts of female identity, that are deployed in feminist politics. . . . That outcome is no basis for the compelling beliefs which all social movements require if they are to mobilize support (Tong, 1989: 232). The dilemma of feminism caught between modernism and post-modernism is expressed by Alcoff (1988: 420) in the following terms:

> If gender is simply a social construct, the need and even the possibility of a feminist politics becomes immediately problematic. What can we demand in the name of women if "women" do not exist and demands in their name simply reinforce the myth that they do? How can we speak out against sexism as detrimental to the interests of women if the category is a fiction? How can we demand legal abortions, adequate child care, or wages based on comparable worth without invoking a concept of "woman"?

The solution to this problem, at which a number of feminists seem to have arrived more or less simultaneously, is to regard standpoint epistemologies as transitional legitimations (Harding, 1987). The project of feminist transformation is then grounded not in woman's standpoint, but in feminist agency, that is to say in a conscious political act of choosing to speak for emancipatory goals in concrete sites of struggle. Henceforth, in Felski's (1989: 231) words, it is by their "strategic value" for the political struggles of everyday life that social scientific categories are to be justified. This decision, we should note, makes the dominant principle in the human sciences that of opposition between communities of "us" and "them." It is, as Harding says, a "politics of solidarity" based on "an oppositional consciousness" (1986a: 196). What the consequences of this principle are likely to be we can see in Harding's complaint about the disadvantage for feminists of using traditional approaches. She says, "The very fact that we borrow from these theories often has the unfortunate consequence of diverting our energies into endless disputes with the nonfeminist defenders of these theories: we end up speaking not to other women but to patriarchs" (Harding, 1986b: 16). Similarly, there is Hartsock's turn away from conversation, because she believes that women are not yet in a position to participate as equals in academic discourse. She concludes that conversation "will not work," because it would "only reinforce previous power relations" (Hartsock, 1987: 200–01). Who we speak to and who we would rather not speak to, and what we talk about and what we do not talk about, are evidently issues of great practical as well as theoretical importance in science today.

LAST RITES: THE DEATH OF MODERN SOCIOLOGY

◆ ◆ ◆

The problematic nature of professional speaking and hearing has not always been thought of as an important issue for sociological theory, even when it is recognized as a serious practical concern. . . . In the language games of an ideal scientific community, communication is reciprocal. That is to say, the communication roles of sender and receiver of signs can potentially always be reversed. Any receiver at one moment can become a sender at a later point in time, and so on. But what happens if the "sender" declines to speak, because the audience is deemed to be incapable of an appropriate response? Or, what happens if the "receiver" will not listen, because the sender is judged to represent a discredited authority? On these occasions, we must suppose, dialogue comes to an end.

Lyotard notes that shared language games are the minimum relations required for any community to exist, including communities of scientists. Scientific dialogue is the social bond that constitutes the community of science producers. In the present moment between modernism

and post-modernism we should be aware of the effects upon that bond of delegitimating others' capacities to speak and hear. Erecting barriers to unwanted messages creates an exclusive field of discourse. The benefit from this is that specialized problems internal to the discourse can be pursued at greater length than would otherwise be the case. The disadvantage is that it becomes difficult to conduct debates between different approaches, because "them" outside the discourse are not taken seriously or have been rendered practically invisible.

Women have experienced that kind of invisibility for a long time, of course, which is why the feminist project has been so important for the recovery of neglected issues in sociology. . . . However, today there is another question that looms large in our future. Are we witnessing the creation of a second form of closed discourse, which is merely the mirror image of that which went before? Toril Moi, a socialist feminist literary critic, has concluded that: "Articulated in isolation, the emphasis on female difference comes disturbingly to echo the very patriarchal prejudices against which the champions of women's equality are struggling" (1988: 6). If that is so, and if tendencies toward articulation in isolation become stronger among sociologists too, then the consequence would be less a sociology remade by feminism, and more a division of sociology. The latter, coming on top of earlier and still unresolved divisions in the discipline, must deepen the crisis in the modern concept of sociology. . . .

It was noted above that, according to Lyotard, modern science is legitimated by two kinds of meta-narratives of progress, namely meta-narratives of emancipation and meta-narratives of unified knowledge. It was also shown how both types of meta-narratives are incorporated in an undifferentiated manner into the modern concept of sociology described, for example, by Giddens. It was further noted that this concept is unstable, as evidenced by the widespread practice of agonistic delegitimation. . . .

The high point of the meta-narrative of the unification of knowledge in sociology was undoubtedly Parsonian systems theory. That grand synthesis neglected difference and pluralism . . . , and it was soon broken by a variety of pluralizing forces, including nationalism and feminism. The latter approaches were allied with important social movements, and they were legitimated by ideologies of emancipation from American neo-imperialism and from male hegemony. Such meta-narratives of emancipation can be the bases for unified sociological traditions. But they cannot provide the basis for a spontaneous unification of sociology. That is because movements of emancipation are always movements for social change, in which the members of different social categories will have different interests. As long as sociologists are drawn from a variety of social backgrounds and have a range of social experiences, then their different interests in change will give rise to sociological divisions, varying in intensity over time to be sure, but never completely resolved. During periods of tension those divisions may lead to the discipline becoming structured along lines of polycentric closure.

Polycentric closure is a form of science in which the process of knowledge production itself has the capacity to create the absence of scientific knowledge. To see how this can happen we need only consider the consequences for Canadian sociology of the macro-sociological boundaries of "The Great Canadian Identity Trap" (Brym, 1989: 495). The exclusion of micro-sociology from "Canadian" sociology by legislators such as Brym does not seem to have diminished the activities of Canadian symbolic interactionists, who maintain a lively presence within the discipline. What it has done, however, is to diminish the possibilities for critical mediation between micro-sociology and macro-sociology. In several other countries, the micro-macro debate was a major focus of attention during the past decade. In Canada that debate could not flourish, because one side of the problem was not even a part of the "Canadian" discourse. . . .

The recent micro-macro debate in sociology has been important, because it is part of a serious effort by modernist sociologists to regain the goal of theoretical unification as outlined, for example, by Giddens. The bifurcation of sociology into micro and macro fields since the 1960s has been more than a minor inconvenience. It has been a formidable problem for all those who take seriously the classical ambition of sociology, to provide a coherent and therefore integrated account of social life.

The current rush of general theorizing—by Giddens, Alexander, Touraine, and others—is the result of a broad international awareness of the severity of the crisis that now exists in modern sociology's definition of itself. The examples of sociological delegitimation described above suggest that the claims which are sometimes made in this connection for a new trend toward convergence in the discipline should be treated with caution. Giddens's modernist vision of a more cohesive social theory seems feasible only if we ignore the effects of feminist epistemology (e.g., Smith), nationalism (e.g., Brym), and the displacement of centre and periphery in professional institutions (reported by Wellman . . .). In other words, we would have to ignore some of the most powerful forces that shaped Canadian sociology in recent years, and which continue to influence the development of sociology in Canada and in other countries. The drift of the present paper is that it is already too late for brave attempts at rescuing the project of modern sociology.

In the absence of a genuinely unifying paradigm, the legitimation of any particular theoretical approach entails the delegitimation of other approaches. This situation has existed for more than two decades now, and the result has been the normalization of sociological delegitimation. That development must increase the barriers that any attempt at theoretical integration would have to overcome, before it could be successful across the discipline. Delegitimation leads to a weakening of the links between speakers and hearers, and to a narrowing of the social spaces within which particular knowledges circulate. It is therefore difficult to see how a trend toward sociological decomposition can be reversed, short of universal terror, once the process of delegitimation has been set into motion under conditions of polycentric closure. The history of modern sociology is coming to an end.

Comment on "Authority and Incredulity"

Bonnie Fox
University of Toronto

◆ ◆ ◆

Sociology is indeed in crisis. Our discipline rewards people who spend their time manipulating data—usually badly and to address half-baked hypotheses—while world events prove the inadequacies of our theories and enormous social problems scarcely catch our attention. David Cheal's assessment of sociology's predicament, however, is not useful: Cheal conjures up nonexistent difficulties, ignores real failures, and implicitly promotes an epistemological position that compounds current problems. After commenting in greater detail on Cheal's argument, I critically review some of the issues raised and arguments made by post-modernist theorists.

Cheal argues from the post-modernist assumption that knowledge is "discursive practice" which aims to achieve authority based on belief. Modernist sociology has lost credibility, according to Cheal, because its assumption of the progress of social change is wrong, and its goal of producing a unified theory has not been realized. Accordingly, a post-modernist sociology should embrace a plurality of theoretical paradigms. Indeed, the many current delegitimations of old sociological truths contribute to theoretical diversity. Posing a threat to these developments, however, are a disciplinary power structure capable of silencing its critics and, far more important to Cheal, a tendency by sociology's most profound critics—feminists—to erect barriers to theoretical diversity by "delegitimating others' capacities to speak and hear." Worse, Cheal argues, feminist sociologists write from a particular standpoint, not because they share a common set of experiences, but because their political project requires them to act as if there were a "women's experience." In short, Cheal argues, the problem facing soci-

ology today is that of "polycentric closure" caused by the increasing social diversity of sociologists.

Consider the argument (aside from its sexist, racist innuendo). First, a basic assumption of post-modernism—that all knowledge claims are mere discourses, or sets of ideas of the status of a conversation—is violated within Cheal's argument: On what basis besides a test against empirical reality can he assert that sociology is wrong in its claim that history is progressive? The assumption, if true, is also problematic for Cheal's vision of a proliferation of understandings, because the absence of standards of judgment about the validity of arguments and theories would mean that personal power, and power accruing to groups by virtue of their race, sex, and class, would determine whose ideas and arguments were published and accorded the status of sociological wisdom. The power of entrenched interests is already a barrier to good sociological work; it would be much more so in a post-modernist intellectual world.

Second, it is bizarre to blame relatively powerless feminist scholars for hindering debate among sociologists. As recently as the 1960s, women students of sociology faced a body of "knowledge" so androcentric that the social world it referenced (for example, family life as portrayed in sociology texts) was virtually unrecognizable to us. Our response has been to criticize accepted wisdom, showing the distortion necessary in any account of social reality that springs only from the vantage point of white, middle-class men, and to begin the task of rewriting sociology from a different set of experiences, moved by different questions, and often employing different methods. This has been an exciting period, in which new understandings emerged, dispelling old

From Bonnie Fox, "Comment on 'Authority and incredulity,'" *Canadian Journal of Sociology* 15(3) 1990, pp. 336–340.

misconceptions, discrediting powerful theoretical perspectives, and pushing against all sorts of boundaries.

It is not surprising that our discovery of the bankruptcy of much of the sociological tradition has led many women sociologists to assume, and some to proclaim, that women write from a privileged point of view. While this claim appears to be true with respect to criticizing the sociological literature we inherited, many feminists understand it to be an untenable epistemological position in general. In any event, the strength of women's contributions, and even the certainty with which women criticize established sociological wisdom, can hardly be stifling to debate: Women are only a minority of sociology faculty and an even smaller minority of powerful "gatekeepers." What *has* hindered debate is the passivity of most of our male colleagues, who—unlike Cheal—have not bothered to read their feminist colleagues' critiques and contributions. How can they be silenced by us? They haven't even heard us.

The specifics of Cheal's argument aside, the trendy post-modernist current, which has moved beyond literary criticism and into social science, deserves serious attention. Its appeal is easy to understand: post-modernism criticizes the epistemological assumptions at the heart of the scientific model on which much of traditional sociology was purportedly built, and it problematizes and theorizes subjectivity, a topic virtually ignored by sociologists and badly handled by social psychologists. On both counts, post-modernism is a very attractive intellectual enterprise to feminist social scientists. Accordingly, one can get a good sense of the merits and problems of post-modernism in the feminist literature (which Cheal references).

Important to the various schools of thought within post-modernism is an assumption about subjectivity: that there is no *essential self*. That is, the idea of an "essence at the heart of the individual which is unique, fixed and coherent and which makes her what she is" (Weedon, 1987: 32) is rejected. Post-modernists assert instead that subjectivity is a social construct. As it has been conceptualized since the Enlightenment, subjectivity is a product of humanist discourse. In individuals' lives, subjectivity is "precarious, contradictory and in process, constantly being reconstituted in discourse each time we think or speak" (Weedon, 1987: 33).

Interpreted in its best light, the claim that subjectivity is a social construct asserts only that what it means to be human (or female, or male) comes from the popular discourses (or ideologies) in which we are immersed—and not from something given in our biology. At least half true—in denying biological determinism—this interpretation still involves a false separation of culture and biology. Interpreted in the light of post-modernist writing, however, the claim is even more problematic. It implies that individuals are like pieces of clay, continually reshaped by every engagement in conversation, reading of a text, etc. This assumption is not unlike functionalist sociology's crude notion of socialization, according to which individuals are simply shaped to fit adult roles. The problem in both instances is the absence of a notion of individuals' active, thoughtful engagement with discourses, or ideas (and the world). A related problem is the absence of a notion of the individual's psychic development. In short, the individual is assumed to be overdetermined (Alcoff, 1988) and without agency. Post-modernism thus avoids shedding insight on the very complex individual/society relationship which it claims to address.

Post-modernist writers typically present their position on subjectivity as the only alternative to the simpleminded, reductionist assumption of a human nature determined by biology and produced through evolution (see Alcoff, 1988; Poovey, 1988). In feminist theory, for example, the problematic alternative would be the "cultural feminist" position that women are by nature different (e.g., more nurturant) than men. An essential (biologically determined), stable self and one totally constructed by discourse are not, however, the only possibilities. A more sociologically sophisticated conception holds our subjectivity (or sense of self) to be created in the many social interactions and experiences that constitute our personal histories, from infancy through adult-hood. Moreover, such a conception assumes that we are active in this process of our own constitution. And it recognizes that while we are not psychically fixed after some critical point, neither do we enter every adult interaction with the social environment as pieces of human putty.

The alternative epistemological positions on the issue of subjectivity become clear in the case of gender. Post-modernist principles, for example, dictate the conclusion that women do not exist, that there is no set of experiences common to females—in short, that gender is not a social reality. "Women" are a product of discourse; gender exists in language only (Alcoff, 1988; see for example, Flax, 1987; Poovey, 1988 . . .). Cheal quotes Alcoff's (1988) statement of this position, but he fails to acknowledge her criticism of it.

Indeed, this is an impossible position for feminist scholars. That every woman's life experiences are different from those of her sisters—especially because of race and class differences—lends credence to the claim that women do not exist outside of discourse (Poovey, 1988). The concept "Woman," however, achieves its significance by the persistence with which our society treats females differently from males. It is the perpetual creation of difference to which gender refers and that "Woman" signifies. Unfortunately, these differences exist in more than language. The incontestable reality of gender has been documented in decades of writing and research on the frequent incidence of violence against women in the form of battery and rape; the norm of women's primary responsibility for child care and housework, even when women work full-time outside the home; and stubborn pay discrepancies. The psychic consequences of gender are also documented. (The serious study of gender can never ignore the individual/society relationship.)

Aside from the issue of subjectivity, post-modernist thinkers have thrown open to debate claims about knowledge, truth, and even reality that are usually taken for granted. They question that reason in general, and the scientific method in particular, can provide the foundations of knowledge, and that the knowledge gained through reason and empirical study represents something real about the world (Flax, 1987). Such profound skepticism derives from the belief that language does not transparently reflect reality, but instead "*constitutes* social reality for us" (Weedon, 1987: 22, my emphasis), and from a doubt that reason involves universal qualities that transcend people's material existence (Flax, 1987).

It is important to interrogate bodies of knowledge and the methods that produced them. It is especially valuable to "tackle the fundamental questions of how and where knowledge is produced and by whom, and . . . what counts as knowledge" (Weedon, 1987: 7). But to abandon reason is insane. In a particularly good critique of post-modernist critics of science, Mary Hawkesworth (1989: 545) noted that "those who abandon themselves to intuition conceive and give birth to dreams, not to truth." One might add, less ambitiously, that they lose the possibility of understanding the world. Of course, the post-modernist claim is that there *is* no reality beyond discourse (cf. Weedon, 1987).

"The world is more than a text," however (Hawkesworth, 1989: 643). In the case of gender, again, arguing that the gendered division of labour exists in people's minds, and ignoring its institutional and structural basis is problematic—bad social science, disastrous political analysis. And it would be extremely problematic to assume a relativist position on the matter of rape.

In assuming that language constitutes the patterns that social scientists assume to exist in the social world, post-modernism calls on us to abandon a constructive search for an understanding of social organization. Deconstruction becomes an end in itself. In Jane Flax's (1987: 643) words, "If we [post-modernists] do our work well, 'reality' will appear even more unstable, complex and disorderly than it does now." Meanwhile, the immediate effect that the post-modernist current has had on social science is a dangerous abandonment of the study of society for the examination of texts, even sociology texts.

A General Introduction

. . . Although theorists challenge each other; it is usually difficult to confirm or disprove a theory. Theories are interpretations of reality; they are not research hypotheses which can be tested with empirical data.

Theorists not only chart and explain social reality; often they also question it. Many theorists take a "negative-critical" view of social institutions. They do not believe that this is the best of all possible worlds: they point to injustices and inequalities among human beings and hope that their ideas can contribute to ending this state of affairs. Controversies among theorists are not only about ways of interpreting reality, but also about prospects for changing it.

Several metaphors are often used to talk about theories. They are said to be constructed or built; theorists make theoretical frameworks, constructions of concepts that are connected to each other. A second commonly used metaphor is visual; theories are perspectives or points of view that focus on some aspect of social reality.

A third metaphor portrays theory as a flowing, changing river, with a mainstream and more controversial countercurrents. The mainstream is formed by ideas that are widely accepted among intellectuals at major universities and publishing houses; the countercurrents are formed by critical and dissenting scholars. Historically, the mainstream has usually been non-Marxist and the major countercurrent, Marxist. There are times when the currents are sharply separated, as in the 1950s, and other times—such as the end of the twentieth century—when they swirl together. Even when they were separate, they were fluid currents, not watertight pipelines. It is a good idea not to think of sociological traditions as completely rigid, distinct systems of ideas; theories have always influenced each other.

Overall, the entire enterprise of theory results in a complex and ever-changing set of overlapping as well as contested ideas. Theorists borrow from each other, recontextualize other theorists' concepts in new frameworks, adapt theory to new empirical and political issues, and challenge each other. A number of questions appear in many theories and form points of connection.

1. What is the nature of modern society, and to what extent is capitalism its key characteristic?

2. How are different types of institutions connected to each other in societies? More specifically, what is the impact of technology, the economy, and culture on each other and on other institutions?

3. How can we best picture the interplay of micro and macro levels of action? By "micro" we mean individual actions and small-scale interactions and by "macro" we mean institutions at the level of societies, nations, and the global system.

4. What is the mix of agency (purposeful human action) and structure (constraining limits) in outcomes? To what extent do human beings "make their own history" individually and collectively, and to what extent is it "made for them" by circumstances inherited from the past?

5. What is the mix of class (economic position) and status (other bases of identity such as racial/ethnic group, gender, and religion) in individual and collective outcomes? How are identities formed? How do identities become the basis of collective action?

6. How do human beings construct social reality?

Source: Roberta Garner, reprinted from *Social Theory, Volume 1, From the Beginnings to the 1960s: A Reader*, edited by Roberta Garner, Ontario: Broadview Press, 2004, pp. xi–xii. Reprinted by permission of Broadview Press.

Unit Twelve

METHODS
Introduction: Positivism and Research Methods

◆ ◆ ◆

You may recall that Auguste Comte coined the term "sociology." Therefore, it is not a surprise that sociological methods are to some extent similar to his vision of doing research. He wanted to shape the science of society similar to that of the natural sciences in an attempt to explain the past development of humankind and to predict its future course. He argued that the study of the social world should be based on reasoning and observation as the only legitimate means of attaining knowledge.

Comte argued that similar to the natural sciences, sociology can draw on three methods of observation, experimentation, and comparison in order to set the task of explaining the laws of progress and social order. Although he acknowledged the importance of observation and use of experimentation for understanding the social world, he viewed the scientific method of

inquiry of central importance to sociologists as that of comparison. The method of comparing humans to animals gives us precious clues to the first germs of social relations. Of course, comparisons within the human species are even more central to sociology. Comte insisted that the sociological method of inquiry is distinct from the natural sciences by its fourth method, the historical method. Historical comparisons throughout the time in which humanity has evolved are at the very core of sociological inquiry. Sociology is nothing if it is not informed by a sense of historical evolution.

Auguste Comte's philosophy of knowledge is called **positivism.** Basically, for positivists, scientific explanation is both deductive and inductive. A **deductive** expla-

nation attributes events to a general law. One starts from an abstract concept or a theoretical proposition and moves toward concrete events or empirical evidence. For example, Durkheim's general law was that division of labour increases in relation to the increase in moral and physical density of the population. Thus, the antecedent conditions (i.e., moral and physical density of the population) explain the phenomenon in question (i.e., division of labour). Researchers can then empirically test this general law by evaluating levels of division of labour in different countries, or in the same country across time, in order to see if division of labour varies in those places or time in moral and physical density of the population. An **inductive** explanation starts from specific observation of an event and moves toward a theoretical proposition. For example, Durkheim noticed that men, single individuals, and/or Protestants are more likely to commit suicide than their counterparts. From these observations he concluded that suicide rates vary inversely to individuals' integration to society.

Positivists suggest that there are two main approaches for evaluating a theory. **Confirmation** involves use of empirical evidence in order to provide support for the truth of a scientific theory. **Falsification** involves use of evidence to show that a theory is actually incorrect. The falsification method is advantageous to the confirmation method because if we confirm a theory, we do not know if it is supported by evidence since the next research project may reject it. However, if we falsify a theory through evidence, we can be confident that the theory is inaccurate because it was rejected at least once. In sum, for positivists, a theory is scientific if it can be tested. That is, scientific and nonscientific theories can be distinguished through their use of empirical evidence.

Since Comte's time, sociological methods have evolved. Some sociologists, including Max Weber, have argued that methods of studying human subjects are different from those of studying natural objects. For example, human subjects play an active role in the inquiry compared to objects in natural sciences. Similarly, social and cultural values play an important role in determining what questions are to be asked, what subjects are to be studied, and how to interpret the findings. Sociologists focus instead on **empathetic understanding** as the only way of studying human subjects. For example, Weber defined sociology as a science that is interested in understanding human action. He argued that understanding human motives, values, attitudes, and behaviours is possible if we develop an empathetic understanding ("verstehen" in German) of those motives. Thus, like the visitor from outer space, we must penetrate into the minds of our actors to understand the world as they understand it. For example, if you see a man is chopping wood, you tend to interpret this as meaning that he wants to get fuel for his fire. If you observe that a person bursts into tears, you tend to interpret that this person must have just suffered a bitter disappointment. We understand that the captain went down with his ship because we view him as faithful to his idea of honour. We understand that a mother may spank her child because the child was behaving unbearably bad. We understand that children respect their parents because of custom and tradition. In all these cases we explain an event by the subjective meanings we associate with human actions.

Therefore, although positivism is dominant in the social sciences, it is only one among many methods of scientific research methods. Moreover, various methods can be used to complement our understanding of the social world. All methods of research are interested in finding a satisfying explanation of some aspect of human reality. This understanding is achieved through the use of theories, or statements and explanations applicable to the widest possibility of phenomena. In the end, however, such general statements must be testable.

We should also remember that scientific exercise is cultural. The scientific community decides what problems are important, the best ways of testing a theory or interpreting the evidence, and which theory is most correct. Furthermore, government agencies, corporate groups, and publishing companies all have a hand in deciding the merits of a research project and explaining certain evidence. Some research projects are not funded or are not published because interest groups may not think the project is important. These gatekeepers and cultural limitations are important in deciding what is scientific or not.

Sociological research is either **quantitative** or **qualitative** (see box insert). As we alluded above, quantitative research is based on methods modelled after the natural sciences. It uses methods of experiment, observation, and comparison. Its language includes **independent** (cause) and **dependent** (effect) **variables**. A variable is simply a concept that varies in amount, quantity, or quality (e.g., income, marital status, religiosity). For example, we may state that students whose parents have higher education are more likely to have higher education themselves. In this example, parents' educational level is the independent variable, and students' educational level is the dependent variable. We immediately notice that a causal phenomenon comes before the outcome. That is, **temporal order** is an important aspect of causal order—the cause must come before the effect. As well, we notice that the proposition states an **association** between the independent and dependent variable. That is, the two phenomena are said to be related to each other.

Finally, in establishing a causal order we should make sure that the relationship between the independent and dependent variable is not **spurious**, meaning that both variables are caused by something else. For example, one may argue that cohabiters are more likely to abuse their partner than married people. However, this may not be due to cohabitation, per se. Cohabiters and violent individuals are both generally younger. Thus, young age "causes" both cohabitation and abusiveness. The original relationship between cohabitation and abuse was thus spurious—it was a mirage.

Qualitative research includes **participant observation** and nonparticipant observation and historical-comparative research. Qualitative researchers rely on interpretative methods of investigation. It is a method of study based on the viewpoint of the person(s) under study. The focus is on the subjective meanings and perceptions of the subjects themselves. The subjects are observed in their own territory and studied on their own terms. Researchers are involved in intimate and prolonged field experience in order to identify reappearing patterns among the subjects. Moreover, researchers need to reflect on their own involvement in order to identify and minimize the effect of their own values, perceptions, and interests in the research process. Furthermore, they evaluate the credibility of their findings by appraising their own level of involvement, familiarity, theoretical knowledge, and good investigative skills. Researchers also provide detailed notes on their methods of data gathering, analysis, and interpretation. Finally, they present the evidence in the form of words, images, documents, observations, themes, motifs, and generalizations.

You may have noticed that social scientists gather and use information, data, and evidence in a variety of ways. In addition to experiments (see the introductory chapter), observation, and field research, they also collect data through surveys, interviews, government statistics, and content analysis of documents. Whatever method used, depending on the type of research (qualitative or quantitative), they tend to follow certain steps (see box insert). In both methods, researchers interact with the theory, and in each step, theory guides them and/or is modified through the research process.

Despite the dominance of positivism and quantitative approaches in sociology, Baldus argued that positivism has experienced a crisis from within. Many recent books and articles written by positivists have shown a profound unease about the current state of theory and research in sociology. This crisis is based on three problems: deficiencies in sociological theories, organizational and institutional rigidities of the profession, and technical flaws in research methods. He further stated that many sociological findings, research, and theories are trivial and tautological (based on circular reasoning), failing to show any general law as argued by positivists. Positivist-based research is also misleading in that social scientists do not report insignificant findings, such findings are not published, and social scientists fail to replicate results in different populations. Such deficiencies may give an illusion of orderly laws that govern human condition. In fact, Baldus indicated, the (social) world is not based on linear evolution and relationships and is complex and chaotic. He concluded that we experience theoretical stagnation and the positivist method cannot help us out of this crisis. According to Baldus, there is little hope for improvement in positivist sociology and perhaps it should be abandoned.

Lenski responded by highlighting that the core of positivism is a belief that scientific data must be based on, tested by, and grounded in sensory experiences, whether directly or indirectly. Second, any scientific statement should be formulated in a way that can be **falsified.** Finally, there has to be interaction between **theory** and empirical reality. Our research should be based on a theoretical framework and used to modify or reject a scientific statement. These core elements of positivism suggest that it is not deterministic but is based on probability. According to Lenski, Baldus seemed to view positivism as deterministic and does not appreciate its probabilistic aspect. Moreover, because of scientific knowledge acquired through positivistic knowledge, we have been able to use the past in order to guide our future. Although our predictive abilities have not been perfect, there have been many cases where the future was predicted based on information acquired in the past. Nevertheless, we have a long way to go in order to develop a macrosociology that can account for the past and present and predict the future.

QUESTIONS

1. Identify a sociological explanation that has helped you understand past and present and allows you to predict a future event with certain probability.
2. Do you think it is useful to study sociology? Why?
3. Among the various sociological methods, which appeals to you? Why?
4. Select a topic of interest. What would be the steps for researching this topic? What specific research method do you think is appropriate for studying it?
5. What role does theory play in doing research?
6. What is positivism?
7. In reading the debate, which side of the argument makes more sense to you? Why?
8. What are the limitations of positivism as applied to human or social behaviour?
9. What do you think are the implications of scientists only reporting "significant" evidence for theory building?

Positivism's Twilight?

Bernd Baldus
University of Toronto

◆ ◆ ◆

After the long lull that followed the positivism debate of the 1960s and early 1970s there has been a recent upsurge in books and articles examining past achievements and future directions of positivist sociology. During the past two years alone, five papers in major American sociological journals (Lenski, 1988; Jasso, 1988; Collins, 1989; Gans, 1989; Blalock, 1989) have dealt with this subject. In addition, several books have looked at the current state of sociological theory (Turner, 1988) and empirical research (Blalock, 1984; Duncan, 1984; Lieberson, 1985).

Unlike the earlier debate, however, where opponents generally belonged to neatly divided ideological camps, these contributions represent an entirely internal critique . . . the participants are all positivist sociologists. Two decades ago, positivists on one side confronted Marxist and hermeneutic critics on the other. Accusations of dogmatism and unscientific research met charges of conservatism and misguided empiricism. The outcome, if one can assess it so briefly, was a politically deeply divided discipline. Positivist sociology has taken firm charge of sociology departments and major journals in the United States, while in Canada it has remained the dominant partner in an uneasy cohabitation with various other approaches to sociology. The homogeneity of the participants in the current debate is, in part, a reflection of this division. But it also represents a significant change. During the earlier positivism debate, the need to close ranks against a common enemy made internal criticism a rare event. The current debate marks the first time that there has been extensive doubt and soul searching among positivists themselves. . . .

But just below the surface of self-congratulatory rhetoric is a deep sense of existential *angst*. After three decades of positivist sociology its vital signs are not good. With the exception of Münch and Jasso who seem, respectively, unaware or disregardful of any problems, all authors share a profound unease about the current state of sociological theory and research and offer sometimes scathing critiques of its practices and results.

THE POSITIVIST PROMISE
◆ ◆ ◆

What is the problem? The basic objectives of positivism or logical empiricism in the social sciences were set out by Hempel (1949, 1954, 1965), Nagel (1961), and Popper (1959), among others. They laid the foundations of the modern positivist doctrines for social research, revising significantly the positivism of the Vienna Circle of the 1920s. They believed that social processes followed the same orderly, linear, and observable causality that governed the natural world. Consequently, there should be a single scientific approach modelled after the successful natural sciences but applicable to all disciplines, natural and social alike. It was the task of the social sciences to explain and predict social processes through searching for universal social laws, analogous to those known, for example, to physics or chemistry. These should specify conditional relationships between events in which the presence of one (cause) would be necessarily and regularly followed by the other (effect), so that the latter could be logically derived from the former. Such laws should initially be obtained through deductive theorizing and given a hypothetical form which could subsequently be confirmed or falsified by suitable empirical evidence (Hempel, 1949: 459, 460).

There were two further, corollary objectives: cumulation and application. Scientific progress should lead the discipline gradually from the observation of limited causal relationships to more general or covering laws which

From Bernd Baldus, "Positivism's twilight?" *Canadian Journal of Sociology* 15(2) 1990, pp. 336–340.

revealed hierarchies of determining conditions and improved our ability to explain and predict accordingly. In everyday sociological practice it became customary to assume that such theoretical cumulation would emerge naturally from the additive results of empirical research. This view largely replaced the more stringent requirements for the deliberate deductive derivation of theories of higher generality set by positivist philosophers. That was never acceptable to purists like Popper who dismissed it as the "big pot" theory—the belief that, as each researcher added a small portion of empirical wisdom, the big pot of theoretical knowledge would gradually fill on its own. But it was very convenient for positivist sociologists. It hallowed them to de-emphasize deductive theorizing in favor of the technology of testing. Social laws were rarely explicitly invoked. General sociological theory was left to evolve on its own, and attendant problems were neglected. Sociologists concentrated instead on the statistical analysis of hypotheses derived with a minimum of theoretical conjecture, and with little concern for their interrelatedness. This view provided the inspiration for the myriad of fragmented empirical studies of independent-dependent variable relationships, strung together by a few sentences passing for theory, which have made up the bulk of positivist sociology. Cumulation and prediction, in turn, were expected to allow the increasing application of positive knowledge for the purpose of guiding or changing social processes in accordance with externally set political priorities.

The dilemma facing this program some thirty years later is that it has failed to produce what it promised. During this time, leading sociology journals have been filled with thousands of studies based on positivist principles, and statistical techniques and mathematical modelling have advanced to the level of an esoteric art. But the laws of social behaviour which this massive research effort was supposed to reveal have remained elusive. Instead of looking confidently at a body of tested general laws, sociology is more divided than ever. . . .

Cumulation has not taken place. Sociological theory "has not advanced nearly as much as it has proliferated" (Lenski, 1988: 165). And with regard to application, Scott and Shore concluded as early as 1979 that

> based on the analyses and commentaries of sociologists who have studied the uses of sociology for public policy in America today, we find that the goal of identifying and studying sociological questions pertinent to formulate workable, politically feasible policies and programs has been adjudged unsuccessful. (Scott and Shore, 1979: 3)

THE LACK OF THEORETICAL CUMULATION
◆ ◆ ◆

The participants in the current debate attribute this state of affairs to three general problems: deficiencies in sociological theory; organizational and institutional rigidities of the profession; and technical flaws in research methods. As regards theory, most authors agree that little progress has been made. . . . What new theory there is, is often vaguely worded, unfalsifiable, and highly compartmentalized. For want of theoretical advances, theory courses tend to retrace standard histories of the founding figures of the discipline, centering around the "Holy Trinity"— Marx, Weber, and Durkheim (Lenski, 1988:165).

But the remedies the authors offer are not likely to cure the malaise. Some, like Lenski and Turner, limit themselves to advocating warmed-up positivist commonplaces of the 1950s: define variables more clearly, specify the relationship between them more unambiguously, formulate theories more rigorously (i.e., algebraically), and engage in more careful data collection and analysis. Only where authors set out deliberately to demonstrate how "state of the art" theorizing should be done does one get a sense of the real frustrations which plague the positivist paradigm. In their attempt to force reality into a procrustean bed of cause-effect formalism, the resulting hypotheses abound with formulations of universal conditional relationships between variables which are obscure, culturally or historically relative, or tautological. Blau, for instance, offers the following "theoretically deduced prediction": "the more intersecting social circles are the greater is the likelihood of intergroup associations" (Blau, 1988: 54), surely a candidate for a near-perfect empirical correlation. Hechter suggests a number of similarly circular hypotheses, all derived from his *rational choice theory* of group solidarity: "The less extensive a group's obligations, the greater the members' scope to engage in independent action" (1988: 65). . . .

That trivial and tautological hypotheses have become something of an involuntary trademark of positivist sociological theory may not be the fault of individual authors. Instead, it may reflect an intrinsic inability of positivist formalism to come to grips with an exceedingly complex social reality which can not be changed through further refinements in defining variables and specifying relations between them.

None of the authors who examine the current state of sociological theory is willing to draw such conclusions. In spite of their misgivings, they cling to the positivist paradigm. Only Collins appears to be prepared to abandon at least some of the ambitions of the positivist program. He suggests that, faced with a recalcitrant and vexatious social world, sociology should downgrade laws to "principles" and cumulation to "coherence," and tolerate a theory with "fuzzy edges" based on tacit and informal understandings. However, this is not a significant revision of positivist sociology, but an escape from the dilemma that the hypotheses keep refusing to fit the facts. Collins' basic commitment to finding "abstract and universal principles" (1989: 133) and to "reach the degree of approximate and pragmatic success the natural sciences have achieved" (1989: 134) remains intact. He is not willing to abandon the "formulation of generalized explanatory principles, organized into models of the underlying processes that generate the social world" (1989: 124).

Fifty years earlier, Hempel had already dismissed the idea of a sociology with fuzzy edges. While acknowledging that many empirical observations in the social sciences were probabilistic and had not yet reached the status of a general law, he admitted such results only as "explanation sketches" that were to be raised to the level of a law by further research (Hempel, 1949: 465). He rightly recognized that the positivist method was indivisible and allowed for no compromise. There could not be one science for natural and another, watered-down one for social processes.

METHODOLOGICAL DIFFICULTIES

◆ ◆ ◆

If the treatment of sociological theory in this debate fails to suggest reasons for the lack of theoretical cumulation during the three decades during which positivism has dominated sociology, the critique of positivist methods by Blalock (1984, 1989) and Duncan (1984)—both among the leading positivist methodologists—is incisive and often devastating. And although their critique does ultimately not transcend the limits of the positivist paradigm, it brings us closer to an understanding of the problems that are at the core of the debate. . . .

But although neither [Blalock and Duncan] mention it directly, it is also clear that the lack of theoretical progress as such has pushed positivist research in these directions. The over quantification about which both authors complain has become a convenient escape. As it became clear that research was not producing the expected laws of social behaviour positivist sociology began to construct a surrogate world of data, methods and models which maintained the illusion of a law-governed and predictable social world. An excess of techniques disguised the inability to arrive at a verified theory of social life. . . .

This trend brought about an increasing quantification of sociological research, leading Gans (1989: 14) to refer to the *American Sociological Review* as "a methodological journal for quantitative sociologists not able or willing to work through the yet more technical articles in *Sociological Methodology*." More important, the desire to see the social world behave in accordance with their presuppositions began to transform positivists' view of social reality itself. Blalock notes the widespread tendency of "finding" causal relationships by covering up inadequate data with sophisticated statistical analysis (1989: 450), by ignoring simplifications in the construction of theoretical models and research designs (1984: 102, 105), by assuming that variables which could not be measured for practical reasons could also be disregarded on theoretical grounds (1989: 455), by losing sight of the tentativeness of findings (1989: 456), or by judiciously selecting variables and *ex post facto* explanations (1984: 136, 137). . . .

Ultimately, the pressure to make a unwieldy reality conform to an inappropriate theoretical paradigm leads researchers to mask or overlook important aspects of reality. . . .

The illusion of an orderly law-governed world is further strengthened by the homogeneity of samples, the tendency in the social sciences of reporting only "significant" results (Isaac and Griffin, 1989: 877), and the almost complete lack of replication. Blalock notes that subjects in social science research tend to be from similar backgrounds, and that powerless groups disproportionally end up as research subjects because they are conveniently accessible. Together with the increasing reliance on fewer data sets because of reduced funding and the high cost of data collection, this artificially diminishes the diversity of data sources and obscures the complexity of the social processes studied. The tendency not to replicate research in different populations has a similar effect (Blalock, 1989: 456). The few examples of cross-cultural replication (e.g., Nelson and Kagan, 1972) illustrate the possible consequences: what may have been easily taken for a universal law of behavior (a very high rate of competitive egotism in problem-solving among American children) revealed its cultural origins when the same design produced a much higher level of cooperation among Canadian Native and rural Mexican children.

LINEAR CAUSALITY AND CHAOTIC REALITY

◆ ◆ ◆

Nowhere is the tendency of positivist research to turn a blind eye to its own problems more evident than in the way it has dealt with unmeasured or omitted variables.

This is not just a technical problem; it is ultimately at the heart of the entire debate. The complexity of social processes, acknowledged by most authors, raises the prospect of a potentially infinite causal regress. Causal explanation of the kind advocated by positivist sociology necessarily requires choice and simplification, and the omission of a large part of the variables that caused an event under study.

Positivists have devised a variety of ways of dealing with this fact: from the use of constants and *ceteris paribus* conditions to the statistical calculation of measurement errors and unexplained variance. All of these have been based on the view that unmeasured and omitted properties of an event were a residual, temporary problem: a messy irritant that stood in the way of elegant causal conjectures and would be removed eventually through more complex research designs and more sophisticated equations. In the meantime, it could be safely neglected. . . .

Why does the problem of omitted variables continue to plague positivist sociology? Long-term cumulation and the resulting improvement of our knowledge of social processes should at least have begun to reduce their number. What if the persistent failure to bring our propositions closer to the status of laws means that we are not dealing with a temporary problem, but an inherent indeterminacy of social processes? As early as 1976 May warned that the assumption of linear causality on which positivist theorizing so typically rests may not at all be suitable for an analysis of social processes. . . .

Since then, the physical sciences themselves have undergone something of a revolution: the discovery that many natural processes are chaotic and unpredictable, from cloud formation, weather patterns or the fluctuation of wildlife populations, to the red spot on Jupiter, the random drip of a faucet, or the turbulence of a stream. This has led to a move away from the Newtonian linear physics that dominated experimental and applied science, toward a new theory of chaos where the movements of pendulums, fluids, or gases may still be patterned around attractors, but follow indeterminate and unstable trajectories.

If the outcome of many natural events is inherently uncertain, this must surely be the norm for social ones. From this vantage point, the consistently probabilistic nature of the causal relationships that the social sciences have found is not a temporary, but a permanent characteristic; not a flaw, but a natural property. Causal sequences in the social world have all the typical attributes associated with mathematically chaotic processes. Small and seemingly insignificant changes in the present lead to major and unpredictable consequences in the future. Social events are not only the result of complex causal chains, but generate highly complex patterns of consequences. Social causal series frequently follow the erratic, oscillating, and tumultuous course one encounters in chaotic systems. Most important with regard to the positivist paradigm, however, is the fact that as non-linear processes they are often analytically intractable. Their indeterminacy and their disorderly nature is a built-in feature *that cannot be improved by collecting additional evidence*. And the exponential amplification of even very small initial measurement errors in a series of causal events will make prediction over longer time periods grossly inaccurate.

This problem is very different from the critique positivists had to respond to in the positivism debate of two decades ago. Then, the question was whether positivist research deliberately ignored the political dimension in what it was doing, and whether the reality it studied could be better analyzed through statistical measurement or through empathetic understanding. On the more, mundane level of everyday departmental politics, the battlelines were usually drawn around the issue of "numbers." None of this is at stake here. The basic problem that the chaotic nature of social processes poses for positivist theory is that the interpretation of social life as rule-bound and subject to a deterministic, linear causality may be profoundly unsuitable for the analysis of the subject matter which sociology faces.

THE POSITIVIST RESPONSE
◆ ◆ ◆

None of the authors who participate in the current debate seem to be aware of this. Only Collins, Blalock, and Duncan address the non-linearity of social processes directly. . . .

None of the practical remedies offered by these authors involve a re-examination of positivism itself. Instead, they all advocate more of the same. Occasionally, that opinion is completely disjointed from the very shortcomings of sociological research which they had earlier identified. Blalock, who had just outlined the limitations of mathematical modelling (1989: 457) and deplored the tendency towards overly technical analyses in sociology (1984: 133) proceeds to prescribe a heavy dose of both to graduate sociology students (1989: 458). Jasso, who thinks it is only a matter of time before sociology will embrace the "economy" of purely mathematical formulation, admits that "there may be need for a new albeit transitional specialty within sociology—reciprocal translation between English and mathematics" (1988: 8). Lenski does not even consider that necessary: "If theory construction can be improved sufficiently in the years ahead, we will arrive at the point where algebraic formulations of most theories become routine" (1988: 167n). . . .

OUTLOOK
◆ ◆ ◆

All this suggests that while there is little hope for future advances of positivist sociology, its practitioners have no intention of relinquishing the field. Much is at stake. A generation of sociologists has now been trained in positivist methods, and has created professional career paths and reward structures on its own terms. The lure of the "respect and other rewards that modern societies accord the sciences and its practitioners" (Lenski, 1988: 170) has a powerful hold on positivists' imaginations, even if no one else takes their claim to it seriously. And in a process well documented by Blalock and Duncan, positivist sociology, like so many other professions, has tended to become immune to the recognition of flaws in its work. In their critique of time-series research Isaac and Griffin observe that

> Conventional practices and assumptions are . . . seldom examined by quantitative analysis in the context of actual research practice or in the development of time-series methodology. Thus, these strategies have become institutionalized, portraying and projecting "correct" quantitative research practice. (Isaac and Griffin, 1989: 874).

If this assessment is accurate, we are likely to see a discipline which, in the absence of theoretical advances, relies for its survival increasingly on the institutional and organizational momentum it has built up, and continues to produce large numbers of studies, that are strong in statistics and wanting in theoretical consequence, and are of little or no benefit to anyone, except to their authors' career interests. That this could go on for a long time is shown by the related discipline of psychology which continues to prosper by probing for "laws of behaviour" through analyses of variance with first-year students, although the procedure is scandalous even by positivism's own standards (Blalock, 1989: 456).

Data say only what researchers ask them to say. And what they ask depends on their theoretical intent. An appropriate theoretical understanding of the social world is therefore crucial. Without it, methods become sterile and self-serving, and sociology comes to resemble the medieval alchemists' quest for the elixir of life or the perpetual motion machine. Alchemists, too, were decidedly practical people with a bend for empirical, experimental work. They, too, were at times heavily funded by credulous authorities who had been promised the stone of wisdom, or just plain gold. But they were guided by the belief that the vapours, liquids, and minerals they worked with embodied death and resuscitation, body and soul, and the pervasive spirit that was the universal manifestation of God. Consequently, their work remained fragmented and theoretically non-cumulative, and their methods deteriorated into learned humbug designed to prevent replication and to conceal the essential weakness of their results. They made important discoveries in chemistry, mechanics, and magnetism, but these were fortuitous by-products of an illusive theoretical enterprise, and their importance for the subsequent growth of science was unintended and unrecognized at the time. Contemporary positivist sociology has comparable characteristics, and has produced comparable spin-offs—statistical as well as descriptive—which will advance the discipline in the future. The bulk of its activities, however, have been spent in the pursuit of a theoretically misguided image of the social world.

An alternative theoretical paradigm would understand society no longer as a Newtonian system of fixed cause-effect mechanisms, but as an organic and evolving system whose dynamics are often non-linear and indeterminate. Such a view would restore the individual's role as the central actor in the creation of the social world, as opposed to being an agent of immutable social or biological forces. But this role is curtailed by human limits to analyze and predict, limits which are not just practical and therefore subject to eventual technical solutions, but stem from irresolvable problems of measuring and forecasting complex and variable environments. As a result, human behavior frequently leads to unforeseeable consequences, and social institutions often turn out to be less than optimal. Small random or blind variations build up and are amplified through positive feedback to produce major societal change that cannot be anticipated in advance. And the cumulative effects of such processes make the course of social evolution itself indeterminate and non-directional.

In the context of such a paradigm, statistical analysis would continue to help sociology sort speculation from fact. But it would do so free from the deformations caused by the search for a non-existent clockwork of cause-effect interactions. Sociology would accept probabilistic results as the normal and satisfactory outcome of its investigations. The analysis of distributions and event trajectories—often ephemeral and unstable—which can be only broadly located around attractors would take the place of the positivist quest for the eventual completion of a pyramid of causal links that connect each social fact to the ultimate determinants of social order. Sociology would concentrate on describing the social world as it is, and on understanding how it came to be that way. Neither its descriptive nor its historical/analytic focus would be burdened by the presumption of finding social laws. Suggestions for change would be very much part of its tradition. But like other sciences dealing with similarly chaotic subject matters, such as evolutionary biology or metereology, sociology would maintain no pretensions of knowing the future, ending a fatal proclivity for social prediction that goes back to the beginnings of modern positivism in the nineteenth century, and to which Marx succumbed just as much as Comte and Spencer. The work on a theory of chaos in the natural sciences could provide important clues for such an effort. But unless such an alternative paradigm appears, the current theoretical stagnation of sociology is not likely to end.

Commentary and Debate: Positivism's Future—and Sociology's

Gerhard Lenski
University of North Carolina

◆ ◆ ◆

The most serious problems with Baldus's (1990) paper stem from the ambiguous and misleading nature of his discussion of two basic issues:

1. What is positivism?
2. In what sense or senses of that term can those whom he attacks be considered positivists?

These lead to a number of other issues which can be addressed more briefly:

3. Are contemporary "positivists" (to use Baldus's label for the moment) in sociology committed to a linear view of social processes as Baldus (pp. 151, 161) claims?
4. Has the course of social evolution been nondirectional as Baldus (p. 161) argues?
5. What, if anything, can sociologists say about the future?
6. Does Baldus, and do others like him, confuse the goals and methods of the social sciences with those of the humanities?
7. And, finally, what is the basic cause of sociology's current ills?

In the pages that follow, I will address each of these issues sequentially.

First, *What is positivism?* Look up the term in any standard reference work or dictionary and it quickly becomes evident that it has a variety of meanings. Baldus is not unaware of this, but he fails to draw the obvious conclusion, namely, that he must specify which of the various meanings he objects to and which, if any, he approves of. In the absence of approving statements concerning *any* aspect of positivism, one can only conclude that he finds positivism objectionable in all its manifestations.

What, then, is positivism? First, and foremost, as Abraham Kaplan (1968) and others have noted, it is an *evolving* philosophy of science, and like any evolving entity it has been characterized by elements of continuity, innovation, and extinction. The heart of the philosophy—and the one element that has persisted unaltered from the Comtean period—is the belief that scientific knowledge must be based on, tested by, and grounded in sensory experience, directly or indirectly (as with the use of the electron microscope or images transmitted by telescopes in space), and that neither intuition, logical reasoning, moral imperatives, or divine revelation can substitute for this. This has been the primary article of faith on which the whole of modern science rests.

As a corollary of this, positivists have concluded that statements about the sensory world that purport to be scientific (i.e., hypotheses and theories) must be formulated in such a way that they can be *falsified*. This, in turn, means that the concepts and relationships contained in such statements must be as unambiguous as possible. This concern with clarity and precision in the formulation of principles has led to the development of countless devices and techniques designed to reduce uncertainties. Most importantly, for present purposes, it has led to concern with problems of measurement and to the use of mathematical formulations to minimize ambiguities in statements about relationships among variables (e.g., $E = Mc^2$). In the social sciences and in population biology, the effort to minimize ambiguity led to the adoption of statistics, which have enabled researchers to replace vague and indefinite terms, such as "some," "many," or "most," with precise values, such as "27 percent" or "89 percent." This, in turn, gave rise to interest in probability theory

From Gerhard Lenski, "Positivism's future—and sociology's," *Canadian Journal of Sociology* 16(2) 1991, pp. 187–194.

and a growing recognition of the need for probabilistic formulations of theories and hypotheses. Though these developments met with some resistance, most of it came from critics of positivism, not its advocates.

Another corollary of the assumption that scientific knowledge must be based on, tested by, and grounded in sensory experience is the belief in the need for frequent interaction between theory and research. Theory must stimulate research, and research must lead back to modifications of theory when results do not conform fully to expectations generated by the latter.

Beyond these core characteristics, positivism has meant certain other things. For Comte, it apparently meant a belief that lawful regularities of a deterministic nature, similar to those that had been found prior to his day in physics and astronomy, governed the social world and that the task of sociologists was to identify these laws. Many others since his day have obviously shared this naive and overly optimistic view of what the social sciences can achieve.

Baldus seems not to appreciate the degree to which the shift from determinism to probabilism has been led by proponents of positivism as they sought to improve the fit between theory and data. Or, to be a bit more precise, he seems not to appreciate the extent to which the advocacy of probabilism has a reflected commitment to core elements of positivism rather than their abandonment. As the statistical mode of thinking with its concern for stochastic processes made its impact felt, growing numbers of social scientists came to see their task as one of explaining distributional patterns within *populations* (i.e., aggregations of individuals), not the characteristics of specific individuals. This has meant that they have been compelled to think in variable and probabilistic terms. As a consequence, therefore, if chaos theory proves of value in the social sciences, as Baldus believes, it will simply be re-enforcing and extending a process that has long been under way. . . .

This brings me to the second of the basic issues mentioned earlier: *In what sense or senses of the term "positivism" are those of us whom Baldus attacks "positivists?"* Had he dealt with this question forthrightly, he would have discovered that he was creating a straw man, and this would have left him with a vastly more daunting task—that of challenging the *contemporary* conception of sociological positivism.

Based on what I know of the work of Blalock, Collins, Duncan, Lieberson, Turner, and the others whom Baldus attacked, all are positivists in the fundamental sense of believing that knowledge claiming to be scientific in nature must be based on sensory experience. (I also share this view.) More than that, most of us have repeatedly argued, as a corollary of this, the need for greater rigor in the formulation of theories and hypotheses. Several even pioneered in the introduction of new and more rigorous methodologies of the kinds that Baldus apparently finds objectionable.

Few, if any of us, need to be lectured on the need for formulations of theory and research designs that take account of indeterminate and probabilistic relationships. In my own case, I would merely note that already in the first edition of *Human Societies,* published more than twenty years ago, no less than five separate discussions of probabilism are listed in the index (Lenski, 1970: 522). Furthermore, if those citations are checked, one finds that they refer to discussions of three basic types: (1) explanations of probabilism, (2) endorsements of probabilism combined with rejections of determinism, and (3) applications of the probabilistic perspective to the question of what can be said about the future. This approach has been maintained consistently in all five of the subsequent editions of *Human Societies,* the latest of which concludes with the assertion that humans today are confronted with a number of critical choices that will profoundly effect the quality of life in the future. It is true, however, that my coauthor and I also say (Lenski and Lenski: 428) that there are limits on what is possible—and that these are "set by our genetic heritage on the one hand and the natural constraints of the biophysical environment on the other." Thus, we part company with the Utopian views that some (Baldus?) seem to favour, namely, that all things are possible and only social consciousness needs to be altered.

What, then, are we to conclude about those whom Baldus attacked in his paper, "Positivism's twilight?" Are they positivists, or aren't they? By now, it should be clear that the problem is not as simple as he made it out to be. They (we) are and they (we) aren't positivists, both at the same time. It all depends on your definition of the term. . . .

Are neopositivists committed to a linear view of social processes as Baldus (pp. 151, 161) *claims?* This third question is not easily answered, since it is unclear precisely what Baldus means by his use of the term "linear." If, by this, he means that neopositivists deny the existence of reciprocal causation, he is clearly wrong. Thirty years ago, Blalock (1961: 55–57) was discussing the subject in *Causal Inferences in Nonexperimental Research* and discussions of nonrecursive systems and feedback have been standard topics in graduate methods training courses for years. Even introductory texts by neopositivists now employ such concepts (see, for example, the numerous citations to feedback in the index of Lenski and Lenski: 487). Neopositivists need no sermons on this from critics.

If, alternatively, Baldus means that neopositivists believe that relationships are all quantitatively linear, once again he is dead wrong. In fact, it may well be that the majority of the relationships that neopositivists have reported in recent decades have been described by them as nonlinear in nature, a development that led to increasing interest in nonrecursive models, quadratic equations, interaction terms, and outliers in statistical analyses.

Has the course of social evolution been nondirectional, as Baldus claims? If so, what are we to make of the evidence of the more or less continuous growth of world population since the end of the hunting and gathering era ten thousand years ago? What of the advances in technology within the world system of societies? The millennia-long increase in productivity? In wealth (though often not in standards of living)? In the division of labor? In urban populations? Are these mere figments of the imaginations of misguided positivists and evolutionists? And, if they are not, can we disregard them as sociologically irrelevant?

As these examples suggest, Baldus, like many in our discipline today, needs to become more precise in his assertions, because statements that may be true when applied to one data set may be utterly false when applied to others. Thus, while it is correct to say that long-term trends of the kinds I just cited cannot be found in many individual societies, perhaps most, this does not mean that such trends have not been present in the world system of societies. On the contrary, as my wife and I have indicated in a discussion that we titled, "The Great Paradox," trends in the world system of societies seem *not* (repeat *not*) to have paralleled those in the majority of individual societies (Lenski and Lenski, 1987: 54–55). On the contrary, because of a process of intersocietal selection, trends in the world system of societies resemble those found in a small, but powerful minority of societies. . . .

While admittedly, some of the efforts to apply neopositivistic principles have been pretentious and some have led to incorrect views of the social world, this does not mean that the principles themselves are flawed, as Baldus argues. It simply means that they have been applied by fallible human beings. Also, it does not mean that the social sciences are permanently burdened with such mistaken views of the social world as may result from the work of neopositivists; on the contrary, as the shift from determinism to probabilism indicates, the positivist tradition has built-in self-corrective mechanisms.

What, if anything, can sociologists say about the future? In the absence of any positive statement by Baldus on the subject, and in view of his insistence on the indeterminate nature of the future one can only infer that he believes that there is nothing we can legitimately or usefully say on the subject. While sharing his belief that the course of social evolution is indeterminate (see, for example, the closing paragraphs of Lenski and Lenski), there are many useful things that social scientists *can* say about the future. I base this on an assumption that was stated best some years ago by the noted biologist, René Dubos (1968: 270) when he wrote, "The past is not dead history; it is the living material out of which man makes the present and builds the future." In other words, careful analyses of the past and present can yield valuable clues concerning the future. In other words, careful analyses of the past and present can yield valuable clues concerning future.

While the failure of most of Marx's predictions serve as a continuing reminder of the hazards inherent in social forecasting, the record of the social sciences is not without impressive achievements. Most sociologists today seem to have forgotten Gaetano Mosca's (1939 [1896]: 281ff.) remarkable predictions concerning collectivist societies of the future—predictions that grew directly out of his theory and made at a time when no collectivist society existed. Twenty years before the Russian Revolution, he accurately forecast the rise and nature of the new class whose characteristics Milovan Djilas (1957) was to describe so vividly more than half a century later.

Another striking example of successful forecasting is provided by the oft-criticized convergence hypothesis of Clark Kerr and his associates (1960). In it, they anticipated the causes and essential nature of the dramatic changes that were to come in eastern Europe more than a quarter century later, and their predictions, like Mosca's, grew directly out of a falsifiable theory. Much the same can be said of Randall Collins' (1986) more recent forecast in "The Future Decline of the Russian Empire." These and other examples of successful social forecasting (many of which, like those just noted, go well beyond extrapolations from existing trends) indicate that one cannot assume that because the course of social evolution is ultimately indeterminate (since no theory can possibly take into account all of the factors at work—especially nonhuman forces, such as plagues and other natural catastrophes—and all their possible inter-actions), social scientists have nothing of value to say about the future.

Does Baldus, and do others like him, confuse the task and methods of the social sciences with those of the humanities? I think they do. In my opinion, an important and valuable division of labor has evolved in the academic world in the last hundred years or so. As a consequence of this, the humanities and the social sciences have come to focus on different facets of the human condition—facets that are equally important. The humanities serve as a continuing reminder of the unique-ness of every person, every group, every event, and every sequence of events. In contrast, the social sciences remind us that these unique entities and occurrences are influenced to a considerable degree by various recurring and repetitive forces and influences that generate inter-esting and important patterns, many of which recur within definable parameters. Thus, the basic goals of the social sciences and the humanities are *complementary* in nature, and the methods that are appropriate to each should be determined by the nature of their respective tasks In effect, the task of one is to remind us that the glass is half empty; the task of the other is to remind us that it is also half full.

Finally, what is the basic cause of sociology's current ills? That sociology has serious problems today cannot be denied; here I agree completely with Baldus. We even seem to agree on many of the manifestations or symptoms, such as the tendency of researchers to ignore important theo-retical problems when they involve variables that cannot be quantified (Baldus: 155), the homogeneity of samples and the resulting inattention to preindustrial and nonin-dustrial societies (Baldus: 156), and the lack of theoretical cumulation, especially in the case of theories of societies and their development (Baldus: 152).

I believe, however, that the cause of these problems lies not with our commitment to positivism or neoposi-tivism, but with the nature and quality of our theory, espe-cially our macrosociological theories. What sociology badly needs today is macrosociological theory, or theories, having four ingredients:

1. *Comprehensiveness*: theory that seeks to explain all of the more important characteristics of the entire uni-verse of important social phenomena—past as well as present;[1]
2. *Structural coherence*: theory that employs cover-ing principles to structure and organize otherwise disjointed and fragmented sets of middle-range

hypotheses, thus providing an intelligible taxonomic "map" of the universe of human societies, the basic organizing units in the social world;[2]
3. *Falsifiability*: theory whose concepts and hypotheses have clear, unambiguous, and research-relevant oper-ationalizations that enable theorists and researchers alike to agree on the implications of test results for the theory itself;
4. *Open-endedness*: theory that can be modified and grow in response to research; this assumes that there is meaningful interaction between theory and research, but that is possible only when theoretical concepts and hypotheses are operationally unam-biguous and theory is falsifiable.

If sociologists ever come to recognize that the demanding standards of science must be applied in *theory construction* as well as in research design, many or most of the more serious problems to which Baldus referred in his paper are likely to disappear. But don't hold your breath waiting for this. Our leading macrosocial theorists still seem to prefer the much too relaxed standards to which we and they have so long been accustomed, and some even make them a badge of honor.

NOTES

◆ ◆ ◆

1. The importance of this is hard to exaggerate, since the power of theories is primarily a function of the range and diversity of phenomena they are able to explain. By narrowing the scope of our theories, we have not only reduced their power (hence, the widespread criticism that sociology is little more than common sense dressed up in arcane jargon), we have denied ourselves the opportunity to gain the kinds of insights that come only from wider ranging, theory-guided cross-national and transhistorical comparisons.
2. What I am referring to here are the kind of covering principles found in evolutionary biology and contem-porary physics, that provide me basis for their respec-tive taxonomic "maps" of species and of panicles. Properly used, covering principles enable one to avoid both the misguided universalism of "grand theory" and the noncumulative particularism of abstracted empiricism. (Abstracted empiricism today includes not only the kinds of analyses of survey data that Mills [1959] warned of, but also the particularism evident in most area studies and in much of historical

sociology.) Covering principles enable one to develop multi-layered theory in which a very small number of basic principles having universal applicability identify major divisions within the field of study (e.g., plants vs. animals) in which a larger number of principles of more limited applicability also operate, and these, in turn, serve as covering principles that identify lesser subdivisions (e.g., vertebrates vs. invertebrates) in which still other principles of even more limited applicability operate.

Steps in the Research Process

THE STEPS
◆ ◆ ◆

Conducting research requires following a sequence of steps. The exact sequence and steps vary somewhat with the type of social research . . . but there are essentially seven major steps. The steps vary slightly by whether a study involves a quantitative or a qualitative approach and data.

Quantitative Approach

The process of conducting a quantitative study begins with a researcher selecting a topic. Quantitative researchers typically start with a general area of study or issue of professional or personal interest, such as the effects of divorce, reasons for delinquency, impact of homelessness, or how elites use the media. However, a topic is too broad for conducting a study. This is why the next step is crucial. The researcher must narrow it down to, or focus on, a specific *research question* that can be addressed in the study. Often this requires a careful review of the *research literature* . . . and developing hypotheses . . . that frequently come from *social theory*. . . .

For example, a broad topic—reasons for delinquency—becomes the focused researcher question: Are teenaged East Asian immigrant males who have strong ties to their home culture and who are not assimilated into the new society more likely to engage in delinquent acts than those with weak ties who have assimilated? A rather vague topic, reasons for delinquency, is focused into a specific reason (i.e., degree of assimilation) for a specific group of people (i.e., teenaged immigrant males from East Asia) that is used to pursue the next step, to *design a study*. . . . Designing the study requires making decisions about the type of case or sample to select, how to measure relevant factors, and what research technique (e.g., questionnaire, experiment) to employ. At this stage as well, theory informs decision making.

After designing the study, a researcher begins to *collect data*. A quantitative researcher will very carefully record and verify information, almost always in the form of numbers, and usually transfers the data into computer-readable format. Once the data are all collected, the researcher begins the fifth step, to *analyze data*. . . . This typically involves manipulating the data or numbers using computer software to create many charts, tables, graphs, and statistics. Often the research ends up with a large quantity of computer-generated output that provides the researcher with a condensed picture of the data. The researcher next has to give meaning to or *interpret the data*. By looking at the analyzed data, using background knowledge on the research topic and question, and drawing on theory, a researcher answers the original research question. A researcher also considers alternative interpretations of the data, compares the results of this study with previous studies, and draws out its wider implications. The researcher will be prepared for the final step, to *inform others*. This means writing a report about the study in a specific format . . . and presenting a description of the study and results to professional audiences and in one or more publications (see Figure 12.1).

Qualitative Approach

. . . Qualitative researchers begin with a self-assessment and reflections about themselves as situated in a sociohistorical context. It is a highly self-aware *acknowledgment of social self* or of a researcher's position in society. Qualitative researchers do not narrowly focus on a specific question, but ponder the theoretical-philosophical *paradigm* . . . in an inquisitive, open-ended settling in process as they *adopt a perspective*. Like the quantitative researcher, a qualitative researcher will *design a study* . . . , *collect data* . . . , *analyze data* . . . , and *interpret data*. The qualitative researcher is likely to collect, analyse, and interpret data simultaneously, going back and forth between these steps. He or she also tends to build new theory as well as draw on existing theory during these steps. At the *interpret data* stage, many quantitative researchers test hypotheses they previously developed whereas qualitative researchers tend to create new concepts and emphasize constructing theoretical interpretations. The last step, to *inform others,* is similar for both approaches, but here again, the report styles to present result other people vary by approach. . . . (See Figure 12.2.)

The neat seven-step process shown in Figures 12.1 and 12.2 are oversimplified. In practice, researchers rarely complete step 1, then leave it to move to step 2, and so on. Research is an interactive process in which steps blend into each other. A later step may stimulate reconsideration

Figure 12.1 Steps in the Quantitative Research Process

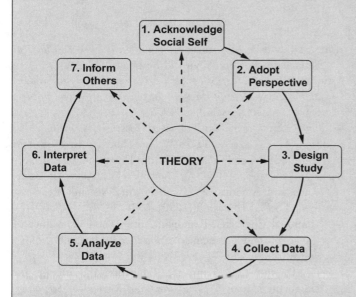

Figure 12.2 Steps in the Qualitative Research Process

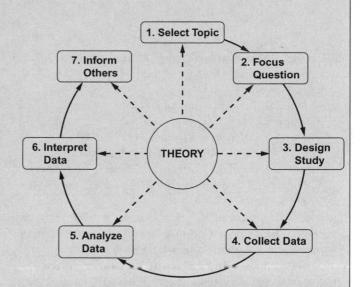

of a previous one. The process is not strictly linear; it may flow in several directions before reaching an end. Research does not abruptly end at step 7. It is an ongoing process, and the end of one study often stimulates new thinking and fresh research questions.

The seven steps are for one research project. A researcher applies one cycle of the steps in a single research project on a specific topic. Each project builds on prior research and contributes to a larger body of knowledge. The larger process of scientific discovery and accumulating new knowledge requires the involvement of many researchers in numerous research projects all at the same time. A single researcher may be working on multiple research projects at once, or several researchers may collaborate on one project. Likewise, one project may result in one scholarly article or several, and sometimes several smaller projects are reported in a single article.

Source: Neuman, W. Lawrence, *Social Research Methods: Qualitative & Quantitative Approaches.* Published by Allyn and Bacon, Boston, MA. Copyright © by Pearson Education. By Permission of the publisher.

Bibliography

Abercrombie, N., S. Hill, and B. S. Turner. *The Dominant Ideology Thesis.* London: George Alien and Unwin, 1980.

Acock, A. C., and D. H. Demo. *Family Diversity and Well-Being.* Newbury Park, CA: Sage, 1994.

Adams, C. F., D. Landsbergen, and D. Hecht. "Organizational Impediments to Paternity Establishment and Child Support." *Social Science Review* 72 (1994): 109–26.

Adamson, C. "God's Continent Divided: Politics and Religion in Upper Canada and the Northern and Western United States, 1775 to 1841." *Comparative Studies in Society and History* 36, no. 3 (1994): 417–46.

Albanese, C. L. *American Religious History: A Bibliographical Essay.* Washington, DC: United States Department of State: Currents in American Scholarship Series, 2002.

Alcoff, L. "Cultural Feminism versus Post-Structuralism: The Identity Crisis in Feminist Theory." *Signs* 13, no. 3 (1988): 405–36.

Allen, S. M., and A. J. Hawkins. "Maternal Gate-Keeping: Mothers' Beliefs and Behaviors that Inhibit Greater Father Involvement in Family Work." *Journal of Marriage and the Family* 61 (1999): 99–212.

Allen. W. D., and M. Connor. "An African American Perspective on Generative Fathering." In *Generative Fathering: Beyond Deficit Perspectives,* edited by A. J. Hawkins and D. C. Dollahite. Newbury Park, CA: Sage, 1997.

Altemeyer, B. *Enemies of Freedom: Understanding Right-Wing Authoritarianism.* San Francisco: Jossey-Bass, 1988.

Ambert, A. "An International Perspective on Parenting: Social Change and Social Constructs." *Journal of Marriage and the Family* 56 (1994): 529–43.

Anderson, A., and J. Frideres. *Ethnicity in Canada: Theoretical Perspectives.* Toronto: Butterworths, 1985.

Anderson, M. *Imposters in the Temple: American Intellectuals Are Destroying Our Universities and Cheating Our Students of Their Future.* New York: Simon and Schuster, 1992.

Anderson, M., and P. Hill Collins. *Race, Class and Gender.* 2nd ed. Belmont, CA: Wadsworth, 1995.

Anisef, P. *The Critical Juncture: Realization of the Educational and Career Intentions of Grade 12 Students in Ontario.* Toronto: Ontario Ministry of Colleges and Universities, 1975.

Applebee, A. N. *Curriculum as Conversation: Transforming Traditions of Teaching and Learning.* Chicago, IL: University of Chicago Press, 1996.

Arendell, T. *Fathers and Divorce.* Thousand Oaks, CA: Sage, 1995.

Armstrong, P., and H. Armstrong. *Theorizing Women's Work.* Toronto: Garamond Press, 1990.

Ashley, D., and D. M. Ornstein. *Sociological Theory; Classical Statements.* Boston: Allyn and Becon, 1998.

Astin, A. W. *The Power of Protest: A National Study of Student and Faculty Disruption with Implications for the Future.* San Francisco: Jossey-Bass, 1975.

—. *Four Critical Years.* San Francisco: Jossey-Bass. 1986.

Atkinson, A. B. *Incomes and the Welfare State: Essays on Britain and Europe.* Cambridge: Cambridge University Press, 1995.

Baer, D., E. Grabb, and W. A. Johnson. "The Values of Canadians and Americans: a Critical Analysis and Reassessment." *Social Forces* 68 (1990): 693–713.

—. "National Character, Regional Culture, and the Values of Canadians and Americans." *Canadian Review of Sociology and Anthropology* 30 (1993): 13–36.

Baer, D. E., and R. D. Lambert. "Education and Support for Dominant Ideology." *The Canadian Review of Sociology and Anthropology* 19, no. 2 (1982): 173–95.

—. "Socialization into Dominant vs. Counter Ideology among University-Educated Canadians." *The Canadian Review of Sociology and Anthropology* 27 (1990): 487–504.

Baker, P., and M. Copp. "Gender Matters Most: The Interaction of Gendered Expectations, Feminist Course Content, and Pregnancy in Students' Course Evaluations." *Teaching Sociology* 25 (1997): 29–43.

Baldus, B. "Positivism's Twilight?" *Canadian Journal of Sociology* 15 (1990): 149–63.

Baldwin, E. "The Mass Media and the Corporate Elite." *Canadian Journal of Sociology* 2, no. 1 (1977a): 1–27.

—. "On Methodological and Theoretical 'Muddles' in Clement's Media Study." *Canadian Journal of Sociology* 2, no. 2 (1977b): 215–22.

Bartley, M., D. Blane, and S. Montgomery. "Socioeconomic Determinants of Health; Health and the Life Course: Why Safety Nets Matter." *British Medical Journal* 314 (1997): 1194.

Bartley, M., D. Blane, and G. Davey Smith. "Introduction: Beyond the Black Report." *Sociology of Health and Illness* 20, no. 5 (1998): 563–77.

Baruch, G. K., and R. C. Barnett. "Consequences of Fathers' Participation in Family Work: Parent's Role Strain and Well-Being." *Journal of Personality and Social Psychology* 51 (1986): 983–92.

Baudrillard, J. *Simulations.* New York: Semiotext, 1983.

Bauman, Z. *Legislators and Interpreters.* Ithaca, NY: Cornell University Press, 1987.

—. "Is There a Postmodern Sociology?" *Theory Culture and Society* 5, no. 2–3 (1988a): 217–36.

—. "Sociology and Postmodernity." *Sociological Review* 36, no. 4 (1988b): 790–813.

Becker, G. S. *The Economic Approach to Human Behaviour*. Chicago: University of Chicago Press, 1976.

Becker, H. "On Becoming a Marijuana User." *American Journal of Sociology* 59 (1953): 235–42.

—. *Outsiders: Studies in the Sociology of Deviance*. New York: Free Press, 1963.

Belsky, J., and B. L. Volling. "Mothering, Fathering, and Marital Interaction in the Family Triad During Infancy." In *Men's Transitions to Parenthood: Longitudinal Studies of Early Family Experience*, edited by P. W. Berman and F. A. Pedersen. 37–63. Hillsdale, NJ: Erlbaum, 1987.

Bellamy, L., and N. Guppy. "Opportunities and Obstacles for Women in Canadian Higher Education." In *Women and Education*, edited by J. Gaskell and A. McLaren. 2nd ed., 163–92. Calgary: Detselig, 1991.

Berkman, L. F. "The Role of Social Relations in Health Promotion." *Psychosomatic Research* 57 (1995): 245–54.

Berkowitz, S. D. "Structural and Non-Structural Models of Elites: A Critique." *Canadian Journal of Sociology* 5, no. 1 (1980): 13–31.

—. "Corporate Structure, Corporate Control, and Canadian Elites." In *Models & Myths in Canadian Sociology*, edited by S. D. Berkowitz. 233–62. Toronto: Butterworths, 1984.

Berman, Russell A. "Peristroika for the University." *Telos* 81 (Fall 1989): 115–21.

Bernard, J. "The Good Provider Role: Its Rise and Fall." *American Psychologist* 36 (1981): 1–12.

Bernstein, R., A. Chadha, and R. Montjoy. "Overreporting Voting: Why It Happens and Why It Matters." *Public Opinion Quarterly* 65 (2001): 22–44.

Blais, A., E. Gidengil, R. Nadeau, and N. Nevitte. *Anatomy of a Liberal Victory: Making Sense of the Vote in the 2000 Canadian Election*. Peterborough, ON: Broadview, 2002.

Blais, A., E. Gidengil, N. Nevitte, and R. Nadeau. "Where Does Turnout Decline Come From." *European Journal of Political Research* 43 (2004): 221–36.

Blalock, H. M. Jr. *Causal Inferences in Nonexperimental Research*. Chapel Hill, NC: University of North Carolina Press, 1961.

—. *Basic Dilemmas in the Social Sciences*. Beverly Hills, California: Sage, 1984.

—. "The Real and Unrealized Contributions of Quantitative Sociology." *American Sociological Review* 54 (1989): 447–60.

Blau, P. M. "Structures of Social Position and Structures of Social Relations." In *Theory Building in Sociology*, edited by J. H. Turner. Newbury Park, California: Sage, 1988.

Bloland, H. G. "Postmodernism and Higher Education." *Journal of Higher Education* 66 (1995): 521–59.

Bloom, A. *The Closing of the American Mind: How Higher Education Has Failed Democracy and Impoverished the Souls of Today's Students*. New York: Simon and Schuster, 1987.

Bolaria, B. S., and P. S. Li. *Racial Oppression in Canada*. Toronto: Garamond, 1988.

Bonacich, E. "A Theory of Ethnic Antagonism: The Split Labor Market." *American Sociological Review* 37 (1972): 545–559.

—. "Advanced Capitalism and Black/White Relations in the United States: A Split Labor Market Interpretation." *American Sociological Review* 41 (1976): 34–51.

Bordo, S. "Anorexia Nervosa: Psychology as the Crystallization of Culture." In *Unbearable Weight: Feminism, Western Culture and the Body*. Berkeley: University of California Press, 1993.

Bourdieu, P. *Outline of a Theory of Practice*. Cambridge: Cambridge University Press, 1977.

Bowles, S., and H. Gintis. *Schooling in Capitalist America*. New York: Basic Books, 1976.

Bowles, G., and R. D. Klein. "Introduction: Theories of Women's Studies and the Autonomy/Integration Debate." In *Theories of Women's Studies*, edited by G. Bowles and R. D. Klein, 126. Boston: Routledge Kegan Paul, 1983.

Bowling, B., and C. Phillips. *Racism, Crime and Justice*. London, ON: Pearson Education, 2002.

Boyd, M., J. Goyder, F. E. Jones, H. A. McRoberts, P. Pineo, and J. Porter. *Ascription and Achievement: Studies in Mobility and Status Attainment in Canada*. Ottawa: Carleton University Press, 1985.

Brantingham, P. J., and P. L. Brantingham. *Environmental Criminology*. Beverly Hills, CA: Sage, 1981.

Brayfield, A. "Juggling Jobs and Kids: The Impact of Employment Schedules on Fathers' Caring for Children." *Journal of Marriage and the Family* 57 (1995): 321–32.

Breton, R. "Academic Stratification in Secondary Schools and the Educational Plans of Students." *Canadian Review of Sociology and Anthropology* 7, no. 1 (1970): 17–34.

Breton, R., W. W. Isajiw, W. E. Kalbach, and J. G. Reitz. *Ethnic Identity and Equality: Varieties of Experience in a Canadian City*. Toronto: University of Toronto Press, 1990.

Brown, D. *PACE Ten Years On: A Review of the Research*. London, U.K.: Home Office, 1997.

Brym, Robert. "The Canadian Capitalist Class." In *Social Inequality in Canada: Patterns, Problems and Policies*, edited by J. Curtis, E. Grabb, N. Guppy and S. Gilbert. 36–52. Scarborough: Prentice-Hall Canada Inc., 1988.

—. "The Great Canadian Identity Trap." *Canadian Journal of Sociology* 14, no. 4 (1989): 493–99.

Brym, R. J., and B. J. Fox. *From Culture to Power: The Sociology of English Canada*. Toronto: Oxford University Press, 1989.

Brym, R. J., and J. Myles. "Social Science Intellectuals and Public Issues in English Canada." *University of Toronto Quarterly* 58, no. 4 (1989): 442–51.

Buehler, C., A. Krishnakumar, G. Stone, C. Anthony, S. Pemberton, J. Gerard, and B. K. Barber. "Interparental Conflict Styles and Youth Problem Behaviors: A Two-Sample Replication Study." *Journal of Marriage and the Family* 60 (1998): 119–32.

Bullock, H. A. "Urban Homicide in Theory and Fact." *Journal of Criminal Law, Criminology, and Police Science* 45 (1955): 565–75.

Bunn, D. N., S. B. Caudill, and D. M. Gropper. "Crime in the Classroom: An Economic Analysis of Undergraduate Cheating Behavior." *Journal of Economic Education* 23 (1992): 197–207.

Bunyan, T. "The Cycle of UK Racism: Stop and Search, Arrest and Imprisonment." *Statewatch* 9 (1999): 1–4.

Burden, C. "Voter Turnout and the National Election Studies." *Political Analysis* (2000): 389–98.

Campbell, C., and G. Szablowski. *The Superbureaucrats: Structure and Behaviour in Central Agencies.* Toronto: Macmillan, 1979.

Carroll, M. "Who Owns Democracy? Explaining the Long-Running Debate over Canadian American Value Differences." *The Canadian Review of Sociology and Anthropology* 42, no. 3 (2005): 267–82.

Casper, L. M., and M. O'Connell. "Work, Income, the Economy, and Married Fathers as Child-Care Providers." *Demography* 35 (1998): 243–50.

Chafetz, J. S. *Sex and Advantage: A Comparative, Macro-Structural Theory of Sex Stratification.* Totowa, NJ: Rowman and Allenheld, 1984.

—. *Gender Equity: A Theory of Stability and Change.* Newbury Park, CA: Sage, 1990.

—. "Feminist Theory and Sociology." *Annual Review of Sociology* 23, 97 (1997): 120.

—. "Structure, Agency, Consciousness and Social Change in Feminist Theories." *Current Perspectives in Social Theory* 19 (1999): 145–64.

—. "Building Feminist Theory and Research Methodology." *Journal of Family Issues* 25, no. 7 (2004): 963–77.

Chafetz, J. S., and A. G. Dworkin. *Female Revolt: Women's Movements in World and Historical Perspective.* Totowa, NJ: Rowman and Allenheld, 1986.

Chappell, N. "Health care reform: Implications for Seniors." *Journal of Aging Studies* 11 (1997):171–75.

Chodorow, N. *The Reproduction of Mothering: Psychoanalysis and the Sociology of Gender.* Berkeley: University of California Press, 1978.

Clark, S. D. *Movements of Political Protest in Canada.* Toronto: University of Toronto Press, 1959.

—. *The Developing Canadian Community.* 2nd ed. Toronto: University of Toronto Press, 1968.

Clement, W. *The Canadian Corporate Elite: An Analysis of Economic Power.* Toronto: McClelland and Stewart, 1975a.

—. "Inequality of Access: Characteristics of the Canadian Corporate Elite." *The Canadian Review of Sociology and Anthropology* 12, no. 1 (1975b): 33–52.

—. "Overlap of the Media and Economic Elites." *Canadian Journal of Sociology* 2, no. 2 (1977): 205–14.

—. "A Critical Response to 'Perspectives on the Class and Ethnic Origins of Canadian Elites.'" *Canadian Journal of Sociology* 15, no. 2 (1990): 179–85.

Cole, D. *No Equal Justice: Race and Class in the American Criminal Justice System.* New York: New Press, 1999.

Cole-Hamilton, I., and T. Lang. *Tightening Belts: A Report on Impact of Poverty on Food.* London, U.K.: The London Food Commission, 1986.

Collins, P. *Black Feminist Thought: Knowledge, Consciousness, and the Politics of Empowerment.* Boston: Unwin, Hayman, 1990.

Collins, R. *The Credential Society: An Historical Sociology of Education and Stratification.* New York: Academic Press, 1979.

—. *Weberian Social Theory.* Cambridge: Cambridge University Press, 1986.

—. *Sociology: Prescience or Antiscience.* American Sociological Review 54 (1989): 124–39.

Collins, R., J. S. Chafetz, R. L. Blumberg, S. Coltrane, and J. Turner. "Toward an Integrated Theory of Gender Stratification." *Sociological Perspectives* 36 (1993): 185–216.

Coltrane, S. "Household Labor and the Routine Production of Gender." *Social Problems* 36 (1989): 473–90.

Commission on Systemic Racism. *Report of the Commission on Systemic Racism in the Ontario Criminal Justice System.* Toronto: Queen's Printer for Ontario, 1995.

Connell, R. W. "Why Is Classical Theory Classical?" *American Journal of Sociology* 102 (1997): 1511–57.

Cooksey, E. C., and M. M. Fondell. "Spending Time with His Kids: Effects of Family Structure on Fathers' and Children's Lives." *Journal of Marriage and the Family* 58 (1996): 693–707.

Cowan, C. P., and P. A. Cowan. "Men's Involvement in Parenthood: Identifying the Antecedents and Understanding the Barriers." In *Men's Transitions to Parenthood: Longitudinal Studies of Early Family Experience*, edited by P. W. Berman and F. A. Pedersen. 145–74. Hillsdale, NJ: Erlbaum, 1987.

Cox, M. J., M. T. Owen, and V. K. Henderson. "Marriage, Adult Adjustment and Early Parenting." *Child Development* 60 (1989): 1015–24.

Crook, S., J. Pakulski, and M. Waters. *Postmodernization: Change in Advanced Society.* London, U.K.: Sage, 1992.

Curtis, J. "Voluntary Association Joining: A Cross-Nation & Comparative Note." *American Sociological Review* 36, no. 5 (1971): 872–80.

Curtis, J., D. Baer, and E. Grabb. "Nations of Joiners: Explaining Voluntary Association Membership in Democratic Societies." *American Sociological Review* 66, no. 6 (2001): 783–805.

Curtis, J., E. Grabb, and D. Baer. "Voluntary Association Membership in Fifteen Countries: A Comparative Analysis." *American Sociological Review* 57 (1992): 139–52.

Curtis, J., E. Grabb, and N. Guppy, eds. *Social Inequality in Canada.* 4th ed. Scarborough: Pearson, 2004.

Curtis, J., and L. Tepperman. "What Is Sociology?" In *Sociology: A Canadian Perspective,* edited by L. Tepperman and J. Curtis, 2–31. Don Mills, ON: Oxford University Press, 2004.

Curtis, J. E., and R. D. Lambert. "Educational Status and Reactions to Social and Political Heterogeneity." *The Canadian Review of Sociology and Anthropology* 13, no. 2 (1976): 189–203.

Daly, M., G. J. Duncan, G. A. Kaplan, and J. W. Lynch. "Macro-to-Micro Links in the Relation Between Income Inequality and Mortality." *The Milbank Quarterly* 76, no. 3 (1998): 315–402.

Davey-Smith, G. "Income Inequality and Mortality—Why Are They Related—Income Inequality Goes Hand in Hand with Underinvestment in Human-Resources." *British Medical Journal* 312 (1996): 987–89.

Davey-Smith, G., I. Neaton, D. Wenworth, R. Stamler and J. Stamler. "Mortality Differences between Black and White Men in the U.S.: Contribution of Income and Other Risk Factors among Men Screened for the MRFIT." *The Lancet* 351 (1998): 934–39.

Davis, K., and W. Moore. "Some Principles of Stratification." *American Sociological Review* 10 (1945): 242–49.

Davis, S. F., C. A. Grover, A. H. Becker, and L. N. McGregor. "Academic Dishonesty: Prevalence, Determinants, Techniques, and Punishments." *Teaching Psychology* 19 (1992): 16–20.

Delaney, T. *Contemporary Social Theory.* New Jersey: Pearson/Prentice Hall, 2005.

Deming, J., and M. Hamilton. "Methodist Revivalism in France, Canada, and the United States." In *Amazing Grace,* edited by G. Rawlyk and M. Noll, 121–53. Montreal and Kingston: McGill-Queen's University Press, 1994.

Demo, D. H. "Parent-Child Relations: Assessing Recent Changes." *Journal of Marriage and the Family* 54 (1992): 104–17.

Dennison, J. "The Canadian Community College in the 1980s: Strategies for Survival." *Canadian Journal of Education* 9, no. 2 (1984): 139–53.

Denzin, N. K., and Y. S. Lincoln. "The Discipline and Practice of Qualitative Research." In *Handbook of Qualitative Research,* edited by N. K. Denzin and Y. S. Lincoln. 2nd ed., 1–28. Thousand Oaks, CA: Sage, 2000.

Djilas, Milovan. *The New Class.* New York: Praeger, 1953. [1957].

Dobash, P. R., R. E. Dobash, M. Wilson, M. Daly. "The Myth of Sexual Symmetry in Marital Violence." *Social Problems* 39 (1992): 71.

Doherty, W. J., E. E. Kouneski, and M. F. Erickson. "Responsible Fathering: An Overview and Conceptual Framework." *Journal of Marriage and the Family* 60 (1998): 277–92.

Dougherty, Kevin. "The Effects of Community Colleges: Aid or Hindrance to Socioeconomic Attainment?" *Sociology of Education* 60 (April 1987): 86–103.

Downey, D. B., J. W. Ainsworth-Damell, and M. J. Dufur. "Sex of Parent and Children's Well-Being in Single-Parent Households." *Journal of Marriage and the Family* 60 (1998): 878–93.

Drache, D., and T. Sullivan, eds. *Health Reform: Public Success, Private Failure.* Routledge, London, U.K., 1999.

Dray, P. *At the Hands of Persons Unknown.* New York: Random House, 2003.

Dubos, R. *So Human an Animal.* New York: Scribner's, 1968.

Dumont, C. W. Jr. "Toward a Multicultural Sociology: Bringing Postmodernism into the Classroom." *Teaching Sociology* 23 (1995): 307–20.

Duncan, O. D. *Notes on Social Measurement.* New York: Russel Sage Foundation, 1984.

Durkheim, E. *Suicide: A Study in Sociology.* New York: Free Press, 1951.

—. *Education and Sociology.* New York: The Free Press, 1956.

—. *The Division of Labour in Society.* New York: Free Press, 1964.

Ehrenreich, B., and D. English. *For Her Own Good: 50 Years of the Experts' Advice to Women.* Garden City, NY: Anchor Press, 1978.

Engel, R., J. Shepard, M. Calnon, and T. J. Bernard. "Theory and Racial Profiling: Shortcomings and Future Directions in Research." *Justice Quarterly* 19, no. 2 (2002): 249–73.

Engels, F. *The Origin of the Family, Private Property and the State.* New York: International Publishers, 1970.

Epstein, C. F. *Deceptive Distinctions: Sex, Gender and the Social Order.* New Haven, CT: Yale University Press, 1988.

Esping-Andersen, G. *The Three Worlds of Welfare Capitalism.* Princeton, NJ: Princeton University Press, 1990.

—. *Social Foundations of Postindustrial Economies.* Oxford: Oxford University Press, 1999.

Etzkowitz, H. "The Contradictions of Radical Sociology." *Critical Sociology* 15, no. 2 (1988): 95–113.

Evans, P. "Government Action, Social Capital and Development: Reviewing the Evidence on Synergy." *World Development* 24, no. 6 (1996): 1119–32.

Evers, F., and S. Gilbert. "Outcomes Assessment: How Much Value Does University Education Add?" *Canadian Journal of Higher Education* XXI (1991): 53–76.

Farganis, S. "Social Theory and Feminist Theory: The Need for Dialogue." *Sociological Inquiry* 56 (1986): 50–68.

Federal. *Report on the Health of Canadians.* Ottawa: Minister of Supply and Services, 1996.

Feldman, K. A. "Grades and College Students' Evaluations of their Courses and Teachers." *Research in Higher Education* 4 (1976): 69–111.

—. "Identifying Exemplary Teachers and Teaching: Evidence from Student Ratings." In *Effective Teaching in Higher*

Education: Research and Practice, edited by R. P. Perry and J. C. Smart, 1–31. New York: Agathon, 1996.

Feldman, S. S., S. C. Nash, and B. G. Aschenbrenner. "Antecedents of Fathering." *Child Development* 54 (1983): 1628–36.

Felski, R. "Feminist Theory and Social Change." *Theory Culture and Society* 6, no. 2 (1989): 219–40.

Finke, R., and R. Stark. "How the Upstart Sects Won America: 1776–1850." *Journal for the Scientific Study of Religion* 28, no. 1 (1989): 27–44.

—. *The Churching of America, 1776–1990*. New Brunswick, NJ: Rutgers University Press, 1992.

Flax, J. "Postmodernism and Gender Relations in Feminist Theory." *Signs* 12, no. 4 (1987): 621–43.

Forget, E. "National Identity and the Challenge of Health Reform in Canada." *Review of Social Economy* 60 (2002): 359–75.

Fox, J., and C. Suschnigg. "A Note on Gender and the Prestige of Occupations." *Canadian Journal of Sociology* 14, no. 3 (1989): 353–60.

Franklin, M. N. "Electoral Engineering and Cross-National Turnout Differences: What Role for Compulsory Voting." *British Journal of Political Science* 29 (1999): 205–16.

Fraser, N. and L. Nicholson. "Social Criticism without Philosophy: An Encounter between Feminism and Postmodernism." *Communication* 10, no. 3-4 (1986): 345–66.

Freire, P. *Pedagogy of the Oppressed*. New York: Continuum Press, 1993.

Freud, S. *New Introductory Lectures on Psychoanalysis*. New York: Penguin, 1964.

Frideres, J. S. *Native Peoples in Canada: Contemporary Conflicts*. Scarborough, ON: Prentice-Hall Canada, 1988.

—. "Racism and Health: The Case of the Native People." In *Health, Illness, and Health Care in Canada*, edited by B. S. Bolaria and H. D. Dickson. 202–20. 2nd ed. Toronto: Harcourt Brace and Company, Canada, 1994.

Furstenberg, F. F. Jr. "Children and Family Change: Discourse Between Social Scientists and the Media." *Contemporary Sociology: A Journal of Reviews* 28 (1999): 10–17.

Furstenberg, F. F. Jr., and K. M. Harris. "When and Why Fathers Matter: Impacts of Father Involvement on the Children of Adolescent Mothers." In *Young Unwed Fathers: Changing Roles and Emerging Policies,* edited by R. I. Lerman and T. J. Ooms. Philadelphia: Temple University Press, 1993.

Furstenberg, F. F. Jr., S. P. Morgan, and P. D. Allison. "Paternal Participation and Children's Well-Being after Marital Dissolution." *American Sociological Review* 52 (1987): 695–701.

Gabor, T., and F. Mata. "Victimization and Repeat Victimization over the Life Span." *International Review of Victimology* 10 (2004): 193–221.

Gans, H. "Sociology in America: The Discipline and the Public." American Sociological Association 1988 Presidential Address. *American Sociological Review* 54 (1989): 1–16.

Gerson, K. *Hard Choices: How Women Decide about Work, Career, and Motherhood*. Berkeley, CA: University of California Press, 1985.

—. *No Man's Land: Men's Changing Commitments to Family and Work*. New York: Basic Books, 1993.

Geyer, M. "Multiculturalism and the Politics of General Education." *Critical Inquiry* 19 (1993): 499–533.

Giddens, A. *Capitalism and Modern Social Theory: An Analysis of the Writings of Marx, Durkheim and Weber*. Cambridge: Cambridge University Press, 1971.

—. *Social Theory and Modern Sociology*. Stanford: Stanford University Press, 1987.

—. *Sociology: A Brief But Critical Introduction*. 2nd ed. New York: Harcourt Brace Jovanovich, Publishers, 1987.

Gigliotti, R. J., and F. S. Buchtel. "Attributional Bias and Course Evaluations." *Journal of Educational Psychology* 82 (1990): 341–51.

Gilbert, P. *Depression: The Evolution of Powerlessness*. Hove: Psychology Press, New York: Guilford, 1992.

Gilbert, S. *Attrition in Canadian Universities. Research Report #1*. Ottawa: Commission of Inquiry on Canadian University Education, 1991.

Gold, A. D. "Media Hype, Racial Profiling, and Good Science." *Canadian Journal of Criminology and Criminal Justice* 45 (2003): 391–99.

Goldman, L. "Student Evaluations of their Professors Rarely Provide a Fair Measure of Teaching Ability." *The Chronicle of Higher Education* 36, no. 47 (1990): B2.

Goldstein, H. "Improving Policing: A Problem-Oriented Approach." *Crime and Delinquency* 25 (1979): 236–58.

Goode, W. J. "Why Men Resist." In *Rethinking the Family: Some Feminist Questions*, edited by B. Thorne and M. Yalom. 131–47. New York: Longman, 1982.

Gottfredson, M., and T. Hirschi. *A General Theory of Crime*. Stanford, CA: Stanford University Press, 1990.

Gottman, J. M. "Toward a Process Model of Men in Marriages and Families." In *Men in Families,* edited by A. Booth and N. Crouter. Hillsdale, NJ: Erlbaum, 1998.

Grabb, E. *Theories of Social Inequality: Classical and Contemporary Perspectives*. Toronto: Holt, Rinehart and Winston of Canada, 1990.

Grabb, E., D. Baer, and J. Curtis. "The Origins of American Individualism: Reconsidering the Historical Evidence." *Canadian Journal of Sociology* 24 (1999): 511–33.

Grabb, E., and J. Curtis. *Regions Apart: The Four Societies of Canada and the United States*. Don Mills, ON: Oxford University Press, 2005.

Grabb, E., J. Curtis, and D. Baer. "Defining Moments and Recurring Myths: Comparing Canadians and Americans after the American Revolution." *Canadian Review of Sociology and Anthropology* 37 (2000): 373–419.

—. "On Accuracy and Big Pictures: Reply to Lipset. *Canadian Review of Sociology and Anthropology* 38 (2001): 101–03.

Gray, M. and M. Caul. "Declining Voter Turnout in Advanced Industrial Democracies, 1950 to 1997: The Effects of Declining Group Mobilization." *Comparative Political Studies* 33 (2000): 1091–1122.

Guidi, S., M. Townsley, and R. Homel. "March Repeat Break and Enter Crimes: An Analysis of Police Calls for Service Data in a Brisbane Region." Paper presented to the Second National Outlook Symposium, Canberra, 1997.

Guidubaldi, J., H. K. Cleminshaw, J. D. Perry, B. D. Nastasi, and J. Lightel. "The Role of Selected Family Environment Factors in Children's Postdivorce Adjustment." *Family Relations* 35 (1986): 141–51.

Guimond, S., and D. L. Palmer. "Type of Academic Training and Causal Attributions for Social Problems." *European Journal of Social Psychology* 20 (1990): 61–75.

—. "Education, Attitude Change, and Social Action." Unpublished manuscript, Royal Military College of Canada, 1993.

Guimond, S., D. L. Palmer, and G. Begin. "Education, Academic Program and Intergroup Attitudes." *The Canadian Review of Sociology and Anthropology* 26, no. 2 (1989): 193–216.

Guppy, N., S. Freeman, and S. Buchan. "Economic Background and Political Representation." In *Social Inequality in Canada: Patterns, Problems and Policies*, edited by J. Curtis, E. Grabb, N. Guppy and S. Gilbert. 394–404. Scarborough: Prentice-Hall Canada Inc., 1988.

Guppy, N., and K. Pendakur. "The Effects of Gender and Parental Education on Participation within Post-Secondary Education in the 1970s and 1980s." *Canadian Journal of Higher Education* 19, no. 1 (1989): 49–62.

Habermas, J. "Modernity versus Postmodernity." *New German Critique* 22 (1981): 3–14.

—. *The Philosophical Discourse of Modernity*. Cambridge, MA: MIT Press, 1987.

Harding, S. *The Science Question in Feminism*. Ithaca, NY: Cornell University Press, 1986a.

—. "The Instability of the Analytical Categories of Feminist Theory." *Signs* 11, no. 4 (1986b): 15–34.

—. "Conclusion: Epistemological questions." In *Feminism and Methodology*, edited by S. Harding. 181–90. Bloomington: Indiana University Press, 1987.

Harris, D. "Driving while Black and All Other Traffic Offences: The Supreme Court and Pretextual Traffic Stops." *Journal of Criminal Law and Criminology* 87 (1997): 544–82.

—. "The Stories, the Statistics and the Law: Why 'Driving while Black' Matters." *Minnesota Law Review* 84 (1999): 265–326.

Harris, K. M., F. E. Furstenberg Jr., and J. K. Manner. "Paternal Involvement with Adolescents in Intact Families: The Influence of Fathers over the Life Course." *Demography* 35 (1998): 201–16.

Harris, M. "Why Men Dominate Women." *The New York Times Magazine*, November 13, 1977.

Hartsock, N. "Rethinking Modernism: Minority vs. Majority Theories." *Cultural Critique* 7 (1987): 187–206.

Harvey, E. "An Independent Review of the *Toronto Star* Analysis of Criminal Information Processing System (CIPS) Data Provided by the Toronto Police Service (TPS)." 2003. Report available on the Toronto Police Service website. http://www.torontopolice.on.ca.

Hassan, I. *The Postmodern Turn*. Columbus: Ohio State University Press, 1987.

Hatch, N. O. *The Democratization of American Christianity*. New Haven: Yale University Press, 1989.

Hawkesworth, M. "Knowers, Knowing, Known: Feminist Theory and Claims of Truth." *Signs* 14, no. 3 (1989): 533–57.

Heath, A. "Were Traditional Labour Voters Disillusioned with New Labour? Abstention at the 1997 General Election." In *British Elections and Parties Review 10*, edited by P. Cowley, D. Denver, A. Russell and L. Harrison. London: Frank Cass, 2000.

Heath, A. and B. Taylor. "New Sources of Abstention?" In *Critical Elections: British Parties and Voter in Long-Term Perspective*, edited by G. Evans and P. Norris. London: Sage, 1999.

Heath, A., R. Jowell, and J. Curtice. *Understanding Political Change*. Oxford: Pergamon, 1991.

Heckelman, J. "Determining Who Voted in Historical Elections: An Aggregated Logit Approach." *Social Science Research* 26 (1997): 121–34.

Hempel, C. G. "The Function of General Laws in History." In *Readings in Philosophical Analysis*, edited by H. Feigl and W. Sellars. New York: Appleton, Century, Crofts, 1949.

—. "A Logical Appraisal of Operationalism." *Scientific Monthly* 79 (1954): 215–20.

—. *Aspects of Scientific Explanation*. New York: Free Press, 1965.

Hendrickson, M. W., ed. *The Morality of Capitalism*, 2nd ed. New York: Foundation for Economic Education, 1996.

Henry, F., and E. Ginzberg. *Who Gets the Work? A Test of Racial Discrimination in Employment*. Toronto: The Urban Alliance on Race Relations and the Social Planning Council of Metropolitan Toronto, 1985.

Henry, F., C. Tator, W. Mattis, and T. Rees. *The Colour of Democracy: Racism in Canadian Society*. 2nd ed. Toronto: Harcourt Brace, 2000.

Herrnstein, R. J. "Still American Drama." *The Public Interest* 98 (1990): 3–17.

Hetherington, E. M., M. Cox, and R. Cox. "Effects of Divorce on Parents and Children." In *Nontraditional Families: Parenting and Child Development*, edited by M. Lamb. Hillsdale, NJ: Erlbaum, 1982.

Hewitt, E. C. *A Treatise on Pedagogy for Young Teachers*. New York: Van Antwerp Bragg, and Co., 1884.

Hill Collins, P. "Learning from the Outsider Within: The Sociological Significance of Black Feminist Thought." *Social Problems* 33 (1986): 514–30.

—. "Black Women and Motherhood." In *Rethinking the Family: Some Feminist Questions*, edited by B. Thorne and M. Yalom. 2nd ed., 215–45. Boston: Northeastern University Press, 1992.

Hird, M. J. "Gender's Nature: Intersexuality, Transsexuality and the 'Sex/Gender.'" *Feminist Theory* 1, no. 3 (2000): 347–64.

Hirschi, T. *Causes of Delinquency*. Berkeley and Los Angeles: University of California Press, 1969.

Hochschild, A., with A. Machung. *The Second Shift: Working Parents and the Revolution at Home*. New York: Viking, 1989.

Hood, R. *Race and Sentencing: A Study in the Crown Court*. Oxford: Clarendon Press, 1992.

hooks, bell *Feminist Theory: From Margin to Center*. Boston: South End Press, 1984.

—. *Teaching to Transgress: Education as the Practice of Freedom*. New York: Routledge, 1994.

Howarth, C., P. Kenway, G. Palmer, and R. Miorelli. *Monitoring Poverty and Social Exclusion 1999*. York, U.K.: Joseph Rowntree Foundation, 1999.

Howe, P., and D. Northrup. "Strengthening Canadian Democracy—The Views of Canadians." *Policy Matters* 1, no. 5 (2000) 1–104.

Hsieh, C. C., and M. D. Pugh. "Poverty, Income Inequality, and Violent Crime: A Meta-Analysis of Recent Aggregate Data Studies." *Criminal Justice Review* 18 (1993): 182–202. Reprinted in *Income Inequality and Health: The Society and Population Health Reader, Vol. 1*: edited by I. Kawachi, B. Kennedy and R. G. Wilkinson. NY: New Press, 1999.

Humphries, K., and E. Doorslaer. "Income-Related Health Inequalities in Canada." *Social Science & Medicine* 50 (2000): 663–71.

Hunter, A. A. "Class and Status in Canada." In *Introduction to Canadian Society*, edited by G. N. Ramu and S. D. Johnson. Toronto: Macmillan, 1976.

—. *Class Tells: On Social Inequality in Canada*. Toronto: Butterworths, 1986.

Hunter, A. "Formal Education and Initial Employment: Unravelling the Relationship Between Schooling and Skills over Time." *American Sociological Review* 53, no. 3 (1988): 753–65.

Hunter, A., and J. Leiper. "Sex, Schooling and Earnings: Productivity and Credentialism in the Earnings Determination Process." Unpublished paper, McMaster University, 1991.

Ihinger-Tallman, M., K. Pasley, and C. Buehler. "Developing a Middle-Range Theory of Father Involvement Postdivorce." In *Fatherhood: Contemporary Theory, Research, and Social Policy*, edited by W. Marsiglio. 57–77. Thousand Oaks, CA: Sage, 1995.

Inter-University Consortium for Political and Social Research (I.C.P.S.R.). *Class Structure and Class Consciousness Merged Multi-Nation File Code-Book*. Ann Arbor, MI: I.S.P.S.R. [distributor], 1986.

Isaac, L. W., and L. J. Griffin. "A Historicism in Time-Series Analyses of Historical Process: Critique, Redirection, and Illustrations from U.S. Labor History." *American Sociological Review* 54 (1989): 873–90.

Isajiw, W. W. Definitions of Ethnicity. *Ethnicity* 1, no. 2 (1974): 111–24.

—. "Ethnic-Identity Retention." In *Ethnic Identity and Equality: Varieties of Experience in a Canadian City*, edited by R. Breton et al., 34–91. Toronto: University of Toronto Press, 1990.

Jackson, J. "Sociology in Anglophone Canada: Introduction." *Canadian Review of Sociology and Anthropology* 22, no. 5 (1985): 615–18.

Jacoby, R. *The Last Intellectuals: American Culture in the Age of Academe*. New York: Basic Books, 1987.

James, C. "'Up to No Good': Black on the Streets and Encountering Police." In *Racism and Social Inequality in Canada: Concepts, Controversies, and Strategies of Resistance*, edited by V. Satzewich. Toronto: Thompson, 1998.

Jasso, G. "Principles of Theoretical Analysis." *Sociological Theory* 6 (1988): 1–20.

—. "Notes on the Advancement of Theoretical Sociology (Reply to Turner)." *Sociological Theory* 7 (1989):135–44.

Johnston, R. "Canadian Elections at the Millenium." *Choices* 6, no. 6 (2001): 1–52.

Johnston, R. J., and C. J. Pattie. "Is There a Crisis of Democracy in Great Britain? Turnout at General Elections Reconsidered." In *Challenges to Democracy: Ideas, Involvement and Institutions*, edited by K. Dowding, J. Hughes and H. Margetts. Basingstoke: Palgrave, 2001.

Jones, L. "Unemployed Fathers and Their Children: Implications for Policy and Practice." *Child and Adolescent Social Work Journal* (1991): 101–16.

Jones, F. E. "Educational and Occupational Attainment: Individual Achievement." In *Ascription and Achievement*, edited by M. Boyd et al. Ottawa: Carleton University Press, 1985.

Kalter, N., A. Kloner, S. Schreier, and K. Okla. "Predictors of Children's Postdivorce Adjustment." *American Journal of Orthopsychiatry* 59 (1989): 605–18.

Kaplan, A. "Positivism." *International Encyclopedia of the Social Sciences* 12 (1968): 389–95.

Kaplan, G. A., E. R. Pamuk, J. W. Lynch, R. D. Cohen, and J. L. Balfour. "Inequality in Income and Mortality in the United States: Analysis of Mortality and Potential Pathways." *British Medical Journal* 312 (1996): 999–1003 (erratum 31, 1253).

Karabel, Jerome. "Community Colleges and Social Stratification." *Harvard Educational Review* 42 (1972): 521–62.

Kawachi, I., and B. P. Kennedy. "Socioeconomic Determinants of Health: Health and Social Cohesion: Why Care about Income Inequality?" *British Medical Journal* 314 (1997): 1037.

Kawachi, I., B. P. Kennedy, K. Lochner, and D. Prothrow-Stith. "Social Capital, Income Inequality and Mortality."

American Journal of Public Health 87 (1997): 1491–98. Reprinted in *Income Inequality and Health. The Society and Population Health Reader, Vol. 1*, edited by I. Kawachi, B. Kennedy and R. G. Wilkinson. NY: New Press, 1999.

Kelling, G. "The Kansas City Patrol Experiment." Washington, DC: Police Foundation, 1974.

—. *London Labour and the London Poor, Vol. 4: Those That Will Not Work, Comprising Prostitutes, Thieves, Swindlers, and Beggars*. 1862. New York: Dover, 1968.

Kellough, G., and S. Wortley. "Remand for Plea: The Impact of Race, Pre-Trial Detention and Over-Charging on Plea Bargaining Decisions." *British Journal of Criminology* 42, no. 1 (2002): 186–210.

Kennedy, B. P., I. Kawachi, and D. Prothrow-Stith. "Income Distribution and Mortality: Cross Sectional Ecological Study of the Robin Hood Index in the United States." *British Medical Journal* 312 (1996): 1004–07.

Kennedy, W. R. "Grades Expected and Grades Received: Their Relationship to Students' Evaluations of Faculty Performance." *Journal of Educational Psychology* 67 (1975): 109–15.

Kenworthy, L. "Do Social-Welfare Policies Reduce Poverty? A Cross-National Assessment." *Social Forces* 77, no. 3 (1998): 1119–39.

Kerr, C., et al. *Industrialism and Industrial Man*. New York: Oxford University Press, 1960.

Kimura, D. "Sex Differences in the Brain." *Scientific American. Com*. May 13, 2002.

King, V. "Variation in the Consequence of Nonresident Father Involvement for Children's Well-Being." *Journal of Marriage and the Family* 56 (1994): 963–72.

Korpi, W., and J. Palme. "The Paradox of Redistribution and Strategies of Equality: Welfare State Institutions, Inequality and Poverty in the Western Countries." *American Sociological Association* 63 (1998): 661–87.

Ladd, E. C., and S. M. Lipset. *The Divided Academy: Professors and Politics*. New York: Norton Library, 1975.

Lakey, J., and J. Duncanson. "Groups Walk Out at Race–Crime Summit." *Toronto Star*, April 29, 2003: A1.

LaRossa, R. "Fatherhood and Social Change." *Family Relations* 36 (1988): 451–58.

—. *The Modernization of Fatherhood: A Social and Political History*. Chicago: University of Chicago Press, 1997.

Larson, R. W. "Finding Time for Fatherhood: The Emotional Ecology of Adolescent-Father Interactions." In *Father-Adolescent Relationships*, edited by S. Shulman and W. A. Collins. 7–251. San Francisco: Jossey-Bass, 1993.

Larson, R. W., and M. H. Richards. *Divergent Realities: The Emotional Lives of Mothers, Fathers, and Adolescents*. New York: Basic Books, 1994.

Laurin-Frenette, N. "The Sociology of Social Classes." *The Canadian Review of Sociology and Anthropology* 26, no. 3 (1989): 457–84.

Lennards, J. L. "Education." In *Sociology*, edited by R. Hagedorn. 3rd ed. Toronto: Holt, Rinehart and Winston, 1986.

—. "The Academic Profession in Canada. Final Report to the Social Science and Humanities Research Council of Canada." 1988. Toronto: York University.

Lenski, G. *Human Societies*. 1st ed. New York: McGraw-Hill, 1970.

—. "Rethinking Macrosociological Theory." *American of Sociological Review* 53 (1988): 161–71.

Lenski, G., and J. Lenski. *Human Societies*. 5th ed. New York: McGraw-Hill, 1987.

Lerman, R. I. "A National Profile of Young Unwed Fathers." In *Young Unwed Fathers: Changing Roles and Emerging Policies*, edited by R. I. Lerman and T. J. Ooms. Philadelphia: Temple University Press, 1993.

Levine, J. A., and E. W. Pitt. *New Expectations: Community Strategies for Responsible Fatherhood*. New York: Families and Work Institute, 1995.

Levy-Shiff, R., and R. Israelashvili. "Antecedents of Fathering: Some Further Exploration." *Developmental Psychology* 24 (1988): 434–40.

Lieberson, S. *Making It Count*. Berkeley: University of California Press, 1985.

Lipset, S. M. *The First New Nation: The United States in Historical and Comparative Perspective*. New York: Basic Books, 1963a.

—. *Political Man: The Social Bases of Politics*. Garden City, NY: Doubleday, 1963b.

—. "The Value Patterns of Democracy: A Case Study in Comparative Analysis." *American Sociological Review* 28 (1963c): 515–31.

—. "Revolution and Counter-Revolution: The United States and Canada." In *The Revolutionary Theme in Contemporary America*, edited by T. R. Ford, 21–64. Leamington: University of Kentucky Press, 1965.

—. *Rebellion in the University*. Chicago: University of Chicago Press, 1971.

—. "Historical Traditions and National Characteristics: A Comparative Analysis of Canada and the United States." *Canadian Journal of Sociology* 11 (1986): 113–55.

—. *Continental Divide: The Values and Institutions of the United States and Canada*. New York: Routledge, 1990a.

—. "The Values of Canadians and Americans: A Reply." *Social Forces* 69 (1990b): 267–72.

—. "The Social Requisites of Democracy Revisited." *American Sociological Review* 59 (1994): 1–22.

—. *American Exceptionalism: A Double-Edged Sword*. New York: W. W. Norton, 1996a.

—. 1996b. "Steady Work: An Academic Memoir." *Annual Review of Sociology* 22: 1–27.

—. "Defining Moments and Recurring Myths: A Reply." *Canadian Review of Sociology and Anthropology* 38 (2001): 97–100.

Lipset, S. M., and E. C. Ladd. "The Myth of the 'Conservative' Professor: A Reply to Michael Faia." *Sociology of Education* 47 (1974): 203–13.

Long, D. A. "Sociology and a Pedagogy for Liberation: Cultivating a Dialogue of Discernment in Our Classrooms." *Teaching Sociology* 23 (1995): 321–30.

Long, G. L., and E. S. Lake. "A Precondition for Ethical Teaching: Clarity about Role and Inequality." *Teaching Sociology* 24 (1996): 111–16.

Lupri, E., and J. Frideres. "Marital Satisfaction over the Family Life Cycle. *Canadian Journal of Sociology* 6 (1981): 283–306.

Lyons, W., and R. Alexander. "A Tale of Two Electorates: Generational Replacement and Decline of Voting in Presidential Elections." *The Journal of Politics* 62, no. 4 (2000): 1014–34.

Lyotard, J-F. *The Postmodern Condition.* Minneapolis, MN: University of Minnesota Press, 1984.

Mann, C. R. *Unequal Justice: A Question of Color.* Bloomington: Indiana University Press, 1993.

Mann, M. "The Social Cohesion of Liberal Democracy." *American Sociological Review* 35, no. 3 (1970): 423–39.

Marchak, M. Patricia. *Ideological Perspectives on Canada.* 3rd ed. Toronto: McGraw-Hill Ryerson, 1988.

Marsden, P., J. S. Reed, M. Kennedy, and K. Stinson. "American Regional Cultures and Differences in Leisure Time Activities." *Social Forces* 60, no. 4 (1982): 1023–49.

Marsh, H. W. "Students' Evaluations of University Teaching: Dimensionality, Reliability, Validity, Potential Biases, and Utility." *Journal of Educational Psychology* 76 (1984): 707–54.

Marsiglio, W. "Paternal Engagement Activities with Minor Children." *Journal of Marriage and the Family* 53 (1991): 973–86.

Marx, K. *The Critique of Gotha Programme.* New York: International Publisher, 1970.

—. *The Grundrisse.* Introduction by Martin Nicolaus. New York: Vintage Books, 1973.

Marx, K., and F. Engels. *Selected Works, Parts I, II, and III.* Moscow: Progress Publisher, 1962.

—. *The German Ideology.* Moscow: Progress Publisher, 1976.

—. *Capital.* Volumes I, II and III. New York: International Publishers, 1977.

—. Engels. *Pre-Capitalist Socio-Economic Formations.* Moscow: Progress Publisher, 1979.

Mathews, D. G. "The Second Great Awakening as an Organizing Process, 1780–1830: An Hypothesis." *American Quarterly* 21 (1969): 23–43.

Mauer, M. *Race to Incarcerate.* New York: New Press, 1999.

McDonald, M. D., and S. I. Popkin. "The Myth of the Vanishing Voter." *American Political Science Review* 95 (2001): 963–74.

McFarlane, S., R. Beaujot, and T. Haddad. "Time Constraints and Relative Resources as Determinants of Sexual Division of Domestic Work." *The Canadian Journal of Sociology* 25, no. 1 (2000): 61–82.

McKeachie, W. J. *Teaching Tips: A Guidebook for the Beginning College Teacher.* Lexington, MA: Heath, 1978.

McKinney, R. "Toward a Resolution of the Modernist/Postmodernist Debate." *Philosophy Today* 30, no. 3 (1986): 234–45.

McLoyd, V. C. "Socialization and Development in a Changing Economy: The Effects of Paternal Job Loss and Income Loss on Children." *American Psychologist* 44 (1989): 293–302.

—. "The Impact of Economic Hardship on Black Families and Children: Psychological Distress, Parenting, and Socioemotional Development." *Child Development* 61 (1990): 311–46.

McMurtry, J. *Unequal Freedoms: The Global Market as an Ethical System.* Toronto: Garamond Press, 1998.

McPherson, J. *Abraham Lincoln and the Second American Revolution.* New York: Oxford University Press, 1991.

—. "Quebec Whistles Dixie." *Saturday Night Magazine* 113, no. 2 (1998): 13–23, 72.

McQuillan, K., and M. Belle. "Who Does What? Gender and Division of Labour in Canadian Households." In *Social Inequality in Canada*, edited by Curtis et al. 186–98. Scarborough, Canada: Prentice Hall Canada, 1999.

Mead, G. H. *Mind, Self and Society: From the Standpoint of a Social Behaviourist.* Chicago: University of Chicago Press, 1962.

Medsker, L. L. *The Junior College.* New York: McGraw-Hill, 1960.

Meehan, A., and M. Ponder. "Race and Place: The Ecology of Racial Profiling African American Motorists." *Justice Quarterly* 19 (2002): 399–429.

Merton, R. K. *Social Theory and Social Structure.* New York: Free Press, 1968.

Michels, R. *Political Parties.* New York: The Free Press, 1962.

Mies, M. "Towards a Methodology for Feminist Research." In *Theories of Women's Studies*, edited by G. Bowles and R. Klein, 117–139. London: Routledge Kegan Paul, 1983.

Miliband, R. *The State in Capitalist Society.* London: Quartet Books, 1973.

Miller, W. E. "Disinterest, Disaffection, and Participation in Presidential Politics." *Political Behavior* 2, no. 1 (1980): 7–32.

—. "The Puzzle Transformed: Explaining Declining Turnout." *Political Behavior* 14, no. 1 (1992): 1–43.

Mills, C. W. *The Sociological Imagination.* New York: Oxford University Press, 1959.

—. *The Sociological Imagination.* Harmondsworth: Penguin, 1970.

Milner, H. "Civic Literacy in Comparative Context: Why Canadians Should Be Concerned." *Policy Matters* 2, no. 2 (2001a): 1–40.

—. "Social Capital, Civic Literacy and Political Participation: Explaining Differences in Voter Turnout." In *Challenges to Democracy: Ideas, Involvement and Institutions*, edited by K. Dowding, J. Hughes and H. Margetts. Basingstoke: Palgrave, 2001b.

—. *Civic Literacy: How Informed Citizens Make Democracy Work.* Hanover: University of New England Press, 2002.

Mishler, W. *Political Participation in Canada: Prospects for Democratic Citizenship.* Toronto: The Macmillan Company of Canada Limited, 1979.

Mishra, R. *The Welfare State in Capitalist Society.* Toronto: University of Toronto Press, 1990.

Mitchell, M., and J. Jolley. *Research Design Explained.* New York: Harcourt Brace Jovanovich, 1992.

Moi, T. "Feminism, Postmodernism, and Style." *Cultural Critique* 9 (1988): 3–22.

Monk-Turner, E. "Sex Differences in Type of First College Entered and Occupational Status: Changes over Time." *Social Science Journal* 22 (1985): 89–97.

—. "Educational Differentiation and Status Attainments: The Community College Controversy." *Sociological Focus* 21, no. 2 (1988): 141–51.

—. "The Occupational Achievements of Community and Four-Year College Entrants." *American Sociological Review* 55, no. 5 (1990): 719–25.

Mosca, G. *The Ruling Class.* Trans. by H Kahn. New York: McGraw-Hill, 1939 [1896].

Mott, F. L., L. Kowaleski-Jones, and E. G. Menaghan. "Paternal Absence and Child Behavior: Does a Child's Gender Make a Difference?" *Journal of Marriage and the Family* 59 (1997): 103–18.

Muntaner, C., and J. Lynch. "Income Inequality, Social Cohesion, and Class Relations: A Critique of Wilkinson's Neo-Durkheimian Research Program." *International Journal of Health Services* 29, no. 1 (1999): 59–81.

Murphy, R. "The Struggle for Scholarly Recognition: The Development of the Closure Problematic in Sociology." *Theory and Society* 12 (1983): 631–58.

Nagel, E. *The Structure of Science.* New York: Harcourt Brace, 1961.

Nagler, M. "Minority Values and Economic Achievement: The Case of the North American Indian." In *Perspectives on the North American Indian,* edited by M. Nagler. Toronto: McClelland and Stewart, 1972.

Nagler, M. *Natives without a Home.* Toronto: Longman Canada, 1975.

Nakhaie, M. R. "Class and Voting Consistency in Canada." *Canadian Journal of Sociology* 17 (1992): 275–301.

—. "Housework in Canada: The National Picture." *Journal of Comparative Family Studies* 26, no. 3 (1995): 409–26.

—. "Asymmetry and Symmetry of Conjugal Violence." *Journal of Comparative Family Studies* 29, no. 3 (1998): 549–68.

—. "Social Origins and Educational Attainment in Canada, 1985 and 1994." *Review of Radical Political Economics* 32, no. 4 (2000): 577–609.

—. "Class, Breadwinner Ideology, and Housework among Canadian Husbands." *Review of Radical Political Economics* 34 (2002): 137–57.

—. "Socio-Economic Statuses, Social Capital and Health of Canadians." *Review of Radical Political Economics.* (2006) In press.

Nakhaie, M. R., and R. Brym. "Political Attitudes of Canadian Professors." *Canadian Journal of Sociology* 24, no. 3 (1999): 329–54.

Nakhaie, M. R., and J. Curtis. "The Effects of Class Positions of Parents on Educational Attainment of Daughters and Sons." *Canadian Review of Sociology and Anthropology* 35, no. 4 (1998): 483–516.

Nakhaie, M. R., and R. Pike. "Social Origins, Social Statuses and Home Computer Ownership and Use." *Canadian Journal of Sociology* 23, no. 4 (1998): 427–50.

Nakhaie, M. R., R. Silverman, and T. LaGrange. "Self-Control and Social-Control: An Examination of Gender, Ethnicity, Class and Delinquency." *Canadian Journal of Sociology* 25, no. 1 (2000): 35–60.

Nelson, L. L., and S. Kagan. "The Star-Spangled Scramble." *Psychology Today* (September 1972), 53–56, 90–91.

Neugebauer, R. "Kids, Cops, and Colour: The Social Organization of Police-Minority Youth Relations." In *Criminal Injustice: Racism in the Criminal Justice System,* edited by R. Neugebauer. Toronto: Canadian Scholars Press, 2000.

Noll, M. *A History of Christianity in the United States and Canada.* Grand Rapids, MI: W.B. Eerdmans, 1992.

Noll, M., N. Hatch, and G. Marsden. *The Search for Christian America.* Westchester: Crossway, 1983.

Normandeau, A. "Crime on the Montreal Metro." *Sociology and Social Research* 71 (1987): 289–92.

Norris, P. "Conclusions: The Growth of Critical Citizens and its Consequences." In *Critical Citizens: Global Support for Democratic Governance,* edited by P. Norris. 257–72. Oxford: Oxford University Press, 1999.

—. *A Virtuous Circle: Political Communications in Postindustrial Societies.* Cambridge: Cambridge University Press, 2000.

Norris, P., J. Curtiee. D. Sanders, M. Scammell, and H. Semetko. *On Message: Communicating the Campaign.* London, U.K.: Sage, 1999.

O'Brien, J., and J. A. Howard. "To Be or Not To Be: The Paradox of Value-Neutrality and Responsible Authority." *Teaching Sociology* 24 (1996): 326–30.

Ogmundson, R. "Perspectives on the Class and Ethnic Origins of Canadian Elites: A Methodological Critique of the Porter/Clement/Olson Tradition." *Canadian Journal of Sociology* 15, no. 2 (1990): 165–77.

—. "Commentary and Debate." *Canadian Journal of Sociology* 17, no. 3 (1992): 313–25.

—. "At the Top of the Mosaic: Doubts about the Data." *American Review of Canadian Studies* Autumn (1993): 373–86.

Ogmundson, R., and J. McLaughlin. "Trends in the Ethnic Origins of Canadian Elites: The Decline of the BRITS?" *The Canadian Review of Sociology and Anthropology* 29, no. 2 (1992): 227–42.

—. "Changes in an Intellectual Elite 1960–1990: The Royal Society Revisited." *The Canadian Review of Sociology and Anthropology* 31, no. 1 (1994): 1–13.

Okin, S. M. *Justice, Gender, and the Family*. New York: Basic Books, 1989.

Olsen, D. *The State Elite*. Toronto: McClelland and Stewart, 1980.

Pammett, J., and L. LeDuc. "Explaining the Turnout Decline in Canadian Federal Elections." http://www.elections.ca./content.asp?section=loi&document=index&dir=tur/tud&lang=e&textonly=false, 2003, accessed January 20, 2006.

Panitch, L. *The Canadian State: Political Economy and Political Power*. Toronto: University of Toronto Press, 1977.

Park, S. M. "Research, Teaching, and Service: Why Shouldn't Women's Work Count?" *Journal of Higher Education* 67 (1996): 46–84.

Parkin, F. *Class Inequality and Political Order*. London, U. K.: Paladin, 1971.

—. *Marxism and Class Theory: A Bourgeois Critique*. London: Tavistock, 1979.

Pattie, C. J., and R. J. Johnston. "Voter Turnout in the British General Election of 1992: Rational Choice, Social Standing or Political Efficacy?" *European Journal of Political Research* 33 (1998): 263–283.

—. "A Low Turnout Landslide: Abstention in the British General Election of 1997." *Political Studies* 49 (2001): 286–305.

—. "Civic Literacy and Falling Electoral Turnout: The United Kingdom 1992–1997." *Canadian Journal of Political Science* 36, no. 3 (2003): 579–99.

Pattison, S. *Financial Post Survey of Industrials*. Toronto: Financial Post, 1985.

Pease, K., and G. Laycock. *Revictimization: Reducing the Heat on Hot Victims*. Canberra: Australian Institute of Criminology, 1999.

Pederson, J. E. "Sexual Politics in Comte and Durkheim: Feminism, History and the French Sociological Tradition." *Signs* 27 (2001): 229–63.

Peterson, R. R. "A Re-Evaluation of the Economic Consequences of Divorce." *American Sociological Review* 61 (1996): 528–36.

Phares, V. "Conducting Nonsexist Research, Prevention, and Treatment with Fathers and Mothers: A Call for Change." *Psychology of Women Quarterly* 20 (1996): 55–77.

Piccone, P. "The Reuniversalization of the University?" *Telos* 81 (Fall 1089): 122–29.

Pleck, E. H., and J. H. Pleck. *Fatherhood Ideal in the United States: Historical Dimensions*. New York: John Wiley, 1997.

Pleck, J. H. "Paternal Involvement: Levels, Sources, and Consequences." In *The Role of the Father in Child Development*, edited by M. E. Lamb. 3rd ed., 66–103. New York: Wiley, 1997.

Poovey, M. "Feminism and Deconstruction." *Feminist Studies* 14, no. 1 (1988): 51–65.

Popay, J., G. William, C. Thomas, and T. Gatrell. "Theorising Inequalities in Health: The Place of Lay Knowledge." *Sociology of Health and Illness* 20, no. 5 (1998): 619–44.

Popper, K. R. *The Logic of Scientific Discovery*. New York: Basic Books, 1959.

Porter, J. *The Vertical Mosaic: An Analysis of Social Class and Power in Canada*. Toronto: University of Toronto Press, 1965.

—. "Research Biography of a Macrosociological Study: The Vertical Mosaic." In *Macrosociology: Research and Theory*, edited by J. Coleman et al., 149–82. Boston: Allyn and Bacon, 1970.

—. "Power and Freedom in Canadian Democracy." In *Measure of Canadian Society: Education, Equality and Opportunity*, J. Porter, Chapter 9, 207–40. Toronto: Gage, 1979.

Porter, J., M. Porter, and B. R. Blishen. *Stations and Callings: Making It through the School System*. Toronto: Methuen, 1982.

Potvin, M. "Some Racist Slips about Quebec in English Canada between 1995 and 1998" *Canadian Ethnic Studies* 32 (2000): 1–26.

Powell, R. W. "Grades, Learning, and Student Evaluation of Instruction." *Research in Higher Education* 7 (1977): 193–205.

Presser, H. B. "Shift Work and Child Care among Young Dual-Earner American Parents." *Journal of Marriage and the Family* 50 (1988): 133–48.

Presthus, R. *Elite Accommodation in Canadian Politics*. Toronto: Macmillan of Canada, 1973.

Putnam, R. *The Comparative Study of Political Elites*. Englewood Cliffs, NJ: Prentice-Hall., 1976.

Putnam, R. D. "Bowling Alone: America's Declining Social Capital." *Journal of Democracy* 6 (1995): 65–78.

—. *Bowling Alone: The Collapse and Renewal of American Community*. New York: Simon and Schuster, 2000.

Putnam, R. D., R. Leonardi, and R. Y. Nanetti. *Making Democracy Work: Civic Traditions in Modern Italy*. Princeton, NJ: Princeton University Press, 1993.

Quandango, J. "Theories of the Welfare State." *Annual Review of Sociology* 13 (1987): 109–28.

Quinn, J. "New Jersey Shooting Spurred Real Reform." *Toronto Star*, October 21, 2002: A6.

Rabow, J., and A. C. R. Hernandez. "The Price of the GPA Perspective: An Empirical Study of 'Making the Grade.'" *Youth and Society* 19 (1988): 363–77.

Rankin, J., J. Quinn, M. Shephard, S. Simmie, and J. Duncanson. "Singled Out: An Investigation into Race and Crime." *Toronto Star*, October 19, 2002a: A1.

—. "Police Target Black Drivers." *Toronto Star*, October 20, 2002b: A1.

—. "Black Crime Rates Highest." *Toronto Star*, October 26, 2002c: A1.

—. "Life and Death on Mean Streets." *Toronto Star*, October 27, 2002d: A1.

Raphael, D. 1999. "Health Effects of Economic Inequality." Canadian Review of Public Policy 44 (1999): 25–40.

Rapping, E. 1994. "Growing Pains." *The Women's Review of Books* 12: 25–26.

Rawlyk, G., and M. Noll. "Introduction." In *Amazing Grace*, edited by G. Rawlyk and M. Noll, 15–25. Montreal and Kingston: McGill-Queen's University Press, 1994.

Reed, J. S. *One South*. Baton Rouge: Louisiana State University Press, 1982.

—. "New South or No South? Regional Culture in 2036." In *The South Moves into the Future,* edited by J. Himes, 225–35. Tuscaloosa: University of Alabama Press, 1991.

Reed, J. S., and D. V. Reed. *1001 Things Everyone Should Know about the South*. New York: Broadway, 1996.

Reitz, J. "Language and Ethnic Community Survival." In *Ethnicity and Ethnic Relations in Canada*, edited by R. M. Bienvenue and J. E. Goldstein. 105–23. Toronto: Butterworths, 1985.

Rettig, K. D., D. H. Christensen, and C. M. Dahl. "Impact of Child Support Guidelines on the Economic Well-Being of Children." *Family Relations* 40 (1991): 167–75.

Rich, H. "The Vertical Mosaic Revisited: Toward a Macro-Sociology of Canada." *Journal of Canadian Studies* 11 (1976): 14–31.

—. "Observations on 'Class and Ethnic Origins of Canadian Elites' by Richard Ogmundson." *Canadian Journal of Sociology* 16, no. 4 (1991): 419–423.

Richer, S. "The Equality to Benefit from Schooling: The Issue of Educational Opportunity." In *Social Issues: Sociological Views of Canada,* edited by D. Forcese and S. Richer. 336–74. Scarborough: Prentice Hall Canada, 1982.

Riley, D. *Am I that Name?* Minneapolis: University of Minnesota Press, 1988.

Risman, B. J. "Intimate Relationships from a Microstructural Perspective: Men Who Mother." *Gender and Society* 1 (1987): 6–32.

Ritzer, G. *Contemporary Sociological Theory*. 3rd ed. Toronto: McGraw-Hill Inc., 1992.

Roberts, J., and A. Doob. "Race, Ethnicity, and Criminal Justice in Canada." In *Ethnicity, Crime, and Immigration: Comparative and Cross-National Perspectives, Vol. 21,* edited by M. Tonry. Chicago: University of Chicago Press, 1997.

Romano, R. *Race Mixing: Black-White Marriage in Postwar America*. Cambridge, MA: Harvard University Press, 2003.

Rosenberg, M. W., and K. Wilson. "Gender, Poverty and Location: How Much Difference Do They Make in the Geography of Health Inequalities?" *Social Science & Medicine* 51 (2000): 275–87.

Rosenblum, K., and T. M. Travis. *The Meaning of Difference: American Constructions of Race, Sex and Gender, Social Class and Sexual Orientation*. 3rd ed. New York: McGraw-Hill, 2003.

Ross, R. J. S., and K. C. Trachte. *Global Capitalism: The New Leviathan*. Albany, NY: State University of New York, 1990

Rothenberg, P. S. *Race, Class and Gender in the United States: An Integrated Study*. 4th ed. New York: St. Martin's, 1998.

Rutenberg, T. "Learning Women's Studies." In *Theories of Women's Studies*, edited by G. Bowles and R. D. Klein, 72–78. Boston: Routledge Kegan Paul, 1983.

Sacco, V. F., and L. W. Kennedy. *The Criminal Event*. 3rd ed. Toronto: Nelson, 2002.

Sangren, S. Rhetoric and the Authority of Ethnography: "Postmodernism" and the Social Reproduction of Texts. *Current Anthropology* 29, no. 3 (1988): 405–35.

Sapolsky, R. M. *Why Zebras Don't Get Ulcers: A Guide to Stress, Stress-Related Disease and Coping*. 2nd ed. NY: WH Freeman, 1998.

Saxena, N. "Citizens' Dialogue Experience: Follow-Up Survey Results." Canadian Policy Research Networks. Public Involvement Network, 2003.

Scheper-Hughes, N. *Death without Weeping: The Violence of Everyday Life in Brazil*. Berkeley, CA: University of California Press, 1992.

Schneider, A. G. "Social Religion, the Christian Home, and Republican Spirituality in Antebellum Methodism." In *Perspectives on American Methodism: Interpretive Essays*, edited by R. E. Richey, K. E. Rowe and J. Miller Schmidt, 192–208. Nashville: Abingdon Press, 1991.

Scott, R. A., and A. R. Shore. *Why Sociology Does Not Apply*. New York: Elsevier, 1979.

Seidman, S. "The End of Sociological Theory." In *The Postmodern Turn: New Perspectives on Social Theory*, edited by S. Seidman. Cambridge: Cambridge University Press, 1994.

Sennett, R., and J. Cobb. *The Hidden Injuries of Class*. Knopf, New York, 1973.

Shain, B. *The Myth of American Individualism*. Princeton: Princeton University Press, 1994.

Sherman, L., P. R. Gartin, and M. E. Buerger. "Routine Activities and the Criminology of Place." *Criminology* 27 (1987): 27–55.

Silverstein, L. B. "Fathering is a Feminist Issue." *Psychology of Women Quarterly* 20 (1996): 3–37.

Skocpol, T. *Diminished Democracy*. Norman: University of Oklahoma Press, 2003.

Sloss, S. G. "Comment: Is Computer-Based Testing a Solution to Students' Cheating?" *Teaching Sociology* 23 (1995): 58–59.

Smith, D. "Women's Perspective as a Radical Critique of Sociology." *Sociological Inquiry* 44, no. 1 (1974): 7–13.

—. "An Analysis of Ideological Structures and How Women Are Excluded." *Canadian Review of Sociology and Anthropology* 12, no. 4 (1975): 353–69.

—. "A Sociology for Women." In *The Prism of Sex*, edited by J. Sherman and E. Torton Beck. 135–87. Madison: University of Wisconsin Press, 1979.

Smith, D. E. *The Conceptual Practices of Power: A Feminist Sociology of Knowledge.* Boston: Northeastern University Press, 1990.

Smith, D. H. "Voluntary Action and Voluntary Groups." *Annual Review of Sociology* 1 (1975): 247–70.

Smith, P. *Higher Education in America: Killing the Spirit.* New York: Penguin Books, 1990.

Sprague, J., and D. Kobrynowicz. "A Feminist Epistemology." In *Handbook of the Sociology of Gender,* edited by J. S. Chafetz, 25–43. New York: Plenum, 1999.

"Sociology's Long Decade in the Wilderness." *New York Times,* May 28, 1989.

Sprague, J., and M. K. Zimmermann. "Overcoming Dualisms: A Feminist Agenda for Sociological Methodology." In *Theory on Gender/Feminism on Theory,* edited by P. England, 255–80. New York: Aldine De Gruyter, 1993.

Stacy, J., and B. Thorne. "The Missing Feminist Revolution in Sociology." *Social Problems* 32 (1985): 301–16.

Stanley, L., and S. Wise. *Breaking Out: Feminist Consciousness and Feminist Research.* Boston: Routledge Kegan Paul, 1983.

Stephens, L. S. "Will Johnny See Daddy this Week? An Empirical Test of Three Theoretical Perspectives of Postdivorce Contact." *Journal of Family Issues* 17 (1996): 466–94.

Stoecker, R., J. Mullin, M. Schmidbauer, and M. Young. "Integrating Writing and the Teaching Assistant to Enhance Critical Pedagogy." *Teaching Sociology* 21 (1993): 332–40.

Straits, B. C. "The Social Context of Voter Turnout." *Public Opinion Quarterly* 54, no. 1 (1990): 64–73.

Straus, M., R. Gelles, and C. Smith. *Physical Violence in American Families: Risk Factors and Adaptations to Violence in 8,145 Families.* New Brunswick: Transaction Publishers, 1990.

Swaddle, K., and A. Heath. "Official and Reported Turnout in the British General Election of 1987." *British Journal of Political Science* 19 (1989): 537–51.

Syme, S. L. "Social and Economic Disparities in Health: Thoughts about Intervention." *The Milbank Quarterly* 76, no. 3 (1998): 492–505.

Tanner, J., and S. Wortley. The Toronto Youth Crime and Victimization Survey: Overview Report. Toronto: Centre of Criminology, "There Is No Racism. We Do Not Do Racial Profiling." *Toronto Star,* October 19, 2002: A14.

Taylor, K. W. "Racism and Canadian Immigration Law." Paper presented at the meetings of the Canadian Sociology and Anthropology Association. Kingston, ON. 1991. Also forthcoming in *Canadian Ethnic Studies.*

Taylor, R., B. Leashore, and S. Toliver. "An Assessment of the Provider Role as Perceived by Black Males." *Family Relations* 37 (1988): 426–31.

Tedlock, B. 2000. "Ethnography and Ethnographic Representation." In *Handbook of Qualitative Research,* edited by N. K. Denzin and Y. S. Lincoln. 2nd ed., 455–86. Thousand Oaks, CA: Sage.

Tepperman, L. *Social Mobility in Canada.* Toronto: McGraw-Hill Ryerson, 1975.

Tepperman, L., and J. Curtis. *Social Problems: A Canadian Perspective.* Don Mills, ON: Oxford University Press, 2004.

Thompson, B., and S. Tyagi. "Multicultural Education and the Sociological Imagination." *Teaching Sociology* 21 (1993): 192–96.

Thompson, L. "Women's Sense of Fairness." *Journal of Family Issues* 12 (1991): 181–96.

Thompson, L., and A. J. Walker. "The Place of Feminism in Family Studies." *Journal of Marriage and the Family* 57 (1995): 847–65.

Tocqueville, A. *Democracy in America.* Vol. 1: 298–342. New York: Random House, 1945.

Tong, R. *Feminist Thought.* Boulder: Westview Press, 1989.

Tonry, Michael. *Malign Neglect: Race, Crime and Punishment in America.* New York: Oxford University Press, 1995.

Trojanowicz, R., and B. Bucqueroux. *Community Policing.* Cincinnati, OH: Anderson, 1990.

Trower, P., P. Gilbert, and G. Sherling. "Social Anxiety, Evolution and Self-Presentation." In *Handbook of Social and Evaluation Anxiety,* edited by H. Leitenberg, 11–45. NY: Plenum Press, 1990.

Turner, Jonathan H. *Theory Building in Sociology.* Newbury Park, California: Sage, 1988.

Turner, J. H, P. R. Turner, A. Maryanski, K. Allen, P. Colony, C. Powers, S. Fuchs, R. Li and D. Wagner. *The Structure of Sociological Theory.* New York: Wadsworth Publishing Company, 1998.

Turrittin, A. H., P. Anisef, and N. J. MacKinnon. "Gender Differences in Educational Achievement: A Study of Social Inequality." *Canadian Journal of Sociology* 8, no. 4 (1983): 395–419.

Tumin, M. M. "Some Principle of Stratification: A Critical Analysis." *American Sociological Review* 18 (1953): 387–93.

Turrittin, A. H. "Inequalities of Social Class." In *Sociology: An Introduction,* edited by K. Ishwaran. Toronto: Addison-Wesley, 1988.

U.S. Bureau of the Census. *Child Support for Custodial Mothers and Fathers: 1991* (Current Population Reports. Series P60-187). Washington, DC: U.S. Government Printing Office, 1995.

Van Loon, R., and M. Whittington. *The Canadian Political System.* 2nd ed. Toronto: McGraw-Hill, 1976.

Vandello, J., and D. Cohen. "Patterns of Individualism and Collectivism across the United States." *Journal of Personality and Social Psychology* 77, no. 2 (1999): 279–92.

Vattimo, G. *The End of Modernity.* Cambridge: Polity Press, 1988.

Verba, S., K. L. Schlozman, and H. E. Brady. *Voice and Equality: Civic Voluntarism in American Politics.* Cambridge: Harvard University Press, 1995.

Vinick, B. H., and S. Lanspery. "Cinderella's Sequel: Step-mothers' Long-Term Relationships with Adult Stepchildren." Paper presented at the annual meeting of the American Society on Aging, March 1998. San Francisco.

Wagenaar, T. C. "Study in Depth: Sociology versus Other Disciplines." *Teaching Sociology* 21 (1993): 352–62.

—. "Student Evaluations of Teaching: Some Cautions and Suggestions." *Teaching Sociology* 23 (1995): 64–68.

Walker, A. J. "Refracted Knowledge: Viewing Families through the Prism of Social Science." *Journal of Marriage and the Family* 62 (2000): 595–608.

Wallerstein, I. *The Uncertainties of Knowledge.* Philadelphia: Temple University Press, 2004.

Wattenberg, E. "Paternity Actions and Young Fathers." In *Young Unwed Fathers: Changing Roles and Emerging Policies,* edited by R. I. Lerman and T. J. Ooms. Philadelphia: Temple University Press, 1993.

Weast, D. "Alternative Teaching Strategies: The Case for Critical Thinking." *Teaching Sociology* 24 (1996): 189–194.

Weedon, C. *Feminist Practice and Poststructuralist Theory.* Oxford: Blackwell, 1987.

Weiss, S. M. "I Remember Max." *The Chronicle of Higher Education* 23, no. 22 (1982): 56.

Weizman, L. J. *The Divorce Revolution: The Unexpected Social and Economic Consequences for Women and Children in America.* New York: The Free Press, 1985.

Wellman, B. "Letter to the Editor." *Society/Societe* 13, no. 2 (1989): 45–46.

West, C., and D. Zimmerman. "Doing Gender." *Gender and Society* 1 (1987): 125–51.

Westkott, M. "Feminist Criticism of the Social Sciences." *Harvard Educational Reviewer* 49 (1979): 422–30.

Weitzer, R., and S. Tuch. "Perceptions of Racial Profiling: Race, Class and Personal Experience." *Criminology* 40 (2002): 435–56.

Wiesenfeld, K. "Making the Grade: Many Students Wheedle for a Degree as if It Were a Freebie T-Shirt." *Newsweek*, June 17, 1996, 16.

Wigle, D., and Y. Mao. *Mortality by Income Levels in Urban Canada.* Ottawa: Health and Welfare Canada, 1980.

Wilkinson, R. G. *Unhealthy Societies: The Afflictions of Inequality.* London: Routledge, 1996.

—. "Socioeconomic Determinants of Health: Health Inequalities: Relative or Absolute Material Standards." *British Medical Journal* 314 (1997): 591–95.

—. "Income Inequality, Social Cohesion, and Health: Clarifying the Theory—A Reply to Muntaner and Lynch." *International Journal of Health Services* 29, no. 3 (1999a): 525–43.

—. "The Culture of Inequality." In *Income Inequality and Health: The Society and Population Health Reader, Vol. 1,* edited by I. Kawachi, B. Kennedy and R. G. Wilkinson. NY: New Press, 1999b.

Williams, A. P. "Social Origins and Elite Politics in Canada." *Canadian Journal of Sociology* 14, no. 1 (1989): 67–88.

Williams, P. "Social Origins and Elite Politics in Canada: The Impact of Background Differences on Attitudes Toward the Welfare State." *Canadian Journal of Sociology* 14, no. 1 (1989): 67–87.

Williams, R. B., J. Feaganes, and J. C. Barefoot. "Hostility and Death Rates in 10 U.S. Cities." *Psychosomatic Medicine* 57, no. 1 (1995): 94.

Williams, T. "Sentencing Black Offenders in the Ontario Criminal Justice System." In *Making Sense of Sentencing,* edited by J. V. Roberts and D. P. Cole. Toronto: University of Toronto Press, 1999.

Wilson, J. "Review of the Values of Volunteering: Cross-Cultural Perspectives." *American Journal of Sociology* 109, no. 6 (2004): 1540–42.

Wortley, S. "Profiling One Source of Alienation: Both Sides of Debate Get Support in Recent Survey." *Toronto Star,* November 25, 2002: B1.

—. "The Usual Suspects: Race, Police Contact and Perceptions of Criminal Injustice." *Criminology*, forthcoming.

Wortley, S., B. Fischer, and C. Webster. "Vice Lessons: A Survey of Prostitution Offenders Enrolled in the Toronto John School Diversion Program." *Canadian Journal of Criminology* 44, no. 4 (2002): 369–402.

Wortley, S., and J. Tanner. "Data, Denials and Confusion: The Racial Profiling Debate in Toronto." *Canadian Journal of Criminology and Criminal Justice* 45 (2003): 367–89.

Wortley, S., and J. Tanner. "The Good, the Bad and the Profiled: Race, Deviant Activity and Police Stop and Search Practices." Paper presented at the University of Toronto Faculty of Law Conference on Systemic Racism in the Criminal Justice System, Toronto. November 28, 2002. Data, Denials, and Confusion: The Racial Profiling Debate in Toronto.

Wright, P., R. Whittington, and G. E. Whittenburg. "Student Ratings of Teaching Effectiveness: What the Research Reveals." *Journal of Accounting Education* 2 (1984): 5–30.

Wuthnow, R. *The Restructuring of American Religion.* Princeton: Princeton University Press, 1988.

Zemsky, R. "Consumer Markets and Higher Education." *Liberal Education* 79 (1993): 14–17.

Zill, N., D. R. Morrison, and M. J. Coiro. "Long-Term Effects of Parental Divorce on Parent-Child Relationships, Adjustment, and Achievement in Young Adulthood." *Journal of Family Psychology* 7 (1993): 91–103.

Glossary

Achieved status A social position that one assumes as a result of personal choice, by learning skills or gaining credentials. It reflects personal ability and effort.

Alienation The term, as originally used by Karl Marx, refers to loss of control over one's work and product. It is a feeling of powerlessness from other people and from oneself.

Altruist suicide One of Durkheim's classification of suicide that occurs when there is a high level of integration of individuals to the society or community.

Anomie According to Emile Durkheim, anomie is a condition in which society provides little or no moral guidance for individual actions. A state of normlessness.

Ascribed status A social position that one assumes at birth or receives involuntarily later in life.

Assimilation The process by which minority ethnoracial groups lose their distinctive culture and adopt that of the dominant groups.

Association An empirical relationship between two or more phenomena or variables. A change in one variable is statistically related to a change in another variable.

Asymmetry An unbalanced arrangement or distribution.

Authority Power that people perceive as legitimate rather than coercive.

Bivariate Involving two variables.

Bourgeoisie In Marxism, it refers to an individual or a group of people who own the means of production (capital, raw materials, factories, tools, etc.) and who hire workers in order to produce products to sell for profit.

Bureaucracy A rational organization designed to perform tasks efficiently.

Calling A religious duty. The term was used by the Protestants to refer to one's occupation as a religious duty.

Capitalism A system of production in which a small group of people own the means of production, while a large group of people who do not have access to those means of production have to sell their labour power in order to earn enough to subsist. The pressure to produce tends to increase innovation and technological developments, yet helps to produce unemployment, poverty, and inequality.

Capital accumulation According to Marxists, governments have a tendency to help provide opportunities that increase accumulation of wealth and capital for capitalists.

Capitalist See Bourgeoisie.

Charter groups The two original Europeans groups (British and French) whose rights and privileges (such as language rights) are enshrined in the Canadian constitution.

Charisma Extraordinary qualities in individuals that can turn an audience into followers.

Class Generally, it means an individual's relative location in a society based on wealth, power, prestige, or other valued resources. Marxists view class as individuals' relationship to the organization of production. Weberians refer to class in terms of an individuals' access to life chances.

Class conflict Antagonism between social classes in a society. Marx used this term to refer to the struggle between capitalists and workers because of their clash of interests.

Coercion According to Marxists, governments will use their legal, political, military, or police force to ensure stability for investment and capital accumulation.

Cohabitation Sharing of a household by unmarried couples.

Collective conscience A body of beliefs and sentiments that are common to all members of a society.

Colonialism The process by which a nation becomes rich and powerful at the expense of political and economic control of other nation(s).

Colonization The process by which a country takes over another country by force of arms and governs that country without people's consent.

Communism A social system where there is no private ownership of the means of production and no state; all members of the society are economically, politically, and socially equal.

Comparison A method of discovery that builds new knowledge by finding similarities and differences among subjects and places and across time.

Confirmation Involves the use of empirical evidence in order to provide support for the truth of a scientific theory.

Conflict theory Focuses on how social groups have different interests and how such interests produce conflict in society.

Conformist Merton's classification of individuals who accept the societal goals and acceptable means of achieving those goals.

Control A statistical term that refers to holding constant all relevant variables except for the one that we are interested in, to see its effect.

Control theory A criminological theory that explains crime in terms of weak internal control mechanisms developed in childhood in combination with weak or absent social rules.

Corporate (or white-collar) crime Crime committed by a corporation or people in high status positions in the course of their occupations.

Cultural capital A term used by Pierre Bourdieu to refer to people's assets, including their values, beliefs, attitudes, and competence in language and culture.

Cultural relativism The practice of judging a culture by its own standards.

Culture A set of values, norms, mores, and laws, and so on that prevail in a given society or part of it.

Curriculum   All the courses of study offered at a school or university.

Deductive   Attributes events to general law.

Democratic racism   A type of racism that results in unequal outcome when people are treated equally, without paying attention to their differences or unequal conditions.

Dependent variable   A variable that can be changed by another (independent) variable.

Discrimination   Unequal treatment of various groups; actions of the dominant group that deny members of minority groups resources available to other groups.

Division of labour   Task specialization of economic activities.

Dogma   A system of beliefs or a system of doctrine believed to be authoritative and/or maintained by a religious body as true and necessary.

Domination   Institutionalization of control of one group by another.

Double day of work   Often referred to women doing both paid work and housework.

Egalitarian   Believing in political or social equality.

Egalitarianism   A belief in political, economic, and social equality between people (e.g., each person to be treated equally under the law).

Ego   For Freud, it refers to a person's efforts to manage Id's pleasure-seeking desires in society.

Egotistic suicide   Durkheim's classification of suicide that occurs when individuals are least integrated with the society or community.

Empathetic understanding   A rational way of understanding the world by paying attention to actors' motives and emotions.

Enclosure Act   Law passed in England to clear the land for sheep-grazing.

Endogamous marriage   Marriage within the blood clan or group.

Enlightenment   A period in human knowledge when all aspects of human life and work were the subject of critical examination in order to develop an understanding of human society and to further humanity's general progress.

Entrance groups   Late immigrants whose group rights are not enshrined in the Canadian constitution.

Epistemology   The branch of philosophy that critically examines the nature, limits, and validity of human knowledge and understanding.

Equality of condition   A belief in equality of overall distribution of resources.

Equality of opportunity   A view that all individuals should be given an equal chance to compete for higher education, status, and jobs.

Ethnic identity   The extent to which members of an ethnic group differentiate themselves from others, consider themselves as a common people separate from others, and have a positive sense of attachment to their own group.

Ethnocentrism   The practice of judging members of another cultural group by one's own cultural standards; a belief in superiority of one's own culture.

Ethnomethodology   The study of the way people make sense of their everyday life.

Exchange value   Value or product created for exchange in the market.

Exogamy   Marriage outside one's blood clan or one's social type.

Experiment   A research method that investigates the cause and effect relationship in a controlled environment.

Exploitation   The process by which members of one class (e.g., capitalists) extract surplus value or surplus labour from members of another class (e.g., workers).

Extended families   Include several relatives such as grandparents, parents, children, their spouse and their children, all in the same residence.

External control   Type of social control that includes attachment to significant others, commitment or investment in conventional society, involvement in conventional behaviours, and belief in society's values.

Falsification   Involves use of evidence to show that a theory is actually incorrect.

Family violence   Emotional, physical, or sexual abuse of one family member by another member.

Fatalistic suicide   Durkheim's classification of suicide that occurs when individuals have no way out of the undesirable situation they are in.

Feminist theory   The evaluation and explanation of why women have less power and resources than men and how to challenge and transform such imbalance.

Feudalism   A social system prevalent in the Middle Ages where land and resources are owned by the nobility, state, and landlords, and main producers are attached to the land.

Frequency   A statistical term referring to a number of similar events or categories.

Functionalist theory   Explanation of a particular social institution by its functions and how it meets the need of the system and/or helps the survival of larger society.

Gender identity   Culturally appropriate male and female traits and personalities.

Generalized others   Widespread cultural norms and values that guide individuals' self-evaluation.

Hegemony   A type of domination. The subordinate classes' consensus to the dominant class is achieved through control over their thinking process; ideological control.

Hidden curriculum   Subtle presentation of cultural values and norms that prevails in schools and classes.

Hierarchy   Ranked positions within a society or social system.

Human capital   One's skill and productivity.

Hypothesis An unverified statement of the relationship between two or more variables.

I According to George Herbert Mead, "I" is an aspect of the self that is the source of novelty and self-actualization.

Id According to Freud, it refers to the basic pleasure-seeking desires of human beings.

Ideology A set of charged normative and descriptive beliefs that justify and/or challenge the existing order of society.

Independent variable A variable that causes change in another (dependent) variable.

Individualism Contrast to egalitarianism; the right of individuals to challenge important beliefs and institutions.

Inductive Starts from the observation of an event and moves toward theoretical proposition.

Infant mortality rate The number of deaths in the first year of life for each thousand live births in a year.

Inner-worldly ascetics Thinking that most problems stem from physical involvement in the world and that doubt and temptation within the individual causes suffering.

Innovationist Merton's classification of individuals who accept societal goals but not the means to achieve those goals. They pursue less acceptable means of acquiring societal goals.

Institutional completeness Raymond Breton's term for the complexity and number of organizations that meets the needs of members of a group or society.

Institutional racism The established rules, procedures, and practices that directly and deliberately prevent full and equal involvement of the minority group members in society.

Instrumentalist state theory A Marxist type of explanation that focuses on the linkage between individuals occupying key state positions and upper classes.

Internal control Type of social control that refers to early parental childrearing and school practices that can help inhibit a child's undesirable immediate act and ensure internalization of values and lessons that prevent future deviances.

Intersection model A theoretical framework that views humans as governed by multiple identities and life worlds.

Intersexuality An individual showing biological characteristics of both sexes.

Interval variable A ranked variable with equal distance between categories.

Laissez faire Nonintervention of the state into economic activities; greater liberty of trade and business.

Law A set of formally codified legal rules or norms that either forbid or permit specific behaviours or relationships among people.

Liberalism A belief in the importance of the individual as opposed to a collective entity; resistance to state control of economic life.

Legitimation A process by which subordinate groups have semblance of power without much substance.

Liberty Conditions in which individuals have immunity and are protected from arbitrary exercise of authority or power.

Life expectancy The average length of time that a person can expect to live.

Logistic regression A statistical technique that estimates the probability of an event.

Macrostructure Large-scale social structures.

Matriarchy A hierarchical social organization where women are in control of social, political, and economic institutions of society.

Matrilineal A system where descent is traced through the mother.

Me An aspect of the personality that according to George Herbert Mead, refers to the organized set of attitudes assumed by an individual.

Mean Statistical term used to describe the sum of all the scores divided by the number of scores.

Mechanical solidarity According to Emile Durkheim, it refers to shared morality among members, helping social bonds in traditional societies.

Median The score that divides a distribution into equal parts.

Metanarratives General or grand narratives or theories that explain everything.

Microstructures Patterns of social interactions in a given situation.

Minority A category of people distinguished by physical and/or cultural traits and who are often disadvantaged.

Monogamy Marriage between two partners.

Mores Set of norms that must be followed because the survival of the society may depend on them.

Multiculturalism Policies designed to ensure cultural and ethnic maintenance of ethnic groups and to promote equality of opportunity for all ethnic groups in Canada. Social justice, identity, and engagement are the three pillars of multiculturalism.

Multivariate A method of studying a phenomenon by explaining it through two or more variables.

Necessary labour The amount of work needed to meet one's basic needs.

Neoliberal See neoliberalism.

Neoliberalism A philosophy or set of economic policies and views that desire to intensify and expand the market, by increasing the frequency of transactions and minimizing the role of governments.

Norms Institutionalized values.

Nuclear families Independent institutions established through marriage and include parents and children.

Objectivity Personal neutrality in conducting social research.

Observation A method of discovery that searches for similarities and differences based on observation of subjects or events.

Ontology A branch of knowledge that deals with philosophical theory of reality.

Ordinary (least square) regression A statistical technique that summarizes information and minimizes error of prediction.

Organic solidarity According to Emile Durkheim, the social bonds created due to interconnectedness in division of labour.

Oppression The act of keeping individuals or groups in subjugation through the unjust of force or authority; the state of being in subjugation.

Other-worldly mystics Viewing salvation as being reached through the separation of one's self from body.

Paralogy Jean-Francois Lyotard's views on the tendency in scientific research to undermine itself and previous knowledge.

Participant observation A systematic method of involvement and observation of people's routine activity.

Patriarchy Social organization where males dominate females.

Patrilineal A system where descent is traced through the father.

Pedagogy The theory of how to teach.

Performativity Lyotard's view that science is more interested in efficiency than the truth.

Pluralist View of the state system suggesting that it is made of a great variety of people and interest groups that help ensure that everyone gets a fair and representative voice in its management and decision-making process.

Polygamy A form of marriage that unites three or more people.

Polytheism Beliefs in many gods.

Populism A view that espouses direct political participation of the people in the government.

Positivism The application of natural science methods to social science.

Postmodern After modernism.

Postmodernism A theoretical framework that believes knowledge is socially constructed, developed by multiple life worlds, and questions grand theories.

Power Refers to one's ability to influence others and reach a goal even against opposition from those who are subject to power.

Prediction A method of scientific research that allows researchers to predict future events based on events that occurred in the past.

Prejudice Negative judgment of individuals on the basis of assumed characteristics of the group to which the individual belongs. A biased attitude based on an unfavourable attitude toward a group.

Primary deviance The first deviant act before the labelling process.

Protestant ethic A belief system among Protestants that according to Max Weber, includes hard work in order to glorify God on Earth. Also a belief in predestination.

Qualitative research A method of gathering information that is not numeric, includes participant and nonparticipant observation, and historical-comparative research.

Quantitative method A method of gathering numeric information, based on methods of natural science, and uses methods of experiment, observation, and comparison.

Quiet Revolution Social changes in Quebec that included educational expansion, industrialization, and urbanization.

Racial profiling A greater level of criminal justice surveillance of a particular racial or ethnic group compared to others.

Racism The belief that one group sharing certain physical characteristics is innately superior to another group with different characteristics.

Ratio variable A ranked variable with equal distance between categories and a true zero point.

Rationalization Weber's term for the movement toward the development of human thought based on systematic accumulation of evidence as in the form of impersonal authority common in bureaucracies.

Rebel Merton's classification of deviance in which individuals reject both societal goals and means of achieving those goals and substitute their own new goals and means.

Reformation Protestant reformation.

Reserve army of labour A part of the labour force that is drawn into the labour market when needed by capitalists and is pushed out of that market when no longer needed. Women and minority ethnoracial groups are said to constitute such a flexible labour supply.

Retreatist Merton's classification of deviance in which individuals reject both societal goals and means of achieving those goals and withdraw from the society.

Second shift Refers to domestic work performed by women in addition to doing paid work.

Secondary deviance The extent of deviance that is due to labelling the individual as deviant.

Serfs Group of people who worked on the landlord's land and kept a share of the output for themselves.

Sexism A belief that one's own sex is innately superior to the other.

Sex-segregated occupations The extent to which any occupation is concentrated by males or females. The higher the concentration of one of the sexes in one occupation, the more that occupation is sex-segregated.

Significant others Most important individual(s) in one's life.

Slavery Economic organization in which some individuals are the property of other individuals. Slaves can be bought and sold at the owner's wish.

Social capital A feature of social life that includes trust, networks, and associational participation. These features are used by individuals to secure more resources.

Social construction of reality The process by which people actively shape reality through social interaction.

Social structure Relatively stable pattern of social behaviour; large-scale and long-term patterns of organization in a society. These organizations are external to individuals and influence their behaviour and thoughts.

Socialism   An economic system in which the means of production are collectively owned.

Socialization   The learning of certain attributes and becoming a participant in society.

Socioeconomic status   One's social status in the stratification hierarchy based on education, occupation, and income.

Sociology   A science that constructs theories about social relationships composing society.

Sociological imagination   An imagination that allows for creative thinking, which enables an individual's awareness in relationship to the wider society.

Split labour market   Division of the economy into two sectors—primary and secondary. The primary sector is more unionized and capital intensive with high-paying jobs than the secondary sector. Often subordinate group members work in the secondary economic sector.

Sponsored mobility   A type of social mobility that is based on ascription and family connections.

Spurious relationship   An apparent though false relationship between two or more variables that is in fact due to a third variable.

Standard deviation   Measure of dispersion based on deviation from the mean.

Standpoint theory   The view that knowledge depends on one's social context and position.

Status   The relative prestige or position of an individual and its negative and positive perception by others.

Stereotype   A simplified belief about characteristics of a social group. Such belief minimizes a group's differences and maximizes its similarities. It exaggerates based on too little information.

Stratification   The existence of inequality between groups of people in a society based on their access to material and nonmaterial resources.

Street crime   Crime committed by ordinary individuals.

Super-Ego   According to Freud, it refers to the internalized values and norms of a culture that keep in check Id's pleasure-seeking drives.

Surplus labour   The labour used to produce products over and above what is needed for subsistence.

Surplus products   The products produced over and above what is needed for subsistence; when production outpaces consumption.

Surplus value   According to Marx, it is the difference between wages paid to the worker and the value created by the worker in the act of producing commodities.

Symbolic interactionism   The theory that is interested in finding how face-to-face interaction between individuals helps explain human behaviours, produces shared meaning and stable social systems.

Symmetry   Balanced proportion or distribution; equal correspondence between the opposite halves of a figure or pattern.

Systematic racism   Practices that systematically discriminate against one or more racial groups because of their colour of skin, religion, language, or nationality.

Tautology   Circular reasoning; saying the same thing in different words.

Techniques of neutralization   Justification and rationalization of deviant behaviour.

Temporal order   Refers to a principle of causal order where the cause of a phenomenon must take place before its effect.

Theory   Ideas or tentative explanations about social relations.

Transsexual   People who feel they are one sex though biologically they are the other.

Transexuality   See transsexual.

Treaty groups   First Nation Aboriginals with treaty rights.

Treaty status   Certain privileges and obligations passed onto the aboriginal people of Canada by their ancestors who signed treaties with the Canadian government.

Universalism   The doctrine that states that rules should apply to all equally and without restriction.

Urbanization   Type of enlightenment in which people are uprooted from their village communities and entered into urban areas.

Use value   Value of things created for self-consumption.

Values   Abstract principles that guide human actions.

Variance   A measure of dispersion around the mean.

Visible minority   Official government classification of non-white and non-Caucasian groups.